MANAGING INDUS
KNOWLEDGE

Creation, Transfer and Utilization

edited by

Ikujiro Nonaka and David J. Teece

SAGE Publications

London • Thousand Oaks • New Delhi

First published 2001

SAGE Publications Ltd
6 Bonhill Street
London EC2A 4PU

SAGE Publications Inc
2455 Teller Road
Thousand Oaks, California 91320

SAGE Publications India Pvt Ltd
32, M-Block Market
Greater Kailash – I
New Delhi 110 048

British Library Cataloguing in Publication data

A catalogue record for this book is available
from the British Library

ISBN 0 7619 5498 8
ISBN 0 7619 5499 6 (pbk)

Library of Congress catalog record available

Typeset by Mayhew Typesetting, Rhayader, Powys
Printed and bound in Great Britain by Athenaeum Press, Gateshead

MANAGING INDUSTRIAL
KNOWLEDGE

Contents

Preface

This volume of collected papers came out of the second and third annual University of California, Berkeley, Forums on Knowledge and the Firm held in autumn 1998 and 1999. Berkeley is a great centre of learning and in the past has excelled at linking together different disciplines and cultures. The Knowledge Forums were no exception, bringing together faculty members from across disciplines and continents, as well as senior executives from around the world.

The Forums have self-consciously endeavoured to advance several themes, which the editors trust are reflected in this book. One is that knowledge assets now form the basis of competitive advantage among global firms. The ability to create, protect, transfer and utilize knowledge assets is at the core of commercial progress and wealth creation today. Second, knowledge management involves much more than the development and deployment of new IT-based knowledge management systems. Third, we believe that the amount of disturbance technological and marketplace innovation is delivering is such that society needs new frameworks and models to explain the practices and future requirements of knowledge-based firms and organizations. Fourth, because of the poor state of knowledge about knowledge management, it is important at this stage to generate new ideas and frameworks rather than focus on the rigorous empirical testing of hypotheses. There will be plenty of scope for that later.

The co-editors wish to thank the financial sponsors of the forums, which have included Fuji Xerox, Xerox Corporation, Fujitsu Limited, Fujitsu Research Institute, Fujitsu Business Systems, and Eisai Corporation, as well as grant funds from the Alfred P. Sloan Foundation and the Air Force Office of Scientific Research. The Institute of Management, Innovation and Organization (IMO) at University of California Berkeley was not just a financial sponsor, but also provided the able staff to make it happen. These included Anita Patterson, Athena Katsaros, Janet Mowery, Stuart Graham, Satoshi Akutsu and Ryoko Toyama. We would like to especially thank Patricia Murphy, the Assistant Director of IMO. Without her selfless dedication, keen eyes, infinite patience and warm heart, neither the forums nor this book were possible.

Ikujiro Nonaka
David J. Teece

Introduction

Ikujiro Nonaka and David J. Teece

Historical Background

Perhaps one of the most remarkable developments of our time is the 'discovery' that knowledge is the key, not just to economic progress, but also to business and corporate success. This discovery is in many ways simply a rediscovery. At least with respect to economic progress, economic historians have long recognized that technological progress is the key to prosperity. However, with respect to firm-level competitive advantage, widespread recognition that knowledge is the key has come much more recently.

Understanding that knowledge is an asset and needs to be protected is nevertheless not new. In past centuries, alchemists and artisans alike would frequently endeavour to protect their 'industrial' secrets. Indeed, the patent system had its origins in the desire to protect the design and trade secrets of the guildsmen. Even the American Constitution (Article I, Section 8) recognized the benefits of inventions by authorizing Congress to enact patent legislation, which it did in 1790. In the nineteenth century, Britain imposed restrictions on the migration of skilled craftsmen to the Continent in a vain effort to keep the knowledge associated with the Industrial Revolution at home.

While there has been a small group of academics and others consistently beating the drum as to the importance of knowledge assets, widespread realization that this is the main game is quite recent. Indeed, some might say it is still emergent. There is also a great tendency to try and squeeze new developments into old frameworks. This frequently leads to the dismissal of 'inconvenient' facts and ideas as they are too hostile to traditional frameworks and theories. However, the failure to properly conceptualize just how firms and management are impacted by the growing importance of knowledge assets is likely to have costly consequences, especially to incumbent firms.

Intangible Assets, Tangible Assets and Information

At the outset, we wish to point out that this is a book about *knowledge* management, not simply *information* management. This is an important distinction, which is too frequently overlooked. Information is data. Sometimes it is old, sometimes it is new. New information modifies the expectations of the recipient. For example, information that oil prices have increased is most important – it will affect expectations about the profitability of oil companies and the strength of the economy. Knowledge, on the other hand, involves the understanding of how something works. Clearly, knowledge might be impacted by the arrival of new information; but it fundamentally involves the understanding of interrelationships and behaviour. It is context-dependent.

Knowledge assets are intangible and quite different from tangible assets. These differences are summarized in Table I.1. First, knowledge has aspects of what economists refer to as 'public goods' – consumption by one individual does not reduce the amount left for another. This is especially true for scientific knowledge. One engineer's use of Newton's laws does not subtract from the ability of others to use the same laws. However, the distinction erodes quickly as one moves towards industrial knowledge and away from scientific knowledge. While multiple use need not take away from knowledge – indeed, it may well be augmented in the process of learning by using – the economic value may well decline with simultaneous use by multiple entities. This is saying little more than the obvious. Imitators can dramatically lower the market value of knowledge by augmenting its supply in the market. Competition simply drives down the price, even though the utility of the product has not declined.

Relatedly, while knowledge does not wear out, as do most physical assets (tractors, trucks, refrigerators and even disk drives), it is frequently exposed to rapid depreciation because of the creation of new knowledge. Thus, leading-edge products in the computer industry are often obsolete in a matter of months rather than years. In fact, the depreciation may be so radical that a technological breakthrough drops the value of current practice technology to zero, or very nearly so.

Transfer costs are also rather different for intangible and tangible assets. Intangible assets can sometimes be moved around at low cost, as when a secret formula or a piece of software code is transferred over a secure network. However, whether the transfer is complete or not depends on the sophistication and absorptive capacity of the receiver. Frequently, transfer costs are quite high, even within the same organization. Indeed, knowledge transfer tools are being developed to lower such costs, but their efficacy is problematical. Generally, transfer costs increase as the tacit portion increases. The costs of transferring tangible assets can be either high or low; the main difference is that they can usually be readily calibrated. This is not the case for intangible (knowledge) assets.

An important difference between intangible and tangible assets is the availability and enforceability of property rights. Physical assets (land, cars, ships, jewellery) are generally well protected. Ownership is relatively easy to define and the 'boundaries' of the property relatively easy to ascertain. Not so with intangibles. One normally thinks of different forms

Table I.1   *Differences between intangible assets and tangible assets*

	Knowledge (intangible) assets	Physical (tangible) assets
How public it is	Use by one party need not prevent use by another	Use by one party prevents simultaneous use by another
Depreciation	Does not 'wear out'; but usually depreciates rapidly	Wears out; may depreciate quickly or slowly
Transfer costs	Hard to calibrate (increases with the tacit portion)	Easier to calibrate (depends on transportation and related costs)
Property rights	Limited (patents, trade secrets, copyrights, trademarks, etc.) and fuzzy, even in developed countries	Generally comprehensive and clearer, at least in developed countries
Enforcement of property rights	Relatively difficult	Relatively easy

of intellectual property (patents, trade secrets, trademarks, copyrights) as providing comprehensive protection, but this is not so. There can be 'holes' and 'gaps' in intellectual property (IP) coverage. Moreover, some forms of IP (patents and copyrights) eventually expire and cannot be extended. This is generally nor so for physical assets.

Patents, trade secrets and trademarks provide protection in different ways. The strongest form of intellectual property is the patent. A valid patent provides rights for exclusive use by the owner, although, depending on the scope of the patent, it may be possible to invent around it, albeit at some cost. Trade secrets do not provide rights of exclusion over any knowledge domain, but they do protect covered secrets in perpetuity. Trade secrets can well augment the value of a patent position. Different knowledge mediums (software, printed matter, semiconductor masks) qualify for different types of intellectual property protection. The degree to which intellectual property keeps imitators at bay may depend also on other external factors, such as regulations that may block or limit the scope for 'invent around' alternatives. Table I.2 summarizes general characteristics of legal forms of protection in the United States. Accordingly, knowledge assets and their management cannot be just an afterthought to traditional ways of managerial and economic thinking. They lie at the core of competitive advantage. It is necessary, therefore, to begin thinking from first principles about how to design and manage knowledge-based firms and organizations.

The Future of the Business Firm

In the old economy, the challenge inside the firm was to coordinate the physical items produced by different employees. This was mainly a

Table I.2 Characteristics of legal forms of protection in the USA

Considerations	Copyright	Trade secret	Patent	Trademark	Mask works*
National uniformity	Yes	No	Yes	Yes	Yes
Protected property	Expression of idea	Secret information	Invention	Goodwill	Semiconductors
Scope of protection	Exclusive right to reproduce, prepare derivative works, publicly distribute, display and perform	Right to make, use and sell secret and protect against improper use or disclosure	Right to exclude others from making, using, selling	Proscribes against misrepresentation of source	
Effective date of protection	Creation of work	From date of conception or receipt of secret information	Patent application date	Use and/or filing date of US application issuing as principal registration on or after 16/11/89	First commercial exploitation
Cost of obtaining protection	Low	Low	Moderate	Low	Low
Term of protection	Life of author plus 50 years or 70 years	Possibility of perpetual protection; or termination at any time by improper disclosure or individual development by others	20 years	Perpetual if used correctly and diligently policed	10 years
Cost of maintaining protection	Nil	Moderate	Moderate	Moderate	Nil
Cost of enforcing rights against violators	Moderate	High	High	Moderate	Moderate

* Semiconductor industry only.

problem of managing the production and physical flow of (interi
products. In the knowledge economy, the challenge is to build, ci
and integrate the knowledge assets of many thousands of individua
much more formidable task. It also involves creating an environme
which knowledge accumulates and is shared at low cost. Clearly this
be enabled by some of the new groupware products available today.
Meanwhile, the new Internet-enabled economy is leading to the proliferation of new electronic marketplaces, making transactions in standardized
and quasi-standardized products even more efficient. As the scope of the
marketplace expands, firms are being left with the functions they can
perform better than the market. Of these, the creation, protection and use
of difficult to imitate knowledge assets are central.

Put differently, the raison d'être for integrated firms lies in their knowledge creation, accumulation, protection and deployment capabilities, as
compared to pure market-instigated arrangements. If firms can draw forth
and synthesize the knowledge capabilities of individuals better than
markets, they will be around a century from now. Otherwise, they will not,
and organization will take place by electronic markets that will entirely
usurp the basic functions of the executive and business organizations as we
know them today.

At least for the meantime, business firms are likely to survive. However,
they will need to be good at knowledge management if they are to provide
something that the new Internet-enabled marketplaces do not. Honing
their knowledge creation and transfer skills is obviously key and so it is the
focus of much of the material in this book.

A Brief Synopsis of the Book[1]

There is no way the editors can adequately summarize the contributions of
individual authors, and so no attempt to do so has been made here. Rather,
a few opening observations and comments are made on each piece, merely
to help put each chapter in context.

Part I Knowledge creation, organization and leadership

Chapter 1   I. Nonaka, R. Toyama and N. Konno, SECI, Ba, and
Leadership: A Unified Model of Dynamic Knowledge Creation

Nonaka, Toyama and Konno outline a firm-level model of knowledge
creation. In their conceptualization, the organization is not merely an
information processing machine, but an entity that creates knowledge by
virtue of its actions and interactions with its environment and new synthesis of existing firm-specific capabilities. Knowledge is seen as humanistic

and relational, not just abstract. Knowledge is created by means of a dynamic that involves the interplay between the explicit and tacit – the knowledge-conversion process. The creation process is self-transcending – you cannot do it without others or at least stimulus from the outside. The process also requires a physical context. 'Ba' offers such a context. It is a Japanese word meaning a specific time and place. It is related to the concept of communities of practice, but is different in a much as *ba* is a place where new knowledge is created, not just shared.

To create new knowledge, top management must create a vision and communicate it throughout the firm. This vision helps give direction to the knowledge-creating process. It is also important to success that knowledge producers know where to find know-how inside the firm. Creation also requires navigating between order and chaos; it also requires diverse ideas and thinking, both inside the firm and in the marketplace.

Chapter 2 *J.S. Brown and P. Duguid,* Structure and Spontaneity: Knowledge and Organization

Brown and Duguid recognize that formally structured organizations are better able to support innovation than spontaneous ones. They note the emergence of virtual corporations; they also observe high rates of mergers in the global economy. They reject the notion that there is spontaneity in markets but not in firms. At the same time, they remind us that knowledge does not flow easily inside firms. Barriers appear to exist between departments and divisions, between inside and outside, and among individuals. They set out to describe the challenge of organizing knowledge inside firms, while constantly recognizing that firms can outcompete self-organizing structures. Indeed, many successful structures that appear to be self-organizing turn out, on further examination, to have formal structure and are not pure market structures. The authors point out that knowledge often lies not with individuals, but is distributed among an ensemble of people working together. 'Knowing how' is learned by practice.

The authors also distinguish between declarative knowledge – knowing about something – versus dispositional knowledge, which implies the ability to respond to actual situations and get things done. The latter is more valuable and is not a stepchild of theory. A component of know-how is the ability to work with other people. In terms of internal transfer, the authors find this facilitated less by the conversion of the tacit to the explicit than by the alignment of practices and goals among internal communities.

Chapter 3 *C.O. Scharmer,* Self-transcending Knowledge: Organizing Around Emerging Realities

Scharmer shows that self-transcending knowledge is the ability to sense the presence of potential or to see what does not yet exist, and is usually associated with artists rather than business managers. This chapter argues that discussions about knowledge management need to expand beyond the familiar distinction between explicit and tacit knowledge by including self-transcending knowledge. Such knowledge includes an epistemology in which focus occurs on that which transcends the current self towards the ultimate common ground that is prior to subject–object distinctions – that is, action–intuition; an infrastructure that evolves during the interplay of shared action, shared reflection and formation of shared will; a conversational complexity of generative dialogue; a strategy of precognition or the ability to strategize and organize around not yet embodied knowledge; and an experience of the self that becomes part of a larger social breathing rhythm across generations and civilizations.

Chapter 4   C.J. Nemeth and L. Nemeth, Understanding the Creative Process: Management of the Knowledge Worker

In this chapter, Nemeth and Nemeth explore the dimensions of the creative process in contrast to problem solving or mere intelligence. It contrasts creative traits with many others considered essential for high morale and effectiveness within the firm and concludes that companies that want to encourage creative thought might need to embrace playfulness, the visions of children and diversity in personality, style and ideas. Without company support, creative individuals will either seek employment elsewhere or conform at serious cost to their potential contributions and the creative needs of the company.

Chapter 5   K. Peng and S. Akutsu, A Mentality Theory of Knowledge Creation and Transfer: Why Some Smart People Resist New Ideas and Some Don't

Peng and Akutsu propose a mentality theory to explain the problem of resisting new ideas. They argue that blame should be partly placed on mentality, particularly epistemology-driven mindsets. Defining mentality as the psychological stances that result as a reaction to new information, the chapter suggests that mentality is a major factor in understanding people's attitudes and behaviour around new ideas and new knowledge in general. Initial evidence from cultural psychology points to linear thinking and dialectical thinking mentalities. Both mentalities are based on rational principles rooted in different epistemologies. By studying these two mentalities among respondents in Japan and the United States, this chapter confirms that different epistemologies fascinate different kinds of mentalities and provide a concrete means of measuring mentality. The chapter concludes with an overview of the role that cultural psychology could play in knowledge creation and transfer, as well as its managerial implications.

Part II Firms, Markets and Innovation

Chapter 6 D.J. Teece, Strategies for Managing Knowledge Assets: The Role of Firm Structure and Industrial Context

This chapter argues that competitive advantage flows from the creation, ownership, protection and use of knowledge assets that are difficult to imitate. Superior performance, therefore, depends on the ability of firms to be good at innovation, protecting intangible knowledge assets and using them. The latter obviously conceals complicated processes surrounding:

1 the integration of intangibles with other intangibles, and with tangible assets;
2 the transfer of intangibles inside the firm;
3 the astute external licensing of technology wherever appropriate.

   This set of activities requires management to refocus priorities, build organizations that are highly flexible to accommodate such activity and display an uncommon level of entrepreneurial drive. The new norms required for success are already evident in many of the high-tech industries in the United States, Europe and Japan.

Chapter 7 R.M. Grant, Knowledge and Organization

In this chapter, Grant talks about knowledge and its application to production, and how this offers considerable scope for advancing both the role of alternative economic institutions and the design of company structures. As competition intensifies and the pace of change accelerates across most business sectors, the coordination requirements for firms become increasingly complicated. Firms need to simultaneously pursue multiple performance goals: cost, efficiency, quality, innovation and flexibility. Explicit consideration of the knowledge management requirements of these complicated coordination patterns can offer insight into the choice and design of organizational structures.

Chapter 8 C. Leadbeater, How Should Knowledge Be Owned?

Leadbeater shows us that the managerial focus of knowledge-based theories of the firm is too narrow. The ability of firms to compete in the knowledge-driven economy will depend on how their internal capabilities combine with a wider policy framework that conditions that activities. The implications of the knowledge-driven economy for public policy extend well beyond familiar issues that are to do with fiscal incentives for research and development, standards of public education or business links with universities. It will raise much more fundamental issues about how economies should be organized to increase the productivity of their knowledge.

This chapter considers the importance of innovative forms of ownership for the growth of the knowledge-driven economy. It calls for a hybrid economic culture that offers everyone the chance to compete via a world-class basic education system, as found in Japan and Germany, but also encourages radical innovation by means of an open, liberal and entrepreneurial culture, as is found in California.

Chapter 9   F.E. Murray, Following Distinctive Paths of Knowledge: Strategies for Organizational Knowledge Building within Science-based Firms

This chapter by Murray offers a framework based on control theory to distinguish between the state of knowledge and the processes that shape knowledge within the firm. It then turns to the literature on the sociology of science and technological trajectories to probe basic processes in the production of scientific knowledge. Building a taxonomy of knowledge paths that represent different ways in which knowledge-building processes can be used together, the chapter concludes with an outline of the organizational implications of these different paths. Such a knowledge path analysis suggests that the costs of search and assembly, their organizational requirements and the likelihood of success are crucial considerations in a firm's decision making about where to search for knowledge and how to assemble it. Knowledge paths require a cluster of organizational processes and shed light on how to building a new path when there are dramatic shifts in the external knowledge context of the firm. Knowledge evolution will be at the heart of sustainable competitive advantage for knowledge-based firms.

Chapter 10   H.W. Chesbrough and K. Kusunoki, The Modularity Trap: Innovation, Technology Phase Shifts and the Resulting Limits of Virtual Organizations

Chesbrough and Kusunoki develop a contingency framework that firms may use to align their organizational strategy with the technology they are pursuing. They argue that the character of technology is not static, but, rather, evolves from a 'integral' to a 'modular' type before cycling back. As the technology shifts from one phase to the other, the optimal organizational configuration of the firm must also shift if the firm is to continue to capture value from its innovation activities. Given difficulties of this process, however, the chapter also offers a conceptual framework of organizational traps that helps explain how and why a firm fails to capture value from innovation after technology phase shifts. The framework is applied to the Japanese hard disk drive industry.

Part III   Managing Knowledge and Transformation

Chapter 11   C.E. Lucier and J.D. Torsilieri, Can Knowledge Management Deliver Bottom-line Results?

Lucier and Torsilieri show that, in a study of 108 companies, no correlation was found between systematic management of knowledge and improved bottom-line performance. It is argued that these results require that firms set out not to manage knowledge, but to integrate it into management. Many traditional management practices remain valid, but firms must be more explicit about the link between the improved creation and use of knowledge and the benefits to customers and shareholders, and a new view of change underscoring a dynamic set of activities must be adopted. Future knowledge management will evolve from two present schools of thought: sharing-enabled knowledge and results-driven knowledge management.

Chapter 12   S. Kulkki and M. Kosonen, How Tacit Knowledge Explains Organizational Renewal and Growth: the Case of Nokia

Kulkki and Kosonen argue that the contextually embedded and future-oriented nature of knowledge may explain growth in terms of organizational dynamism and renewal, even on an international and global scale. The dynamic nature of knowledge as a growth engine is derived from its tacitness.

This chapter looks at the Nokia Corporation because it achieved its exceptional growth and renewal capability while it profitably transformed itself from a diversified European conglomerate into a focused global telecommunications company. The Nokia case shows that the emergence of individual knowledge – and, consequently, organizational tacit knowledge – may be accelerated if the company offers opportunities for individuals to learn and experience demanding new things by stretching them. The Nokia case also demonstrates ways of acting that cause individuals to be interested in, and concerned about, the future.

Chapter 13   H. Naito, Knowledge is Commitment

Naito shows that knowledge creation is an approach for solving new or historically unresolved issues, with socialization forming the most important knowledge-creation activity. This article considers a variety of ways in which the Japanese pharmaceutical company Eisai has benefited from a knowledge-creation perspective. From its practical application, an important conclusion is that middle managers hold the key to knowledge creation by facilitating socialization, externalization and combination. Articulation of goals and mission will become even more important in an age of increasing diversity of values.

Chapter 14   K. Kikawada and D. Holtshouse, The Knowledge Perspective in the Xerox Group

Kikawada and Holtshouse examine domains in which knowledge is shown to be at work within business. They also take a look at the paths that brought Xerox and Fuji Xerox to a common view on knowledge. Xerox and Fuji Xerox hold the view that an ability to leverage knowledge resources will be critical to every company's future success. The companies' experience in managing documents and the knowledge they embody provide a valuable basis for playing a leadership role in this field.

Chapter 15   H. Takeuchi, Towards a Universal Management of the Concept of Knowledge

Takeuchi shows how knowledge management originally reflected three different approaches represented by European, American and Japanese companies respectively that is now becoming synthesized to form a universal management concept of knowledge.

This chapter particularly concentrates on the Japanese approach, which is less about measuring and managing knowledge than creating knowledge – that is, capturing knowledge gained by individuals and spreading it to others in the organization. According to this approach, exemplified in the works of Ikujiro Nonaka, knowledge involves emotion, values, hunches; companies should seek to create rather than manage knowledge; and all members in an organization are involved in creating knowledge, with middle managers serving as key knowledge engineers.

Takeuchi concludes that, as more Western organizations turn towards knowledge creation and more Japanese firms emphasize measurement, knowledge management may turn out to be the most universal management concept ever.

Chapter 16   D.J. Teece and I. Nonaka, Research Directions for Knowledge Management

Knowledge management can become an umbrella for integrating important work in accounting, economics, entrepreneurship, organizational behaviour, philosophy, marketing, sociology and strategy. Major areas for future research include: the assembling of evidence to test the proposition that firm-level competitive advantage in open economies flows from difficult-to-replicate knowledge assets; further quantification of the value of intangible assets; understanding of generic inputs, idiosyncratic inputs and profitability; and exploring the importance of entrepreneurial versus administrative capabilities.

The authors hope that, ultimately, researchers and practitioners can devise a new paradigm drawing on transdisciplinary research, expansion of the unit of analysis for knowledge-based theories and practices, and a more sophisticated 'group' epistemology. Building a solid philosophical foundation will prove the key to the development of a unified theory.

Note

1   This section was written with the assistance of Dr Josef Chytry.

PART I
KNOWLEDGE, CREATION AND LEADERSHIP

---

1 SECI, *Ba* and Leadership: a Unified Model of Dynamic Knowledge Creation

Ikujiro Nonaka, Ryoko Toyama and Noboru Konno

As Alvin Toffler (1990) said, we are now living in a 'knowledge-based society', where knowledge is the source of the highest-quality power. In a world where markets, products, technology, competitors, regulations and even societies change rapidly, continuous innovation and the knowledge that enables such innovation have become important sources of sustainable competitive advantage. Hence, management scholars today consider knowledge and the ability to create and utilize knowledge to be the most important source of a firm's sustainable competitive advantage (Cyert, Kumar and Williams, 1993, Drucker, 1993, Grant, 1996a, Henderson and Cockburn, 1994, Leonard-Barton, 1992 and 1995, Nelson, 1991, Nonaka, 1990, 1991 and 1994, Nonaka and Takeuchi, 1995, Quinn, 1992, Sveiby, 1997 and Winter, 1987). The raison d'être of a firm is to continuously create knowledge. Yet, despite all the talk about 'knowledge-based management' and despite the recognition of the need for a new knowledge-based theory that differs 'in some fundamental way' (Spender and Grant, 1996) from the existing economics and organizational theory, there is very little understanding of how organizations actually create and manage knowledge.

This is partially because we lack a general understanding of knowledge and the knowledge-creating process. The 'knowledge management' that academics and businesspeople talk about often means just 'information management'. In the long tradition of Western management, the organization has been viewed as an information-processing machine that takes and processes information from the environment to solve a problem and adapts to the environment based on a given goal. This static and passive view of the organization fails to capture the dynamic process of knowledge creation.

Instead of merely solving problems, organizations create and define problems, develop and apply new knowledge to solve the problems, then, further, develop new knowledge in the process of problem solving. The organization is not merely an information-processing machine, but an entity that creates knowledge by virtue of action and interaction (Cyert and March, 1963, and Levinthal and Myatt, 1994). It interacts with its environment, reshapes the environment, and even itself, in the process of knowledge creation. Hence, the most important aspect of understanding a firm's ability concerning knowledge is its dynamism in continuously creating new knowledge out of existing firm-specific abilities, rather than the stock of knowledge (such as that concerning a particular technology) that a firm possesses at one point in time (Barney, 1991, Lei, Hitt and Bettis, 1996, Nelson, 1991, Teece, Pisano and Shuen, 1997, and Wilkins, 1989).

With this view of the organization as an entity that creates knowledge continuously, we need to re-examine our theories of the firm – how it is organized and managed, interacts with its environment and how its members interact with each other. Our goal in this chapter is to understand the dynamic process by means of which an organization creates, maintains and exploits knowledge. The sections that follow discuss basic concepts related to the organizational knowledge-creating process, how such a process is managed and how one can lead such a knowledge-creating process. Knowledge is created in the spiral that goes through pairs of seemingly antithetical concepts such as order and chaos, micro and macro, part and whole, mind and body, tacit and explicit, self and other, deduction and induction, and creativity and control. We argue that the key to leading the knowledge-creating process is dialectic thinking, which transcends and integrates such contradictions (see Figure 1.1).

What is Knowledge?

In our theory of the knowledge-creating process, we adopt the traditional definition of knowledge as 'justified true belief'. However, our focus is on the 'justified' rather than the 'true' aspect of belief. In traditional Western epistemology (the theory of knowledge), 'truthfulness' is the essential attribute of knowledge. It is the absolute, static and non-human view of knowledge. This view, however, fails to address the dynamic, humanistic and relative dimensions of knowledge.

Knowledge is dynamic as it is created in social interactions among individuals and organizations. Knowledge is context-specific, because it depends on a particular time and space (von Hayek, 1945). Without a context, it is just information, not knowledge. For example, '1234 ABC Street' is just information. Without context, it does not mean anything. However, when put into a context, it becomes knowledge: 'My friend David lives at 1234 ABC Street, which is next to the library.'

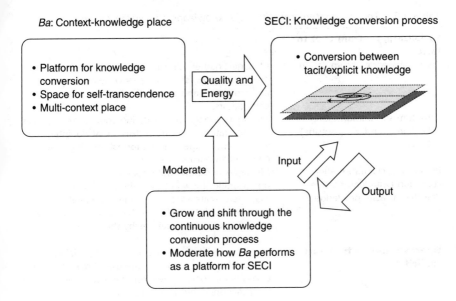

Figure 1.2   *Three elements of knowledge creating process*

Table 1.1 lists the factors that characterize the four knowledge conversion modes.

Socialization

Socialization is the process of converting new tacit knowledge through shared experiences. As tacit knowledge is difficult to formalize and often time- and space-specific, it can be acquired only through shared experience, such as spending time together or living in the same environment.

Socialization typically occurs in a traditional apprenticeship. Apprentices learn the tacit knowledge needed in their craft as being exposed to hands-on experiences rather than from written manuals or textbooks. Socialization may also occur in informal social meetings outside the workplace, where tacit knowledge such as a worldview, mental models and mutual trust can be created and shared. It also occurs beyond organizational boundaries. Firms often acquire and take advantage of the tacit knowledge embedded in customers or suppliers by interacting with them.

Externalization

The process of articulating tacit knowledge as explicit knowledge is externalization. When tacit knowledge is made explicit, knowledge is crystallized, thus allowing it to be shared by others, and it becomes the basis of new knowledge.

Concept creation in new product development is an example of this conversion process. Another example is a quality control circle, which

Table 1.1   *The factors that constitute the knowledge conversion modes*

Socialization – from tacit to tacit	
Tacit knowledge accumulation	Managers gather information from sales and production sites, share experiences with suppliers and customers and engage in dialogue with competitors.
Extra-firm social information collection (wandering outside)	Managers engage in 'wandering about', getting ideas for corporate strategy from daily social life, interaction with external experts and informal meetings with competitors outside the firm.
Intra-firm social information collection (wandering inside)	Managers find new strategies and market opportunities by wandering about inside the firm.
Transfer of tacit knowledge	Managers create a work environment that allows peers to understand the craftsmanship and expertise from practice and demonstrations by the master.
Externalization – from tacit to explicit	Managers facilitate creative and essential dialogue, the use of 'abductive thinking', the use of metaphors in dialogue for concept creation, the involvement of the industrial designers in project teams.
Combination – from explicit to explicit	
Acquisition and integration	Managers are engaged in planning strategies and operations, assembling internal and external data by using published literature, computer simulation and forecasting.
Synthesis and processing	Managers build and create manuals, documents and databases for products and services and build up material by gathering management figures and/or technical information from throughout the company.
Dissemination	Managers engage in the planning and implementation of presentations to transmit newly created concepts.
Internalization – from explicit to tacit	
Personal experience. Real-world knowledge acquisition	Managers engage in 'enactive liaisoning' activities with functional departments. Members of cross-functional development teams work on overlapping product development, search for and share new values and thoughts, and share and try to understand management visions and values through communications with fellow members of the organization.
Simulation and experimentation. Virtual world knowledge acquisition	Managers facilitate prototyping, benchmarking and the challenging spirit within the organization. Managers form teams as a model and conduct experiments and share results with the entire department.

Source: Adapted from Nonaka, Byosiere, Borucki and Konno, 1994.

allows employees to make improvements on the manufacturing process by articulating the tacit knowledge accumulated on the shop floor from years on the job. The successful conversion of tacit knowledge into explicit knowledge depends on the sequential use of metaphor, analogy and models.

Combination

This is the process of converting explicit knowledge into more complicated and systematic sets of explicit knowledge. Explicit knowledge is collected from inside or outside the organization and then combined, edited or processed to form new knowledge. The new explicit knowledge is then disseminated among the members of the organization.

Creative use of computerized communication networks and large-scale databases can facilitate this mode of knowledge conversion. When the comptroller of a company collects information from throughout the organization and puts it together in a context to make a financial report, that report is new knowledge in the sense that it is a synthesis of information from many different sources in one context. The combination mode of knowledge conversion can also include the 'breakdown' of concepts. Breaking down a concept such as a corporate vision into operationalized business or product concepts also creates systemic, explicit knowledge.

Internalization

The process of embodying explicit knowledge as tacit knowledge is internalization. Via internalization, explicit knowledge created is shared throughout an organization and converted into tacit knowledge by individuals.

Internalization is closely related to 'learning by doing'. Explicit knowledge, such as product concepts or manufacturing procedures, has to be actualized in action and practice. For example, training programmes can help trainees to understand an organization and themselves. By reading documents or manuals about their jobs and the organization and reflecting on them, trainees can internalize the explicit knowledge in such documents to enrich their tacit knowledge base. Explicit knowledge can also be embodied in simulations or experiments that trigger learning by doing.

When knowledge is internalized to become part of individuals' tacit knowledge base in the form of shared mental models or technical know-how, it becomes a valuable asset. This tacit knowledge accumulated at the individual level can then set off a new spiral of knowledge creation when it is shared with others in socialization.

How the modes interact in knowledge creation

As stated above, knowledge creation is a continuous process of dynamic interactions between tacit and explicit knowledge. Such interactions are

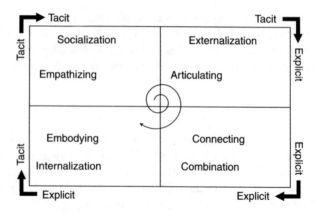

Figure 1.3   *The SECI process*

Source: Adapted from Nonaka and Takeuchi (1995)

shaped by shifts between different modes of knowledge conversion, not just one mode of interaction. Knowledge created by each of the four modes of knowledge conversion interacts in the spiral of knowledge creation. Figure 1.3 shows the four modes of knowledge conversion and the evolving spiral movement of knowledge that occurs in the SECI process.

It is important to note that the movement through the four modes of knowledge conversion forms a *spiral*, not a circle. In knowledge creation, the interaction between tacit and explicit knowledge is amplified by each of the four modes of knowledge conversion. The spiral becomes larger in scale as it moves up the ontological levels. Knowledge created in the SECI process can trigger a new spiral of knowledge creation, expanding horizontally and vertically across organizations. It is a dynamic process, starting at the individual level and expanding as it moves through communities of interaction that transcend sectional, departmental, divisional and even organizational boundaries. Organizational knowledge creation is a never-ending process that upgrades itself continuously.

This interactive spiral process takes place both intra- and inter-organizationally. Knowledge is transferred beyond organizational boundaries and knowledge from different organizations interacts to create new knowledge (Badaracco, 1991, Inkpen, 1996, Nonaka and Takeuchi, 1995, and Wikstrom and Normann, 1994). By means of this dynamic interaction, knowledge created by the organization can trigger the mobilization of knowledge held by outside constituents, such as consumers, affiliated companies, universities or distributors. For example, an innovative new manufacturing process may bring about changes in the suppliers' manufacturing process, which in turn trigger a new round of product and process innovation at the organization. Another example is the articulation of tacit knowledge possessed by customers that they themselves have not been able to articulate. A product works as the trigger to elicit tacit

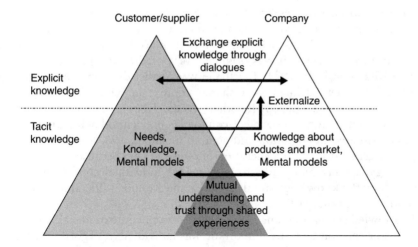

Figure 1.4   *Creating knowledge with outside constituents*

knowledge when customers give meaning to the product by purchasing, adapting, using or even not purchasing it. Their actions are then reflected in the innovative process of the organization and so a new spiral of organizational knowledge creation starts again. Figure 1.4 shows how the organization interacts with outside constituents to create knowledge.

It should also be noted that knowledge creation is a self-transcending process, in which one reaches out beyond the boundaries of one's own existence (Jantsch, 1980). In knowledge creation, one transcends the boundary between self and other, inside and outside, past and present. In socialization, self-transcendence is fundamental because tacit knowledge can only be shared in direct experiences, which go beyond individuals (Nishida, 1921). For example, in the socialization process, people empathize with their colleagues and customers, which diminishes barriers between individuals. In externalization, an individual transcends the inner and outer boundaries of the self by committing to the group and becoming one with it. Here, the sum of the individuals' intentions and ideas fuse and become integrated with the group's mental world. In combination, new knowledge generated via externalization transcends the group in analogue or digital signals. In internalization, individuals access the knowledge realm of the group and the entire organization. This again requires self-transcendence, because one has to find oneself in a larger entity.

Ba – the shared context for knowledge creation

Knowledge needs a context to be created. Contrary to the Cartesian view of knowledge, which emphasizes the absolute and context-free nature of knowledge, the knowledge-creating process is necessarily context-specific in terms of who participates and how they participate. Knowledge needs a physical context if it is to be created: 'there is no creation without place' (Casey, 1997: 16). '*Ba*' (which roughly means 'place') offers such a context.

Based on a concept that was originally proposed by the Japanese philosopher Kitaro Nishida (1921, 1970) and was further developed by Shimizu (1995), *ba* is here defined as a shared context in which knowledge is shared, created and utilized. In other words, *ba* is a shared context in cognition and action. Knowledge cannot be understood without understanding situated in cognition and action (Suchman, 1987). In knowledge creation, generation and regeneration of *ba* is the key, because *ba* provides the energy, quality and places to perform the individual conversions and move along the knowledge spiral (Nonaka and Konno, 1998, and Nonaka, Konno and Toyama, 1998).

In knowledge creation, one cannot be free from context. Social, cultural and historical contexts are important for individuals (Vygotsky, 1986) because such contexts give the basis for one to interpret information to create meanings. As Friedrich Nietzsche argued, 'there are no facts, only interpretations'. *Ba* is a place where information is interpreted to become knowledge.

Ba does not necessarily mean a physical space. The Japanese word '*ba*' means not just a physical space, but a specific time and space. *Ba* is a time–space nexus or, as Heidegger expressed it, a locationality that simultaneously includes space and time. It is a concept that unifies physical space, such as an office space, virtual space, such as e-mail, and mental space, such as shared ideals.

The key concept to understanding *ba* is 'interaction'. Some of the research on knowledge creation focuses mainly on individuals, based on the assumption that individuals are the primary driving forces of creation. For example, quoting Simon's 'All learning takes place inside individual human heads' (Simon, 1991: 125), Grant (1996b) claims that knowledge creation is an individual activity and that the primary role of firms is to apply existing knowledge. However, such an argument is based on a view of knowledge and human beings as static and inhuman. As stated above, knowledge creation is a dynamic human process that transcends existing boundaries. Knowledge is created by means of the interactions among individuals or between individuals and their environments, rather than by an individual operating alone. *Ba* is the context shared by those who interact with each other and, via such interactions, those who participate in *ba* and the context itself evolve through self-transcendence to create knowledge (see Figure 1.5). Participants of *ba* cannot be mere onlookers. Instead, they are committed to *ba* by action and interaction.

Ba has a complicated and ever-changing nature. It sets a boundary for interactions among individuals, yet its boundary is open. Because there are endless possibilities to one's own contexts, a certain boundary is required for a meaningful shared context to emerge, yet *ba* is still an open place where participants with their own contexts can come and go and the

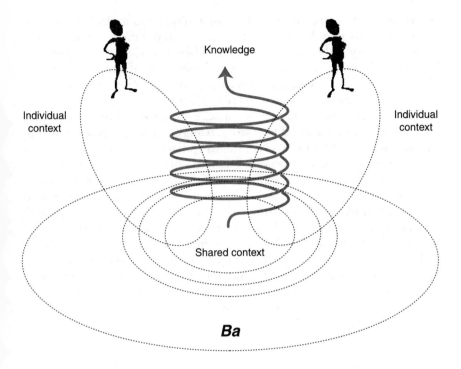

Figure 1.5   Ba *as shared context*

shared context (that is, *ba*) can continuously evolve. By providing a shared context in motion, *ba* sets binding conditions for the participants by limiting the way in which the participants view the world. Yet, it also provides participants with higher viewpoints than their own.

Ba lets participants share time and space, yet it transcends time and space. In knowledge creation – especially in socialization and externalization – it is important for participants to share time and space. A close physical interaction is important in sharing the context and forming a common language among participants. Also, as knowledge is intangible, boundaryless and dynamic and cannot be stocked, *ba* works as the platform of knowledge creation by collecting the applied knowledge of the area into a certain time and space and integrating it. However, because *ba* can be a mental or virtual place as well as a physical place, it does not have to be bound to a certain space and time.

The concept of *ba* seemingly has some similarities to the concept of 'communities of practice' (Lave and Wenger, 1991, and Wenger, 1998). Based on the apprenticeship model, the concept of communities of practice argues that members of a community learn by participating in the community of practice and gradually memorizing jobs. However, there are important differences between the concepts of communities of practice and *ba*. While a community of practice is a place where the members learn knowledge that is embedded in the community, *ba* is a place where new knowledge is created. While learning occurs in any community of practice, *ba* needs energy to become an active *ba* where knowledge is created. The boundary of a community of practice is firmly set by the task, culture and history of the community. Consistency and continuity are important for a community of practice, because it needs an identity. In contrast, the boundary of *ba* is fluid and can be changed quickly as it is set by the participants. Instead of being constrained by history, *ba* has a 'here and now' quality as an emerging relationship. It is constantly moving; it is created, functions and disappears according to need. *Ba* constantly changes, as the contexts of participants and/or the membership of *ba* change. In a community of practice, changes take place mainly at the micro (individual) level, as new participants learn to be full participants. In *ba*, changes take place at both the micro and the macro levels, as participants change both themselves and *ba* itself. While the membership of a community of practice is fairly stable and it takes time for a new participant to learn about the community to become a full participant, the membership of *ba* is not fixed – participants come and go. Whereas members of a community of practice belong to the community, participants of *ba* relate to the *ba*.

There are four types of *ba*:

1   originating *ba*;
2   dialoguing *ba*;
3   systemizing *ba*;
4   exercising *ba*.

They are defined by two dimensions of interactions (see Figure 1.6). One dimension is the type of interaction – that is, whether the interaction takes place individually or collectively. Another dimension is the media used in such interactions – that is, whether the interaction is in the form of face-to-face contact or virtual media, such as books, manuals, memos, e-mails or teleconferences. Each *ba* offers a context for a specific step in the knowledge-creating process, though the respective relationships between single *ba* and conversion modes are by no means exclusive. Building, maintaining and utilizing *ba* is important to facilitate organizational knowledge creation. Hence, one has to understand the different types of *ba* and how they interact with each other.

Originating ba

This is defined by individual and face-to-face interactions. It is a place where individuals share experiences, feelings, emotions, and mental models. It mainly offers a context for socialization, since an individual face-to-face interaction is the only way to capture the full range of physical senses and psycho-emotional reactions such as ease or discomfort, which are important elements in sharing tacit knowledge. Originating *ba* is an

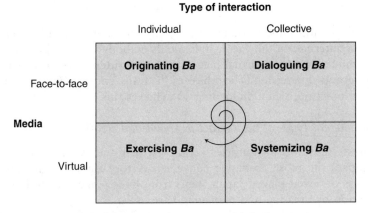

Figure 1.6　Ba, *the shared space for interaction*

existential place in the sense that it is the world where an individual transcends the boundary between self and others, by sympathizing and/or empathizing with others. From originating *ba* emerge care, love, trust, and commitment, which form the basis for knowledge conversion among individuals.

Dialoguing ba

This type of *ba* is defined by collective and face-to-face interactions. It is the place where individuals' mental models and skills are shared, converted into common terms, and articulated as concepts. Hence, dialoguing *ba* mainly offers a context for externalization. Individuals' tacit knowledge is shared and articulated through dialogues among participants. The articulated knowledge is also brought back into each individual, and further articulation occurs through self-reflection. Dialoguing *ba* is more consciously constructed than originating *ba*. Selecting individuals with the right mix of specific knowledge and capabilities is the key to managing knowledge creation in dialoguing *ba*.

Systemizing ba

This third type of *ba* is defined by collective and virtual interactions. Systemizing *ba* mainly offers a context for the combination of existing explicit knowledge, because explicit knowledge can be relatively easily transmitted to a large number of people in written form. Information technology, such as on-line networks, groupware, documentation and databanks, offer a virtual collaborative environment for the creation of systemizing *ba*. Today, many organizations use such things as electronic mailing lists and newsgroups by means of which participants can exchange necessary information or answer each other's questions to collect and disseminate knowledge and information effectively and efficiently.

Exercising ba

Defined by individual and virtual interactions, exercising *ba* mainly offers a context for internalization. Here, individuals embody explicit knowledge that is communicated via virtual media, such as written manuals or simulation programs. Exercising *ba* synthesizes the transcendence and reflection that come in action, while dialoguing *ba* achieves this via thought.

How the different types of ba *interact in knowledge creation*

Let us illustrate how a firm utilizes various *ba* with the example of Seven-Eleven Japan, the most profitable convenience store franchiser in Japan. The success of Seven-Eleven Japan stems from its management of knowledge creation by creating and managing various *ba*.

Seven-Eleven Japan uses the shop floors of the 7,000 stores around Japan as originating *ba*. Store employees accumulate tacit knowledge about customers' needs in face-to-face interactions. Long-term experiences in dealing with customers give store employees unique knowledge and insight into the local market and their customers. They often say that they can just 'see' or 'feel' how well certain items will sell in their stores, although they cannot explain why.

To promote the use of its stores as originating *ba*, Seven-Eleven Japan gives its employees extensive on-the-job training (OJT) on the shop floor. Every new employee is required to work at Seven-Eleven stores in various functions for about two years in order to accumulate experience in dealing directly with customers and managing Seven-Eleven stores. Another instrument that is used to create originating *ba* is '*burabura shain*' (walking-around employees), whose task is to wander about the stores and socialize with customers to acquire new knowledge in the field.

Their tacit knowledge about the customers is then converted into explicit knowledge in the form of 'hypotheses' about market needs. As local employees are the ones who hold tacit knowledge about their local markets, Seven-Eleven Japan lets them build their own hypotheses about the sales of particular items by giving them the responsibility for ordering items to be stocked in their stores. For example, a local worker can order more beer than usual based on the knowledge that the local community is having a festival.

To facilitate hypothesis-building, Seven-Eleven Japan actively grows and utilizes dialoguing *ba*, where tacit knowledge of local employees is externalized into explicit knowledge in the form of hypotheses by means of dialogues with others. Several employees are responsible for ordering merchandise instead of just one manager. Each employee is responsible for certain merchandise categories and, in discussions with others who are responsible for other categories, they can build hypotheses that fit changing market needs.

Another instrument to facilitate hypothesis-building is the use of field counsellors, who visit the local stores regularly to enter into dialogues with owners and employees and advise them on placing orders and managing stores. The goal is for owners and employees to articulate their tacit knowledge. If a field counsellor notices a unique hypothesis, such as new ways to display merchandise at one store, they may share that hypothesis with other stores.

The hypotheses built on the shop floor are shared throughout the company via various dialoguing *ba*. Field counsellors report on the knowledge built at the stores to their zone managers, who then disseminate that knowledge to other field counsellors. Zone managers from across Japan meet at the headquarters in Tokyo every week, where success stories and problems at local stores are shared with Seven-Eleven's top management and other zone managers. Field counsellors also have weekly meetings in which they and staff members from the headquarters, including the top management, share knowledge.

The cost of maintaining such *ba* is not small. To hold such meetings in Tokyo every week, it has been estimated that Seven-Eleven Japan spends about 18 million dollars per year on travel, lodging and related costs. However, the company emphasizes the importance of face-to-face interaction.

The hypotheses built at the dialoguing *ba* stage are tested by actual sales data, which are collected, analysed and utilized in a state-of-the-art information system. The system works as systemizing *ba*, where explicit knowledge in the form of sales data are compiled, shared and used by the headquarters and local stores.

The explicit knowledge compiled in systemizing *ba* are immediately fed back to stores by the information system so that they can build new hypotheses that suit the reality of the market better. By using the point-of-sale data and its analysis, store employees test their hypotheses about the market every day at their local stores, which work as exercising *ba*. In exercising *ba*, knowledge created and compiled in systemizing *ba* is justified by being compared to the reality of the world, and the gap between the knowledge and the reality then triggers a new cycle of knowledge creation.

Ba exists at many ontological levels and these levels may be connected to form a greater *ba*. Individuals form the *ba* of teams, which in turn form the *ba* of the organization. Then, the market environment becomes the *ba* for the organization. As stated above, *ba* is a concept that transcends the boundary between micro and macro. The organic interactions at these different levels of *ba* can amplify the knowledge-creation process.

Because *ba* often acts as an autonomous, self-sufficient unit that can be connected with other *ba* to expand knowledge, it seems to work in a similar way as a modular system or organization, in which independently designed modules are assembled and integrated to work as a whole system (Baldwin and Clark, 1997, Grant, 1999, and Sanchez and Mahoney, 1996). However, there are important differences between a modular organization and *ba*. Knowledge, especially tacit knowledge, cannot be assembled in the same way that modules are assembled into a product. In a modular system, information is partitioned into visible design rules in a precise, unambiguous and complete way. 'Fully specified and standardized component interfaces' (Sanchez and Mahoney, 1996) make the later integration of modules possible. However, relationships among *ba* are not necessarily known *a priori*. Unlike the interfaces among modules, the relationships among *ba* are not predetermined and clear.

The coherence among *ba* is achieved by means of organic interactions among *ba* based on the knowledge vision rather than a mechanistic concentration in which the centre dominates. In organizational knowledge creation, neither micro nor macro dominates. Rather, they interact with each other to evolve into a higher self. The 'interfaces' among *ba* also evolve along with *ba*. Interactive organic coherence of various *ba* and individuals that participate in *ba* has to be supported by trustful sharing of knowledge and continuous exchanges between all the units involved to create and strengthen the relationships.

For example, Maekawa Seisakusho (a Japanese industrial freezer manufacturer) consists of 80 'independent companies' that operate as autonomous and self-sufficient *ba*. These companies interact with each other organically to form Maekawa as a coherent organization. Some of the independent companies share office space and work closely together. Individual employees of the different independent companies often spend time together and form informal relationships, out of which a new project or even a new independent company can be created. When they encounter problems too large to deal with alone, several independent companies form a group to work on the problem together. Such interactions among independent companies are created and managed voluntarily, not by a plan or order from the headquarters.

Knowledge assets

At the basis of a knowledge-creating process are knowledge assets. We define these assets as 'firm-specific resources that are indispensable to creating value for the firm'.

Knowledge assets are inputs, outputs and moderating factors of the knowledge-creating process. For example, trust among organizational members is created as an output of the process and, at the same time, it moderates how *ba* functions as a platform for the whole process.

Although knowledge is considered to be one of the most important assets for a firm wanting to create a sustainable competitive advantage today, we do not yet have an effective system and tools for evaluating and managing knowledge assets. Although a variety of measures have been proposed (Edvinsson and Malone, 1997, and Stewart 1997), existing accounting systems are inadequate for capturing the value of knowledge assets, owing to the tacit nature of knowledge. Knowledge assets must be

Experiential knowledge assets	Conceptual knowledge assets
Tacit knowledge shared through common experiences	Explicit knowledge articulated through images, symbols, and language
• Skills and know-how of individuals • Care, love, trust, and security • Energy, passion, and tension	• Product concepts • Design • Brand equity
Routine knowledge assets	**Systemic knowledge assets**
Tacit knowledge routinized and embedded in actions and practices	Systemized and packaged explicit knowledge
• Know-how in daily operations • Organizational routines • Organizational culture	• Documents, specifications, manuals • Database • Patents and licences

Figure 1.7 *Four categories of knowledge assets*

built and used internally in order for their full value to be realized, because they cannot be readily bought and sold (Teece, in this volume). We need to build a system to evaluate and manage the knowledge assets of a firm more effectively.

Another difficulty in measuring knowledge assets is that they are dynamic. They are both inputs and outputs of the organization's knowledge-creating activities and, hence, they are constantly evolving. Taking a snapshot of the knowledge assets that the organization owns at one point in time is never enough to evaluate and manage them properly.

To understand how knowledge assets are created, acquired and exploited, we propose to categorize them as four types (Figure 1.7):

1 experiential
2 conceptual
3 systemic
4 routine.

Experiential knowledge assets

These consist of shared tacit knowledge, which is built by means of shared, hands-on experience among the members of the organization, and between the members of the organization and its customers, suppliers or affiliated firms.

Skills and know-how that are acquired and accumulated by individuals in experiences at work are examples of experiential knowledge assets. Emotional knowledge, such as care, love and trust, physical knowledge, such as facial expressions and gestures, energetic knowledge, such as the sense of existence, enthusiasm and tension, and rhythmic knowledge, such as improvisation and entrainment, are also examples of such knowledge assets.

Because they are tacit, experiential knowledge assets are difficult to grasp, evaluate or trade. Firms have to build their own knowledge assets from their own experiences. Their tacitness is what makes experiential knowledge assets the firm-specific, difficult-to-imitate resources that give a sustainable competitive advantage to a firm.

Conceptual knowledge assets

These consist of explicit knowledge articulated via images, symbols and language. They are based on the concepts held by customers and members of the organization.

Brand equity, which is perceived by customers, and concepts or designs, which are perceived by the members of the organization, are examples of conceptual knowledge assets. As they have tangible forms, conceptual knowledge assets are easier to grasp than experiential knowledge assets, though it is still difficult to grasp what customers and organizational members perceive exactly.

Systemic knowledge assets

These assets consist of systematized and packaged explicit knowledge, such as explicitly stated technologies, product specifications, manuals and documented and packaged information about customers and suppliers. Legally protected intellectual properties, such as licences and patents, also fall into this category.

A characteristic of systemic knowledge assets is that they can be transferred relatively easily. This is the most 'visible' type of knowledge asset and current knowledge management focuses primarily on managing systemic knowledge assets, such as intellectual property rights.

Routine knowledge assets

The tacit knowledge that is routinized and is embedded in the actions and practices of the organization make up its routine knowledge assets.

Know-how, organizational routines and organizational culture in carrying out the daily business of the organization are examples of routine knowledge assets. By means of continuous exercises, certain patterns of thinking and action are reinforced and shared among organizational members. Sharing the background of, and 'stories' about, the company also helps members form routine knowledge. A characteristic of routine knowledge assets is that they are practical knowledge.

The role of knowledge assets in knowledge creation

The four types of knowledge assets described above form the basis of the knowledge-creating process. To manage knowledge creation and exploitation effectively, a company has to 'map' its stocks of knowledge assets. However, cataloguing the existing knowledge is not enough. As stated above, knowledge assets are dynamic, and new knowledge assets can be created from existing ones.

Leading the Knowledge-creating Process

In the previous section, we presented a model of the organizational knowledge-creating process consisting of three elements: SECI, *ba* and knowledge assets. Using its existing knowledge assets, an organization creates new knowledge through the SECI process that takes place in *ba*. The knowledge created then become the knowledge assets of the organization, which become the basis for a new spiral of knowledge creation. Now we turn our attention to how such a knowledge-creation process can be managed.

The knowledge-creation process cannot be managed in the traditional sense the word, which centres on controlling the flow of information (von Krogh, Nonaka and Ichijo, 1997, and Nonaka and Takeuchi, 1995). Managers can, however, lead the organization to actively and dynamically create knowledge by providing certain conditions. In this section, we discuss the roles of top and middle managers in leading a dynamic knowledge-creating process. Especially crucial to this process is the role of knowledge producers – that is, middle managers who are at the intersection of the vertical and horizontal flows of information in the company and interact with others to create knowledge by participating in, and leading, *ba*. In knowledge creation, 'distributed leadership' – as seen in 'middle up and down' management (Nonaka and Takeuchi, 1995) – is the key, because it cannot be 'managed' using traditional top-down leadership.

Top and middle management take a leadership role by 'reading' the situation (Maxwell, 1998), as well as leading it, in working on all three elements of the knowledge-creating process. Leaders provide the knowledge vision, develop and promote sharing of knowledge assets, create and energize *ba* and enable and promote the continuous spiral of knowledge creation (see Figure 1.8). Especially important is the knowledge vision, which affects all the three layers of the knowledge-creating process.

Providing the knowledge vision

To create knowledge dynamically and continuously, an organization needs a vision that synchronizes the entire organization. It is top management's role to articulate the knowledge vision and communicate it throughout and outside the company.

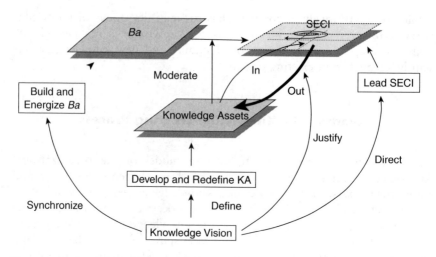

Figure 1.8 *Leading knowledge creating process*

The knowledge vision defines what kind of knowledge the company should create in what domain. The knowledge vision gives a direction to the knowledge-creating process and the knowledge created by it by asking such fundamental questions as 'What are we?', 'What should we create?', 'How can we do it?', 'Why are we doing this?' and 'Where are we going?' In short, it determines how the organization and its knowledge base evolve in the long term. As knowledge has no boundaries, any form of new knowledge can be created regardless of the existing business structure of the company. Therefore, it is important for top management to articulate a knowledge vision that transcends the boundaries of existing products, divisions, organizations and markets.

The knowledge vision also defines the value system that evaluates, justifies and determines the quality of knowledge the company creates. The aesthetic value of higher aspiration expands the boundary of knowledge creation. Together with organizational norms, routines and skills, the value system determines what kinds of knowledge are to be needed, created and retained (Leonard-Barton, 1995, and Nonaka, 1985). It also fosters spontaneous commitments of those who are involved in knowledge creation. To create knowledge, organizations should foster their members' commitment by formulating an organizational intention, as commitment underlies the human knowledge-creating activity (Polanyi, 1958).

Serving as a bridge between the visionary ideals of the top and the chaotic reality of those on the front line, the middle then has to break down the values and visions created by the top into concepts and images that guide the knowledge-creating process with vitality and direction. Middle managers work as knowledge producers to remake reality or 'produce new knowledge', according to the company's vision.

Developing and promoting the sharing of knowledge assets

Based on the knowledge vision of the company, top management has to facilitate dynamic knowledge creation by taking a leading role in managing the three elements of the knowledge-creating process. First, top management has to develop and manage the knowledge assets of the company, which form the basis of its knowledge-creating process. Many companies have created the position of chief knowledge officer (CKO) to perform this function (Davenport and Prusak, 1998). However, the CKO role, so far, has been mostly limited to managing knowledge assets as a static resource to be exploited. Top management has to play a more active role in facilitating the dynamic process of building knowledge assets from knowledge.

As knowledge is boundaryless, top management has to redefine the organization on the basis of the knowledge it owns, rather than by using existing definitions such as technologies, products and markets. Top management and knowledge producers have to read the situation, to determine what kinds of knowledge assets are available to them. It is perhaps even more important to read the situation for the kinds of knowledge they are *lacking*, according to the knowledge vision that answers the question 'Where are we going?'

To do so, they can take an inventory of the knowledge assets and, on that basis, form a strategy to build, maintain and utilize the firm's knowledge assets effectively and efficiently. For example, after studying a hybrid power system that uses an engine and a motor, Toyota realized that it did not have the technology to make the main components of the hybrid system, such as the battery, motor, converter and inverter. Realizing that it lacked knowledge assets that could determine the future of the firm, the top management of Toyota undertook research, development and production of the hybrid system internally.

It is also important to have knowledge producers who know where to find the knowledge and personnel that will enable the firm to create and exploit its knowledge. It is often difficult for a large organization to determine exactly what it knows. Top management has to foster and utilize knowledge producers who can keep track of the firm's knowledge assets and make use of them when they are needed.

It should be noted that knowledge assets – especially routine knowledge assets – can hinder as well as foster knowledge creation. Organizations are subject to inertia and it is difficult for them to diverge from the course set by their previous experiences (Hannan and Freeman, 1984). Successful experience leads to excessive exploitation of the existing knowledge and, in turn, hinders the exploration of new knowledge (March, 1991, 1999). Therefore, current capabilities may both impel and constrain future learning and actions taken by a firm (Peteraf, 1993). Core capabilities may turn into 'core rigidities' (Leonard-Barton, 1992) or a 'competence trap'

(Levitt and March, 1988), which hinder innovation rather than promote it. To avoid rigidities and traps, a firm can use an R&D project that requires knowledge that is different from the existing knowledge assets as an occasion for challenging current knowledge and creating new knowledge (Leonard-Barton, 1992).

Building, connecting and energizing *ba*

Ba can be built intentionally or created spontaneously. Top management and knowledge producers can build *ba* by providing physical space, such as meeting rooms, cyberspace, such as a computer network, or mental space, such as common goals. Forming a taskforce is a typical example of intentional building of *ba*. To build *ba*, leaders also have to choose the right mix of people to participate in and promote their interaction. It is also important for managers to 'find' and use spontaneously formed *ba*, which changes or disappears very quickly. Hence, leaders have to read the situation in terms of how members of the organization are interacting with each other and with outside environments in order to quickly capture the naturally emerging *ba*, as well as form *ba* effectively.

Further, various *ba* are connected with each other to form a greater *ba*. For that, leaders have to facilitate the interactions among various *ba* and the participants, based on the knowledge vision. In many cases, the relationships among *ba* are not predetermined. Which *ba* should be connected in which way is often unclear. Therefore, leaders have to read the situation to connect various *ba* as the relationships among them unfold.

However, building, finding and connecting *ba* is not enough for a firm to manage the dynamic knowledge-creation process. *Ba* should be 'energized' to give energy and quality to the SECI process. For that, knowledge producers have to supply necessary conditions, such as autonomy, creative chaos, redundancy, requisite variety, love, care, trust and commitment.

Autonomy

Autonomy increases the chances of finding valuable information and motivating organization members to create new knowledge. Not only does self-organizing increase the commitment of individuals, but it also can be a source of unexpected knowledge. By allowing the members of the organization to act autonomously, the organization may increase the chances to access and utilize the knowledge held by its members (Grant, 1996a, 1996b, and Wruck and Jensen, 1994).

A knowledge-creating organization with autonomy can be depicted as an 'autopoietic system' (von Krogh, 1995, and Maturana and Varela, 1980). Living, organic systems are composed of various organs, which are made up of numerous cells. Relationships between system and organs, and between organs and cells, are neither dominant–subordinate nor whole–part. Each unit, like an autonomous cell, controls all of the changes occurring continuously within itself, and each unit determines its boundary by virtue of self-reproduction. Similarly, autonomous individuals and groups in knowledge-creating organizations set task boundaries for themselves in pursuit of the ultimate goal expressed by the organization.

In the business organization, a powerful tool for creating autonomy is provided by the self-organizing team. An autonomous team can perform many functions, thereby amplifying and sublimating individual perspectives to higher levels. Researchers found that a use of cross-functional teams that involve members from a broad cross-section of different organizational activities is very effective in the innovative process (Clark and Fujimoto, 1991, and Imai, Nonaka and Takeuchi, 1985). At NEC, autonomous teams have been employed to foster the expansion of its technology programme. Sharp uses its 'Urgent Project System' to develop strategically important products. The team leader is endowed by the President with responsibility for the project and the power to select their team members from any unit in Sharp.

Creative chaos

Creative chaos stimulates the interaction between the organization and its external environment. Creative chaos is different from complete disorder; it is intentional chaos introduced to the organization by leaders to evoke a sense of crisis among the members of the organization by proposing challenging goals or ambiguous visions.

Creative chaos helps to focus people's attention and encourages them to transcend existing boundaries to define a problem and resolve it. Facing chaos, organization members experience a breakdown of routines, habits and cognitive frameworks. Periodic breakdowns, or 'unlearning', provide an important opportunity for them to reconsider their fundamental thinking and perspectives (Hedberg, 1981, and Winograd and Flores, 1986). The continuous process of questioning and re-evaluating existing premises energizes *ba* and hence fosters organizational knowledge creation. Some have called this phenomenon creating 'order out of noise' or 'order out of chaos' (Prigogine and Stengers, 1984, and von Foerster, 1984). It is important for leaders to read the situation to introduce creative chaos into *ba* in the right place at the right time and lead the creation of order out of chaos so that the organization does not fall into complete disorder.

For example, when the development team of Toyota Prius came up with a plan to improve fuel efficiency by 50 per cent, which was ambitious enough in itself, the top management rejected the plan and set a new goal to increase it by 100 per cent instead. This put the team into turmoil and it eventually discarded its original plan to use the direct-injection engine and developed the world's first commercially available hybrid car.

Redundancy

'Redundancy' here means the *intentional* overlapping of information about business activities, management responsibilities and the company as a whole.

Redundancy of information speeds up the knowledge-creating process in two ways. First, sharing redundant information promotes the sharing of tacit knowledge, because individuals can sense what others are trying to articulate. Redundant information enables individuals to transcend functional boundaries to offer advice or provide new information from different perspectives to others. Second, redundancy of information helps members of an organization to understand their role in it, which, in turn, functions to control the direction of their thinking and actions. Thus, it provides the organization with a self-control mechanism for achieving a certain direction and consistency.

Acknowledging redundancy of information is also necessary to realize the 'principle of redundancy of potential command' – that is, each part of an entire system carries the same degree of importance and has the potential to become its leader (McCulloch, 1965). At Maekawa Seisakusho, different people take leadership in turn during the course of a project, from research and prototype-building to implementation. The person whose abilities can best address the issues or problems at hand takes the leadership role to drive the project forward, guaranteeing 'the right man in the right place' in each phase of the project. Redundancy of information makes such a style of management possible and allows team members to recognize the strengths of their colleagues. By rotating through different positions and roles within the team, such as leader, support and others, specialists gain additional knowledge in related fields as well as management skills and knowledge. In short, redundancy facilitates transcendence between leaders and subordinates, generalists and specialists, and creators and users of knowledge.

Redundancy of information, however, increases the amount of information to be processed and can lead to information overload. It also increases the cost of knowledge creation, at least in the short run. Leaders have to read the situation to deal with the possible downside of redundancy by making it clear where information can be located and where knowledge is stored within the organization.

Requisite variety

Creation lies on the border between order and chaos. Requisite variety helps a knowledge-creating organization maintain the balance between order and chaos. An organization's internal diversity has to match the variety and complexity of the environment in order to deal with challenges posed by the environment (Ashby, 1956). To cope with many contingencies, an organization has to possess requisite variety, which should be a minimum for organizational integration and a maximum for effective adaptation to environmental changes.

Requisite variety can be enhanced by combining information differently, flexibly, and quickly, and by providing equal access to information throughout the organization. When an information differential exists within the organization, organization members cannot interact on equal terms, which hinders the search for different interpretations of new information. An organization's members should be able to know where information is located, where knowledge is accumulated and how information and knowledge can be accessed at the highest speed. Kao Corporation, Japan's leading maker of household products, utilizes a computerized information network to give every employee equal access to corporate information as the basis for opinion exchanges among organizational units with different perspectives.

There are two ways to realize requisite variety. One is to develop a flat and flexible organizational structure in which the different units are interlinked with an information network, thereby giving an organization's members fast and equal access to the broadest variety of information. Another approach is to change the organizational structure frequently and/ or rotate personnel frequently, thereby enabling employees to acquire interdisciplinary knowledge to deal with the complexity of the environment.

Love, care, trust and commitment

Fostering love, care, trust and commitment among members of an organization is important because those qualities form the foundation of knowledge creation (von Krogh, 1998, and von Krogh, Ichijo and Nonaka, 2000). For knowledge (especially tacit knowledge) to be shared and for the self-transcending process of knowledge creation to occur, there should be strong love, caring and trust among an organization's members. As information creates power, an individual might be motivated to monopolize it, hiding it even from their colleagues. However, because knowledge needs to be shared to be created and exploited, it is important for leaders to ensure that there is an atmosphere in which an organization's members feel safe sharing their knowledge. It is also important for leaders to cultivate commitment among organization members to motivate the sharing and creation of knowledge based on the knowledge vision.

To foster love, care, trust and commitment, knowledge producers need to be highly inspired and committed to their goal. They also need to be selfless and altruistic. They should not try to monopolize the knowledge created by the organization or take credit for other members' achievements. Also, knowledge producers need to be positive thinkers. They should try to avoid having or expressing negative thoughts and feelings. Instead, they should have creative and positive thoughts, imagination and the drive to act.

Promoting the SECI process

An organization's leadership should also promote the SECI process. Following the direction provided by the knowledge vision, knowledge producers promote organizational knowledge creation by facilitating all four modes of knowledge conversion, although their most significant contribution is made in externalization. They synthesize the tacit knowledge of front-line employees, top management and outside constituents, such as customers and suppliers, to make it explicit and incorporate it into new concepts, technology, products or systems. To do so, knowledge producers should be able to reflect on their actions. As Schön (1983) states, when a person reflects while in action, they become independent of established theory and technique and are able to construct a new theory of the unique case.

Another important task for knowledge producers is to facilitate the knowledge spiral across the different conversion modes and on different organizational levels. To facilitate the knowledge-creating process effectively, knowledge producers need to read the situation in terms of where the spiral is heading and what kind of knowledge is available to be converted, both inside and outside the organization. With this reading, knowledge producers need to improvise to incorporate necessary changes in the knowledge-creating process. Improvisation is an important factor in dynamic knowledge creating, especially when dealing with tacit knowledge (Weick, 1991). Knowledge producers should be able to improvise and facilitate improvisation by the participants in the knowledge-creation process.

Knowledge producers need to be able to create their own concepts and express them in their own words and, thus, should be able to use language effectively. Language here includes tropes (such as metaphor, metonymy, synecdoche), 'grammar' and 'context' for knowledge and non-verbal visual language, such as design. Each mode of knowledge conversion requires different kinds of language for knowledge to be created and shared effectively. For example, non-verbal language, such as body language, is essential in the socialization process because tacit knowledge cannot be expressed in articulated language. In contrast, clear, articulate language is essential in the combination process, because knowledge has to be disseminated and understood by many people. In externalization, tropes such as metaphor, metonymy and synecdoche are effective in creating concepts out of vast amounts of tacit knowledge. Therefore, knowledge producers should carefully choose and use language that is appropriate to the process of knowledge creation.

Conclusion

In this chapter, we have discussed how organizations manage the dynamic process of knowledge creation, which is characterized by dynamic interactions among organization members, and between organization members and the environment. We proposed a new model of the knowledge-creating process to understand the dynamic nature of knowledge creation and to manage such a process effectively. Three elements – the SECI process, *ba* and knowledge assets – have to interact with each other organically and dynamically. The knowledge assets of a firm are mobilized and shared in *ba*, where tacit knowledge held by individuals is converted and amplified by the spiral of knowledge in socialization, combination, externalization and internalization.

We have also discussed the role of leadership in facilitating the knowledge-creating process. Creating and understanding the knowledge vision of the company, understanding the knowledge assets of the company, facilitating and utilizing *ba* effectively and managing the knowledge spiral are the important roles that managers have to play. Especially important is the role of knowledge producers – the middle managers who are at the centre of the dynamic knowledge-creating process.

All three elements of the knowledge-creating process should be integrated under the leadership so that a firm can create knowledge continuously and dynamically. The knowledge-creating process should become a discipline for organization members in terms of how they think and act in finding, defining and solving problems.

In this chapter we have focused primarily on the organizational knowledge-creating process that takes place within a company. We described this process as the dynamic interaction between organization members and between organization members and the environment. However, the process is not confined within the boundaries of a single company. The market – where the knowledge held by companies interacts with that held by customers – is also a place for knowledge creation. It is also possible for groups of companies to create knowledge. If we further raise the level of analysis, we arrive at a discussion of how so-called national systems of innovation can be built. For the immediate future, it will be important to examine how companies, governments and universities can work together to make knowledge creation possible.

References

Argyris, C., and Schön, D.A. (1978) *Organizational Learning*. Reading, MA: Addison-Wesley.

Ashby, W.R. (1956) *An Introduction to Cybernetics*. London: Chapman & Hall.

Badaracco, J.L., Jr (1991) *The Knowledge Link: How Firms Compete through Strategic Alliances*. Boston: Harvard Business School Press.

Baldwin, C.Y., and Clark, K. (1997) 'Managing in an age of modularity', *Harvard Business Review*, Sep./Oct, 75 (5): 84–94.

Bateson, G. (1973) *Steps to an Ecology of Mind*. London: Paladin.

Bateson, G. (1979) *Mind and Nature: A Necessary Unity*. New York: Bantam Books.

Barney, J.B. (1991) 'Firm resources and sustained competitive advantage', *Journal of Management*, 17 (1): 99–120.

Brown, J.S., and Deguid, P. (1991) 'Organizational learning and communities-of-practice: toward a unified view of working, learning, and innovation', *Organization Science*, 2 (1): 40–57.

Casey, E.S. (1997) *The Fate of Place: A Philosophical History*. Berkeley, CA: University of California Press.

Choo, C.W. (1998) *The Knowing Organization: How Organizations Use Information to Construct Meaning, Create Knowledge, and Make Decisions*. Oxford: Oxford University Press.

Clark, K.B., and Fujimoto, T. (1991) *Product Development Performance: Stragegy, Organization, and Management in the World Auto Industry*. Boston, MA: Harvard Business School Press.

Cohen, M.D., and Bacdayan, P. (1994) 'Organizational routines are stored as procedural memory: evidence from a laboratory study', *Organization Science*, Dec.: 554–68.

Cyert, R.M., Kumar, P.K., and Williams, J.R. (1993) 'Information, market imperfections and strategy', *Strategic Management Journal*, 14 (Winter Special): 47–58.

Cyert, R.M., and March, J.G. (1963) *A Behavioral Theory of the Firm*. Englewood Cliffs, NJ: Prentice Hall.

Daft, R.L., and Weick, K.E. (1984) 'Toward a model of organizations as interpretation systems', *Academy of Management Review*, 9 (2): 284–95.

Davenport, T.H., and Prusak, L. (1998) *Working Knowledge*. Boston: Harvard Business School Press.

Dierickx, I., and Cool, K. (1989) 'Asset stock accumulation and sustainability of competitive advantage', *Management Science*, 35: 1504–11.

Dodgson, M. (1993) 'Organizational learning: a review of organizations as interpretation systems', *Organizational Studies*, 14: 375–94.

Dopson, S., and Stewart, R. (1990) 'What is happening to middle management?', *British Journal of Management*, 1: 3–16.

Drucker, P. (1993) *Post-Capitalist Society*. London: Butterworth Heinemann.

Duncan, R., and Weiss, A. (1979) 'Organizational learning: implications for organizational design', in B.M. Staw (ed.), *Research in Organizational Behavior*, Vol. 1. Greenwich, CT: JAI Press. pp. 75–123.

Edivinsson, L., and Malone, M.S. (1997) *Intellectual Capital*. New York: Harper Business.

von Foerster, H. (1984) 'Principles of self-organization in a socio-managerial context', in H. Ulrich and G.J.B. Probst (eds), *Self-organization and Management of Social Systems*. Berlin: Springer-Verlag. pp. 2–24.

Gleick, J. (1987) *Chaos*. New York: Viking Press.

Gouldner, A.W. (1954) *Patterns of Industrial Bureaucracy*. Glencoe, IL: The Free Press.

Grant, R.M. (1996a) 'Prospering in dynamically-competitive environments: organizational capability as knowledge integration', *Organization Science*, 7: 375–87.

Grant, R.M. (1996b) 'Toward a knowledge-based theory of the firm', *Strategic Management Journal*, 17 (Winter Special): 109–22.

Grant, R.M. (1999) 'Knowledge and organization'. Working Paper, Georgetown University.

Hannan, M.T., and Freeman, J.H. (1984) 'Structural inertia and organizational change', *American Sociological Review*, 49: 149–64.

von Hayek, F.A. (1945) 'The use of knowledge in society', *The American Economic Review*, 35: 519–30.

Hedberg, B. (1981) 'How organizations learn and unlearn', in P. Nystrom and W. Starbuck (eds), *Handbook of Organizational Design*. New York: Oxford University Press.

Henderson, R., and Cockburn, I. (1994) 'Measuring competence: exploring firm-effects in pharmaceutical research', *Strategic Management Journal*, 15 (Winter Special): 63–84.

Imai, K., Nonaka, I. and Takauchi, H. (1985) 'Managing the new product development process: how Japanese companies learn and unlearn', in K.B. Clark, R.H. Hayes and C. Lorenz (eds), *The Uneasy Alliance: Managing the Productivity-technology Dilemma*. Boston, MA: Harvard Business School Press. pp. 337–81.

Inkpen, A.C. (1996) 'Creating knowledge through collaboration', *California Management Review*, 39 (1): 123–40.

Jantsch, E. (1980) *The Self-organizing Universe*. Oxford: Pergamon Press.

Johnson-Laird, P.N. (1983) *Mental Models*. Cambridge: Cambridge University Press.

Kogut, B. and Zander, U. (1996) 'What firms do? Coordination, identity, and learning', *Organization Science*, 7 (5): 502–18.

von Krogh, G. (1995) *Organizational Epistemology*. New York: St Martin's Press.

von Krogh, G. (1998) 'Care in knowledge creation', *California Management Review*, 40 (3): 133–53.

von Krogh, G., Nonaka, I., and Ichijo, K. (1997) 'Develop knowledge activists!', *European Management Journal*, 15 (5): 475–83.

von Krogh, G., Ichijo, K., and Nonaka, I. (2000) *Enabling Knowledge Creation*. New York: Oxfird University Press.

Lave, J., and Wenger, E. (1991) *Situated Learning – Legitimate Peripheral Participation*. Cambridge: Cambridge University Press.

Lei, D., Hitt, M.A., and Bettis, R. (1996) 'Dynamic core competences through meta-learning and strategic context', *Journal of Management*, 22 (4): 549–69.

Leonard-Barton, D. (1992) 'Core capabilities and core rigidities: a paradox in managing new product development', *Strategic Management Journal*, 13 (5): 363–80.

Leonard-Barton, D. (1995) *Wellsprings of Knowledge*. Boston, MA: Harvard Business School Press.

Levinthal, D., and Myatt, J. (1994) 'Co-evolution of capabilities and industry: the evolution of mutual fund processing', *Strategic Management Journal*, 15 (Winter Special): 45–62.

Levitt, B., and March, J.G. (1988) 'Organizational learning', *Annual Review of Sociology*, 14: 319–340.

Machlup, F. (1983) 'Semantic quirks in studies of information', in F. Machlup and U. Mansfield (eds), *The Study of Information*. New York: John Wiley & Sons. pp. 641–71.

March, Jim (1991) 'Exploration and exploitation in organizational learning', *Organization Science*, 2 (1): 101–23.

March, Jim (1999) *The Pursuit of Organizational Intelligence*. Malden, MA: Blackwell Publishers.

Maturana, H.R., and Varela, F.J. (1980) *Autopoiesis and Cognition: The Realization of the Living*. Dordrecht, Holland: Reidel.

Maxwell, J.C. (1998) *The 21 Irrefutable Laws of Leadership: Follow Them and People Will Follow You*. London: Thomas Nelson.

McCulloch, W. (1965) *Embodiments of Mind*. Cambridge, MA: The MIT Press.

Merton, R.K. (1940) 'Bureaucratic structure and personality', *Social Forces*, 18: 560–68.

Nelson, R.R. (1991) 'Why do firms differ, and how does it matter?', *Strategic Management Journal* 12 (Winter Special): 61–74.

Nishida, K. (1921) *An Inquiry into the Good*. Abe, M., and Ives, C. (trans) (1990). New Haven/London: Yale University.

Nishida, K. (1970) *Fundamental Problems of Philosophy: The World of Action and the Dialectical World*. Tokyo: Sophia University.

Nonaka, I. (1988) 'Toward middle-up-down management: accelerating information creation', *Sloan Management Review*, 29 (3): 9–18.

Nonaka, I. (1990) *Chishiki-Souzou no Keiei* (A Theory of Organizational Knowledge Creation). Tokyo: Nihon Keizai Shimbun-sha (in Japanese).

Nonaka, I. (1991) 'The knowledge-creating company', *Harvard Business Review*, November–December: 96–104.

Nonaka, I. (1994) 'A dynamic theory of organizational knowledge creation', *Organization Science*, 5 (1): 14–37.

Nonaka, I., Byosiere, P., Borucki, C.C., and Konno, N. (1994) 'Organizational knowledge creation theory: a first comprehensive test', *International Business Review*, 3 (4): 337–51.

Nonaka, I., and Kigyo, S. (1985) *Corporate Evolution: Managing Organizational Information Creation*. Tokyo: Nihon Keizai Shimbunsha.

Nonaka, I., and Kiyosawa, T. (1987) *3M no Chousen* (The Challenge of 3M). Tokyo: Nihon Keizai Shinbunsha (in Japanese).

Nonaka, I. and Konno, N. (1993) 'Chisiki beesu sosiki' (knowledge-based organization), *Business Review*, 41 (1): 59–73 (in Japanese).

Nonaka, I., and Konno, N. (1998) 'The Concept of "*ba*": building a foundation for knowledge creation', *California Management Review*, 40 (3): 1–15.

Nonaka, I., Konno, N., and Toyama, R. (1998) 'Leading knowledge creation: a new framework for dynamic knowledge management', 2nd annual knowledge Management Conference, Haas School of Business, University of California Berkeley. 22–24 September.

Nonaka, I., and Takeuchi, H. (1995) *The Knowledge-creating Company*. New York: Oxford University Press.

Peters, T.J. (1987) *Thriving on Chaos*. New York: Alfred A. Knopf.

Peteraf, M.A. (1993) 'The cornerstones of competitive advantage: a resource-based view', *Strategic Management Journal*, 14: 179–91.

Pinchot, G., III (1985) *Intrapreneuring: Why You Don't Have to Leave the Corporation to Become an Entrepreneur*. New York: Harper & Row.

Polanyi, M. (1958) *Personal Knowledge*. Chicago, IL: University of Chicago Press.

Polanyi, M. (1966) *The Tacit Dimension*. London: Routledge & Kegan Paul.

Porras, J.I., and Collins, J.C. (1994) *Built to Last: Successful Habits of Visionary Companies*. New York: Harper Collins.

Prahalad, C.K., and Hamel, G. (1990) 'The core competence of the corporation', *Harvard Business Review*, 68 (3): 79–91.

Prigogine, I. (1980) *From Being to Becoming: Time and Complexity in the Physical Sciences*. San Francisco: W.H. Freeman & Co.

Prigogine, I., and Stengers, I. (1984) *Order Out of Chaos: Man's New Dialogue with Nature*. New York: Bantam Books.

Quinn, J.B. (1992) *Intelligent Enterprise: A Knowledge and Service-based Paradigm for Industry*. New York: The Free Press.

Sanchez, R., and Mahoney, J.T. (1996) 'Modularity, flexibility, and knowledge management in product and organization design', *Strategic Management Journal*, 17 (10): 63–7.

Schoenhoff, D.M. (1993) *The Barefoot Expert*. Westport, CN: Greenwood Press.

Schön, D.A. (1983) *The Reflective Practitioner*. New York: Basic Books.

Selznik, P. (1949) *TVA and the Grass Roots*. Berkeley, CA: University of California Press.

Senge, P.M. (1990) *The Fifth Discipline: The Age and Practice of the Learning Organization*. London: Century Business.

Shakai Keizai Seisansei Honbu (1998) *Shin Nihon-gata Sangyou, Kigyou Keiei Saikouchiku heno Teigen*, Shakai Seisansei Honbu (in Japanese).

Shimizu, H. (1995) '*Ba*-principle: new logic for the real-time emergence of information', *Holonics*, 5 (1): 67–79.

Simon, H.A. (1945) *Administrative Behavior*. New York: Macmillan.

Simon, H.A. (1973) 'Applying information technology to organization design', *Public Administration Review*, 33: 268–78.

Simon, H.A. (1983) *Reason in Human Affairs*. Stanford, CA: Stanford University Press.

Simon, H.A. (1991) 'Bounded rationality and organizational learning', *Organization Science*, 2: 125–34.

Spender, J.C. (1996) 'Making knowledge the basis of a dynamic theory of the firm', *Strategic Management Journal*, 17 (Winter Special): 45–62.

Spender, J.C., and Grant, R.M. (1996) 'Knowledge and the firm: overview', *Strategic Management Journal*, 17 (Winter Special): 5–9.

Stewart, Tom (1997) *Intellectual Capital: The New Wealth of Organizations*. New York: Doubleday.

Suchman, L. (1987) *Plans and Situated Actions: The Problem of Human-machine Communication*. New York: Cambridge University Press.

Sveiby, K. (1997) *The New Organizational Wealth*. San Francisco: Berret-Koehler.

Takeuchi, H., and Nonaka, I. (1986) 'The new *new* product development game', *Harvard Business Review*, July–Aug.: 137–46.

Taylor. F.W. (1991) *The Principles of Scientific Management*. New York: Harper.

Teece, D.J. (2001) 'Strategies for managing knowledge assets: the role of firm structure and industrial context', in David J. Teece and Ikujiro Nonaka (eds), *Managing Industrial Knowledge*. London: Sage.

Teece, D.J., Pisano, G., and Shuen, A. (1997) 'Dynamic capabilities and strategic management', *Strategic Management Journal*, 18 (7): 509–33.

Toffler, A. (1990) *Powershift: Knowledge, Wealth and Violence at the Edge of the 21st Century*. New York: Bantam Books.

Tsoukas, H. (1996) 'The firm as a distributed knowledge system: a constructionist approach', *Strategic Management Journal*, 17 (Winter Special): 11–25.

Vygotsky, L. (1986) *Thought and Language*. Cambridge, MA: The MIT Press.

Weick, K.E. (1991) 'The non-traditional quality of organizational learning', *Organizational Science*, 2 (1): 116–24.

Wenger, E. (1998) *Communities of Practice: Learning, Meaning, and Identity*. Cambridge: Cambridge University Press.

Whitehead, A.N., as recorded in L. Price (1954) *Dialogues of Alfred North Whitehead*. Boston, MA: Little, Brown and Company.

Wikstrom, S., and Normann, R. (1994) *Knowledge and Value: A New Perspective on Corporate Transformation*. London: Routledge.

Wilkins, M. (1989) *The History of Foreign Investment in the United States to 1914*. Cambridge, MA: Harvard University Press.

Winograd, T., and Flores, F. (1986) *Understanding Computers and Cognition: A New Foundation for Design*. Reading, MA: Addison-Wesley.

Winter, S.G. (1987) 'Knowledge and competence as strategic assets', in D.J. Teece (ed.), *The Competitive Challenge: Strategies for Industrial Innovation and Renewal*. Cambridge, MA: Ballinger. pp. 159–84.

Wruck, K.H., and Jensen, M.C. (1994) 'Science, specific knowledge, and total quality management', *Journal of Accounting and Economics*, 18: 247–87.

2   Structure and Spontaneity: Knowledge and Organization

John Seely Brown and Paul Duguid

Knowledge in the Firm

The 'information economy' steamrollers ahead, by many accounts undermining venerable institutions as it goes along. Yet, its implications for business organization remain unclear. Some futurists predict that the hierarchical organization of the industrial economy, or 'second wave', will give way to 'flat' organizations, 'hollow' companies, 'virtual' firms or 'electronic cottages' in the 'third wave'. With ever more 'perfect' information provided by IT, some predict outsourcing and subcontracting will shrink firms until, in most cases, they are little more than a self-organizing network of individual entrepreneurs. The structure of formal organization, according to these arguments, is giving way before the spontaneity of self-organizing markets.[1]

The evidence for this one-directional trajectory from structure to spontaneity, however, is not quite so clear cut. Confident predictions that the firm is shrinking and subcontracting confront daily announcements of mergers and consolidations. In June of 1998, the US Justice Department's lawyers testified before Congress that the year was on track for the first 2-trillion-dollar year for mergers. Seven of history's ten largest mergers had occurred in the first six months. This testimony came before the giant mergers of Chrysler and Mercedes, Deutsche Bank and Bankers Trust, Citibank and Travelers, and Exxon and Mobil (*New York Times*, 1998).

No doubt some of these examples actually provide evidence of the difficulties large organizations can face today. Several of the late-1990s mergers do suggest dinosaurs herding together in the face of likely extinction. Bank mergers, for example, probably reflect the precarious future of conventional banking, while car manufacturers and 'big oil' seem to be consolidating in response to significant overcapacity. However, many other merging companies look less like dinosaurs and more like phoenixes – transformed organizations rising from the ashes of old business models. These might include examples of 'convergence', such as AT&T's absorption of TCI or Time-Warner's of Turner Broadcasting. They surely include Internet-driven combinations, such as MCI's merger with WorldCom, IBM's takeover of Lotus, AT&T's purchase of IBM's Global Network and, especially, AOL's capture of Netscape. Meanwhile, Microsoft, a still-growing giant, always stands prepared to expand by buying access to both new markets and new ideas.

Other evidence that there is room for firms to expand as well as shrink in the new economy comes from the dramatic growth of small start-ups. However virtual the organizations, firms are still hiring in Silicon Valley. The title of 'fastest growing company ever' is eagerly pursued and changes hands frequently. It is true that most of these businesses are several orders of magnitude smaller than General Motors was in its heyday. None the less they indicate that there is still life left in formal organization and collective practice. Most significant from our point of view, the more inventive and innovative start-ups seem to depend heavily on closely (rather than loosely) knit groups of interdependent workers (Cusumano and Yoffie, 1998, and Newman, 1998).

The distance between predictions that the formally structured enterprise is irrelevant and evidence that it still has life indicates, we suspect, continuing uncertainty about what it is that firms actually do. In contrast to a variety of neoclassical accounts that portray the firm as an approximation of the market, in this chapter we endorse the 'knowledge-based' view of the firm. Knowledge, we argue, is not necessarily best served by spontaneous organization.[2]

To make this argument, we first look briefly at notions of self-organization – its strengths as well as its limits. We point to historical evidence of the contributions of organizations and institutions to the development of knowledge.[3] However, we reject both a simple binary division between hierarchies and markets and the implicit assumptions that there is spontaneity and only epiphenomenal structure in markets or that there is structure and consequently little spontaneity in firms (Duguid and da Silva Lopes, 1999). These pairs are not mutually exclusive categories. Arguments about the importance of organization do not detract from claims made for the extraordinary power and spontaneity of self-organization.

Elsewhere we have looked outside the firm to argue that organizations represent areas of intensive husbandry in a broader, complex-adaptive 'ecology'.[4] Here, we want to turn inside to suggest that, within, firms offer useful structuring resources for the experimentation, improvisation and inventiveness that occur in their midst. We hope to give due acknowledgement to both the structure and the spontaneity within firms and the synergistic relationship between the two.

Consequently, we also argue that many knowledge-based accounts, in stressing the firm's particular ability to add value by organizing knowledge, often oversimplify the internal structure of the firm and underestimate its internal diversity. If the organization were – as some knowledge-based arguments suggest – a unitary 'knowledge system', we would expect knowledge to flow within it. However, the organizational literature is full of laments about the difficulty of moving insights from R&D to production, from customer service to sales and marketing, from line management to staff, from top to bottom, from bottom to top and so on. You do not have to read far in the literature before coming across the lament of Hewlett Packard's CEO that if only HP knew what HP knew it would be far more successful.[5]

We suggest, then, that some knowledge-based views actually under-estimate the challenge of organizing knowledge. Only by recognizing the internal divisions that exist in all but the smallest organizations, we argue, is it possible to see why organizing knowledge is, on the one hand, so important, yet, on the other, so difficult. So a principal goal here is to provide an account of the internal 'texture' of all but the smallest firms (any firm that has an internal division of labour is likely to have the sorts of internal divisions that we talk about). We address this in terms of the diverse communities that develop around the multiple practices within most organizations.[6]

Concluding, then, that firms are neither imperfect knowledge markets nor unitary knowledge systems, we discuss the implications of our view for organization theory and organizational communication.

Organization and Self-organization

Disintermediation, demassification and disaggregation have become watchwords of cyberspace. New technologies, it is argued, are breaking collectives down into individual units. Contracting entrepreneurs are replacing formal organizations. Any form of coherence and coordination beyond the individual should result from self-organizing systems, not from hierarchical governance. Hence, the firm has little future (see, for example, George Gilder (1994) for disintermediation, Alvin Toffler (1980) for demassification and Nicholas Negroponte (1996) for disaggregation).

Curiously, many who argue for self-organization can sound less like economists or technologists and more like entomologists as bees, ants and termites, as well as bats and other small mammals, provide much of the evidence for the self-organizing case. In a related vein, others draw examples from 'artificial life', the systems of which are themselves usually modelled on insect- and animal-like behaviour (see Kelly, 1994, for bees, Clark, 1997, for termites, Dawkins, 1986, and Turkle, 1996, for artificial life). While all these provide forceful models, it is important to recognize their limits. Humans and insects show many intriguing similarities, but these should not mask their important differences.

In particular, most champions of complicated adaptive systems, particularly those of artificial life, say relatively little about the importance to human behaviour of deliberate social organization. To pursue the analogies from entomology or artificial life much further, we would need to know what might happen if insects decided to form a committee, bats to pass a law or artificial agents to organize a strike or join a firm.

Ants moving across a beach, for example, do exhibit elaborate, collective patterns that emerge as each individual adjusts to the environment and its immediate neighbour. In this way, they recall aspects of human behaviour – of, for example, the uncoordinated synchronicity of sunbathers on the same beach seeking the sun or trying to keep sand from blowing into their sandwiches. However, unlike the sunbathers, ants do not construct coastal highways to reach the beach or beachfront restaurants and shops to provide food or farms to supply the shops. Neither do they establish regulations to limit roads, shops and farming or courts to rule on the infringement of private property rights or, indeed, regulations or property rights at all.

As a result of this institution-building, humans are probably more resilient in the face of diminishing provisions from their local ecology. (Failure to factor in the contribution of human organization to human survival has undermined many a gloomy Malthusian prediction.) By organizing together, people have found out how to produce more food out of the same areas of land, extend known energy resources and search for new ones, establish new regions for human endeavour, hold natural forces at bay and design the very technology that is now paradoxically invoked as the end of organization. In all such cases, organization has helped to foster and focus humanity's most valuable resource: its infinitely renewable knowledge base (North, 1981).

Humanity has relied on organization not merely to harness advantage, but to ward off disasters produced by the downside of self-organizing behaviour. For example, it is widely accepted that establishing and continually adjusting socially acknowledged property rights has limited the 'tragedy of the commons'. Establishing certain trading regulations has prevented markets from spontaneously imploding. (As Shapiro and Varian point out in *Information Rules*, 1999, even in an information economy, conventional antitrust rules and monopoly regulation have a place.) Such institutional constraints help channel self-organizing behaviour and knowledge production in productive rather than destructive directions. This ability may be one of humanity's greatest assets.

It is easy to cite the undeniable power of spontaneous organization as a way to damn formal organization. Undoubtedly, in the hands of von Mises or Hayek, analysis of self-organization has helped reveal not just the limits but also the dangers of formal organization (von Hayek, 1988). In particular, it has helped show the folly of planning economies or ignoring markets. These arguments do not, however, necessarily reject planning or non-market behaviour on a more local scale. Formal organization, as shown by Fukuyama and Shulsky (1997), is particularly useful for goal-driven behaviour, high reliability and tight coordination, as well as, we will argue, knowledge creation and innovation. In all, it makes no more sense to demonize formal organization in the abstract than it does to demonize self-organizing systems. Rather, we believe, each is best deployed to restrain the other's worst excesses. As Orton and Weick (1990) suggest, the

nship between tightly coupled and loosely coupled systems is
cal, not dichotomous.

Organization and Technology

While it is often acknowledged that humans distinguish themselves from
most other lifeforms by the increasingly sophisticated technologies they
design, it is less often noted that they also distinguish themselves by
designing sophisticated social institutions. Yet, it is important to note the
ways in which these technologies are themselves the outcome of institutional endeavour. Even new technology remains profoundly enmeshed in
modern institutional structures. In the welter of private-sector Internet
expansion, it is easily forgotten that the Net itself is not the product of self-
organization – it required government initiative in tandem with major
business investment.

Nevertheless, some people align new technology with self-organization,
creating an implicit opposition between technology, individual freedom
and self-organization on one side and formal organization, individual
subjection and institutions on the other. New technology, this opposition
assumes, will ultimately lead society back to the 'electronic cottage', the
'electronic frontier' or the 'global village', where there will be no further
need for modern-day institutions and organizations (see Toffler, 1980, for
the electronic cottage, Rheingold, 1993, for the electronic frontier, and
McLuhan, 1962, for the global village).

Though many such arguments implicitly hark back to an earlier era of
the cottage economy, frontier expansion and village society, there is little
historical evidence for such claims. The last great period of technological
innovation, by contrast, illustrates the significance of institutions and
organizations to technological innovation. The early nineteenth century
gave us the bicycle, train and steamship, as well as the telegraph, photo-
graph and power-driven printing press, which together helped to transform
transportation and communication in the first half of the century. This
period also produced the slide rule and prototypes of the calculator and
computer. The latter part of the century then saw, among other things, the
refinement of the electric motor and dynamo, and the development of
the typewriter, carbon paper, mimeograph, filing cabinet, telephone, film,
record player, punch-card processor, internal combustion engine, motor-
cycle, car and airplane, along with numerous dramatic advances in
materials, engineering, chemistry and physics.

Yet, it is plausibly argued that the creative energies of the nineteenth
century are evident less in industry, science or the arts than in the new kinds
of social institution that developed. Among these are the modern research
university, private research laboratory, public library, post office, limited
liability company, modern business organization, modern government

agency and unions. Indeed, the economic historian Douglass North (1990) suggests that an absence of adequate institutions caused the century-long lag between the dawn of the Industrial Revolution and the late-nineteenth century's dramatic technological and economic expansion. Similarly, Alfred Chandler, the business historian, claims that half of this expansion resulted from organizational, not technological, innovation. New universities played a vital role in the advancement of scientific knowledge. New business organizations were critical to marshalling the means for capital- and resource-intensive exploration and innovation. Governments oversaw the expansion and stability of markets. In Chandler's apt phrase, nineteenth-century technological advances were products of the 'visible hand' of organization, not just the invisible hand of the market (1977).

More recently, the economist Paul David (1990) has brought a similar argument to bear on the modern economy to explain the 'productivity paradox' – that huge investments in new technology have had barely any effect on national productivity. David's argument suggests that the struggle to develop third-wave institutions and organizations adequate for a new economy may be restraining the potential of technological innovation and investment. While it does suggest the inevitable limits of current institutions and organizations, this argument does not support the idea that institutions and organizations will not be needed at all in the third wave (Sichel, 1997).

If nothing else, these arguments portray a complicated relationship between organizations and technology that pictures of new technology vanquishing old institutions and 'empowering' individuals grossly over-simplify. While communications technology has dispersed power and control in some sectors, in others it has clearly led to centralization and concentration. Fukuyama and Shulsky point, for instance, to the extra-ordinary success of firms such as Wal-Mart, Federal Express and Benetton, which have used technology to centralize decision making and significantly disempower their peripheries. In other sectors, the trend has also been towards concentration. Perhaps most paradoxically, the mergers of com-munications firms, both those involved in content (the movies, broadcast media and publishing, in particular) and those involved in infrastructure (telecommunications, software and hardware) suggest that, where new technology is used most intensively, there are pressures towards concen-tration as well as dispersal. Elsewhere, some firms that pursued decentral-ization, federation and subsidiarity are now recentralizing. For example, Royal Dutch Shell – one of the most well known and widely applauded decentralizers of the 1990s – announced that it would centralize its 'treasury', for which decentralization had been too costly and inefficient. More generally, *The Economist*'s 'Intelligence Unit' reports a trend towards 'shared services' in large companies and what they described reads very much like recentralization.

So, the relationship between improving technologies and shrinking organizations was not linear in the past, just as it is not today. The telegraph, typewriter and telephone, which launched the communications revolution, allowed the growth and spread of the giant firms of industrial capitalism as well as the proliferation of small businesses (Innis, 1951). Similarly, today, the emergence of small, adaptable firms may not point in any simple way to market disaggregation. Some research into small firms and start-ups highlights the symbiosis between large and small. Research indicates that many important relations between firms, let alone within them, are not ultimately self-organizing, market relations. Increasingly, they reflect the way firms are embedded in interorganizational networks (Powell, Koput and Smith Doerr, 1996, Kreiner and Schultz, 1993, and Walker, Kogut and Shan, 1997). Even where interfirm relations are extremely competitive, cross-sector cooperation and agreements are often highly significant. In the cut-throat world of silicon chip manufacture, for example, firms continuously cross-licence one another's patents and even engage in joint research via Sematech, a supra-organizational body.

So, the classic antithesis between hierarchy and market – even when hedged with the notion of 'hybrids' – seems inadequate to describe the nature of contemporary organizational configurations. The more recent antithesis between hierarchy and technology appears to be more a product of wishful thinking than any identifiable pattern. The limits of both arguments indicate the need to explore further the relationship between organization and knowledge.

Knowledge in organizations

Following other 'knowledge-based' accounts, we are suggesting that, in certain cases, organizations may handle the development of knowledge more effectively than markets. Though Davenport and Prusak (1998), for example, talk of 'knowledge markets', there are several reasons for it being difficult to create a market in knowledge or information. They have been well examined elsewhere, so we will not repeat the arguments here, beyond saying that knowledge is, in several ways, distinct from the sorts of commodities that markets handle well.[7]

Instead, we want to stress that, contrary to many neoclassical assumptions, knowledge often lies not with individuals but distributed among an ensemble of people working together. Thus, at this level, the market's role is at least partially pre-empted and forms of deliberate (rather than self-) organization may become as significant. Here we have in mind not the sorts of declarative knowledge that individuals can, as the name suggests, declare on examination – what the philosopher Gilbert Ryle (194) called 'knowing that'. Instead, we are concerned with dispositional knowledge – Ryle called this 'knowing how'. Dispositional knowledge entails an ability to respond to actual situations and get things done rather than only talk about them in the abstract.

'Knowing how', Ryle notes, is learned by practising, by doing things. Inevitably, such knowledge is therefore often dismissed as 'mere' practical knowledge, on the assumption that it is inferior to the theoretical kind. Doing seems less cerebral than thinking. However, the distinction between 'knowing how' and 'knowing that' does not support a simple separation between practice and theory. Thinking, after all, is a kind of doing. Ryle himself was practising philosophy, just as a doctor practises medicine or a theoretical physicist practises theoretical physics. In each of these cases, the ability to do these things – the dispositional knowledge, rather than the ability to talk about them – is acquired in practice itself. Consequently, as Ryle argues, 'Intelligent practice is not a step-child of theory. On the contrary, theorizing is one practice amongst others and is itself intelligently or stupidly conducted.'

Moreover, the practice makes critical distinctions among knowledge. A management theorist is a practitioner, but their practice is the practice of theorizing, whereas a manager's is the practice of managing. Both might have similar 'know that', but, as a result of their different practices, the way each puts it to work – the 'know how' of each – will be quite different.

Social practice

'Know how' begins, Ryle suggests, in practice. Most practices that people engage in, particularly work practices, are, to some extent, social practices – those that join people in interdependent activity. Thus, 'know how' more often than not reflects an ability to work with other people.

Indeed, even when people are assumed to work alone, their work is often social in character.[8] A study of Xerox repair technicians undertaken by the anthropologist Julian Orr (1996) shows that, though the work of these 'reps' is, in theory, individual, in practice, they work together, sharing ideas and insights, circulating information and covering for one another. Orr shows that, despite the individual character of their job, the reps meet constantly in their own time to keep informed and up to date and often collaborate to solve difficult problems. Similar studies of how work is actually conducted (rather than how it appears from job descriptions and manuals) confirm that the dispositional knowledge within a group, while often invisible, is significantly collective and can give rise to what Weick and Roberts refer to as aspects of a 'collective mind' (see Hutchins, 1991, Suchman, 1996a, 1996b and 1996c, and Whalen and Vinkhuyzen, 2000).

Consequently, as well as being dispositional, this sort of practice-based knowledge is often both distributed and partial. It is also likely to be improvisational. As we have already indicated, it is *dispositional* because it is revealed more in the situated practice (Lave, 1988, and Seely Brown, Collins and Duguid, 1995) of getting things done than in declarative statements about practice. It is *distributed* because it often needs several or all of the members of a group working together to get things done. It is *partial* because, while each member of the group may have a part of the whole, no one is likely to have it all. Though group members may apparently learn the 'same' things, the different skills and backgrounds of each result in each knowing different things or knowing them in different ways. Shared experience does not lead to identical knowledge for all in the way that all might have identical tools. Community knowledge is often more like a piece of music than a piece of equipment. Different players have distinct parts, and only the ensemble can produce the complete piece.[9]

Finally, it is likely to be *improvisational* for a couple of reasons. First, it requires the coordination in practice of group members. In this way, work is often like jazz improvisation, with each member of the group adapting their activity spontaneously to harmonize with the others and the underlying theme. Second, while most workplace activity is seen as a function of routine, in fact, as Arthur Stinchcombe (1990) argues, it is more a function of *routinization* – the reduction in practice of unpredictable events to the prescriptions of organizational routine and group capabilities. In this way, the routine of group 'know how' resembles that of basketball players, who continually adapt routine plays to the actual demands of the game. As Orr's work in particular shows, work groups continually find inventive and resourceful ways to get things done when the world defies routine prediction. This sort of routinization becomes particularly important when rapidly changing environments continuously challenge routine. Then practice-based improvisation becomes an important indicator of ecological change, although, as we explain later, it is often invisible to, or ignored by, organizations.[10]

Communities of practice

These groups that form around practice and, in the process, develop collective, dispositional knowledge are examples of what Lave and Wenger describe as 'communities of practice'. Shared practice, they argue, enables participants over time to develop a common outlook on, and understanding of, their work and how it fits into the world around them, thereby joining them together in an informal community.[11] Members will also share the sort of judgement that tells them not only what to do, but also when to do it and when it is well done.[12] They are likely to share a 'warranting' structure, too, a sense of what is important or interesting, deserves attention, is valid and, by contrast, what is not. Thus, when, as Orr shows, members of such a community share 'war stories', though these may be opaque to outsiders, within the group they can be densely freighted with knowledge, insight and community endorsements. The opacity and density themselves provide an implicit warrant that alerts other group members to the significance of what is told. While Orr (1996) describes the reps' knowledge-exchanging narratives as 'war stories', he notes that the reps themselves make an important, warranting distinction. They use the term 'war stories' primarily for the sort of banter, swaggering and braggadocio common to all work groups and to distinguish such talk from the more important knowledge exchanges.

In presenting this picture of communities and community knowledge, we do not want to dismiss or diminish the idea of personal, private knowledge. Indeed, far from overlooking the individual, our purpose is to elaborate the landscape in which, as a result of practice, individuals frame their identity. Lave and Wenger developed the notion of a 'community of practice' to honour the process by which individuals form their identities in relation to social identities of membership. At the centre of their argument is a characterization of learning as the process of engaging in practice and, thereby, becoming a member of a social group of practitioners. As Lave and Wenger argue, it is at the level of the community, the level at which practice is shared, that individual identities are principally forged.

Identity, Community, Organization

Issues of organizations and knowledge are closely intertwined with questions of individuals and identity. A shared worldview is a prerequisite for sharing understanding, insights, information and knowledge – for the sorts of shared, dispositional knowledge we have just described. A person's worldview is, moreover, a central aspect of their identity. Consequently, the level in society at which identity is shared is the level at which knowledge flows most easily. As Kogut and Zander (1996) argue, by understanding the formation of identity in organizations, we can understand the flow of knowledge.

The critical question then becomes, at what level of society is identity shared? In a survey of the great sociological pioneers, Kogut and Zander argue that Marx located identity at the level of class, Durkheim at the level of society and Weber at the level of the modern organization. Following Weber, and reflecting many other knowledge-based arguments, Kogut and Zander offer the firm as the critical locus of identity formation and, consequently, knowledge flow. They therefore regard the firm as a 'social community'. Similarly, Grant (1996) regards it as a 'knowledge system', Tsoukas (1996) as a 'discursive community', Kreiner and Lee (1999) as a single 'community of practice' and Daft and Weick (1984) as an interpretive system. These views echo earlier organizational sociologists who portrayed the firm as a system of cooperation into which individuals are socialized (Barnard, 1938, and Whyte, 1956).

Though for most people, work, is undoubtedly important to identity formation, there are, none the less, a couple of reasons to question whether or not the firm is the central concern.[13] Theoretically, it seems unlikely, given the enormous range of firms, that they should somehow form a single level of identity formation in modern society. So, we need to enquire how joining an organization – particularly modern, far-flung organizations – provides a shared identity or a common discourse community.

Furthermore, if firms are indeed some sort of discursive community in which members share sufficient aspects of identity to share knowledge, it becomes important, as we noted earlier, to ask, why does knowledge stick in organizations? Some, like Szulanski (1996), trace this internal stickiness to individual failings, such as a 'recipient's lack of absorptive capacity'. Yet, knowledge often seems to stick for more systemic reasons – between, for example, particular units, sections or levels of an organization. So, for instance, we have elsewhere discussed the difficulty of getting knowledge to flow from R&D into production in organizations such as Xerox. Cole discusses the difficulty of transferring 'best practices' within Hewlett Packard. Barley (1996) and Cole (1998) note the difficulty technicians face in getting their ideas taken seriously and Sitkin and Stikel (1996) show the confusion and distrust that can arise when assumptions of uniformity actually confront organizational diversity in practice. If organizations are single, unitary communities and confer an organization-wide shared identity, it is hard to find a systemic reason for these problems.

If, however, we accept that identity formation – what Bruner calls 'learning to be' – occurs in practice, then practice is clearly a central part of the process of identity formation. Thus, by extension, the locus of social identity formation becomes, as Lave and Wenger argue, the level at which practice is interdependent. Now the community of practice within an organization, rather than the organization as a whole, presents itself as the level at which organizational identity is significantly formed. In turn, the community of practice also becomes a critical subdivision within organizations of multiple practice. Once the subdivisions within an organization appear, it is easier to see why knowledge might stick.

Interdependent practice, we are arguing, is the process by means of which shared identity develops – a process that is clearly more complicated than simply joining or belonging to an organization and that points not to membership in an organization as a whole as most significant, but to membership in the community of practice. Here it is perhaps helpful to distinguish different notions of membership. On the one hand, there is the sort of membership one acquires by joining a club or a political party – membership that requires little more by way of process than a declaration of affiliation. Such declarations alone can hardly endow significant features of identity. Joining a business has some aspects of this sort of membership. For example, an affiliation is acquired on the first day of work and lost on the first day of separation. However, that sort of affiliation cannot induct people into the richness of a single discourse community. Nor does such a binary notion of membership (you are either 'in' or 'out') offer an explanation of the process of joining such a community. Also, it does not indicate how, whatever the process, joining a firm unites the newcomer and the old-timer, who may work a thousand miles away in unrelated firm activities, into a single community.

Given the range of communities, practices and, thus, locally produced knowledge systems in any large organization, enacting organizational coherence can be remarkably difficult. As Chesbrough and Teece (1996) point out, 'Some competencies may be on the factory floor, some in the R&D labs, some in the executive suites.' Consequently, most organizations try to limit the task by restricting the scope of their search to areas where they expect to find useful knowledge. Inevitably – given the ubiquity of improvisation and invention in communities of practice – while understandable, such restrictions are likely to miss a good deal that might be useful. Leonard-Barton's *Wellsprings of Knowledge* (1995) provides an extreme example of this, discussing a takeover in which the buyer sought to capture the sophisticated knowledge of a competitor by acquiring primarily its advanced equipment and highly trained engineers. Only after the deal was settled and the target company's other employees laid off did it become clear that 'the most critical operating knowledge' was actually held by the now departed line employees (Lester, 1998).

Moving

If the firm were a unitary knowledge system or discourse community, then, as we have suggested, whatever the difficulties of identifying useful knowledge, the task of moving it would be relatively easy. However, it is not, for knowledge tends to stick at the boundaries of practice. Nonaka and Takeuchi suggest that if knowledge is made explicit, it can cross these boundaries. Our own argument suggests, however, that when knowledge moves it has less to do with exchanging explicit (or declarative) knowledge and more to do with aligning the practices of different communities. It is by coordinating practices between communities that they come to share a certain amount of knowledge and understanding. Thus, for example, as Lester, following Sabel, points out, one of the unexpected consequences of 'just-in-time' or 'inventoryless' production was that the direct integration of suppliers and manufacturers aligned the practices between them and, as a result, produced a 'rich flow' of insight and understanding across the production process (Davenport and Prusak, 1998).

Ultimately, then, we see the organizational role as developing the processes to take advantage of (by giving structure to) the practices that develop spontaneously within. Allowing practice to evolve unchecked only leads to increasing fragmentation. Checking it too firmly leads to rigidity. We suspect that several of the problems that business process re-engineering has encountered may come from looking too exclusively at the structuring of process and, thus, ignoring the practices that give life and adaptability to these processes. Aligning processes, like exchanging explicit knowledge, has only limited value unless you work to align the underlying practices.

Structuring Spontaneity: Taking Advantage of Incoherence

From our perspective, then, we see organizations as having a critical role to play in structuring fragmented practice. To fully play that role, organizations need to recognize that they are not coherent wholes battling the incoherence of the world around them. Divisions of knowledge, understanding, worldview and practice fall within them, too. They must thus take advantage of their own incoherence. That advantage comes from having a privileged view on the various practices within and the possibilities and potential for weaving these together into complementary innovations – of products, processes or practices.

Clearly, from this perspective (in contrast to information-based perspectives), the solution to fragmentation is not simply to build a better intranet, deploy Lotus Notes or develop a 'knowledge warehouse' to try to find out 'what HP knows'. Rather, it involves working on two fronts. One is to support the internal development and circulation of knowledge within communities of practice. The other is to then pursue fruitful alignments of changing practice between communities. In closing, we point briefly to some examples of how organizations can provide such supports and alignments without unduly restricting the emergence of local 'know how'.

Within

Supporting knowledge within communities inevitably requires first recognizing their existence. They are not simply the teams or units listed on an organizational chart. They are, rather, groups that develop spontaneously and often informally around shared, coordinated practice. (Focus on 'community', therefore, is often misleading. Practice is more revealing.) Consequently, it is often the informal aspects of community practice that benefit from support.

Xerox has tried to do this in responding to the work practices of its 'reps', which Orr helped uncover. For some, the organization provided two-way radios to honour the continuous communication that the reps developed into a resource. More ambitiously, elsewhere it developed a database to store the tips and insights that Orr found reps continuously shared.

One of the difficulties of developing such databases is that it is quickly overwhelmed, losing specificity and value in proportion to its indiscriminate growth. As a frustrated manager at Andersen Consulting told Davenport and Prusak (1998: 7) in just such circumstances, 'We've got so much knowledge . . . in our Knowledge Xchange repository that our consultants can no longer make sense of it.' To remain useful for the reps, input into the database had to be judiciously filtered in accordance with the reps' community judgements rather than some 'objective' judgement about what they needed to know. So the reps, in effect, ran a 'peer review' process. A small group was charged with reviewing and refining submissions. That way, the database remained uncluttered, while anyone looking for a tip knew that what they found had been warranted as valuable by the selection process.

Between

The greater challenge lies in brokering knowledge across the borders that lie between practices. Earlier, we described the principal task as one of aligning practice. Here, we focus on ways to do this by brokering arrangements. We describe briefly three different aspects of brokering – participation, translation and boundary objects.

Brokering by participation

Although we have in general described the communities within an organization as though they were mutually exclusive, in almost all organizations there is, in fact, a great deal of overlap among communities. Some people may belong to several communities. Consequently, they are in a position to broker knowledge between the different communities to which they belong. By virtue of their diverse identities, they are able to work in and understand the interests of each.

In an analysis of the diffusion of knowledge across networks, the sociologist Mark Granovetter (1976) noted that overlaps are hard to develop in communities with strong internal ties as these tend to preclude external links. Thus, Granovetter pointed to the 'strength of weak ties', suggesting that it was often people loosely linked to several communities who facilitated the flow of knowledge among them.[19]

These participating brokers often create informal channels between communities. Organizational hierarchies, however, may pay attention primarily to more formal channels. Yet, knowledge that seems sticky in formal channels may leak quite readily via valuable back channels. Consequently, there are significant risks in overformalizing the relations within a firm. The outcome may endanger or completely sever the sorts of weak and informal ties that build unexpected but productive bridges across organizations.

Brokering by translation

Organizational translators are those who can frame the interests of one community in terms of another's practice-shaped worldview. Such a position requires a broad understanding of all the communities involved. Unlike a practitioner, a translator is not necessarily a member of either community. Thus, external mediators and consultants often find themselves providing translation. None the less, translators must be sufficiently knowledgeable about the work of the communities involved to be able to translate.

The mere presence of a translator may itself make evident the mutual unintelligibility of the groups involved, revealing to participants that ideas are failing to flow not simply because of obtuseness or uncooperative behaviour (standard accusations), but because the worldviews of the participants are mutually unintelligible, even with the best of intentions. In this way, breakdowns in communication can be instructive and a catalyst for breakthrough.

Translation, however, requires trust – a trust that must develop at just that point, the intercommunal boundary, where trust can be hardest to win. Yet, participants must be able to rely on translators to carry negotiation back and forth, not only in one direction. The difficulty of doing this makes translators extremely valuable, extremely powerful and, equally, extremely difficult to find (Latour, 1992, Star and Griesener, 1989).

It may be because trust and power are such tendentious issues for translation that people outside the central power structure of an organization can make very useful translators. Davenport and Prusak (1998) point, for example, to the informal brokering of this sort that organizational librarians can play.

Brokering through boundary objects

What Leigh Star (1989) calls 'boundary objects' offer another highly resourceful way to forge coordinating links among communities, bringing them, intentionally or unintentionally, into negotiation. Like brokers, boundary objects lie on the boundaries of more than one community, though, in this case, they are objects, not people (see also Star and Griesener, 1989).

Boundary objects are objects of interest to each community involved, but are viewed or used differently by each. They can be physical objects, technology, business processes, phase gates or techniques shared by different communities. Around these, each can come to understand what is common and what is distinct about another community, its practices and worldview. By bringing background assumptions to the fore, boundary objects not only help to clarify attitudes of other communities. They can also make a community's own presuppositions apparent to itself, encouraging reflection and 'second-loop' learning (Argyris and Schön, 1978).

Essentially, boundary objects help communities engage in mutual negotiation. Sometimes this negotiation is quite explicit. More often it is a process of implicit, reciprocal adjustment, as communities learn to accommodate and adjust to one another in interlocking practices without the coordination ever being a direct subject for discussion. Such negotiation is evident in the way that people around a table can silently arrange who sits where, how much space to take up, who speaks when and so forth. When informal negotiation breaks down, formal negotiation is needed to sort things out. In most circumstances, the implicit form is socially more acceptable. To demand explicit negotiation may appear confrontational. Indeed, formal negotiation often begins only when informal negotiation has broken down, and been moving to the formal can put an end to further informal negotiation.

Contracts are classic, though highly explicit, examples of boundary objects. They develop as different groups converge, via negotiation, on an agreed meaning that has significance for all. More generally, documents play a similar role, though the negotiation involved is usually more implicit. Within an organization, where contracts rarely play much of a role, forms, lists, memos and mission statements, as well as plans and blueprints and other organizational documents, make significant boundary objects. Transparent within groups, these can become opaque between them. Such opacity helps focus attention on differences in worldviews as each tries to understand the others' idiosyncratic use of these shared, coordinating documents.

To help produce intercommunal negotiation, organizations can seed the border between communities with boundary objects. These can be as formal as mission statements or as informal as a Dilbert cartoon. The idea-fermenting metaphors that Nonaka (1991) describes draw some of their power from being boundary objects. On the one hand, these work within groups to spark ideas. On the other, once a group has found one metaphor particularly powerful, that metaphor may also serve to foster under-standing between groups. Of course, not just any metaphor will do. The skill lies in finding the right metaphor – one that generates creative and coordinating responses among communities. Indeed, finding or crafting the right boundary object is an organizational skill.

Conclusion

Our aim here has been to reach an understanding of aspects of the relationship between knowledge and organization. For this, we suggest, it is important to look beyond the simple binaries of hierarchy and market, organization and individual, or structure and spontaneity. We have tried to disrupt these oppositions by inserting among them the notion of the community of practice and focusing on the role of practice in generating both knowledge and identity. In the variegated picture of the organization this brings to light, we believe it is possible to see more clearly the role of knowledge in organizations and of organizations in organizing knowledge.

Notes

This chapter has developed ideas that first appeared in the article 'Organizing knowledge' in 1988 in the *California Management Review* 40 (3): pp. 90–111.

1   For the notion of 'waves' and the 'electronic cottage', see Alvin Toffler (1980), *The Third Wave*. New York: William Morrow. While Toffler's work mostly precedes the 'digital' age, it, like McLuhan's, has been revived by the *Wired* generation. For arguments about the organization, see, among others, Samuel E. Bleeker (1994), 'The virtual organization', *Futurist*, 28 (2): pp. 9–14; William Davidow and Michael S. Malone (1982), *The Virtual Corporation: Structuring and Revitalizing the Corporation for the 21st Century*. New York: HarperCollins; Robert Killoren and Raymond W. Eyerly (1997), 'The brave new world of virtual organization: creating distributed environments for research administration', *SRA Journal* 29 (1–2): pp. 25–32; Thomas W. Malone and Robert J. Laubacher (1998), 'The dawn of the e-lance economy: are big companies becoming obsolete?', *Harvard Business Review*, Sept.–Oct.: pp. 145–52; Thomas W. Malone, Joanne Yates, and Robert Benjamin (1987), 'Electronic markets and electronic hierarchies', *Communications of the ACM*, 30 June: pp. 484–97; A. Mowshowitz (1997), 'On the theory of virtual organization', *System Research and Behavioral Science*, 14 (6): pp. 373–85; Charles Handy (1992), 'Balancing corporate power: a new federalist paper', *Harvard Business Review*, Oct.–Nov.: pp. 59–72.

2   Among the accounts that approximate the market, we would include Ronald Coase's transaction cost approach and its development by Oliver Williamson. See R.H. Coase (1937), 'The nature of the firm', *Economica*, NS 4 (16): 386–405; and Oliver E. Williamson (1981), 'The economics of organization: the transaction cost approach', *American Journal of Sociology*, 87 (3): 548–77. The knowledge-based literature grows daily. Special issues of several journals have been dedicated to it, including *California Management Review*, Spring 1998 (edited by Robert E. Cole), and *Strategic Management Journal*, Winter 1997 (edited by Robert M. Grant and J.C. Spender), and *Organization Science* (1997), 7 (5). Among other articles and books that we have found particularly useful in framing the argument in this chapter are Kenneth J. Arrow (1984), 'Information and economic behavior', in K. Arrow, *Collected Papers*, Cambridge, MA: Harvard University Press, pp. 136–52; Gary S. Becker and Kevin M. Murphy (1993), 'The division of labor, coordination costs, and knowledge', in Gary S. Becker, *Human Capital: A Theoretical and Empirical Analysis, with Special Reference to Education*, 3rd ed., Chicago: University of Chicago Press (1994), pp. 229–322; Lisa Bud-Frierman (ed.), *Information Acumen: The Understanding and Use of Knowledge in Modern Business*, London: Routledge; Kathleen Conner and C.K. Prahalad (1996), 'A resource-based theory of the firm: knowledge versus opportunism', *Organizational Science*, 7 (5): pp. 477–501; Thomas Davenport and Laurence Prusak (1998), *Working Knowledge: How Organizations Manage What They Know*, Boston, MA: Harvard Business School Press; Bruce Kogut and U. Zander (1993), 'Knowledge of the firm and the evolutionary theory of the multinational corporation', *Journal of International Business Studies*, 24 (4): pp. 625–45; Bruce Kogut and U. Zander (1993), 'Knowledge and the speed of the transfer and imitation of organizational capabilities: an empirical test', *Organization Science*, 6 (1): pp. 76–92; Bruce Kogut and U. Zander (1992), 'Knowledge of the firm, combinative capabilities, and the replication of technology', *Organization Science*, 3 (3): pp. 383–97; Kristian Kreiner (1998), 'Knowledge and mind: the management of intellectual resources', in R. Garud and J. Porac (eds), *Knowledge, Cognition, and Organizations*, Greenwich, CT: JAI Press;

Dorothy Leonard-Barton (1995), *Wellsprings of Knowledge: Building and Sustaining the Sources of Innovation*, Cambridge, MA: Harvard Business School Press; Ikujiro Nonaka (1991), 'The knowledge creating company', *Harvard Business Review*, Nov.–Dec.: pp. 96–104; Ikujiro Nonaka and Hirotaka Takeuchi (1995), *The Knowledge-creating Company: How Japanese Companies Create the Dynamics of Innovation*, New York: Oxford University Press; J.C. Spender (1996), *Industry Recipes: The Nature and Sources of Managerial Judgement*, Oxford: Blackwell; J.C. Spender (1996), 'Competitive advantage from tacit knowledge? Unpacking the concept and its strategic implications', in B. Moingeon and A. Edmondson (eds), *Organizational Learning and Competitive Advantage*, London: Sage, pp. 56–73; Karl Weick and K. Roberts (1993), 'Collective mind and organizational reliability', *Administrative Science Quarterly*, 38: pp. 357–81.

3   A distinction between organizations and institutions is made most clearly by North, who sums up the difference in the phrase, 'institutions are the rules, organizations are the players'. See, for example, Douglass C. North (1992), *Transaction Costs, Institutions, and Economic Performance*, San Francisco, CA: Institute for Contemporary Studies.

4   Or, as D.H. Robertson put it in 1923, firms create 'islands of conscious power' amid 'oceans of unconscious coordination' (Robertson quoted in Mark C. Casson (1997), *Information and Organization: A New Perspective on the Theory of the Firm*, Oxford: Clarendon Press, p. 78. See Brown and Duguid, 'Organizing knowledge'; J.C. Spender and Robert M. Grant (1996), 'Knowledge and the firm: overview', *Strategic Management Journal*, 17 (Winter Special): pp. 1–9, for the notion of husbandry applied to the firm.

5   For the stickiness and leakiness of knowledge, see Brown and Duguid, 'Knowledge and organization: the perspective of practice', in preparation. As we explain there, understanding and dealing with stickiness strikes us as one of the most critical managerial challenges. The remark about HP appears widely in the organizational knowledge literature. O'Dell and Grayson trace it to Jerry Junkins, CEO of Texas Instruments, who said, 'If TI only knew what TI knows.' It was then echoed by Lew Platt, chairman of HP, who said, 'I wish we knew what we know at HP.' See Carla O'Dell and C. Jackson Grayson (1988), 'If only we knew what we know: identification and transfer of internal best practice', *California Management Review*, 40 (3): pp. 154–74.

6   The notion of 'community of practice' is now widespread in organizational literature. Its *locus classicus* is Jean Lave and Etienne Wenger (1991), *Situated Learning: Legitimate Peripheral Participation*, New York: Cambridge University Press; and Etienne Wenger (1998), *Communities of Practice*, New York: Cambridge University Press. We employed the concept of organizational innovation in John Seely Brown and Paul Duguid (1991), 'Organizational learning and communities of practice: towards a unified view of working, learning, and innovation', *Organization Science*, 2 (1): pp. 40–58.

7   See, for example, Arrow, 'Information and economic behavior'; J.C. Spender (1996), 'Making knowledge the basis of a dynamic theory of the firm', *Strategic Management Journal*, 17 (Winter Special): pp. 45–62; Hardimos Tsoukas (1996), 'The firm as a distributed knowledge system: a constructionist approach', *Strategic Management Journal*, 17 (Winter Special): pp. 11–25. These arguments, we believe, also challenge those who see organization in terms of information. See, for example, Casson, *Information and Organization*.

Like many technological arguments, these information-centred ones under-estimate the social challenge of human communication. Indeed, Casson offers a neoclassical account of language and human communication that bears almost no relation to, and draws nothing from, the science of linguistics. Mark C. Casson (1996), 'Economics and anthropology: reluctant partners', *Human Relations*, 49 (9): pp. 1151–80.

8   In a famous example, the philosopher Jean-Paul Sartre noted that the lone waiter in a café models his behaviour on that of other waiters: 'He returns, trying to imitate in his walk the inflexible stiffness of some kind of automaton while carrying his tray with the recklessness of a tightrope walker by putting it in a perpetually unstable, perpetually broken equilibrium which he perpetually re-establishes by a light movement of the arm and hand. . . . We need not watch long before we can explain it: he is playing *at being* a waiter in a café. . . . [T]he waiter plays with his condition in order to *realize it*' (Jean-Paul Sartre (1969), *Being and Nothingness*, translated by Hazel E. Barnes, London: Methuen).

9   Weick and Roberts make a similar point about the collective mind, which 'is not indexed by within-group similarity of attitudes'. See Karl Weick and K. Roberts (1993), 'Collective mind and organizational reliability', *Administrative Science Quarterly*, 38: pp. 357–81.

10 Environmental economists place significant emphasis on the notion of routine (see Richard R. Nelson and Sidney G. Winter (1982), *An Evolutionary Theory of Economic Change*, Cambridge, MA: Belknap Press of Harvard University Press; Giovanni Dosi and Richard Nelson (1994), 'An introduction to evolutionary theories in economics', *Journal of Evolutionary Economics*, 4: pp. 153–72). They tend, however, to accept a 'canonical' view of routines, as if they were carried out as specified. As we have argued elsewhere, such a view conceals a great deal of what work actually involves (see Brown and Duguid, 'Organizational learning and communities of practice').

11 As Wenger shows in *Communities of Practice*, the community's view might be quite different from that of others in the organization.

12 Bruner amplifies this point by quoting Aristotle's *Nichomachean Ethics*: 'It is an easy matter to know the effects of honey, wine, hellebore, cautery, and cutting. But to know how, for whom, and when we should apply these as remedies is no less an undertaking than being a physician.' See Jerome Bruner (1996), *The Culture of Education*, Cambridge, MA: Harvard University Press, p. 44.

13 It is sometimes forgotten in the organization literature that work is not the only locus of identity formation. See, however, Tsoukas (1996), 'Firms as a Distributed Knowledge System', which importantly stresses that work is only a part of a larger whole.

14 See Lave and Wenger, *Situated Learning*; Ryle, *The Concept of Mind*; Bruner, *The Culture of Education*. Their different notions of membership and identity are, in our view, missing from 'networked' views of society, such as those proposed in Manuel Castells' influential work (1994–1998), *The Information Age: Economy, Society, Culture*, 3 vols, Oxford: Blackwell. Castells considers identity primarily in terms of the first type of membership – affiliation – over-looking the contribution of shared practice to a more robust kind of identity.

15 It seems likely that Weick does, too. See the tribute to Lave and Wenger in the opening to (1996) *Sensemaking in Organizations*, Thousand Oaks, CA: Sage, p. xi, and Orton and Weick, 'Loosely coupled systems', p. 216.

16 The pressure to disguise improvisation from organizations leads to what the organizational ethnographer Lucy Suchman describes as 'endless small forms of practical "subversion" taken up in the name of getting work done'. See Lucy Suchman (1998), 'Organizational alignment: a case of bridge-building', a paper presented at the Academy of Management Annual Meeting, San Diego, CA, August 11.

17 Nelson and Winter, *An Evolutionary Theory of Economic Change*, describes R&D and Schumpeterian as a process of searching that helps to drive evolutionary organizational change. In amplifying on this approach, we want to stress the importance of complementarity and coherence seeking in this process.

18 Hayek's strictures against an overarching view of knowledge apply here. See Friedrich von Hayek (1945), 'The use of knowledge in society', *American Economic Review*, 35 (September): pp. 519–30.

19 Granovetter's argument presupposes that for knowledge to spread, groups cannot simply be related as isolated individuals connected by market. They (and, indeed, markets) must be embedded in complicated social systems.

References

Argyris, Chris, and Schön, Donald (1978) *Organizational Learning*. Reading, MA: Addison-Wesley.

Arrow, Kenneth J. (1974) *The Limits of Organization*. New York: Norton.

Barley, Stephen R. (1996) 'Technicians in the workplace: ethnographic evidence for bringing work into organization studies', *Administrative Science Quarterly*, 41: 404–41.

Barnard, Chester I. (1938) *The Functions of the Executive*. Cambridge, MA: Harvard University Press.

Brown, John Seely, Collins, Alan, and Duguid, Paul (1995) 'Situated cognition and the culture of learning', in H. McLellan (ed.), *Perspectives on Situated Learning*. Englewood Cliffs, NJ: Education Technology Books. pp. 19–46.

Chandler, Alfred D. (1977) *The Visible Hand: The Managerial Revolution in American Business*. Cambridge, MA: Harvard University Press.

Chesbrough, Henry W., and Teece, David J. (1996) 'When is virtual virtuous? Organizing for innovation', *Harvard Business Review*, Jan.–Feb.: 65–74.

Clark, Andy (1997) *Being There: Putting Brain, Body, and World Together Again*. Cambridge, MA: MIT Press.

Cole, Robert (1998) *The Quest for Quality Improvement: How American Business Met the Challenge*. Oxford: Oxford University Press.

Cusmano, Michael A., and Yoffie, David B. (1998) *Competing on Internet Time: Lessons from Netscape and Its Battle with Microsoft*. New York: The Free Press.

Daft, R.L., and Weick, Karl E. (1984) 'Toward a model of organizations as interpretation systems', *Academy of Management Review*, 9 (2): 284–95.

Davenport, Thomas and Prusak, Laurence (1998) *Working Knowledge: How Organizations Manage What they Know*. Boston, MA: Harvard Business School.

David, Paul (1990) 'The dynamo and the computer: an historical perspective on the modern productivity paradox', *American Economic Review*, 80 (2): 355–61.

Dawkins, Richard (1986) *The Blind Watchmaker*. New York: Norton.

Duguid, Paul, and da Silva Lopes, Teresa (1999) 'Ambiguous company: institutions and organizations in the port wine trade, 1814–1834', *Scandinavian Journal of Economic History*, 47 (1): 84–102.

Edquist, Charles (1997) *Systems of Innovation: Technologies, Institutions, and Organizations.* London: Pinter.

Fukuyama, Francis, and Shulsky, Abram (1997) *The 'Virtual Corporation' and Army Organization.* Santa Monica, CA: Rand.

Gilder, George (1994) *Life After Television.* New York: Norton.

Granovetter, Mark (1976) 'The strength of weak ties', *American Journal of Sociology*, 78 (6): 1360–80.

Grant, Robert M. (1996) 'Towards a knowledge-based view of the firm', *Strategies Management Journal*, 17 (Winter Special): 109–22.

von Hayek, Friedrich (1988) *The Fatal Conceit: The Errors of Socialism.* Chicago: University of Chicago Press.

Hutchins, Ed (1991) 'Organizing work by adaptation', *Organization Science*, 2 (1): 14–38.

Innis, Harold (1951) *The Bias of Communication.* Toronto: University of Toronto Press.

Kelly, Kevin (1994) *Out of Control: The New Biology of Machines, Social Systems, and the Economic World.* New York: Addison-Wesley.

Kogut, Bruce, Walker, Gordon, and Kim, Dong-Jae (1997) 'Cooperation and entry induction as an extension of technology rivalry', *Research Policy*, 24: 77–95.

Kogut, Bruce, and Zander, U. (1996) 'What do firms do?: co-ordination identity and learning', *Organization Science*, 7 (5): 502–18.

Kreiner, K., and Schultz, M. (1993) 'Informal collaboration in R&D: the formation of networks across organizations', *Organization Science*, 14 (2): 189–209.

Kreiner, Kristian, and Lee, Kristina (1999) 'Knowledge assimilation: mobilizing distributed knowledge', paper presented at the Third World Congress on the Management of Intellectual Capital, Hamilton, Ontario, Jan. 20–22.

Latour, Bruno (1992) 'Where are the missing masses? The sociology of a few mundane artifacts', in W. Bijker and J. Law, *Shaping Technology/Building Society: Studies in Societechnical Change.* Cambridge, MA: MIT Press. pp. 225–58.

Lave, Jean (1988) *Cognition in Practice: Mind, Mathematics and Culture in Everyday Life.* Cambridge: Cambridge University Press.

Lester, Richard (1998) *The Productive Edge: How US Industries Are Pointing the Way to a New Era of Economic Growth.* New York: Norton.

McLuhan, Marshall (1962) *The Gutenberg Galaxy: The Making of Typographic Man.* Toronto: University of Toronto Press.

Negroponte, Nicholas (1996) *Being Digital.* New York: Alfred A. Knopf.

Newman, Susan E. (1998) 'Here, there, and nowhere at all: distribution, negotiation and virtuality', in Postmodern Engineering and Ethnography, in S. Gorenstein (ed.), *Knowledge and Society: Vol II. Researches in Science and Technology.* Stamford, CA: JAI Press.

New York Times, June 17, 1998, p. B1.

Nonaka, Ikujiro (1991) 'The knowledge creating company', *Harvard Business Review*, Nov–Dec.: 96–104.

North, Douglass C. (1981) *Structure and Change in Economic History.* New York: Norton.

North, Douglass C. (1990) *Institutions, Institutional Change, and Economic Performance.* New York: Cambridge University Press.

Orr, Julian (1996) *Talking About Machines: An Ethnography of a Modern Job.* Ithaca, NY: IRL Press.

Orton, J. Douglas, and Weick, Karl E. (1990) 'Loosely coupled systems: a reconceptualization', *Academy of Management Review*, 15 (2): 203–23.

Powell, Walter W., Koput, Kenneth, and Smith Doerr, Laurel (1996) 'Interorganizational collaboration and the locus of innovation: networks of learning in biotechnology', *Administrative Science Quarterly*, 41: 116–45.

Rheingold, Howard (1993) *The Virtual Community: Homesteading on the Electronic Frontier.* Reading, MA: Addison-Wesley.

Rosenberg, Nathan (1994) *Exploring the Black Box: Technology, Economics, and History.* New York: Cambridge University Press.

Ryle, Gilbert (1949) *The Concept of Mind.* London: Hutchinson. p. 26.

Shapiro, Carl, and Varian, Hal R. (1999) *Information Rules: A Strategic Guide to the Network Economy.* Boston, MA: Harvard University Press.

Sichel, Daniel E. (1997) *The Computer Revolution: An Economic Perspective.* Washington, DC: Brookings Institution Press.

Sitkin, Sim B., and Stickel, Darryl (1996) 'The road to hell: the dynamics of distrust in an era of quality', in Roderick M. Kramer and Tom R. Tyler (eds), *Trust in Organizations: Frontiers of Theory and Research.* Thousand Oaks, CA: Sage. pp. 196–215.

Star, Susan L. (1989) 'The structure of ill-structured solutions: heterogeneous problem-solving, boundary objects, and distributed artificial intelligence', in M. Hans and L. Gasser (eds), *Distributed Artificial Intelligence*, vol. 2. Menlo Park, CA: Morgan Kauffman.

Star, Susan L. and Griesener, James R. (1989) 'Institutional economy, "translations" and boundary objects: amateurs and professionals in Berkeley's Museum of Vertebrate Zoology 1907–39', *Social Studies of Science*, 19: 387–420.

Stinchcombe, Arthur L. (1990) *Information and Organization.* Berkeley, CA: University of California Press.

Suchman, Lucy (1996a) 'Representations of work', *Communications of the ACM*, 36 (special issue edited by Lucy Suchman) (9): 33–39.

Suchman, Lucy (1996b) 'Making work visible', *Communications of the ACM*, 36 (special issue edited by Lucy Suchman) (9): 56–64.

Suchman, Lucy (1996c) 'Supporting articulation work', in R. Kling (ed.), *Computerization and Controversy: Value Conflicts and Social Choices*, 2nd edn. San Diego, CA: Academic Press.

Szulanski, Gabriel (1996) 'Exploring internal stickiness: impediments to the transfer of best practice within the firm', *Strategic Management Journal*, 17 (Winter Special): 27–43.

Teece, David J., Rumelt, Richard, Dosi, Giovanni, and Winter, Sidney (1994) 'Understanding corporate coherence: theory and evidence', *Journal of Economic Behavior and Organization*, 23: 1–30.

Toffler, Alvin (1980) *The Third Wave.* New York: Morrow.

Tsoukas, Hardimos (1996) 'The firm as a distributed knowledge system: a constructionist approach', *Strategic Management Journal*, 17 (Winter Special): 11–25.

Turkle, Sherry (1996) *List on the Screen: Identity in the Age of the Internet.* New York: Simon and Schuster.

Walker, Gordon, Kogut, Bruce, and Shan, Weijian (1997) 'Social capital, structural holes and the formation of an industry network', *Organization Science*, 8: 109–12.

Whalen, Jack, and Vinkhuyzen, Erik (2000) 'Expert systems in (inter)action: diagnosing document machine problems over the telephone', in C. Heath, J. Hindmarsh and P. Luff (eds), *Workplace Studies: Recovering Work Practice and Informing Systems Design.* Cambridge: Cambridge University Press.

Whyte, William H. (1956) *The Organization Man.* New York: Simon & Schuster.

3 Self-transcending Knowledge: Organizing Around Emerging Realities

Claus Otto Scharmer

Introduction

Throughout the twentieth century, industry in the so-called developed economies was transformed from one that largely processed raw materials and conducted manufacturing to one that largely processes information and knowledge (Teece, 1998). As a consequence, the logic of competition has shifted from markets with decreasing returns to markets with increasing returns driven by positive feedback loops (Arthur, 1996). According to Arthur, in increasing return markets, that which is ahead tends to stay ahead: 'If knowledge-based companies are competing in winner-takes-most markets, then managing becomes redefined as series of quests for the next technological winner.' Bill Gates is not so much a wizard of technology, says Arthur, 'but a wizard of precognition, of discerning the shape of the next game.' Arthur (1996: 104) compares the new competitive game around emergent markets and technology with casino gambling, where part of the game is to choose which games to play:

> We can imagine the top figures in high tech – the Gateses and Gerstners and Groves of their industries – as milling in a large casino. Over at this table, a game is starting called multimedia. Over at this one, a game called Web services. In the corner is electronic banking. There are many such tables. You sit at one. 'How much to play?' you ask. 'Three billion', the croupier replies. 'Who'll be playing?' We won't know until they show up. 'What are the rules?' 'Those'll emerge as the game unfolds.' 'What are my odds of winning?' 'We can't say. Do you still want to play?'

Leaders confronted with this question face a new challenge. The challenge is to develop the capacity for 'precognition' – the ability to sense and actualize emergent potentials. To do this, leaders must be able to see the sources of emerging realities. This kind of knowledge can be thought of as 'tacit knowledge prior to its embodiment', or 'self-transcending' knowledge.

Self-transcending knowledge – the ability to sense the presence of potential, to see what does not yet exist – is usually associated with artists, not business managers. For example, there are three ways to look at a painter and their work. One can look at the completed painting, one can watch the painter in the process of painting or one can watch the painter before they lift a brush, as they consider the blank canvas. Each structural perspective offers a different type of access to the artist's work.

The completed picture is the explicit reflection of the artist's work. The artist in the process of painting offers insight into the tacit knowledge they bring to the work. The artist in front of their blank canvas senses the emergent painting, much as Michelangelo, talking about his famous sculpture of David, sensed the emergent figure: 'David was already in the stone. I just took away everything that wasn't David.' The ability to see a David where others just see rock is what distinguishes the truly great artist. The same applies to leaders. As J. Jaworski, Chairman of the Centre for Generative Leadership, says, 'The capacity to sense and actualize emergent realities distinguishes great entrepreneurial leaders from the rest' (Jaworski and Scharmer, 1999).

Today, leaders increasingly find themselves standing in front of their own blank canvases. They are faced not only with the challenge of figuring out what in their business environment may contain the potential new 'David', but also with how to take away everything that isn't David. In order to learn to intuit emergent form, leaders have to access a new type of not yet embodied knowledge.

While the knowledge management discussion of the 1990s revolved around the interplay of two forms of knowledge – explicit and tacit (Nonaka and Takeuchi, 1995) – the underlying proposition of this chapter is that the discussion of the next decade will revolve around the interplay of three forms of knowing: explicit, tacit and self-transcending knowledge.

The purpose of this chapter is to introduce the concept of self-transcending knowledge. The remainder is organized into seven sections, which introduce the concept of self-transcending knowledge and discuss the implications in terms of knowledge types, epistemology, *basho*, infrastructures and requisite conversational complexity. The last section discusses the preceding ones.

Self-transcending Knowledge: the Other Side of Tacit Knowing

At a 1997 meeting in Palo Alto, California, Richard LeVitt, Hewlett-Packard's Director of Quality, explained where HP's corporate quality came from and where he saw it going:

> In the earliest stage we mainly focused on product outcomes and concrete results like product reliability. Though these are important, we realized we could achieve more by shifting our focus upstream toward the processes that precede

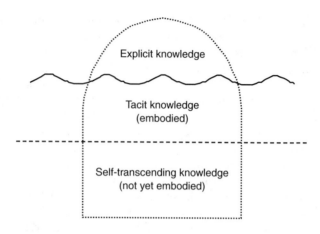

Figure 3.1   *The three forms of knowledge*

and produce the results. The issue was, how can we get our processes right? This stage of managing quality was the heart of the TQM movement in the 1980s.

But once you and your competitors have the processes right, the question is, what will be next? What will be the next basis of competitive advantage? For us, one critical new focus area is how managers can improve their quality of thought – especially their deep thought about customers and the experiences they should have with us.

LeVitt's depiction of HP's shift of focus from results to the processes that produce these results, then from processes to the preceding thought conditions that allowed those processes to emerge, corresponds with the analogy of the painter. Like the painter, who used a different type of knowledge at each stage of creating a painting, each stage of quality management requires a different type of knowledge. When measuring the outcomes of quality, managers need explicit knowledge. When improving process management, like TQM, the overall focus is on knowledge in use – that is, tacit knowledge. However, when moving towards the upstream domain of quality that LeVitt described – improving qualities of thought and customer experience – a manager has to access a different type of knowing. He finds himself in the same situation as the artist. The leverage for improving the quality of thought is not to be found in things that are around him, but within his own self. The lever is in the capacity of the self to see the David hidden within the stone.

Figure 3.1 depicts the three forms of knowledge using the model of an iceberg. Above the waterline is explicit knowledge. Explicit knowledge is the least difficult to disseminate and distribute. Below the waterline are two types of tacit knowledge: tacit embodied knowledge and self-transcending knowledge. Both forms of tacit knowledge are very difficult to disseminate and transfer from one part of the organization to another.

The example of a loaf of bread can be used to ground these distinctions. Certain kinds of information about bread – such as its weight, price and ingredients – are examples of explicit knowledge. The activities of baking and producing the bread are examples of tacit knowledge (Nonaka and Takeuchi, 1995) and the knowledge that enables a particular baker to invent baking bread in the first place is an example of not yet embodied knowledge. This 'self-transcending knowledge' is tacit knowledge prior to its embodiment in day-to-day practices.

The discussion of knowledge management (KM) has evolved historically in three phases, each with a dominant point of view. During phase I, the primary focus was on explicit knowledge. KM revolved around IT solutions. From this vantage point, knowledge was conceived of as a thing. Hence, knowledge could be gathered and stored in remote databanks and IT systems. Knowledge was nothing but information, and knowledge management the processing of information.

In the second phase, the process of knowledge creation took precedence (Nonaka, 1991 and 1994). In this phase, knowledge was conceived of as tacit, embodied in human action. Knowledge, according to Nonaka and Takeuchi (1995), is not a thing, but a process.

In this phase, KM started to revolve around the interplay between explicit knowledge and tacit knowledge. Knowledge creation evolves in a spiralling movement between the explicit and implicit knowledge held by individuals, teams and the organization (Nonaka and Takeuchi, 1995).

However, Nonaka and Takeuchi left one question unanswered: what is the force that drives the knowledge spiral itself? This question leads on directly to the third phase of KM, which focuses attention on the thought conditions that allow processes and tacit knowledge to evolve in the first place. Examples of this form of knowing are what Nonaka and Konno (1998) call 'originating *ba*', what Schön (1983) refers to as 'reflection-in-action', what von Krogh (1998) refers to with his notion of 'care', what Senge (1990) calls 'personal mastery', what Kappler (1993) calls 'presencing', what Jaworski, Gozdz and Senge (1997) refer to as 'emergent fields' and what Scharmer (1999) calls 'not yet embodied' knowledge.

All of these refer to a territory of knowledge formation that is upstream from both explicit and tacit embodied knowledge. It is the kind of knowledge Buber (1970) meant when he talked about the basic word 'I-Thou' and Heidegger (1993) meant when he talked about being as 'coming from absence into presence' and truth as coming from 'concealment into unconcealment' and what the Japanese philosopher Nishida was referring to when he spoke of 'pure experience' (1990) and 'action intuition' (1987). All of these scholars point at a formative state of knowledge that precedes the separation of subject and object, or knower and known, as we will see in the following sections.

Summarizing, the concept of self-transcending knowledge proposes a distinction between two types of tacit knowledge: tacit embodied knowledge on the one hand and not yet embodied knowledge on the other hand.

The distinction is relevant because each of the three forms of knowledge – explicit, tacit embodied and self-transcending – is based on different epistemological assumptions and requires a different type of knowledge infrastructure, as is discussed below. Moreover, the differentiation among markets with decreasing, steady and increasing returns suggests that, in order to successfully compete for increasing returns, market leaders need a new type of knowledge that allows them to 'sense and actualize what wants to emerge' (Jaworski and Scharmer, 1999) – that is, to tap into the sources of not yet embodied knowing.

Mapping the Landscape of Knowledge in Organizations: Twelve Types

The framework outlined below is based on two distinctions – one epistemological and the other ontological (Nonaka and Takeuchi, 1995). The epistemological distinction differentiates among three forms of knowledge: explicit, tacit (knowledge in use) and self-transcending knowledge (not yet embodied knowledge). The ontological distinction differentiates among four levels of corporate action (Scharmer, 2000):

A1: delivering results that create value (performing);
A2: improving the process-based context of performing (strategizing);
A3: reframing the assumption-based context of performing (mental modelling);
A4: re-conceiving the identity-based context of performing (sculpting).

A1 represents the stream of customer-driven value creation. The other three action levels represent underlying streams of 'contextual action' that continually improve the context and input qualities for A1. Combined, both distinctions result in the framework of 12 types of knowledge shown in Table 3.1.[1]

The epistemological distinctions between explicit, tacit and self-transcending knowledge are shown in columns E1, E2 and E3. Based on the differentiation among the three columns of Table 3.1, the historical development of knowledge management can be presented as a play that is enacted on three stages.

Act I: knowledge about things

Act I takes place on a single platform. We will call this platform Stage One. On this stage, knowledge is conceived from the traditional point of view – knowledge is a thing. Thus, knowledge can be gathered and stored in remote databanks and IT systems. Knowledge is nothing but information.

Table 3.1   *Twelve types of knowledge in organizations*

Epistemological/ action type	E1: Explicit knowledge	E2: Tacit knowledge	E3: Self-transcending knowledge
A1: Performing	Know-what	Knowledge in use	Reflection in action
A2: Strategizing	Know-how	Theory in use	Imagination in action
A3: Mental modelling	Know-why	Metaphysics in use	Inspiration in action
A4: Sculpting	Know-who	Ethics/aesthetics in use	Intuition in action

This traditional IT-based view of knowledge still prevails as the dominant view in most contemporary institutions. In Western business schools and universities, for instance, the main emphasis is on conceptual and explicit knowledge, not on building skills and competence for action. Examples of this kind of knowledge are a balance sheet (know-what), accounting rules (know-how), reports based on activity-based costing (know-why) and the purpose statement of a company (know-who). In all these examples, knowledge is conveyed in the same structure – as a piece of information that is separate from the practice or reality it denotes.

The challenge on this stage is related to relevance (Johnson and Kaplan, 1991) – how do these types of explicit knowledge relate and contribute to the capacity to innovate and create value?

Act II: knowledge about doing things

Act II takes place as the interplay between the action on two stages. On the second stage, knowledge is not a thing, but, rather, a process. Knowledge is conceived of as tacit knowledge that is embodied in human action. Thus, Act II is based on the interplay between explicit knowledge (Stage One) and tacit embodied knowledge (Stage Two).

Act II is largely based on the work of Nonaka (1991 and 1994) and Nonaka and Takeuchi (1995). Says Nonaka (1996: 668), 'What I found was that the existing theory of information processing is not enough. The process of innovation is not simply information processing; it's a process to capture, create, leverage and retain knowledge.' In their theory of the knowledge-creating company, Nonaka and Takeuchi present a view of knowledge creation that takes into account both 'stages' – that is, explicit and tacit knowledge. Knowledge develops as it cycles between explicit and tacit forms of knowledge in an evolving 'knowledge spiral'.

Today, Nonaka and Takeuchi's (1995) work has become widely accepted as state-of-the-art. In this view, knowledge is a living process. Examples of this kind of knowledge focus on surfacing:

1   knowledge in use (Lave and Wenger, 1991);
2   theories in use (Argyris and Schön, 1996);

3 culture and metaphysics in use (Schein, 1992, v. Krogh and Roos, 1995);
4 aesthetics in use (de Monthoux, 1993, and Scharmer, 1991).

In all these examples, knowledge is considered to be embodied in day-to-day practices. It is not external to the reality it describes, but in the midst of it (Polanyi, 1966). Hence, knowledge is not about describing, but about enacting the reality it refers to (Argyris, Putnam and Smith, 1985).

However, Nonaka and Takeuchi's (1995) work still does not answer one question: what is the force that drives the knowledge spiral itself?

Act III: knowledge about thought as the origin of doing things

The question 'What is the force that drives the knowledge spiral?' shifts the focus of attention to the third platform. On this stage, knowledge is situated in an incipient, not yet enacted reality that is brought into existence by means of an act of *action intuition* (Nishida) or *self-presencing* (Heidegger). The terms 'action intuition' and 'self-presencing' signify a state of mind that transcends the distinctions between 'inside' and 'outside', between 'I' and 'thou' and between knowing and acting. The focus of attention is on the emergent common ground from which all these distinctions arise in the first place. Thus, Act III is based on the interplay between the three stages, on which the explicit, tacit embodied and not yet embodied forms of knowing are enacted simultaneously.

Self-transcending knowledge is the scarcest resource and the most difficult to attain. Hamel and Prahalad (1994: 46–7) give an example of how it relates to the other two stages of knowledge formation.

> Competition for the future can be linked to pregnancy. Like competition for the future, pregnancy has three stages – conception, gestation, and delivery. These three stages correspond in competition to foresight and intellectual leadership, competition to foreshorten the migration paths, and competition for market position and share. It is the last stage of competition that is the focus of strategy textbooks and strategic planning exercises. Typically, the assumption is that the product or service concept is well established, the dimensions of competition are well-defined and the boundaries of the industry have stabilized. But focusing on the last stage of market-based competition, without a deep understanding of pre-market competition, is like trying to make sense of the process of childbirth without any insight into conception and gestation.
>
> The question for managers to ask themselves at this point is which stage receives the bulk of our time and attention: conception, gestation, or labor and delivery? Our experience suggests that most managers spend a disproportionate amount of time in the delivery room, waiting for the miracle of birth. But as we all know, the miracle of birth is most unlikely, unless there's been some activity nine months previously.

Table 3.2 *Three epistemologies*

Epistemology	E1: Explicit knowledge	E2: Tacit embodied knowledge	E3: Self-transcending knowledge
Type of knowledge	Knowledge about *things*	Knowledge about *doing* things	Knowing about *thought origins* for doing things
Data	External reality	Enacted reality	Not yet enacted reality
Experience type	Observation experience	Action experience	Aesthetic experience
Action–reflection ratio	Reflection without action	Reflection on action	Reflection in action
Truth	Matching reality	Producing reality	Presencing reality
Truth criterion	Can you observe it?	Can you create it?	Can you actualize it?
Perspective	External: view on *objective* reality	Internal: view on *enacted* reality	Both internal and external: view on *not yet enacted* reality
Subject–object relationship	Separation	Unity (after action)	Unity (in action)

Three Underlying Epistemologies

Explicit, tacit and self-transcending knowledge are based on three different bodies of epistemological assumptions – that is, three different relationships between knower and known (see Table 3.2).

Explicit knowledge captures knowledge about things. The data point is observed reality. The experience type is based on observation. The conceptualization is usually based on reflection without action. The criterion for truth is the test, 'Can you observe it?' (see Table 3.2).

Tacit embodied knowledge captures knowledge about things we do (Nonaka and Takeuchi, 1995, and Polanyi, 1966). The data point is enacted reality. The experience type is based on action. Thus, capturing this type of knowledge requires 'reflection on action' – reflecting on one's actions. The ultimate criterion for truth is the test, 'Can you create it?' (Argyris, Putnam and Smith, 1985).

Not yet embodied knowledge captures knowledge about the thought conditions that give rise to the things we do. The focus is on the primary ground from which human action arises in the first place. The data point is not yet enacted reality (Fichte, 1982). The experience type is based on aesthetic or pure experience (Nishida, 1990). In order to capture this most upstream level of social action, we have to reflect as we act or engage in what Schön (1983) calls 'reflection-in-action,' or what Csikszentmihalyi (1991) calls 'flow'. The ultimate criterion for truth is the test, 'Can you actualize it?' (Scharmer, 2000a).

The three forms of knowledge – explicit, tacit embodied and self-transcending – constitute three fundamentally different epistemological stances – that is, three different relationship modes between the knower and the known. Each form of knowledge relates to the reality that it describes from a different point of view.

Explicit knowledge relates to the reality that it denotes from outside. The statement 'this bread costs one dollar' does not enable the knower to actually produce the thing (bread) that the knowledge signifies. The knower produces a statement about, but cannot bring into existence, the known. From this point of view, knowledge represents and denotes a thing.

Embodied tacit knowledge relates to the reality that it signifies from within. Here the knower does not talk about bread but actually bakes and produces bread. Tacit knowledge enables the knower to produce and bring into existence the known. From this point of view, knowledge denotes not a thing, but a living process.

Self-transcending knowledge relates to reality both from within and from outside. The locus of the denoted reality (outside the knower in the case of explicit knowledge and inside in the case of tacit embodied knowledge) is both outside and within the knower. Alternatively, as Nishida puts it, it is neither outside nor inside the knower (Nishida, 1990). From this point of view, knowledge emerges from a *basho* – a field or shared space that gives rise to the process of enacting tacit knowledge in the first place (Nishida, 1987, and Nonaka and Konno, 1998).

Summing up, explicit knowledge is based on the separation of the knower and the known, whereas both forms of tacit knowledge are based on the unity of subject and object. However, this unity differs in one important way. The difference lies in the locus from which the self conceives the unity of subject and object (action). In the case of tacit embodied knowledge, the self conceives of its action after the fact (reflection on action). In the case of self-transcending knowledge, the self conceives of its action while acting. Because aesthetic experiences are often described as being simultaneously inside oneself (acting) and outside of oneself (observing), the various types of self-transcending knowing all qualify as genuine aesthetic experience.[2]

Three *Bashos*, Three Metamorphoses

The shift from the second to the third epistemology – that is, from organizing around tacit embodied to organizing around not yet embodied knowledge – is not only at issue in cutting-edge practices in knowledge management, as we will see below, but is also in contemporary philosophy's transition from 'modern' to 'postmodern' modes of thought. At the heart of this underlying theme of twentieth-century philosophy and that of the thinking of Martin Heidegger, Kitaro Nishida and Friedrich

Nietzsche, is a fundamentally different way of sensing, approaching and conceiving of reality.

Martin Heidegger begins with the question 'Why are there beings at all, and why not rather nothing?' (Heidegger, 1993). With this question, Heidegger tries to conceive of reality from the locus of origin, from a space in which being emerges out of nothing, out of no thing. This locus allows Heidegger to approach reality in a radically different way. From this point of view, reality is not simply 'out there'. Rather, reality is brought forth from absence into presence, from concealment into unconcealment. The process of 'presencing' and disclosing reality is the essence of true thinking.

Kitaro Nishida articulated the same turn from an Eastern point of view. In *An Inquiry into the Good* (1990), he articulates the locus and starting point for his philosophizing as 'pure experience'. This, according to Nishida (1990), has three defining properties. It:

1   precedes the subject–object distinction;
2   conceives reality from within;
3   accomplishes a union of knowledge, feeling and volition.

Reality, according to Nishida, is the self-development of a single system. Reality is that 'which constitutes in itself a single system'. The unifier of reality is the self. This self is not a thing, but an activity. The activity in which the self unites with things is called love. Hence, real knowledge is based on the unity of subject and object – that is, on love (Nishida, 1990).

In his later works, Nishida extended his notion of pure experience into his idea of self-consciousness and later to his notion of '*basho*' – field or shared space. Nishida's *basho* is never a subject or an object, but a place or field of emerging relationships. Alternatively, as Carter (1997) puts it, '*basho* is the given-in-intuition prior to analysis and expression of objectification.' *Basho* is the primal place/field/system that gives rise to knowledge and knowing. Nishida distinguishes among three types of bashos that correspond with the three forms of knowledge introduced above (Carter, 1997, and Wargo, 1972).

The first universal *basho* is what Nishida calls the 'universal of judgement'. It refers, and gives rise, to the content of judgement and knowledge. The second universal *basho* is what Nishida calls the 'universal of self-consciousness'. This *basho* is more fundamental and contains the first *basho*. The second *basho* focuses on how the content of judgement (first *basho*) arises in consciousness and self-consciousness in the first place. It reflects on the relationship and the activity of the self to the content of judgement. The third *basho* is the deepest and most fundamental field. Called 'the intelligible universal', it envelops the first two and moves attention from the self and self-consciousness to acts of consciousness in which the self is no longer the focus.

Nishida's three universal *bashos* relate to the three forms and epistemologies of knowledge as follows. The first *basho* corresponds with the epistemology of explicit knowledge in so far as both focus on objective things in the external world. The second *basho* corresponds with the epistemology of tacit embodied knowledge in so far as both focus on the relationship between content and self, or knower and known, respectively. Both are based on reflection on action. The third *basho* corresponds with the epistemology of self-transcending knowledge in so far as both focus on that which transcends the current self towards the most ultimate common ground that is prior to subject–object distinctions. Both are based on reflection in action or, as Nishida puts it, 'action-intuition'.

Let us close the philosophical investigation of self-transcending knowledge with a quotation from Nietzsche's *Thus Spake Zarathustra* (1982: 137–40). The passage deals with three metamorphosing of the spirit. These can be read as embodiments of the movement through the three *bashos* discussed above:

> Of the three metamorphoses of the spirit I tell you: how the spirit becomes a camel; and the camel, a lion; and the lion, finally, a child.
>
> There is much that is difficult for the spirit, the strong reverent spirit that would bear much: but the difficult and the most difficult are what its strength demands.
>
> 'What is difficult?' asks the spirit that would bear much, and kneels down like a camel wanting to be well loaded. 'What is most difficult, O heroes,' asks the spirit that would bear much, 'that I may take it upon myself and exult in my strength?' Is it not humbling oneself to wound one's haughtiness? Letting one's folly shine to mock one's wisdom?
>
> Or is it this: parting from our cause when it triumphs? Climbing high mountains to tempt the tempter? . . .
>
> Or is it this: loving those who despise us and offering a hand to the ghost that would frighten us?
>
> All these most difficult things the spirit that would bear much takes upon itself: like the camel that, burdened, speeds into the desert, thus the spirit speeds into its desert.
>
> In the loneliest desert, however, the second metamorphosis occurs: here the spirit becomes a lion who would conquer his freedom and be master in his own desert, here he seeks out his last master: he wants to fight him and his last god; for ultimate victory wants to fight with the great dragon.
>
> Who is the great dragon whom the spirit will no longer call lord and god? 'Thou shalt' is the name of the great dragon. But the spirit of the lion says, 'I will.' 'Thou shalt' lies in his way, sparkling like gold, an animal covered with scales; and on every scale shines a golden 'thou shalt.'
>
> Values, thousands of years old, shine on these scales; and thus speaks the mightiest of all dragons: 'All value of all things shines on me. All value has long been created, and I am all created value. Verily, there shall be no more "I will."' Thus speaks the dragon.
>
> My brothers, why is there a need in the spirit for the lion? Why is not the beast of burden, which renounces and is reverent, enough?
>
> To create new values – that even the lion cannot do; but the creation of freedom for oneself for new creation – that is within the power of the lion. The creation of freedom for oneself and a sacred 'No' even to duty – for that, my

brothers, the lion is needed. To assume the right to new values – that is the most terrifying assumption for a reverent spirit that would bear much. Verily, to him it is preying, and a matter for beast of prey. He once loved 'Thou shalt' as most sacred: now he must find illusion and caprice even in the most sacred, that freedom from his love may become his prey: the lion is needed for such a prey.

But say, my brothers, what can the child do that even the lion could not do? Why must the preying lion still become a child? The child is innocence and forgetting, a new beginning, a game, a self-propelled wheel, a first movement, a sacred 'Yes' is needed: the spirit now wills his own will, and he who had been lost to the world now conquers his own world.

Of the three metamorphoses of the spirit I have told you: how the spirit became a camel; and the camel, a lion; and the lion, finally, a child. Thus spoke Zarathustra. And at that time he sojourned in the town that is called The Motley Cow.

In the first metamorphosis, the spirit becomes a camel by submitting completely to external reality, bearing whatever it must: 'What is most difficult, O heroes, asks the spirit that would bear much, that I may take it upon myself and exult in my strength?' The camel relates to reality from outside, which is isomorphic to how the knowledge of the first epistemology (and the first *basho*) relate to the reality that they denote: from outside.

In the second metamorphosis the camel becomes a lion. In the 'loneliest desert' the spirit meets the great dragon, whose name is 'Thou shalt,' but the spirit of the lion says 'I will'. Moving from 'Thou shalt' to 'I will' shifts the origin of action from a reality that is externally based to one that is internally based. The lion relates to his will-based reality from within, which is isomorphic to how the knowledge of the second epistemology (or *basho*, respectively) relates to the reality that it denotes: from within.

In the third metamorphosis the lion finally becomes a child: 'The child is innocence and forgetting, a new beginning, a game, a self-propelled wheel, a first movement.' Moving from a 'sacred No' to a 'sacred Yes' again shifts the relationship mode between self and reality, or knower and known. In order to engage in 'a new beginning, a game, a self-propelled wheel', the self has to transcend the lower self of the lion, stuck in his own 'I will', to reach the emerging movement of the self-propelling wheel. The way the child relates to his 'sacred Yes' is isomorphic to how the knowledge (knower) of the third epistemology relates to reality (known): both from outside and from within at the same time, or, as Nishida puts it, neither-nor.

Learning Infrastructures: the Triadic Spiral of Knowledge Creation

What does all of that have to do with knowledge management?

Everything. Companies, consultants, trainers, and business schools usually have fairly well developed practices for how to manage and disseminate explicit knowledge, slightly less sophisticated practices for how to manage and disseminate tacit embodied knowledge and relatively undeveloped practices for how to manage and disseminate forms of self-transcending knowing. In fact, the very term 'managing knowledge' seems inappropriate at this point. Knowledge management is a typical 'Stage One' term. We can manage databanks, but we cannot manage human experience.

Here I distinguish three types of learning infrastructures.

Type I learning infrastructures

These are based on a one-dimensional process. Type I learning infrastructures include websites, electronic databases, films, books and other forms of self-service media. These learning infrastructures are ideal for disseminating explicit knowledge and are easily scalable and replicable.

Type II learning infrastructures

These infrastructures are based on two-dimensional processes that build on the interplay between action and reflection on action. Examples of Type II learning infrastructures are all sorts of parallel structures in which practitioners reflect and learn from their experience on a regular and repetitive basis (Bushe and Shani, 1991). Schein (1995), for example, describes the institutions of the MIT Learning Consortium as a set of parallel learning structures within and among companies. Type II learning infrastructures are required for all systems that focus on surfacing and disseminating tacit knowledge by sharing experiences. As reflection on action usually requires shared time and shared space among a group of practitioners, Type II learning infrastructures tend to be much more expensive and difficult to scale and replicate.

Type III learning infrastructures

These last infrastructures are based on three-dimensional processes that build on the interplay between shared action (praxis), shared reflection and forming shared will (Scharmer, Versteegen and Käufer, 1998, and Senge and Scharmer, 1997).

Type III infrastructures allow practitioners to repetitively go through the whole cycle of shared praxis, shared reflection and formation of shared will, which then leads again to a new praxis. As the surfacing of both tacit knowledge (shared reflection) and self-transcending knowledge (formation of shared will) requires a very high quality of shared time and space, Type III learning infrastructures are the most expensive and difficult to attain.

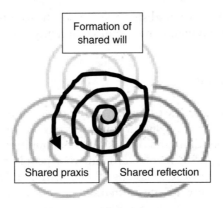

Figure 3.2   *The spiral of self-transcending knowledge creation*

Figure 3.2 depicts the three-dimensional knowledge spiral that enables organizing and strategizing around not yet embodied knowledge. For example, a global health systems company takes its leadership team to three-day off-site meetings every six months. In these meetings, the managers engage in the following three activities: they reflect on their experiences and identify key learnings; work to uncover what truly motivates each individual; and use this knowledge to redefine the agenda of action for the upcoming months.

The more distributed organizations and networks of collaboration become, the more critical Type III learning infrastructures tend to be, because shared praxis, shared reflection and formation of shared will are the glue that keeps distributed networks in synch and together.

Shared praxis

This is everything that people do together. All 'communities of practice' (Wenger, 1998) evolve around what people do together. Everyone who has gone through a real 'action experience' with others knows that, after such an event, the nature of their relationship is different. However, most virtual teams do not qualify for shared experience. Distributed work does not create community. Shared experience does. Only when distributed work is perceived as a shared body of action can the intangible nature of community evolve and manifest.

Shared reflection

This includes all shared experiences and the expression of their underlying themes, puzzles and questions. All 'communities of reflection' revolve around what people reflect on and think about together. However, most discussions and discussion groups do not qualify as shared reflection or communities of reflection. Abstract discussion and the mere transaction of speech acts do not create community. Shared reflection on common experiences does. Only when abstract discussion turns into shared bodies of reflection can the intangible nature of community evolve and emerge.

Formation of shared will

This is the most rare and least tangible of the three sources of networked community building. It happens in conversations in which participants articulate shared aspirations and desires. All 'communities of commitment' (Kofman and Senge, 1993) revolve around what people really care about together. However, most discussions about setting goals, targets and objectives do not qualify as the formation of shared will. Negotiations about targets and objectives do not create community. The formation of shared will does. The difference between the two is that the former is a one-stage process and the latter is a four-stage process.

Negotiating objectives starts where it ends, with negotiating objectives. Shared will formation starts with subjective reality and ends with objective realities. Shared will formation starts with the expression of individual experiences (phase I: individual perspectives); continues with reflecting on common themes, questions and patterns that underlie the various individual perspectives (phase II: dialogue); proceeds with uncovering what the participating individuals truly care about and what they really want to create (phase III: reconceiving purpose); and ends with agreed on leverage points and commitments to act (phase IV: objectives).

Hence, what appears to be the same – the negotiation of objectives and the formation of shared will – is not. The former starts and ends with objectives and objective realities. The latter is a process that uses the eye of the needle of individuality to mould the collective will into a new social sculpture (Beuys, 1992). It starts with intrasubjective realities (phase I), continues with intersubjective (phase II) and trans-subjective (phase III) realities and concludes with redefining objective realities (phase IV). Only when abstract discussions of group objectives turn into a shared body of collective will can the most intangible sphere of community building be actualized (Scharmer, 2000a).

Summing up, the core principles that underlie Type III learning infrastructures are those of wholeness and movement. These interweave and integrate the three domains by:

1 turning distributed labour into shared experience;
2 turning abstract discussions into shared reflection;
3 turning negotiation of objectives into the formation of collective will.

All three represent different aspects of a single underlying process – the process of self-transcending knowledge creation.

Self-reflective speech acts

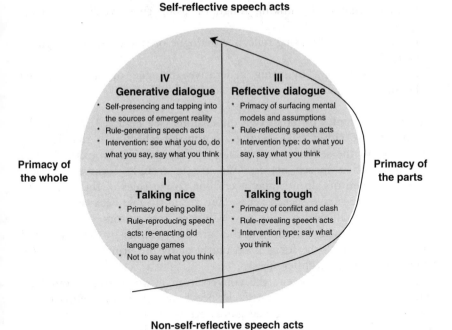

Non-self-reflective speech acts

Figure 3.3   *Four field logics of languaging*

Field Logics of Languaging: Requisite Conversational Complexity

The single most critical issue affecting the success or failure of knowledge infrastructures is whether or not the communication in use has the conversational complexity required to access the particular type of knowledge. Many knowledge management systems fail because they do not meet this criterion. Without the capacity for dialogue, for instance, teams are unable to express their tacit, taken-for-granted assumptions about how reality works.

The model in Figure 3.3 outlines a process archetype that I have seen in numerous management and organizational settings and developed by means of many consulting, action research and community-building experiences (Scharmer, 1999). The model is based on four generic stages and field logics of listening and 'languaging'.

Within each of these four different field logics, people relate to each other at a different level of conversational complexity by using different kinds of language structures:

1   in field logic I, by talking nice or using rule-reproducing language
    games;

2   in field logic II, by talking tough or using rule-revealing language games;
3   in field logic III, by using reflective dialogue or rule-reflecting language games;
4   in field logic IV, by using generative dialogue or rule-generating language games.

The four field logics differ in two dimensions (see Figure 3.3). First, the speech acts are either self-reflective or non-self-reflective – that is, they either refer to the self who is speaking or they do not. An example of a non-self-reflective speech act is, 'We are in trouble because the new Chinese competitors do not play according to the rules of the game.' An example of a reflective speech act is, 'We are in trouble because we failed to meet the challenge of our new Chinese competitors.' Second, the respective speech acts differ in that they are driven either by the primacy of wholeness (in which the focus is on unity) or by the primacy of parts (in which the focus is on differences).

Throughout the full cycle, the conversation moves through four field logics of performed speech acts. Each speech act relates differently to the rules of the underlying language game. Rule-reproducing (talking nice), rule-revealing (talking tough), rule-reflecting (reflective dialogue) and rule-generating (generative dialogue) speech acts produce different kinds of conversations, each of which allows participants to access and communicate different types and layers of knowledge and knowing.

Each of the previously discussed forms of knowledge requires a different level of conversational complexity in order to be accessed and disseminated in organizations (see Figure 3.4). The requisite conversational complexity for creating and disseminating know-what, know-how, know-why and know-who usually tends towards the second field logic of communication (talking tough). In order to access and disseminate the tacit dimension of knowledge in use throughout organizations, conversational complexity must move one quadrant up, to reflective dialogue. Finally, in order to access and enhance the not yet embodied dimension of knowing, the requisite conversational complexity again moves one quadrant up, to generative dialogue. Without the capacity for generative dialogue, teams are unable to tap into the sources of imaginative, inspirative and intuitive knowledge. Thus, without the fourth field logic of languaging, they lack the capacity to innovate by 'sensing and actualizing what wants to emerge' (Jaworski and Scharmer, 1999).

The leadership challenge is to help teams and institutions get 'unstuck' in the first quadrant (talking nice), and increase their capacity to move up across all four quadrants and field logics of conversational action. What sort of interventions or speech acts can help leaders move the field logic up?

In shifting from field logic I to field logic II, the principal leverage is based on reconnecting what we think with what we say. The work of

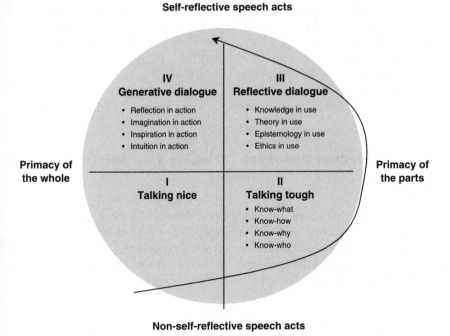

Self-reflective speech acts

IV **Generative dialogue** • Reflection in action • Imagination in action • Inspiration in action • Intuition in action	**III** **Reflective dialogue** • Knowledge in use • Theory in use • Epistemology in use • Ethics in use
I **Talking nice**	**II** **Talking tough** • Know-what • Know-how • Know-why • Know-who

Primacy of the whole ... **Primacy of the parts**

Non-self-reflective speech acts

Figure 3.4   *Field logics of languaging as requisite complexity for knowledge creation*

Argyris (1992) on accessing the 'left-hand column' focuses on these kinds of interventions. An example of this kind of intervention would be to create a space that allows participants to articulate opposing views and confront difficult issues. No learning or genuine knowledge creation will ever occur without moving the field logic from the first to the second quadrant, for field logic I only reproduces what is already known.

The principal leverage in field logic III is based on reconnecting what we think and say with what we do. The work of Argyris and Schön (1996), Schein (1992 and 1993), Isaacs (1993) and Srivastva and Cooperider (1990) addresses this issue and focuses on 'double loop learning' (Argyris and Schön), 'taken for granted assumptions' (Schein), 'containers of conversation' (Isaacs), and 'appreciative enquiry' (Srivastva and Cooperider).

The principal leverage in moving from field logic III to IV is based on reconnecting what we think, say and do with what we see. Examples of this rare event are difficult to summarize. Sometimes they occur, after many days of shared work, as intentional quietness or sacred silence (Isaacs, 1999, and Scharmer, 2000). The issue is how to move from reflective dialogue – that is, from talk that revolves around tacit embodied knowledge to the emergent space of self-presencing (Heidegger) and action-intuition (Nishida) – that is, towards the self-transcending state of knowing.

The four field logics represent four generic attractors that define the rules according to which the drama of human conversation plays out. They differ in the degree of complexity that they are able to capture and represent. The more teams and companies learn to move with ease across all four quadrants or field logics of conversational action, the more they will succeed in turning their customer relationships into shared bodies of imagination, inspiration and intuition for continuous, radical innovation.

Concluding Discussion: Bringing Your Self into Reality

What new insights does the distinction between two types of tacit knowledge – embodied and not yet embodied – add to the discussion? Why not just use the old distinction between explicit and tacit?

We have discussed five distinct areas in which the differentiation between tacit embodied and self-transcending knowledge does, in fact, add new insights.

1 **Epistemology** The theoretical argument is that tacit embodied and self-transcending knowledge are grounded in different epistemologies and, as discussed above, different *bashos*. What Nishida calls the second *basho* – the universal of self-consciousness – corresponds with the epistemology of tacit embodied knowledge in that both focus on the relationship between content and self, or knower and known, respectively. Both are grounded in reflection on action. The third *basho* – the intelligible universal – corresponds with the epistemology of self-transcending knowledge in that both focus on that which transcends the current self towards the ultimate common ground that is prior to subject–object distinctions. Both are based on reflection in action, or, as Nishida puts it, 'action-intuition'.

2 **Praxis** The practical argument is that the managing and nurturing of tacit and self-transcending knowledge requires managers to create different types of learning infrastructures. Tacit knowledge requires Type II infrastructures, which are based on the interplay of action and reflection on action. Self-transcending knowledge requires a Type III infrastructure that evolves during the interplay of shared action, shared reflection and formation of shared will. Thus, managers design and engage in different process types, depending on whether they organize around tacit or self-transcending knowledge.

3 **Requisite conversational complexity** The requisite conversational complexity differs not only for explicit and tacit knowledge, but also for tacit and self-transcending knowledge. Whereas tacit knowledge requires reflective dialogue as the minimum condition of conversational complexity (field logic III), self-transcending knowledge needs

generative dialogue in order to emerge in conversations (field logic IV).

4   **Strategy**   Self-transcending knowledge matters because within increasing return-based competition, nothing counts more than precognition – that is, the ability to strategize and organize around not yet embodied knowledge.

5   **Self**   '*Ba* may also be thought of as the recognition of the self in all', write Nonaka and Konno (1998). I would like to echo this statement from a Fichtean perspective: *ba* may also be thought of as the space that allows you to bring your self into reality. Both sequences – recognizing your self in what surrounds you and bringing your self into reality – are part of a larger social breathing rhythm across generations and civilizations. This breathing rhythm constitutes the social space that allows the self to transcend and jump over the boundaries of its current embodiment.

Thus, there is both theoretical and practical evidence that the concept of self-transcending knowledge constitutes a knowledge type *sui generis*. The more the world economy moves towards the logic of increasing returns and, as a consequence, the leadership challenge becomes one of being 'in front of a blank canvas', the more the capacity to sense and actualize self-transcending knowledge will turn out to be the most critical source of future competitive advantage.

Notes

1   The 12 types of knowledge represent an analytical distinction. In practice, all dimensions of knowledge creation are intertwined. The two cornerstones of the field are the upper left and lower right fields: know-what about results and performance and intuition, which reshapes and reframes itself and all 11 other fields: To test whether or not the framework is a useful device, we have to ask whether the lower left (know-who) and the upper right fields (reflection in action) refer to the same or distinct knowledge types. An example of know-who is to outline the fundamental causes and belief systems (such as shared value standards or purpose statements). Reflection in action is an entirely different form of knowledge that does not refer to things (such as mission statements) but to 'no things' at work. Hence, the framework based on the differentiation among ontological (four streams of action) and epistemological (three forms of knowledge) assumptions does create new distinctions.

2   The term 'aesthetic' refers to those kinds of experiences that meet the following three conditions. The subject of experience sees something (seeing 1), observes their observing at the same time (seeing 2) and closes the feedback loop between 'seeing 1' and 'seeing 2' ('seeing 3'). Hence, in an aesthetic experience, the subject is within (watching something) and outside of themselves (watching themselves) at the same time. Technically speaking, we refer to those experiences as aesthetic experiences that have the property of synchronicity between action and reflection – that is, zero feedback delay.

References

Arthur, W.B. (1996) 'Increasing returns and the new world of business', *Harvard Business Review*, July–Aug.: 100–9.

Argyris, C. (1992) *On Organizational Learning*. Cambridge, MA: Blackwell.

Argyris, C., and Schön, D. (1996) *Organizational Learning II: Theory, Method, and Practice*. New York: Addison-Wesley.

Argyris, C., Putnam, R., and Smith, D. McLain (1985) *Action Science: Concepts, Methods, and Skills for Research and Intervention*. San Francisco: Jossey-Bass.

Beuys, J. (1992) 'Kunst = Kapital', in Rainer Rappmann (ed.), *Achberger Vorträge*. Wangen: Achberger Verlag.

Bohm, D. (1990) *On Dialogue*. Ojai, CA: David Bohm Seminars.

Brown, J.S., and Duguid, P. (1998) 'Organizing knowledge', *California Management Review*, 40 (3): 90–111.

Buber, M. (1970) *I and Thou*. New York: Simon & Schuster.

Bushe, G.R., and Shani, A.B. (1991) *Parallel Learning Structures*. Reading, MA: Addison-Wesley.

Carter, R.E. (1997) *The Nothingness Beyond God: An Introduction to the Philosophy of Nishida Kitaro*, 2nd edn. St Paul, MN: Paragon House.

Cook, S.N., and Seely Brown, J. (1997) 'Bridging epistemologies: the generative dance between organizational knowledge and organizational knowing', working paper, forthcoming in *Organization Science*.

Csikszentmihalyi, M. (1991) *Flow: The Psychology of Optimal Experience*. New York: HarperPerennial.

Fichte, J.G. (1982) *The Science of Knowledge*. Cambridge: Cambridge University Press.

Hamel, G., and Prahalad, C.K. (1994) *Competing for the Future*. Boston, MA: Harvard Business School Press.

Heidegger, Martin (1993) 'What is metaphysics?', in Martin Heidegger and David Farrell Krell (eds), *Basic Writings: From Being and Time to The Task of Thinking*, 2nd edn. San Francisco: Harper.

Isaacs, W. (1993) 'Taking flight: dialogue, collective thinking and organizational learning', *Organizational Dynamics*, Autumn: 24–39.

Isaacs, W. (1999) *Dialogue and the Art of Thinking Together: A Pioneering Approach to Communicating in Business and in Life*. New York: Currency.

Jaworski, J. (1996) *Synchronicity: The Inner Path of Leadership*. San Francisco: Berrett-Koehler.

Jaworski, J., Gozdz, K., and Senge, P. (1997) 'Setting the field: creating the conditions for profound institutional change', working paper, Society for Organizational Learning, Cambridge, MA.

Jaworski, J., and Scharmer, C.O. (1999) 'Leadership in the new economy', working paper, Centre for Generative Leadership, Hamilton, MA.

Johnson, H.T., and Kaplan, R.S. (1991) *Relevance Lost: The Rise and Fall of Management Accounting*. Boston, MA: Harvard Business School Press.

Kappler, E. (1993) 'Gegenwartsfdhigkeit als zentrales Thema von Personalentwicklung', in S. Laske and S. Gorbach (eds), *Spannungsfeld Personalentwicklung*. Vienna: Manz Verlag. pp. 61–74.

Kofman, F., and Senge, Peter (1993) 'Communities of commitment: the heart of learning organizations', *Organizational Dynamics*, Autumn: 5–23.

von Krogh, G. (1998) 'Care in knowledge creation', *California Management Review*, 40 (3): 133–53.

von Krogh, G., and Roos, J. (1995) *Organizational Epistemology*. London: Macmillan; New York: St Martin's.

Lave, J., and Wenger, E. (1991) *Situated Learning: Legitimate Peripheral Participation*. Cambridge: Cambridge University Press.

Leonard, D., and Sensiper, S. (1998) 'The role of tacit knowledge in group innovation', *California Management Review*, 40 (3): 112–32.

de Monthoux, P.G. (1993) 'The spiritual in organizations: on Kandinsky and organizational aesthetics', in S. Laske and S. Gorbach (eds), *Spannungsfeld Personalentwicklung*. Vienna: Manz Verlag. pp. 133–51.

Nietzsche, F. (1982 [1954]) 'Thus spake Zarathustra', in W. Kaufmann (ed. and trans.), *The Portable Nietzsche*. New York: Penguin. pp. 137–40.

Nishida, K., and Dilworth, D.A. (trans. and Intro.) (1987) *Last Writings: Nothingness and the Religious Worldview*. Honolulu: University of Hawaii Press.

Nishida, K., Abe, M., and Ives, C. (trans.) (1990) *An Inquiry into the Good*. New Haven: Yale University Press.

Nonaka, I. (1991) 'The knowledge creating company', *Harvard Business Review*, Nov.–Dec.: 96–104.

Nonaka, I. (1994) 'A dynamic theory of organizational knowledge creation', *Organization Science*, 5 (1): 14–37.

Nonaka, I. (1996) 'Knowledge has to do with goodness, beauty, and truth', in C.O. Scharmer (ed.), 'Crafting architectures of thought: 25 dialogue-interviews on organization studies, strategy, leadership, and controlling in the 21st century', unpublished project report, Vol. III, pp. 667–88.

Nonaka, I., and Konno, N. (1998) 'The concept of "*ba*": building a foundation for knowledge creation', *California Management Review*, 40 (3): 40–54.

Nonaka, I., and Takeuchi, H. (1995) *The Knowledge-creating Company: How Japanese Companies Create the Dynamics of Innovation*. Oxford: Oxford University Press.

Polanyi, Michael (1966) *The Tacit Dimension*. London: Routledge & Kegan Paul.

Scharmer, C.O. (1991) *Ästhetik als Kategorie strategischer Führung*. Stuttgart: Urachhaus-verlag.

Scharmer, C.O. (1999) 'Organizing around not-yet-embodied knowledge', in G. van Krogh, I. Nonaka and T. Nishiguchi (eds), *Knowledge Creation: A New Source of Value*. New York: Macmillan.

Scharmer, C.O. (2000a) 'Presencing: illuminating the blind spot of knowledge and leadership', habilitation thesis, University of Innsbruck, Cambridge, MA.

Scharmer, C.O. (2000b) 'Presencing: shifting the place from which we operate', presented at the Conference on Knowledge and Innovation. Helsinki, Finland.

Scharmer, C.O., Versteegen, U., and Käufer, K. (1998) 'The pentagon of praxis', working paper, Cambridge, MA.

Schein, E.H. (1992) *Organizational Culture and Leadership*, 2nd edn. San Francisco: Jossey-Bass.

Schein, E.H. (1993) 'On dialogue, culture, and organizational learning', *Organizational Dynamics*, Autumn: 40–51.

Schein, E.H. (1995) 'Learning consortia: how to create parallel learning systems for organization sets', working paper, Organizational Learning Center, MIT Sloan School of Management, Cambridge, MA.

Schön, D.A. (1983) *The Reflective Practitioner*. New York: Basic Books.

Senge, P.M. (1990) *The Fifth Discipline: The Art and Practice of the Learning Organization.* New York: Doubleday.

Senge, P.M., and Scharmer, C.O. (1997) 'Von "learning organizations" zu "learning communities"', in H. von Pierer and B. von Oetinger (eds), *Wie kommt das Neue in die Welt?* Munich: Hanser Verlag. pp. 99–110.

Shotter, J. (1993) *Conversational Realities: Constructing Life Through Language.* London: Sage.

Srivastva, S., and Cooperider, D.L. (1990) *Appreciative Management and Leadership: The Power of Positive Thought and Action in Organizations.* San Francisco: Jossey-Bass.

Teece, D. (1998) 'Capturing value from knowledge assets: the new economy, markets for know-how, and intangible assets', *California Management Review*, 40 (3): 55–79.

Torbert, W.R. (1991) *The Power of Balance: Transforming Self, Society, and Scientific Inquiry.* London: Sage.

Wargo, R.J. (1972) 'The logic of Basho and the concept of nothingness in the philosophy of Nishida Kitaso', PhD dissertation, Ann Arbor, University Microfilm International.

Wenger, E. (1998) *Communities of Practice: Learning, Meaning, and Identity.* Cambridge: Cambridge University Press.

4 Understanding the Creative Process: Management of the Knowledge Worker

Charlan Jeanne Nemeth and Lauren Nemeth

Introduction

Only in understanding who tends to be creative and what types of influences stimulate or inhibit the creative process can we hope to find ways to 'manage' it. In fact, 'management' may not be the right word as it implies control and possibly manipulation. It also assumes that one has the knowledge and the power to effect thought processes that lead to creative solutions. However, management of the creative process requires something akin to leadership and inspiration; it also requires an appreciation of 'deviance' – especially in the arena of thoughts, opinions and judgements. Also, the creative process may be better fostered in an environment of respect and engagement than in one of harmony and cohesion.

One of the more fascinating aspects of creativity is that it is not the same as good problem solving, which can be taught more easily. Two elements of creativity are commonly accepted:

1   it is 'novel' – that is, in some sense, it has to be new;
2   it has to be appropriate to the problem.

In other words, a creative solution is unique; it has not been found before. However, there are a number of original or unique or new 'solutions' that do not solve a problem. They may even be bizarre or nonsensical, but still 'appropriate to the problem'. Creativity arguably has a third element (Amabile, 1983), namely that it be heuristic rather than algorithmic. Algorithmic tasks have clear, straightforward paths leading to a solution, whereas heuristic tasks require exploration. In other words, for creativity to occur, the process used to arrive at a solution is not known. If it were known, one might describe this as good problem-solving rather than creativity.

Although creativity is not a step-by-step process, it can still be understood and it can also be facilitated or impeded. Thus, there is a sizable literature that attempts to explain creativity. Some studies have concentrated on 'who' tends to be creative and whether these individuals can be described by typical personality traits. Other studies have concentrated on the mode of thinking that leads to creative outcomes. Still others experimentally manipulate mechanisms to stimulate or impede the process. Yet other studies have tried to understand creativity over the human lifespan. Some of the latter have tracked the accomplishments of 'gifted' children; others have studied highly creative individuals, such as Nobel laureates, in an attempt to understand the process that led to their discoveries.

One of the more intriguing (and consistent) facts about creativity is that it is not the same thing as intelligence (see generally Milgram, 1990). There are both general and specific kinds of intelligence and creativity. General intelligence is characterized by an ability to think abstractly, logically and systematically. Specific intelligences include talent in music or art or mathematics. The general and the specific types of intelligence bear some relationship to each other, but are not highly correlated. The same holds true for creativity. There is general creative thinking that is clever, elegant or surprising (Guilford, 1967, and Mednick, 1962) and leads to imaginative solutions. There is also specific creative ability possessed by people who produce novel and valuable products in the arts, sciences, business or politics, for example. As with intelligence, general and specific creative thought is moderately correlated, but they are not the same thing. Of greater interest is that neither general nor specific intellectual ability appears related to overall creative thinking (Kogan and Pankove, 1972, and Milgram, Moran, Sawyers and Fu, 1987). Further, neither appears related to specific creative talent in a range of arenas (Milgram and Milgram, 1976, and Wing and Wallach, 1971).

Although intelligence, whether general or specific, bears little relationship to general or specific creativity, it is certainly not the case that intelligence plays no part in creative thought or accomplishments. Most studies show a relationship between IQ and creativity up to a moderate baseline; thereafter, there is little or no relationship. What this means is that, up to a slightly better than average IQ, intelligence and creativity are related – the more intelligent one is, the more creative one is likely to be – but additional IQ points above 120 or so do not relate to additional creativity.

Just as creativity requires a certain 'baseline' of intelligence, it also requires 'domain-relevant skills'. It would have been difficult for Charles Townes to develop the maser and laser had he not understood physics and electronics. Domain-relevant skills include a minimum level of factual knowledge and technical proficiency. However, most researchers agree that personality, creative thought processes and motivation also play important roles in creativity and creative accomplishment (Amabile, 1983, and Csikszentmihalyi, 1990). Simonton (1988) also includes the element of persuasion because often creative accomplishment depends on the evaluation and acceptance of 'experts' in a field.

Personality: 'Who' is Creative?

Much of the research on creativity has measured individuals on a host of personality tests (Barron, 1955, and MacKinnon, 1962). One of the more extensive studies used a nomination and rating system to categorize people as highly creative or less creative in their professions (Barron, 1955). The study asked the colleagues of architects, creative writers and mathematicians to rate the creativity of their peers. Generally, these individuals came to a university research setting for a three-day weekend during which they were given a battery of personality tests, observed in a variety of situations and interviewed. Among other indicators, the highly creative women mathematicians, for example, were found to be unconventional. They had 'high intellectual ability, vividness or even flamboyance of character, moodiness and preoccupation, courage and self centredness'. Barron (1955: 68) suggested that 'creative people have an edge to them'. In general, the 'highly creative' were found to have high ego strength and flexibility and achieved successes by means of independent effort rather than conformance. They think and associate ideas in unusual ways.

Other research is highly consistent with this portrayal (Csikszentmihalyi and Getzels, 1973, Albert and Runco, 1986, and MacKinnon, 1964). Personality traits associated with creativity include independence, openness to experience, a lack of interest in social norms and social acceptance and, interestingly, a high value on the activity itself rather than on status or money. The latter is often termed 'intrinsic motivation' and appears to be consistently characteristic of highly creative people.

Independence and lack of interest in social norms and social acceptance are aspects to which we will return repeatedly. They are important for understanding 'who' is creative, but also for understanding how to manage or, more accurately, not manage, highly creative people (Nemeth, 1997). A number of studies have documented the fact that highly creative people are independent and significantly less conforming in experimental settings than less creative people. Of the hundreds of studies on the phenomenon of conformity, most have used some variant of the paradigm developed by Asch (1951). People are shown a series of slides and asked to name which of three figures is equal in length to a standard line. The correct answer is obvious. Alone, individuals have no difficulty recognizing the correct answer. However, when faced with as few as three people who all agree that a different figure is the correct one, fully 35 per cent of the responses tend to agree with the erroneous majority. People abandon the information provided by their own senses and adopt the majority opinion as the correct one, primarily because they assume that 'truth lies in numbers', but also because they fear being a dissenting voice (Deutsch and Gerard, 1955). Highly creative people are much less likely to do this.

Consistent with this behaviour, highly creative people often report that they have pursued their ideas despite advice to the contrary. They were often told that they were wasting their time or valuable resources and had difficulty obtaining funds for their work. Some might view such persistence as rebellion, but I believe it is more likely a willingness to defy the crowd and persist in a given course of action based on a belief in its promise. To illustrate, Nobel laureate Charles Townes repeatedly said that he listened carefully to critics, considered their views and then independently chose what he believed was the proper course of action.

Cognitive Processes: a Style of Thinking

Other approaches to the study of creativity have focused on cognitive or thought processes. Most have emphasized the quality of 'divergent thinking', which involves a consideration of varying perspectives (Guilford, 1967). Here, we need to distinguish between fluency and flexibility, between the sheer number of ideas and the variety of those ideas. This is illustrated by a well-known test for creativity known as the 'uses' test, which asks people to name all the uses of a common object such as a brick. One person might list 'building a road', 'building a house' and 'building a school'. Another might say 'building a house', 'using it as a missile to throw through a window' and 'using it as a doorstop'. Both sets of responses include three ideas – that is, they have the same 'fluency'. However, the former includes only ways of 'building' something, whereas the latter provides a greater variety of ideas and better manifests divergent thinking. Similar to this are Torrance's verbal and non-verbal Tests of Creative Thinking (Torrance, 1966). One non-verbal test is the 'circles' test, which asks people to sketch as many different objects as possible using 36 identical blank circles and give each sketch a name. Again, such products can be scored for fluency (number represented) and flexibility (number of different categories represented).

One of the mechanisms for producing divergent thinking is play. Playfulness is also considered a personality trait and tends to be characteristic of highly creative individuals, who are often described as 'childlike but not childish'. Amabile (1996) considers intellectual playfulness a component of the intrinsic motivation so often evident in highly creative people. They have a passion for their enterprise.

As an enduring personality trait, playfulness has been used to distinguish between highly and less creative children and adolescents (Getzels and Jackson, 1962, and Wallach and Kogan, 1965). There is even suggestive evidence that literal play may facilitate creative thinking, especially the component of flexibility (Piaget, 1951).

As an illustration of such playfulness in the pursuit of a creative accomplishment, I am reminded of my interviews with Donald Glaser, inventor of the 'bubble chamber' for which he received the Nobel Prize in physics. Professor Glaser's 'childlike' goal was to capture cosmic rays in the universe. His fantasy was a transparent bathtub in orbit that would capture these rays. His goal was clear, though there was no exact roadmap of how to achieve it. He could not put a bathtub in orbit, but he could track cosmic rays by creating instability in order to turn tiny microscopic influences into macroscopic recordable things. His idea? A superheated liquid in which liquid and vapour become indistinguishable, which could be made unstable by something as minute as a cosmic ray, which would leave a visible track. After considering various options, such as crystals and clouds, he settled on a superheated liquid in which bubbles would be the visible track – an idea stimulated by watching bubbles in his beer.

Learning from the lifespan

Most of the research on personality and cognitive styles is carefully documented by experiments with substantial samples of people. Research on real-life accomplishment, however, shows only a moderate rather than a strong relationship with creativity as defined by experimental 'creativity tasks'. Thus, case studies and in-depth interviews with highly accomplished people provide additional insights, the above description of the bubble chamber being one. Trying to understand a person over a lifespan is a very complicated undertaking, but is clearly important in any attempt to understand when and why creative thought turns into creative accomplishment.

Interviews with creative people, for example, make clear the importance of the creative person's decision about what problems to focus on. That decision involves determining what is important as well as formulating the problem in a way that will permit its solution. Csikszentmihalyi (1990: 193) noted that creative individuals often point out that the 'formulation of a problem was more important than its solution and that real advances in science and in art tend to come when new questions are asked or old problems are viewed from a new angle'. In my own interviews with Nobel laureates, they repeated the same point. Owen Chamberlain, the founder of the antiproton, for example, noted that his real strength was in knowing a good question. He knew what was worth studying and he had knowledge pertinent to the solution.

Knowing the right questions may be one of the benefits of having a highly creative mentor. There is ample evidence that Nobel laureates tend to be have been trained by Nobel laureates (Zuckerman, 1977). More than half of the 92 studied by Zuckerman were students or collaborators of Nobel laureates. Some researchers have suggested that the reason for this link may be resources (such as funds, facilities) or modelling (styles of thinking and working). However, there is reason to believe that creative mentors, being at the cutting edge of a field themselves, know the important questions – the ones whose answers might lead to a Nobel Prize. In fact, Owen Chamberlain mentioned that one of his teachers, Enrico Fermi, told his class that most of them would win a Nobel prize. They were the best and the brightest and, further, the Nobel Prize is awarded every year. This was the first time, according to Chamberlain, that he took seriously the possibility that he might some day win the prize.

In other interviews, Nobel laureates have commented about the creative process itself. Their insights include recognizing the value of judgement – that is, knowing good ideas from bad ones – and being able to act on the good ones – that is to conduct the experiments. The latter ability is often better recognized by practitioners than researchers. Most entrepreneurs, for example, recognize the importance of knowing a good idea from a bad one and, perhaps even more so, the importance of taking the risk – of acting on the good ideas.

Social Context

Although the preceding discussion has concentrated on individual personality traits and thought processes, it is clear that creativity does not occur in a vacuum. In fact, almost no activity, whether intellectual or social, occurs in a vacuum. One of the more important elements is the impact of the opinions and judgements of others.

The problems with majorities and high status

As mentioned previously, even when an answer is obvious, people are likely to abandon their own position on a question when presented with a majority position that differs from their own, although highly creative people tend to conform less to the judgements of others. Perhaps more important, there is ample evidence that majorities not only cause adoption of their position, right or wrong, but also change the nature of thought processes about the issue. A number of studies have found evidence that majorities induce convergent thinking – that is, consideration of an issue from a single perspective, in this case the perspective posed by the majority. To use one experimental paradigm as an illustration, we (Nemeth and Kwan, 1987) asked individuals in groups of four to name the first three-letter word they saw in a letter string – for example, 'DAMpt'. After short exposure to the string, they all first noticed 'DAM', the word formed by the capital letters from left to right. Then, they were 'informed' that three people in their group had first noticed 'MAD', the three-letter word formed by the backward sequencing of the capital letters. When they were then given a series of ten such letter strings and asked to form all the words they could using the letters in the strings, they tended to find many more words using backward sequencing of letters and fewer words using forward sequencing (such as, 'apt') or mixed sequencing (such as, 'pat'). In other words, in comparison with the responses from a control group that received no information about anyone else's responses, those exposed to a majority view that differed from their own tended to adopt the perspective of the majority to the exclusion of other perspectives.

People react similarly to knowing the positions of persons with high status. There is substantial research showing the power of status to induce movement to its position, right or wrong. As an illustration, Navy bomber crews consisting of a captain, navigator and gunner were asked to solve the following problem:

A man buys a horse for £60, sells it for £70, buys it back for £80 and sells it again for £90. How much profit did he make?

While the problem may appear on the surface to be relatively easy, more than half of bright undergraduates and adults do not solve it correctly. Their answers tend to be £0, £10 or £20. The correct answer is £20.

One might assume that if one person in the group knew the correct answer, the group would adopt that correct answer. However, it turns out that it depends on who has the correct answer.

There is a linear relationship between status and acceptance of an opinion. Thus, the 'captain' was more effective than the 'navigator', who in turn was more effective than the gunner in gaining acceptance of their solutions. Ironically, the navigator was most likely to come up with the correct answer.

It is problematic that people tend to accept the viewpoint of the majority or those with high status and power, whether that viewpoint is right or wrong. Worse, they tend to think about the issue from the perspective posed by the majority or high-status people to the exclusion of other considerations. One should then not be surprised by Professor Warren Bennis of the University of Southern California's estimate that at least seven out of ten people in American business keep their own opinions to themselves when they differ from those of their superiors. Even when subordinates know better, they allow their bosses to make mistakes (Summerfield, 1990).

The usefulness of diversity of viewpoints and dissent

As the above illustrates, there are strong tendencies to agree with a majority or with a person of higher status. Further, people have a tendency to seek concurrence. This tendency has led to American foreign policy 'fiascoes', such as the decision in 1961 by President Kennedy and his advisers to involve the United States in the invasion of the Bay of Pigs (Janis, 1982). Although the President's decision-making group consisted of highly intelligent and accomplished people, they made some very poor decisions. Janis concluded that the culprit was a combination of cohesion, directive leadership, insulation and time pressure. A tight-knit group whose leader has a preferred course of action, which is insulated from other viewpoints and even dissent, especially when under stress and time pressure, is inclined to seek consensus quickly. The resulting decision-making process tends to fall short, considering too few alternatives and less than the full range of information, objectives and contingency plans. As a consequence, the decisions are faulty, sometimes fatal.

Although careful research on these antecedent causes differs (for example, not all cohesive groups show this tendency towards groupthink), the combination of antecedent conditions largely agrees with what we know about creativity. Amabile (1996) has suggested that time pressures can reduce 'intrinsic motivation' and creativity. Further, elements that create cohesive bonds between individuals in a group can often enhance their tendency to agree and confine thinking to the perspective of the majority of members. The element of insulation from others' viewpoints and dissent is the focus of many attempts to improve decision making and creativity.

Techniques for improving creativity

Giving instructions   Most techniques aimed at increasing creativity have in common an attempt to thwart the confining elements of groups. Brain-storming, for example, asks people to generate as many ideas as possible and specifically instructs people to refrain from evaluating or criticizing any viewpoint, including their own (Osborn, 1957). It also encourages them to elaborate on others' views. The literature measuring the efficacy of this technique is somewhat mixed (Taylor, Berry and Block, 1958, and Stroebe and Diehl, 1994), but it is clear that instructions to offer differing views do not ensure that people will do so. In spite of the instructions, they fear criticism, whether it is spoken or not.

Other techniques remove the group from the creative process by having individuals do their creative thinking alone and then come together to select and adopt a preferred solution. Thus, to some extent there is a recognition that the group must agree for any solution to be effectively adopted and implemented. However, the assumption is that the finding of the solution – the creative process itself – is better left to individuals. In summarizing the available literature on this topic, McGrath (1984: 131) argues that 'individuals working separately generate many more, and more creative (as rated by judges) ideas than do groups . . . The difference is large, robust, and general.'

The picture that emerges from the foregoing is that groups tend to be confining and that attempts to increase the diversity of viewpoints often fail. As a result, the best we can do is make groups operate at the level of the sum of their individual creativity, which generally means letting them do their creative thinking apart from others. Work on the value of dissenting viewpoints, however, offers a more optimistic view of the value of conflicting viewpoints and even the value of group decision making for creative thought.

Devil's advocate/dialectical enquiry: mechanisms for dissent? A favoured technique for introducing dissent has been to invoke the devil's advocate. Janis (1982), for example, suggested this as a vehicle for reducing the concurrence-seeking (groupthink) of Cabinet-level foreign policy decision-makers, in order to avoid 'fiascoes'. The idea is to have someone vigorously criticize plans under consideration by a group in the hope that this will foster discussion as well as a consideration of more options and careful scrutiny of those options. A variant on this is dialectical enquiry, in which a counterplan is offered rather than merely criticism of the preferred plan.

Both techniques have been found to be useful (Mason, 1969, and Cosier, 1978), but the findings are mixed with regard to their relative superiority (Katzenstein, 1996). The value of such techniques appears to lie in getting people to 'consider the opposite' or at least a plausible alternative (Hirt and Markman, 1995). However, more recent evidence suggests that the devil's advocate method is less effective than authentic dissent (Nemeth, Connell, Rogers and Brown, 2000). The fact that a person argues for the sake of diversity of viewpoints rather than to express an authentically differing view renders the dissent less effective in stimulating divergent thinking. Perhaps more important, the evidence suggests that there are unintended negative consequences of assigning a devil's advocate. In this study, those exposed to a devil's advocate showed bias in the direction of supporting their initial views. They did not easily abandon or willingly question the correctness of their own positions. Instead, they may have been deluded into believing that they had considered options and alternatives when, in fact, they had focused on supporting their initial position.

The positive role of dissent

Though giving instructions and role-playing dissent have some efficacy, there is considerable evidence that exposure to authentic dissent aids both decision making and creativity. Among the positive contributions made by dissenting viewpoints, two are of particular interest. One is dissent as a liberator; the second is dissent as a stimulator.

Dissent as liberator As outlined above, unanimity mixed with numbers is a powerful combination for inducing agreement and even encouraging thinking from the perspective of the proposed position. People become confused about things as basic as the length of lines or the colour they see when faced with a majority that agrees on a differing view. Many times, they agree with an erroneous judgement simply because it is held by the majority. Most research, however, has documented the importance of unanimity. When the majority view is broken, conformity is dramatically reduced (Allen and Levine, 1969, and Asch, 1951). Of interest, and somewhat contrary to intuition, the 'break' in the majority view can take the form of an ally or an even more extreme dissenter. Most people would predict that having an ally – that is, someone who agrees with you – helps to reduce conformity to an erroneous majority. What is not so obvious is that having someone who disagrees with both you and the majority can also be of great benefit – conformity is significantly reduced.

Another way in which dissenters can be liberators is as a result of observation and modelling. Simple exposure to a dissenting individual – even one who was wrong – liberated individuals to be more independent in a subsequent conformity experiment. In one study, Nemeth and Chiles (1988) asked individuals to identify the colour of some blue slides. One individual repeatedly called the slides 'green'. As predicted, he was disliked, considered unintelligent and believed to have poor colour vision. Subsequently, these individuals were faced with a majority of three other people, all of whom called red slides 'orange'. Among those who had not previously been exposed to the dissenter, conformity was nearly 70 per cent. Among those who had previously been exposed to the dissenter conformity was only around 15 per cent.

Dissent as stimulator   Of perhaps greater practical consequence, dissent has repeatedly been found to stimulate thinking that is more divergent and creative. One illustration comes from the previously described study using the letter string (Nemeth and Kwan, 1987). People shown a series of letter strings, such as 'DAMpt', and asked to name the first three-letter word they notice, will say 'DAM', the word formed by capital letters from left to right. When told that all three of the other individuals in their group had first noticed 'MAD', the word formed by backward sequencing of the letters, they will then tend to look more closely at backward sequencing. Thus, when given a new set of letters and asked to name all the words they can form, they tend to find more words formed by backward sequencing of letters than words formed by forward or mixed sequencing.

Consider one, seemingly slight, change to this information. Suppose you give individuals information that one person in the group first noticed 'MAD' (the word formed by backward sequencing) while the other two, first noticed 'DAM'. Presented with subsequent letter strings, these individuals tend to find more words and find them using all forms of sequencing. They find more words because they detect them using a forward, backward and mixed sequencing of letters. In other words, they manifest divergent thinking and, in the process, find more solutions.

Such results have been documented by dozens of other studies as well. Exposure to minority dissent has been found to stimulate more and better information processing than other forms of dissent discussed (Nemeth and Rogers, 1996). People search for more information on all sides of an issue after exposure to a dissenting minority viewpoint. There is also evidence that people recall information better (Nemeth, Mayseless, Sherman and Brown, 1990). They also detect solutions that otherwise would have gone undetected. They apparently search the visual display more carefully and, in the process, find solutions that they tend not to find without such exposure (Nemeth and Wachtler, 1974). Finally, there is evidence that people think more creatively after being exposed to a dissenting minority viewpoint: their word associations become more original, unique and statistically infrequent. One's usual word association with 'blue' might be 'green' or 'sky'. After exposure to dissent, it is likely it would be more original – such as 'jeans' or 'jazz' (Nemeth and Kwan, 1985, and Nemeth, 1995).

Lessons for Management

The above portrayal of who tends to be creative and how creativity is increased in general suggests several lessons. We contrast these lessons with the corporate cultures often touted as exemplary or visionary. Collins and Porras (1994) list several elements that are considered part of the corporate culture of companies that endure and show profit over long periods of time. In their terms, these are generally cult-like atmospheres in which the powerful forces of unanimity, numbers, status, reward and social interaction foster uniformity of views and action. Some of the practices of those successful companies include the following.

1 **Care in recruitment** They especially look for people who 'fit' the corporate culture. It should be apparent that people who start out with the same values, habits and viewpoints are likely to be highly cohesive, get along and be willing to adhere to company goals and guidelines. They should also be easier to teach, indoctrinate and shape.
2 **Socialization into the company's 'culture'** This happens, for example, in universities, organizations that conduct intense training and, especially, provide numerous occasions for socializing with model citizens of the company. Socialization is aided by a powerful phenomenon that occurs when like-minded people discuss an issue. Literally hundreds of studies have documented the fact that, if individuals are basically in agreement, discussion polarizes their viewpoints – they become more confident of those viewpoints (Moscovici et al., 1969).
3 **Use of mottoes, slogans, language** Many companies have company songs, such as at IBM and Wal-Mart, and some even attempt to use a special language. Disney, for example, uses theatrical terms – a job is a 'part' and being on duty is 'on stage'. These mechanisms help employees identify with the company, develop a sense of cohesion and underscore the importance of uniformity.
4 **Dissent is 'ejected like a virus'** Collins and Porras (1994) suggest that the visionary companies are especially intolerant of dissent. There are many ways to stifle dissent – prescription, rewards and punishment and the opinions of others.

All of the mechanisms mentioned above are powerful tools for achieving high morale and cohesion and promoting effort on behalf of the company. It is well documented that these mechanisms help promote uniformity and with it, harmony and even productivity. However, these mechanisms are unlikely to foster independence, divergent thinking and creativity. Atmospheres of uniformity do not enhance creative thought or the likelihood of finding novel or original solutions. They are also likely to be repugnant to highly creative people who are independent, unconventional, inclined to seek out challenge and even 'on the edge'.

A number of companies have recognized that there are advantages to being different and independent. They use the rhetoric of 'self-renewal' (Motorola) and 'being a pioneer' (Sony). T.J. Watson, the former CEO of IBM, often illustrated the point by recounting the story of the 'wild ducks'. As the story goes, a man on the coast of New Zealand liked to watch the ducks fly south each fall. With good intentions, he began to feed them but found that, over time, they stopped flying south. They fed on what he provided and, after several years, grew so fat and lazy they hardly flew at all. The message? You can make wild ducks tame, but you can never make tame ducks wild again (Watson, 1963). Thus, companies such as General Electric encourage workers to voice their gripes. Pfizer under Edward Steer sent its research and development centre overseas to separate its employees from the executives. Motorola and 3M regularly use teams from different disciplines to encourage a variety of perspectives and improve the quality of thought.

Highly creative people, as we have seen, tend to be independent. They even break rules. In fact, they may need to break rules in order to think creatively. Charles Townes, for example, had to consider the possibility that the second law of thermodynamics did not work. Without breaking axioms, the maser and laser might not have been invented. Children, too, break rules. They continually ask 'Why?' and 'Why not?' I am reminded of the story of Edwin Land's daughter, Candy Land, who wanted to see the results of photographs as soon as they were taken. Luckily her father listened instead of telling her to be more realistic. He found a way to make it happen and became very wealthy in the process (Glazer, 1998). His talent may have been his ability to recognize a good idea when he heard one rather than generating it in the first place. Thus, companies that want to encourage creative thought might well heed the advice to embrace playfulness, the visions of children and, most important, diversity – whether in personality, style or ideas. Without such tolerance or being valued, highly creative people may seek employment elsewhere. Worse, they may respond to the views of others, the dictates of their superiors, the reward structure . . . and become 'tame'.

References

Albert, R.S. (1983) *Genius and Eminence: The Social Psychology of Creativity*. New York: Oxford University Press.

Albert, R.S., and Runco, M.A. (1986) 'The achievement of eminence: a model of exceptionally gifted boys and their families', in R.J. Sternberg and J.E. Davidson (eds) *Conceptions of Giftedness*. New York: Cambridge University Press. pp. 233–41.

Allen, V.L., and Levine, J.M. (1969) 'Consensus and conformity', *Journal of Experimental Social Psychology*, 5: 389–99.

Amabile, T.M. (1983) *The Social Psychology of Creativity*. New York: Springer-Verlag.

Amabile, T.M. (1996) *Creativity in Context*. Boulder, CO: Westview Press.

Asch, S.E. (1951) 'Effects of group pressure upon the modification and distortion of judgment', in H. Guetzkow (ed.), *Groups, Leadership and Men*. Pittsburgh, PA: Carnegie Press.

Barron, F. (1955) 'The disposition toward originality', *Journal of Abnormal and Social Psychology*, 51: 478–85.

Collins, J.C., and Porras, J.J. (1994) *Built to Last: Successful Habits of Visionary Companies*. New York: HarperCollins.

Cosier, R.A. (1978) 'The effects of three potential aids for making strategic decisions on prediction accuracy', *Organizational Behavior and Human Performance*, 22: 295–306.

Csikszentmihalyi, M. (1990) 'The domain of creativity', in M.A. Runco and R.S. Albert (eds), *Theories of Creativity*. Newbury Park, CA: Sage.

Csikszentmihalyi, M., and Getzels, J.W. (1973) 'The personality of young artists: a theoretical and empirical exploration', *British Journal of Psychology*, 64 (1): 91–104.

Deutsch, M., and Gerard, H.B. (1955) 'A study of normative and informational social influence upon individual judgment', *Journal of Abnormal and Social Psychology*, 51: 629–36.

Getzels, J., and Jackson, P. (1962) *Creativity and Intelligence: Explorations with Gifted Children*. New York: Wiley.

Glazer, Rashi (1998) Personal communication.

Guetzkow, H. (ed.) (1951) *Groups, Leadership and Men*. Pittsburgh, PA: Carnegie Press.

Guilford, J.P. (1967) *The Nature of Human Intelligence*. New York: McGraw-Hill.

Hirt, E.R., and Markman, K.D. (1995) 'Multiple explanation: a consider-an-alternative-strategy for debiasing judgments', *Journal of Personality and Social Psychology*, 69: 1069–88.

Janis, I.L. (1982) *Groupthink*, 2nd edn. Boston, MA: Houghton Mifflin.

Katzenstein, G. (1996) 'The debate on structured debate: toward a unified theory', *Organizational Behavior and Human Decision Processes*, 66: 316–32.

Kogan, N. and Pankove, E. (1972) 'Creative ability over a five-year span', *Child Development*, 43: 427–42.

MacKinnon, D.W. (1962) 'The nature and nurture of creative talent', *American Psychologist*, 17: 484–95.

MacKinnon, D.W. (1964) 'The creativity of architects', in C.W. Taylor (ed.), *Widening Horizons in Creativity*. New York: Wiley.

Mason, R.O. (1969) 'A dialectical approach to strategic planning', *Management Science*, 15: B403–B414.

McGrath, J.E. (1984) *Groups: Interaction and Performance*. Englewood Cliffs, NJ: Prentice Hall.

Mednick, S.A. (1962) 'The associative basis of the creative process', *Psychological Review*, 69: 220–32.

Milgram, R.M. (1990) 'Creativity: an idea whose time has come and gone?', in M.A. Runco and R.S. Albert (eds), *Theories of Creativity*. Newbury Park, CA: Sage.

Milgram, R.M., and Milgram, N.A. (1976) 'Creative thinking and creative performance in Israeli students', *Journal of Educational Psychology*, 68: 255–59.

Milgram, R.M., Moran, J.D., Sawyers, J.K., and Fu, V.R. (1987) 'Original thinking in Israeli preschool children', *School Psychology International*, 8: 54–8.

Moscovici, S. (1974) 'Group decision making', in C. Nemeth (ed.), *Social Psychology: Classical and Contemporary Integrations*. Chicago: Rand McNally.

Moscovici, S., and Zavalloni, M. (1969) 'The group as a polarizer of attitudes', *Journal of Personality and Social Psychology*, 12: 124–35.

Moscovici, S., Lage, E., and Naffrechoux, M. (1969) 'Influence of a consistent minority on the responses of a majority in a color perception tast', *Sociometry*, 32: 365–79.

Mucchi-Faina, A. (1994) 'Minority influence: the effects of social status of an inclusive versus exclusive group', *European Journal of Social Psychology*, 24: 679–92.

Myers, D.G., and Lamm, H. (1976) 'The group polarization phenomenon', *Psychological Bulletin*, 83 (4): 602–27.

Nemeth, C. (1995) 'Dissent as driving cognition, attitudes and judgments', *Social Cognition*, 13: 273–91.

Nemeth, C. (1997) 'Managing innovation: when less is more', *California Management Review*, 40: 59–74.

Nemeth, C., and Chiles, C. (1988) 'Modelling courage: the role of dissent in fostering independence', *European Journal of Social Psychology*, 38: 275–80.

Nemeth, C.J., and Kwan, J. (1985) 'Originality of word associations as a function of majority vs. minority influence processes', *Social Psychology Quarterly*, 48: 277–82.

Nemeth, C.J., and Kwan, J. (1987) 'Minority influence, divergent thinking and the detection of correct solutions', *Journal of Applied Social Psychology*, 17: 786–97.

Nemeth, C.J., and Rogers, J. (1996) 'Dissent and the search for information', *British Journal of Social Psychology*, 35: 67–76.

Nemeth, C.J., and Staw, B.M. (1989) 'The tradeoffs of social control and innovation within groups and organizations', in L. Berkowitz (ed.), *Advances in Experimental Social Psychology*, 22. New York: Academic Press. pp. 175–210.

Nemeth, C.J., and Wachtler, J. (1974) 'Creating the perceptions of consistency and confidence: a necessary condition for minority influence', *Sociometry*, 37: 529–40.

Nemeth, C.J., Cornell, J.B., Rogers, J.D., and Brown, K.S. (2000) 'Improving decision making by means of dissent', *Journal of Applied Social Psychology*, in press.

Nemeth, C.J., Mayseless, O., Sherman, J., and Brown, Y. (1990) 'Exposure to dissent and recall of information', *Journal of Personality and Social Psychology*, 58: 429–37.

Osborn, A.F. (1957) *Applied Imagination*. New York: Scribner's.

Piaget, J. (1951) *Play, Dreams and Imitation in Childhood*. New York: Norton.

Runco, M.A., and Albert, R.S. (eds) (1990) *Theories of Creativity*. Newbury Park, CA: Sage.

Simonton, D.K. (1988) 'Creativity, leadership and chance', in R.J. Sternberg (ed.), *The Nature of Creativity*. New York: Cambridge University Press.

Stroebe, W., and Diehl, M. (1994) 'Productivity loss in idea-generating groups', in W. Stroebe and M. Hewstone (eds), *European Review of Social Psychology*, vol. 5. Chichester: Wiley.

Summerfield, F. (1990) 'Paying the troops to buck the system', *Business Month*, May: 77–9.

Taylor, D.W., Berry, P.C., and Block, C.H. (1958) 'Does group participation when using brainstorming facilitate or inhibit creative thinking?', *Administrative Sciences Quarterly*, 3: 23–47.

Torrance, E.P. (1966) *Torrance Tests of Creative Thinking: Norms-technical Manual*. Princeton, NJ: Personnel.

Wallach, M., and Kogan, N. (1965) *Modes of Thinking in Young Children*. New York: Holt, Rinehart and Winston.

Watson, T.J. (1963) *A Business and Its Beliefs: The Ideas That Helped Build IBM*. New York: McGraw-Hill.

Wing, C.W., Jr, and Wallach, M.A. (1971) *College Admissions and the Psychology of Talent*. New York: Holt, Rinehart & Winston.

Zuckerman, H. (1977) *Scientific Elite: Nobel Laureates in the US*. New York: The Free Press.

5 A Mentality Theory of Knowledge Creation and Transfer: Why Some Smart People Resist New Ideas and Some Don't

Kaiping Peng and Satoshi Akutsu

One of the greatest pains to human nature is the pain of a new idea
Walter Bagehot, English economist, *Physics and Politics*, 1872

Introduction

New ideas seem to have characteristics that often make them unpopular. Even proven good ideas may still face obstacles to getting the wider recognition they deserve. For instance, research in management has reported the widespread and longstanding phenomenon of 'the demise of best practice' – that is, proven good business practices find it difficult to be accepted, explored or transferred (Pilkington, 1988, and Szulanski, 1996). Why do people resist new ideas even when they are good ones? What are the rationales for such attitudes and behaviour? Are there any individual and cultural differences in dealing with new ideas? If so, what can be done about it?

In this chapter, we propose a mentality theory to explain the problem of resisting new ideas. Conventional wisdom primarily blames motivational factors, while traditional organizational behaviour studies focus mainly on the structures of knowledge (Szulanski, 1996). Contrary to both of these, we place the blame partly on mentality, particularly epistemology-driven mindsets. We start by demystifying mentality and defining it as the psychological stance that is the result of a reaction to new information. We then suggest that mentality is a major factor in understanding people's attitudes and behaviour towards new ideas and new knowledge in general. We present initial evidence from the field of cultural psychology, suggesting that there are two types of mentality concerning new ideas: linear thinking (LT) and dialectical thinking (DT). We argue that both mentalities are based on rational principles rooted deeply in different epistemologies. We provide an example from our study of these two mentalities among respondents in Japan and the United States. The example serves two purposes: to confirm our theories that different epistemologies fascinate different kinds of mentality and provide a concrete way of measuring mentality. The role that cultural psychology could play in the enterprise of knowledge creation and transfer and the managerial implications of the mentality theory are discussed briefly.

Demystifying Mentality

What is mentality? The notion of mentality in the humanities has often been used to characterize what is distinctive about the thought processes or sets of beliefs of groups or types of people. The French sociologist Lucien Levy-Bruhl (1975) used the mentality construct to describe what he called 'prelogical mentality' in some 'primitive people'. Other conceptions of mentality mention distinctive or strikingly peculiar patterns of discourse or reasoning (Cole and Scribner, 1973) or implicit beliefs (Needham, 1972) or they broadly define mentalities as 'contexts of communication, the nature and styles of interpersonal exchanges or confrontations, the availability and use of explicit concepts of linguistic and other categories in which the actor's self-representations are conveyed' (Lloyd, 1990: 13). However, much of the discussion of mentality in the humanities has been vague and diffuse. Peter Burke (1986) summarized three general features of the mentality approach in the humanities:

1   a focus on the ideas or beliefs of societies rather than of individuals;
2   the inclusion of unconscious as well as conscious assumptions;
3   a focus on the structure of beliefs and their interrelationships, rather than individual beliefs.

We use the concept of mentality in a different way, perhaps in a more psychological way. First, we use the concept of mentality to describe a psychological phenomenon rather than to explain it. In other words, as cultural psychologists, we are not in the business of explaining the ultimate cause of mentality. Instead, we refer to it as a psychological state in which resistance to, or acceptance of, new ideas takes place. We articulate some rationales underlying certain culture-specific mentalities, but only to explain the substantial cultural differences we predict. Although we believe that ecological and historical factors contribute to the development of mentalities in a given culture, these factors are better studied and articulated by anthropologists, historians and other humanities scholars than by psychologists.

Second, we argue that cultures and groups do not think; only individuals do. Individuals construct their culture-specific mentalities in their own idiosyncratic ways. Thus, to explain individual attitudes and behaviour, we should take into account how cultural ideology is represented subjectively for the individual. This approach to mentality encourages us to see individuals as participating in numerous changing cultures, subjected to many kinds of 'cultural influences'. These cultural influences are representational clusters associated with class, ethnicity, religion and organization, rather than simply the 'nation–country–tribe' notions of culture that many scholars in the humanities use (Ames and Peng, 1999).

We do not believe that mentality is pre-wired into people's minds. We assert that mentality is internalized in the process of socialization, which gives rise to individual variation. The mentality approach, as studied in the humanities, has often ignored or played down variations between individuals. In contrast, we think that not everyone in a culture thinks in the way that the culture prescribes; nor do individuals think the same way all the time. In other words, mentality is not static – it can be changed if necessary.

Here we define mentality as a theory-driven psychological stance in reaction to new information. Mentalities often appear as fixed and recurring patterns of thinking and reasoning for people in a given culture in response to particular kinds of stimuli. They are theory-driven processes because mentalities are, to a great degree, based on an individual's beliefs (or implicit theories) of what reality is like and how one comes to know it. Many of these beliefs and theories flow from personal experience within a given context. People from similar cultural or socio-economic groups are more likely to share some cultural or group-specific theories and beliefs by virtue of their participation in the community. However, individuals can also vary in their levels of 'cultural competence'. Therefore, we believe that there are both cultural (or group) and individual differences in people's theories and beliefs about the nature of reality and human knowledge and the appropriate ways to know them. Most important, we believe that such differences in beliefs affect how individuals react to new ideas or new knowledge. People who have a dialectical-thinking mentality are more receptive initially to new knowledge than people who have a nondialectical linear-thinking mentality. However, the linear-thinking mentality may help people to pursue aggressively the practical implications of new ideas when they are proven to be useful.

Contrasting Two Mentalities

We suggest that there are two fundamentally different mentalities for dealing with new ideas: linear thinking and dialectical thinking. Because dialectical thinking is a new concept that we are proposing aids in the study of knowledge creation and transfer, we will start by defining this concept and then contrast it with linear thinking, which we believe influences most people in Western cultures.

What is dialectical thinking? Dialectical thinking, as a psychological concept, refers to a cognitive tendency to concentrate, contemplate and transcend contradiction in ideas or perspectives in a manner that cannot be reduced to mechanistic logic. There are two forms of dialectical thinking – 'synthesizing dialectical thinking' (SDT) and 'compromising dialectical thinking' (CDT). The former is associated with the philosophies of Hegel and Marx and is a highly acclaimed and sophisticated way of reasoning in Western intellectual contexts. The goal of synthesizing dialectical thinking is to identify contradiction and resolve the contradiction by means of synthesis or integration. Compromising dialectical thinking does not focus on resolving contradiction but, rather, on tolerating contradiction. Both forms of dialectical thinking are theory-driven cognitive processes. However, synthesizing dialectical thinking is driven by the belief that a contradiction between the thesis and the antithesis could be resolved by a higher-level synthesis. In contrast, compromising dialectical thinking is guided by the belief that contradictions are permanent and inherent – objects and people are constantly in states of flux and interconnected with other things, including their opposites.

Dialectical thinking has been studied in philosophy and psychology for centuries. In philosophy, dialectical thinking is often associated with Hegel's method of dialectic in which a concept (or thesis) gives rise to its opposite (antithesis) and, as a result of this contradiction, a third view, the synthesis, arises. The synthesis is at a 'higher' level of truth than the first two views. Marx and Engels (Engels, 1884/1942) used the method of dialectic in their analysis of culture and civilizations and exemplified the power of dialectical thinking. In psychology, dialectical thinking is considered to be the most sophisticated mental operation, far beyond Piaget's formal operation in the development of the thought process (Riegel, 1973). Michael Basseches (1980 and 1984; see also Kramer and Woodruff, 1986) found that synthesizing dialectical thinking becomes increasingly important and common in old age. Middle-aged and older people are more likely to accept contradiction in reality and synthesize contradiction in their thinking than young people (Kramer and Woodruff, 1986). There are several allied concepts in psychology that partially capture the essence of dialectical thinking. One popular concept is 'reflective judgement' proposed by John Dewey (1933 and 1938), which refers to the ability to evaluate and integrate existing data and theories into a solution, taking into account the set of conditions under which the problem is being solved (see also King and Kitchener, 1994). Philip Tetlock (1985) proposed a similar concept called 'integrative complexity', which refers to different levels of integration in people's thinking about complicated and contradictory information. The common assumption made by these scholars is that synthesizing dialectical thinking (SDT) is the highest level of thinking, reflecting maturity, complexity, academic training and intelligence beyond the grasp of ordinary people. In this chapter, we focus only on compromising dialectical thinking (CDT), which is more common among ordinary people.

On the other hand, linear thinking is a psychological tendency that shows distaste for ambiguity and contradiction and preference for consistency and certainty. The intellectual orientation of linear thinking reflects three characteristics. First, linear thinkers, usually, are in pursuit of a single truth, believing that there is a fundamental truth in every fact, opinion and person. Linear thinking is usually centred on one or a few overarching principles that guide much of the psychology of linear thinkers. Second, linear thinkers construct counter-arguments in an attempt to find out the single truth. Most linear thinkers have a desire to generate arguments against positions, facts or opinions that they doubt. Finally, linear thinkers prefer behavioural consistency on the part of others as well as themselves. They consider any deviation from the pattern or status quo faulty or disingenuous.

We believe that dialectical mentality and linear mentality have different implications for people's reactions to new ideas and knowledge. On the one hand, dialectical thinking may be more adaptive to new ideas that are still in their infancy, full of contradictions, ambiguous or uncertain. A dialectical approach to dealing with new ideas may enable one to tolerate, even appreciate, some fuzzy characteristics of new ideas. On the other hand, the dialectical approach may be accompanied by a tendency to accept new ideas at face value, failing to reject alternative hypotheses or new ideas that are wrong. Linear thinking is more consistent and congruent with Western scientific reasoning. The linear-thinking approach is undoubtedly useful in many other aspects. Counter-argument construction seems likely to result in more hypotheses and, consequently, more solutions than simple dialectical thinking could. Also, linear thinking's analytic and uncompromising stance may also enable people to act aggressively until the truth (or what is thought to be truth) has been researched. However, linear thinking can also facilitate adversarial and argumentative approaches to new ideas, resulting in the rejection of alternative hypotheses or new ideas that may be right. Hence, the relationship between human mentality and reactions to new ideas turns out to be a dialectical one in nature. Dialectical thinking is good for some pursuits and linear thinking is better for others.

The Rational Foundations of the Two Mentalities

In order to understand the implications of both dialectical thinking and linear thinking, we have to understand the rational principles underlying both mentalities (Peng, 1997, and Peng and Nisbett, 1999). The rational principles of dialectical mentalities are an interconnected set of principles we call 'naïve dialecticism' – a set of folk beliefs about the nature of reality, human life, human knowledge, human beings (including the nature of self, others, relationships and social institutions) and folk epistemologies about the ways of knowing them. It is a cultural–psychological adaptation of a sociological concept – collective representation (Durkheim, 1898).

Such folk beliefs are fundamentally implicit theories in the human mind – explanatory models stored in a person's mind that categorize relationships between objects in the environment, which mediates an individual's psychological functioning (Peng, 1997, and Peng and Nisbett, 1999).

How do people's folk theories affect how they deal with new ideas? Psychologists increasingly recognize that individuals rarely act or function without implicitly or explicitly consulting the available social and cultural wisdom – that is, the shared knowledge and belief systems of the group or groups to which they belong (Wagner, 1997, and Peng, Ames and Knowles, 1999). These shared knowledge systems could be represented by ideas, thoughts, images and theories that members have collectively created and socially communicated to form part of a 'common consciousness' (Wagner, 1997, and Peng, Ames and Knowles, 1999). This pool of knowledge includes some explicit elements, such as cultural models or schemata (Holland and Quinn, 1987), cosmologies (Douglas, 1982) and social representations (Moscovici, 1984). It also contains some implicit knowledge, such as folk ontology and epistemologies (Ames and Peng, 1999, and Peng and Nisbett, 1999) and naïve theories about the world (Murphy and Medin, 1985). Individuals rely on this knowledge to generate, transmit, communicate and store the meanings of the information they process every day. How people understand the meaning of a simple newspaper headline such as 'Teachers Strike Idle Kids' is an example of how much background knowledge determines our understanding. Clearly, we have to rely on our knowledge or theories about the social world to figure out what it means. People from different cultures would be likely to understand the statement differently. A person from a collective culture where labour strikes by teachers are rare, but physical discipline of children is common, may understand this differently from the way someone in the United States would.

In everyday language, people use concept and category to put things together, but what makes a category or concept coherent? Murphy and Medin argue that accounts based on similarity and feature correlation provide inadequate answers because none provides enough constraints on possible concepts or categories. They 'propose that concepts are coherent to the extent that they fit people's background knowledge or naïve theories about the world', 'people's theories of the world embody conceptual knowledge' and 'their conceptual organization is partly represented in their theories' (Murphy and Medin, 1985).

What are the underlying theories of dialectical thinking? We believe that the rational foundation of dialectical thinking is the dialectical epistemology that rests on a tripod – its three legs representing three distinctive principles guiding people's understanding of human life and knowledge. These principles are:

1   the principle of change – reality is not static, but in a process of constant change;

2   the principle of contradiction – reality is not precise and clear, but is full of contradictions;
3   the principle of holism – parts are meaningful in their relations to the whole, and the whole is more than the sum of its parts (Peng, 1997, and Peng and Nisbett, 1999).

Because these principles of reasoning resemble some characteristics of Hegel's dialectics without his idealism and method (thesis, antithesis and synthesis), it has been labeled 'naive dialecticism' (Peng, 1997).

The rational foundations of dialectical thinking are in sharp contrast to those of linear thinking. Linear thinking emphasizes three different principles:

1   the law of identity – if anything is true, then it is true; thus A = A;
2   the law of non-contradiction – no statement can be both true and false; thus A $\neq$ $\neg$ A);
3   the law of the excluded middle – any statement is either true or false; thus (A v B) & $\neg$ (A & B).

The meanings and implications of these logical principles can be better understood by contrasting them with the rational principles of dialectical thinking.

The principle of change suggests that life is a constant passing from one stage of being to another, so that to be is not to be, and not to be is to be. The law of identity, on the other hand, assumes cross-situational consistency – A must be A regardless of the context. If one believes that A is always in a state of change from the state of being A to the state of not being A, A could be A and not be A at the same time. In this sense, the principle of contradiction is a necessary supplement to the principle of change. Hence, a contradiction is inevitable, because it brings a dynamic into reality. Furthermore, if change and contradiction are constant, then a real understanding of truth and reality must be relational or holistic. Hence, for a dialectical thinker, both A and B may be right or wrong or both A and B may equal a third element, C, that is not part of the initial contradiction. The key difference between the law of the excluded middle and the principle of holism is that the former holds that only fixed individual conditions or elements are options for logically correct conclusions and the latter holds that every element in the context is relevant to a possible conclusion.

The Characteristics of New Ideas – the 5Cs Theory

Why does mentality matter to the study of knowledge creation and transfer? One way to understand the relevance of mentality is to understand the characteristics of new knowledge, particularly the dialectical nature of new ideas, such as their ambiguity, contradiction and uncertainty. We believe that these dialectical characteristics are the necessary stimuli that trigger mentality. In other words, mentality is domain-specific. Dialectical mentality and linear mentality affect only the ways people judge and reason about new ideas, not necessarily the other aspects of their lives.

What are the characteristics of new ideas and new knowledge? We propose what we call the 5Cs theory to describe the dialectical nature of new ideas or any new knowledge. We believe this characterization may be applicable to many disciplines and across various domains of new knowledge.

Change

One of the most significant attributes of new ideas is their fluidity. Many times it is difficult to distinguish what is really new and what is not. In other words, a new idea is a process, not a static entity. Development of a new idea is a journey from old knowledge to new knowledge, but the new knowledge is not totally different nor isolated from the old knowledge.

A common misconception about new ideas is that a new idea contains a fundamentally different set of knowledge and is the product of a few genius minds. In actuality, a new idea is based on the old knowledge system and transfers the old one to the new one. Most of the new ideas in science and technology are not the products of a few genius minds, but the result of collective efforts at the right moments. None the less, it is very difficult to make precise predictions about the future of any new idea.

Chaos

Because of the nature of change, new ideas generate chaos. Existing paradigms are challenged, tried, tested, tossed away and often reinvented, redesigned, relocated and refashioned.

An irony is that, although the new knowledge is based on old knowledge, people distort the new information when they try to fit it into an existing paradigm. In this sense, new ideas create chaos – they have their own life that is not immediately comprehended by human rationality. Moreover, the high uncertainty involved in the introduction of new ideas often creates chaos.

Contradiction

Also because of the nature of change, new ideas are often full of contradiction. One example of contradiction comes from the discipline of physics. The Greek philosopher Heraclitus said that everything is in motion, but this claim is contradictory. If an object in motion is at position X at time Y, then at time Y it is not in motion because it is at position X: its motion has been stopped. Therefore, if an object is always in motion, then, at any given time Y, the object, must be both at position X and not at position X (Engels, 1940). Such laws of contradiction may apply to all objects, and may be even more salient and problematical as they apply to new ideas and new knowledge. Contradiction is salient to new ideas because they are novel and more attention-grabbing. However, contradiction in new ideas is also problematical. It makes rejection of new ideas much easier psychologically, which might be one of the most important reasons new ideas are often discounted, marginalized, overlooked and resisted. Thus, new ideas can often be discounted, marginalized, overlooked and resisted.

Co-variation

Any new idea is ultimately related to and affects other information or knowledge. In many ways, a new idea is a revolution that not only changes individual elements or isolated areas, but also has profound effects on other parts of the knowledge system. The history of science has constantly recorded the fact that a new idea in a particular scientific field affected not only the topic in question, but also other knowledge in the field and sometimes other scientific disciplines as well. Such a contagious character led Richard Dawkins to claim that new ideas are 'memes' that replicate themselves in ways similar to what a 'selfish gene' does (Dawkins, 1989).

Context

The last characteristic of new ideas is the importance of context. New ideas can only be understood and appreciated when placed in context. People must understand the context in order to understand the individual elements of an idea. Just as musical notes are meaningful only when people put them together, new ideas are comprehensible only when they are appreciated in context.

We do not assume that these are the only characteristics of new ideas or that all five characteristics must be present in every new idea. We simply suggest that if any one of them is present in a new idea, culture-specific mentality will affect an individual's attitudes and behaviour towards the new idea. A dialectical mentality would lead people to accept – even appreciate – the changing, chaotic, contradictory, co-variate and contextual aspects of a new idea, but linear mentality would lead people to dislike these elements of a new idea and, hence, resist the new idea itself.

Measuring Mentality

How do we know whether or not people have different mentalities and how do we know how mentality affects people's responses to new knowledge and new ideas? Answers to these questions require the development of a measurement of mentality and the analysis of its validity and reliability. We have been working on a variety of ways to measure dialectical thinking and studying its effects on human reasoning and inference (Peng, 1997, and Peng and Nisbett, 1999). This work proceeds from two basic observations. First, different people (within and between nation cultures) have fundamentally different and enduring views of the nature of the world, knowledge and human life. Second, these different stances are predictive of people's social inference and behaviour. We believe this work suggests a number of key implications for the study of knowledge creation and transfer. Most significant are the following two predictions:

1 different attitudes and behaviour towards new knowledge are important consequences of mentality and, while dialectical mentality would lead to greater tolerance of contradiction in new knowledge, linear mentality would lead to less;
2 because the sanctioned mentality differs in different cultures, the mechanism and process of knowledge transfer may vary according to culture – while North American cultures of the United States in particular may esteem synthesizing dialectical thinking, East Asian cultures (those of China and Japan in particular) may esteem compromising dialectical thinking.

Taking measurements

We used two formats to measure mentality. One was a standard attitudes and beliefs questionnaire in which we asked people how much they agreed or disagreed with various ontological and epistemological statements. We initially developed 31 statements, 18 of which were designed to measure dialectical mentality. Here are some examples.

1 The right answer to a question often changes over time.
2 Often, things that seem unrelated are really interconnected.
3 People change a lot depending on who is around them.
4 It is OK to believe two things that contradict each other.

There were 13 items designed to measure linear mentality. The following are some examples of these.

1   Most people's friends and family would all agree on what the person is.
2   Someone's values and beliefs should be consistent and should not change depending on who that person is with.
3   When someone has to make a choice, it's best to pick one and stick with it.
4   People who say they see both sides of an issue just have trouble making up their minds.

Theoretically, linear mentality is the inverse of dialectical mentality. This makes it possible to calculate a single index of dialectical thinking (or linear thinking).

The other format of the dialectical measurement was a forced-choice survey that required people to decide which ontological and epistemological statement they preferred. The rationale for utilizing this format was a concern about dialectical thinking. By virtue of being dialectical, a person might actually believe all the statements and so agree with both the dialectical statements and the linear statements. Although we predicted that dialectical thinkers might not necessarily rate the statements on the previous scale in a dialectical manner, we used the forced-choice format to make people decide between statements. The instruction was clearly stated: 'Consider both, and mark the one that you agree with more.' There follow some examples of the statements.

1A   People are pretty much full of contradiction and inconsistency.
1B   People are pretty much coherent and consistent.
2A   You can learn a lot about people by seeing them away from the influence of their family.
2B   You can learn lots about people by seeing them interact with their family.

The statements were randomly arranged so as to balance any possible order effect in people's responses.

About the participants

In the United States, the questionnaires were randomly distributed to MBA students at the Haas School of Business of the University of California, Berkeley, but only those who agreed to participate after being approached were included in this study. In Japan, the questionnaires were randomly distributed to graduate students at the Department of Commerce of Hitotsubashi University in Tokyo and at the Japan Advanced Institute of Science and Technology in Hokuriku. It was ensured that all respondents had at least several years of working experience. Respondents were offered either $5 or the summary report of the research results for taking about ten minutes to complete the paper-and-pencil tasks. Of the American respondents, 31, and of the Japanese respondents, 34 returned the questionnaire in this pilot study.

The results

As this study was a small-scale pilot study, the sample was relatively small. However, we were pleasantly surprised to find many significant cultural and individual differences in people's responses to the ontological and epistemological statements.

Out of 31 items, cultural differences were significant for 10. Japanese respondents agreed more with dialectical items and American respondents agreed more with linear items. For instance, Japanese respondents were more likely than American respondents to agree with the following dialectical statements.

1 People are constantly changing and are different from one time to the next.
2 It is OK to believe two things that contradict each other.
3 The right answer to a question often changes over time.
4 The best predictor of a person's future behaviour is that person's past behaviour.
5 Often, things that seem unrelated are really interconnected.
6 People change a lot depending on who is around them.

On the other hand, American respondents were more likely than Japanese respondents to agree with the following linear statements.

1 Most people's friends and family would all agree on what the person is.
2 Someone's values and beliefs should be consistent, and should not change depending on who that person is with.
3 When someone has to make a choice, it's best to pick one and stick with it.
4 People who say they see both sides of an issue just have trouble making up their minds.

The significance level test results are listed in Table 5.1.

There were also items that resulted in findings that were inconsistent with the predictions. For instance, the Japanese respondents agreed less than the American respondents with the statement, 'A good leader achieves the group's goals through compromise.' We believe the results may have been skewed by the reaction of Japanese respondents to the economic crisis in Japan at the time, which many Japanese people attributed to too much compromise and too little action among their political and business leaders (Porter and Takeuchi, 1999).

Table 5.1   *Significant cultural differences on dialectical thinking and linear thinking items*

Dialectical items
People are constantly changing and are different from one time to the next.
    US mean = 3.74   Japan mean = 5.03   F = 9.68, sig. = .003
It is OK to believe two things that contradict each other.
    US mean = 4.00   Japan mean = 5.18   F = 7.65, sig. = .007
The right answer to a question often changes over time.
    US mean = 4.65   Japan mean = 6.32   F = 27.54, sig. = .000
The best predictor of a person's future behaviour is that person's past behaviour.
    US mean = 4.42   Japan mean = 5.13   F = 2.93, sig. = .092
Often, things that seem unrelated are really interconnected.
    US mean = 4.87   Japan mean = 6.36   F = 31.05, sig. = .000
People change a lot depending on who is around them.
    US mean = 4.13   Japan mean = 5.82   F = 32.73, sig. = .000
Most seemingly isolated events wind up having a broader impact
    US mean = 4.77   Japan mean = 5.45   F = 3.60, sig. = .063

Linear items
Most people's friends and family would all agree on what the person is.
    US mean = 4.10   Japan mean = 2.62   F = 11.72, sig. = .001
Someone's values and beliefs should be consistent, and should not change depending on who that person is with.
    US mean = 5.52   Japan mean = 3.06   F = 34.34, sig. = .000
When someone has to make a choice, it's best to pick one and stick with it.
    US mean = 4.06   Japan mean = 2.76   F = 10.53, sig. = .002
People who say they see both sides of an issue just have trouble making up their minds.
    US mean = 2.48   Japan mean = 1.82   F = 3.26, sig. = .076
People in different times and different cultures still have basically the same values.
    US mean = 3.48   Japan mean = 2.58   F = 4.13, sig. = .046

The evidence supports our assertions that there are cultural differences in people's beliefs about the nature of the world, knowledge and human life. The Japanese respondents, in general, were more dialectical than American respondents were in their mentalities.

Mentality Matters

A psychological concept is meaningful only when it can describe or predict psychological phenomena. Mentality may be a real set of beliefs that individuals subscribe to and may have strong cultural foundations, but how does it describe or predict people's attitudes and behaviour towards new ideas or new knowledge?

In the same study, we presented five pairs of statements summarizing recent social science research findings that are superficially contradictory yet all plausible. We believe this operationalization of new ideas/new knowledge captures the characteristics of new knowledge and has been proven valid and useful (Peng, 1997, and Peng and Nisbett, 1999). We asked the respondents three questions about new knowledge.

1   How much do you believe these two findings contradict each other?
2   How much do you believe finding A is true?
3   How much do you believe finding B is true?

We predicted that a dialectical mentality would lead people to be less likely to think that the two findings contradicted each other and more likely to believe both findings to be true. If subjects rate both findings as equally true, the two items are less psychometrically 'discriminative'; the smaller the gap, the more dialectical the response. A correlation analysis was conducted to test the relationship between people's mentalities and their responses to new knowledge.

Taking measurements

The same measurement of mentality was used. Two summaries of the dialectical thinking indices were created for each research participant. Index I was the mean of a respondent's endorsements of the dialectical items minus the respondent's endorsements of the linear items. Index II was the total endorsements of dialectical items in the forced-choice format.

Raw materials

The new knowledge was presented in the form of brief descriptions of the findings of scientific studies. The opposing findings were superficially incompatible but were not true contradictions. This left room for a dialectical approach – finding some degree of truth to both findings. The statements about new knowledge were:

Finding 1A: A social psychologist studied young adults and asserted that those who feel close to their families have more satisfying social relationships.
Finding 1B: A developmental psychologist studied adolescent children and asserted that those children who were less dependent on their parents and had weaker family ties were generally more mature.
Finding 2A: A sociologist who surveyed college students from 100 universities claimed that there is a high correlation among female college students between smoking and being skinny.
Finding 2B: A biologist who studied nicotine addiction asserted that heavy doses of nicotine often lead to becoming overweight.
Finding 3A: A health magazine survey found that people who live a long life eat some sorts of white meat, such as chicken.

Finding 3B: A study by a health organization suggests that it is much more healthy to be a strict vegetarian who does not eat meat at all.

Finding 4A: A survey found that older inmates are more likely to be ones who are serving long sentences because they have committed severely violent crimes. The authors concluded that they should be held in prison even in the case of a prison population crisis.

Finding 4B: A report on the prison overcrowding issue suggests that older inmates are less likely to commit new crimes. Therefore, if there is a prison population crisis, they should be released first.

Finding 5A: A group of environmental science undergraduate students examined fuel usage in a large number of developing countries and asserted that recent practices are likely to multiply already worsening environmental problems such as 'global warming'.

Finding 5B: A meteorologist studied temperatures in 24 widely separated parts of the world and asserted that temperatures had actually dropped by a fraction of a degree each of the last five years.

The results

Despite the small sample sizes, we found significant correlations between the mentalities and people's responses to new knowledge. For American respondents, dialectical mentalities were significantly correlated with their judgement of whether or not the two findings were contradictory. Index I, based on an attitude scale of the subject's dialectical beliefs, showed a .45 correlation ($p < .02$) with a dialectical contradiction judgement. Index II (based on the forced-choice format) showed a .43 correlation ($p < .02$). These results indicated that the more dialectical a person's mentality, the less likely it would be that the person thought the two findings contradicted each other. The dialectical measurement was also correlated significantly with people's 'discriminative' tendencies towards the two findings (believing both might be true in effect), but only by the attitude measurement (Index I) and not the forced-choice measurement (Index II). The correlation between Index I and the 'discriminative' tendencies was .41 ($p < .03$).

For Japanese respondents, the results showed much more complicated patterns. Dialectical mentalities were correlated with people's responses to new knowledge, but the correlation was significant only for the forced-choice format and on 'discriminative' tendencies (.42, $p < .02$), indicating that dialectical Japanese respondents were more likely to think both findings were true at the same time.

An interesting observation is that for American respondents, the two types of mentality measurements – attitude scale and forced-choice format – were correlated with each other ($r = .48$, $p < .01$), indicating that there was no fundamental difference between these two measurements of

Table 5.2　*Correlations for two measurements of mentalities and two measurements of dialectical responses to new knowledge*

	American respondents		Japanese respondents	
Independent measurements	Attitude scale	Forced-choice	Attitude scale	Forced-choice
Dependent measurements				
Contraction	.45**	.43*	.19	−.09
Discrimination	.41*	.11	.24	.42*

** = p < .01　　* = p < .05

mentalities. Two kinds of dependent measurements – 'contradiction' and 'discrimination' – were also correlated significantly ($r = .64$, $p < .001$), suggesting that these two measurements may gauge the same psychological phenomenon, which we label 'non-dialectical reactions to new knowledge'. However, for Japanese respondents, the two types of measurements of mentalities were not correlated; nor were the two types of measurements of reactions towards new knowledge. This suggests that:

1　dialectical mentalities can only be measured by the forced-choice format for Japanese respondents, as we hypothesized before beginning the study;
2　judgements about how much two findings contradict each other may be different from judgements about how much two findings may be true at the same time.

The latter may be more indicative of a dialectical attitude among Japanese participants.

All the correlations and their significance levels are listed in Table 5.2, which presents strong support for the existence of mentality effects on people's attitudes and behaviour towards new knowledge. Individuals and cultures do vary in their mentalities, and their mentalities affect how they think about the nature of any new knowledge.

We acknowledge that mentality is not the only factor that affects people's attitudes and behaviour towards new ideas or new knowledge. There are many non-psychological factors that may do this as well as many other cultural and psychological factors. Some factors may be orthogonal to mentality but interact with it in important ways, such as cognitive dissonance, confirmation bias and illusory correlation. For instance, new ideas may cause some people to think 'I didn't know that' or 'I never thought of that', which would contradict their high self-esteem. This may be particularly true for managers, who value competence and vision. An interesting research topic would be how and to what extent dialectical and linear mentality mediates such basic psychological processes.

Managerial Implications of Mentality Theory and Future Directions

What are the managerial implications of mentality theory in knowledge transfer? As we discussed previously, dialectical mentality may be more adaptive to new ideas that are contradictory, ambiguous or uncertain. However, the dialectical mentality may be accompanied by the tendency to accept new ideas at face value. The linear mentality may be adaptive in dealing with knowledge that has been proven valid and useful. However, the linear mentality may be accompanied by adversarial and argumentative approaches. We believe these two types of mentality can be observed in everyday managerial practices.

The mentality theory has implications in most managers' roles and tasks. Consider the seven major factors of management tasks identified by Kraut and others (1989). They are:

1   managing individual performance;
2   instructing subordinates;
3   planning and allocating resources;
4   coordinating interdependent groups;
5   managing group performance;
6   monitoring the business environment;
7   representing one's staff.

The theory suggests that dialectical thinkers would use a holistic approach and linear thinkers a few specific measurable criteria when managing individual performance. Dialectical thinkers would, again, use a holistic approach when instructing subordinates, while linear thinkers would associate a specific task with a specific goal, well-defined responsibility and explicitly stated authority. When planning and allocating resources, dialectical thinkers may be more likely to have their attention diverted, linear thinkers more likely to focus on the one or two most promising projects, all other things being equal. The well-known strategy of Jack Welch at General Electric was to focus only on the number 1 or 2 businesses in the market and ignore all the rest. This strategy differs from that of most Japanese companies, which tend to hoard all existing business and spread their resources among them. Our study suggests that psychological resistance to a linear-thinking strategy like the one implemented at GE is higher among Japanese than Americans, which may be part of reason for Japanese companies finding it so hard to implement 'restructuring'.

Similarly, the theory has implications for other factors as well. Obviously, rigorous studies should be conducted to test hypotheses implied by mentality theory, including the ones discussed here. More important, studies should directly examine the effects of the two mentalities on managers' decisions to adopt new ideas, such as management practice, technology and marketing strategy. In these studies, conditions should be identified that trigger either dialectical mentality or linear mentality.

Conclusions

We suggest that mentality is a major factor in understanding people's attitudes and behaviour towards new ideas and new knowledge in general. Because of the chaotic, changing, contradictory, co-variate and contextual nature of any new knowledge, one of the two types of mentalities – linear thinking or dialectical thinking – would be triggered. Rational foundations of dialectical mentalities are principles of change, contradiction and holism, while linear mentalities are the laws of identity, non-contradiction and the excluded middle. A dialectical mentality may facilitate a more receptive stance than would a linear mentality when dealing with new ideas that are contradictory, ambiguous or uncertain. However, a dialectical mentality may be accompanied by a tendency to accept new ideas at face value. The linear mentality may facilitate a more adversarial and argumentative stance than would a dialectical mentality when dealing with new ideas, resulting in the rejection of new ideas.

There are culturally construed ideologies underlying each mentality, but there is also substantial individual variance within a culture. Using a scale we developed, we found respondents in Japan to be more dialectical than their counterparts in the United States. Individual variances on these two mentalities predicted their reactions to superficially contradictory new research findings. We believe that cultural psychology can play an important role in the study of knowledge creation and transfer.

References

Ames, D., and Peng, K. (1999) 'Making sense of sense-making: a meaning-process approach to cultural psychology', unpublished manuscript. Berkeley, CA: University of California.

Basseches, M. (1980) 'Dialectical schemata: a framework for the empirical study of the development of dialectical thinking', *Human Development*, 23: 400–21.

Basseches, M. (1984) *Dialectical Thinking and Adult Development.* Norwood, NJ: Ablex.

Burke, P. (1986) 'Strengths and weaknesses of the history of mentalities', *History of European Ideas*, vol. VII. Oxford and New York: Pergamon. pp. 439–51.

Cole, M., and Scribner, S. (1973) 'Culture, memory, and narrative', in R. Horton and R. Finnegan (eds), *Modes of Thought.* London: Faber. p. 144.

Dawkins, R. (1989) *The Selfish Gene.* Oxford: Oxford University Press. p. 192.

Dewey, J. (1933) *How We Think: A Restatement of the Relation of Reflective Thinking to the Educative Process.* Lexington, MA: Heath.

Dewey, J. (1938) *Logic: The Theory of Inquiry.* Troy, MO: Holt, Rinehart & Winston.

Douglas, M. (1982) *In the Active Voice.* London: Routledge & Kegan Paul.

Durkheim, E. (1898) 'Representations individuelles et représentations collectives', *Revue de métaphysique*, 6: 275–302.

Engels, F. (1940 [1872–82]) *Dialectics of Nature*. New York: International Publishers.

Engels, F. (1942 [1884]) *The Origin of the Family, Private Property and the State, in the Light of the Researches of Lews H. Morgan*. New York: International Publishers.

Holland, D., and Quinn, N. (1987) *Cultural Models in Language and Thought*. Cambridge: Cambridge University Press.

King, P.M., and Kitchener, K.S. (1994) *Developing Reflective Judgment: Understanding and Promoting Intellectual Growth and Critical Thinking in Adolescents and Adults*. San Francisco: Jossey-Bass.

Kramer, D., and Woodruff, D.S. (1986) 'Relativistic and dialectical thought in three adult age-groups', *Human Development*, 29: 280–90.

Kraut, A., Pedigo, P., McKenna, D., and Dunnette, M. (1989) 'The role of the manager: what's really important in different management jobs', *Academy of Management Executive*, 3 (4): 286–93.

Levy-Bruhl, L. (1975) *The Notebooks on Primitive Mentality*. Oxford: Blackwell. p. 37.

Lloyd, G.E.R. (1990) *Demystifying Mentalities*. Cambridge: Cambridge University Press. p. 13.

Moscovici, S. (1984) 'The phenomenon of social representation', in R. Farr and S. Moscovici (eds), *Social Representation*. New York: Cambridge University Press.

Murphy, G.L., and Medin, D.L. (1985) 'The role of theories in conceptual coherence', *Psychological Review*, 92: 289–316.

Needham, R. (1972) *Belief, Language, and Experience*. Oxford: Blackwell.

Peng, K. (1997) 'Naïve dialecticism and its effects', PhD dissertation, University of Michigan.

Peng, K., and Nisbett, R. (1999) 'Culture, dialectics, and reasoning about contradiction', *American Psychologist*, 54: 741–54.

Peng, K., Ames, D., and Knowles, E. (1999) 'Culture and human inference: perspectives from three traditions', in D. Matsumoto (ed.), *Handbook of Cross-Cultural Psychology*. Oxford: Oxford University Press.

Pilkington, A. (1988) 'Manufacturing strategy regained: evidence for the demise of best practice', *California Management Review*, 41: 31–42.

Porter, M., and Takeuchi, H. (1999) 'Fixing what really ails Japan', *Foreign Affairs*, 78: 66.

Riegel, K.F. (1973) 'Dialectical operations: the final period of cognitive development', *Human Development*, 18: 430–43.

Szulanski, G. (1996) 'Exploring internal stickiness: impediments to the transfer of best practice within the firm', *Strategic Management Journal*, 17: 27–43.

Tetlock, P. (1985) 'Integrative complexity of American and Soviet foreign policy rhetoric: a time-series analysis', *Journal of Personality & Social Psychology*, 49: 1565–85.

Wagner, W. (1997) 'Local knowledge, social representations and psychological theory', in K. Leung, U. Kim, S. Yamaguchi and Y. Kashima (eds), *Progress in Asian Social Psychology*. Singapore: John Wiley & Sons.

PART II
FIRMS, MARKETS AND INNOVATION

---

6 Strategies for Managing Knowledge Assets: the Role of Firm Structure and Industrial Context

David J. Teece

Introduction

There is increasing recognition that the competitive advantage of firms depends on their ability to create, transfer, utilize and protect difficult to imitate knowledge assets. With the liberalization and expansion of markets domestically and internationally, the shift to knowledge assets as the basis of competitive advantage has become compelling. These trends have created a business environment in the United States and in many other developed countries where components/inputs are available to all firms everywhere at similar prices. Even if all components/inputs do not trade, firms are free to locate so as to access them at low cost. Fuelled by a free market philosophy and assisted by new information technology, these developments having a levelling effect with respect to competitive advantage. The trend is well established and unlikely to be reversed in societies where openness to trade is the dominant ethos. In this chapter, certain general implications are distilled.

Managerial challenges that flow from the centrality of knowledge and intellectual property are rather different from those of a bygone era where physical assets were key to competitive advantage. Furthermore, there are also major differences in knowledge management requirements from situation to situation, according to the underlying cost and demand logic at work, the appropriability regimes the firm operates, the importance of compatibility standards, the nature of innovation at issue and the richness of the technological opportunities facing the firm. This chapter is an analysis of knowledge management requirements in these different contexts. However, first, some background.

Creating Value with Knowledge Assets

The nature of knowledge assets is that they cannot be readily bought and sold. Because of this they must be built in-house by firms and they frequently must also be exploited internally in order that their full value will be realized by the owner. This observation flows from the fact that the market for know-how is far from complete and, where it exists, it is far from 'efficient'. This condition derives from the absence of commodity-like markets for knowledge assets – a condition that arises in part from the nature of knowledge itself and, in particular, the difficult to articulate and codify 'tacit dimension' (Teece, 1981).

These transactional difficulties are mainly associated with organizational knowledge. Personal knowledge can, of course, be more readily bought and sold. Transactions in personal knowledge occur every day, when particular (individual) talent is hired and fired. Organizational knowledge or organizational competence is a different matter, being embedded as it is in organizational processes, procedures, routines and structures. Such knowledge cannot be moved into an organization without the transfer of clusters of individuals with established patterns of working together. This is most frequently accomplished by means of personal relations or alliances, joint ventures and mergers and acquisitions of business units. Thus, when Ford Motors in the United States became committed to making smaller cars in the United States, it turned to its European subsidiaries for help. The subsidiaries transferred design and production groups to the US to help establish small car design and manufacturing competence in North America.

In short, the absence of a well-developed market for knowledge renders it imperative that firms innovate internally. Put differently, innovation cannot be outsourced in its entirety, even though internal efforts can be successfully augmented by technology transfer and external acquisition activities (Chesbrough and Teece, 1996). Specification of the internal environment and processes adapted to support rapid innovation is, of course, a topic on which much is written and a good deal is understood. Accordingly, this topic need not detain us further here, despite its great importance. Rather, attention is given to several related aspects of knowledge management, namely extracting value by:

1 disembodied transfer inside the firm (internal technology transfer and utilization);
2 disembodied external transfer;
3 bundled sale of technology (embodied in an item or device).

However, first, a basic observation. Much knowledge is of limited commercial value unless it is bundled in some way. A line of software code is of little utility until it is combined with other pieces of software to constitute a program. For example, units of software smaller than applets cannot typically be bought and sold due to the absence of markets (due possibly to high transaction cost) and/or their primitive state. Accordingly, know-how does not usually command significant value until it is embedded in products. Only then can its value be fully extracted.

There are exceptions. Even when it is not an item of sale, knowledge assets relating to production processes can generate great value inside the firm. The internal technology transfer and use of process know-how is less compromised by the absence of a market for know-how. Indeed, the very essence of a large, integrated firm can be traced, in substantial measure, to its capacity to facilitate the (internal) exchange and transfer of knowledge assets and services, assisted and protected by administrative processes (Teece, 1980, 1982). I shall examine various modes of extracting value from knowledge as each raises distinctive knowledge management issues.

Transferring Knowledge Assets

In the 1960s and 1970s, knowledge transfer inside the firm was viewed as being mainly one way – out from research and development to the divisions, then out from the country of origin to the rest of the world. Now, if not then, the flow is in all directions. Research and development is no longer as centralized organizationally as it used to be. Moreover, the sources of knowledge are diffused geographically, requiring flows from the periphery to the centre, and from one node on the periphery to another.

Given that technology transfer inside the firm is not significantly impeded by proprietary concerns, one would think that technology transfer and use inside the firm would be straightforward. However, this is definitely not the case. As Lew Platt, former CEO of Hewlett-Packard (HP), once put it, 'If only HP knew what HP knows, we would be three times more productive!' (Cole, 1998). The large size of many enterprises, their global reach, the importance of knowledge to competitiveness, the distributed nature of competence within the firm and the availability of tools to assist knowledge transfer has sharpened the competitive importance of accomplishing knowledge transfer inside the firm.

We know very little about how to do this. Economists and other social scientists frequently have a poor grasp of this topic and are often content to assume that the transfer is costless, when clearly it is not (Teece, 1976). Managers are not much better informed, although top management in many companies (such as British Petroleum and Hewlett-Packard) has flagged the importance of knowledge transfer issues. Moreover, the knowledge that needs to be transferred is not simply technological. Knowledge about competitors, customers and suppliers is also a part of the mix. So is managerial experience. Such knowledge is often embedded in operating rules and practices, in customer, supplier and competitor anks and the company's own history. As mentioned earlier, there is an important tacit dimension, which is difficult to transfer, without transferring people.

n the information age, there is both the need and the opportunity to match information and knowledge needs with availability in ways that have hitherto been impossible. Knowledge, which is trapped inside the minds of key employees, in filing drawers and databases, is of little value if it is not supplied to the right people at the right time. Information 'float' – the time elapsing between knowledge discovery/creation and transfer/use – is extremely costly, at least in opportunity cost terms. Indeed, the technology leader could turn out to be viewed as the laggard in the marketplace if its competitors can transfer technology and manage information float better. As Gomory and Schmitt (1988, p. 1131) noted over a decade ago

> If one company has a three-year [development and manufacturing] cycle and another has a two-year cycle, the company with the shorter cycle will have its process and design into production and the product in the market one year before the other. The firm with the shorter cycle will appear to have newer products with new technologies. In fact, both companies will be working from the same storehouse of technology.

Casually formed networks no longer suffice to diffuse best practice and new knowledge more generally. As Larry Prusak asks, if the coffeepot was a font of useful knowledge in the traditional firm, what constitutes a virtual one? How do we manage face time in a firm of tens of thousands? The requirement is to use information and technology creatively. Corporate intranets and the Internet itself can help facilitate the flow of such information. However, as discussed below, information itself rarely constitutes knowledge, so IT tools are never the entire solution. Moreover, knowledge and competence are often widely diffused in an organization. Some may lie in research and development laboratories, some on the factory floor, some in executives' heads. Often what is critical is the capacity to weave it all together. Firms cannot eschew the need for cross-functional and geographical integration without paying a heavy penalty in the marketplace.

While proprietary barriers to internal knowledge transfer are typically absent, within the firm, transfer is not friction free and costless, as noted above. Merely finding the person or group with the knowledge one needs is often quite difficult. In addition, issues such as absorptive capacity, rooted in education and experiences, social, professional and hierarchical contexts, also appear to be important (Brown and Duguid, 1998). 'Gatekeepers', 'translators', 'internal knowledge brokers' and other specialists in technology transfer are often needed to effectuate transfer.

External transfer – from one organization to another – occurs either as a consequence of deliberate transfer (under learning and know-how agreements), inadvertent transfer (such as spillovers in the context of alliances) or imitative activities of competitors. Clearly the external flow of that knowledge protected by intellectual property rights (such as trade secrets) is impeded (to the extent that intellectual property law is effective or deemed to be so), as compared to flows inside the firm. However, intellectual property law does not protect much knowledge and, in some cases, proprietary concerns may be minimal. Then, it may be correct, as Brown and Duguid (1998: 102) claim, that 'knowledge often travels more easily between organizations than it does within them'. Their claim appears to derive from the observation that knowledge moves differently within communities then it does between them: 'Within communities, knowledge is continuously embedded in practice and, thus, circulates easily' (1998: 100). This is undoubtedly true, but, as a general matter, internal transfer ought to be easier.[1]

The external transfer of technology is frequently aided by licensing and technology transfer agreements. These not only remove intellectual property barriers, but they also call for technology transfer assistance. The challenges associated with such external transfers are significantly softened (as compared to the internal challenge) by the absence of a requirement for the subsequent transfer of updates and improvements. It is substantially easier to transfer a known technology for which there is operating and transfer experience than it is to constantly and continuously transfer that which is state of the art.

Information and Knowledge Management

Much of the excitement around knowledge management has been propelled by advances in information technology (IT). However, information transfer is not knowledge transfer; and information management is not knowledge management, although the former can certainly assist the latter. IT alone will rarely be the source of sustained competitive advantage – in part, because competitors can frequently replicate it.

Indeed, the very success of IT in making information accessible at low cost itself highlights the difference between information and knowledge. Individuals and organizations now frequently suffer from information overload. Just as the winner of a national quiz show may never go on to do anything beyond the mediocre, so a corporation with excellent IT systems might have trouble competing. Knowledge is not primarily about facts and what we refer to as 'content'. Rather, it is more about 'context'.

Knowledgeable people and organizations can frame problems and select, integrate and augment information to create understandings and answers. Knowing how to select, interpret and integrate information into a useable body of knowledge is a far more valuable individual and organizational skill than simply being able to know the answer to a discrete question or a

---

BOX 6.1

Information management masquerading as knowledge management?

There are three broad objectives frequently advanced by the 'knowledge' management movement:

- the creation of 'knowledge' repositories (data warehouses) for:

  1 external information, particularly competitive intelligence and best practice;
  2 internal information, such as internal research reports;
  3 informal internal knowledge-like discussion databases;

- to deliver improved 'knowledge' access and, hence, reuse by means of the development of user-friendly and analytical tools;
- to enhance the organization's knowledge environment, including the willingness of individuals to freely share their knowledge and experiences.

---

series of questions. A Bloomberg or Reuters newsfeed is information. The opinions of the leading analysts and commentators, putting the news into context and enabling it to be used to create value, is more akin to knowledge.

Accordingly, data warehousing and datamining exercises are useless, if they are without other knowledge and other sense-making organizational processes (see Davenport, Delong, and Beers, 1998, for examples of knowledge management projects). This is not surprising, given the tacit nature of much organizational knowledge. IT assists in the storage, retrieval and transfer of codified knowledge, but, unassisted by other organizational processes, the productivity benefit it gives is likely to be limited. Accordingly, the view advanced here is that 'knowledge' management as it is frequently defined (see Box 6.1) is too narrowly positioned to warrant the use of the term 'knowledge management'. Efficiently organized information is not knowledge. It is simply efficiently organized information, little more – albeit a helpful tool.

None the less, the combination of IT and co-aligned organizational processes can significantly enhance learning and competitive advantage. In addition, the conversion of tacit to codified or explicit knowledge assists in knowledge transfer and sharing, thereby possibly helping to make the firm more innovative and productive. Once knowledge is made explicit, it is easier to store, reference, share, transfer and, hence, redeploy. Cutting the other way is that fact that once it is codified, it is sometimes harder to protect. Once data is held electronically, it can be sent almost anywhere in the world in seconds. In the wrong hands, it can 'leak out' comprehensively and quickly. Indeed, Edwin Mansfield's (1985) survey indicated that knowledge leaked out of firms with considerable speed even then. However, the absence of strong intellectual property protection is usually not sufficient to warrant managerial strategies in favour of suppressing the conversion of tacit knowledge into explicit knowledge, as such suppression harms the owner's ability to use, reuse and combine such knowledge. Moreover, in most jurisdictions, there is some form of trade secret protection, thereby providing a medium of protection against the misappropriation of explicit knowledge (Teece, 2000a).

Knowledge Management and the Design of Firms

Structural issues

The migration of competitive advantage away from tangible assets to intangible ones helps highlight some fundamental aspects of the business firm. Firms are sometimes portrayed as organizations designed to protect specific physical, locational and human capital assets (Williamson, 1985). The protection of asset values from recontracting hazards will be an enduring feature of the business enterprise. In the global economy, it is intangible capital which is pre-eminent; but, in addition to protecting such capital against recontracting hazards, one must also focus on generating, acquiring, transferring and combining such assets so as to meet customers' needs.

In order to be successful in these activities, firms and their management must be entrepreneurial. They must exhibit capabilities that I have labelled elsewhere as dynamic. Entrepreneurial firms are organized to be highly flexible and responsive (Teece, 1996, 1998a). That, in turn, requires a set of attributes, which include:

1 **flexible boundaries** a presumption in favour of outsourcing and alliances (the only situation where this presumption ought to be overturned is innovation itself, as discussed above);
2 **high powered incentives** to encourage an aggressive response to competitive developments;
3 **non-bureaucratic decision making** decentralized or possibly autocratic and self-managed to the extent possible;
4 **shallow hierarchies** both to facilitate quick decision making and rapid information flow from the market to decision makers;
5 **an innovative and entrepreneurial culture** that favours rapid response and the nurturing of specialized knowledge.

As Charles Leadbeater (1998) points out, orthodoxy from both the left and the right does not always find the new emphasis on entrepreneurship agreeable. The left has demonized entrepreneurs as profit-hungry exploiters of the weak and the poor. Many orthodox economists on the right have no place for the entrepreneur in their intellectual frameworks. In the perfectly competitive world of equilibrium economics, the entrepreneur is superfluous. It is mainly in the Austrian school that one finds a ready acceptance for the critical role of the entrepreneur in economic development. More recently, the role of entrepreneurship in management has begun to be recognized (Teece, 1998b).

The modern corporation, as it accepts the challenges of the new knowledge economy, will need to evolve into a knowledge-generating, knowledge-integrating and knowledge-protecting organization. While many companies have performed these functions with proficiency for decades, if not centuries, the global transformations taking place are quite radical in their implications for management of many orthodox philosophy enterprises, requiring and enabling an entirely new level of proficiency in knowledge management. In the new economy, significant premiums are being placed on the entrepreneurial capacities of management and on the capacities firms develop for building, protecting, transferring and integrating knowledge – both productive and customer knowledge. The ability of an organization to exhibit dynamism is critical to success. Without the organizational capacity to make sense of the evolving reality, the corporation will fall on hard times. Entrepreneurial leaders must be able to make good decisions based on limited information. They must understand the evolving needs of customers in market contexts that are changing at high speed.

Compensation and employment issues

If hierarchy is antithetical to the performance of knowledge-based firms, how can one gain confidence that members of the organization are working for the organization, not against it? The answer lies, in part, with performance pay and equity-based compensation systems. Providing clear performance-based metrics facilitates high autonomy and, if it is well designed, it also facilitates goal congruence. Equity provides a sense of membership and belonging.

The use of equity pay to provide incentive for management at all levels is becoming more widespread, but is more common in the US and significant reliance on it there tends to be mainly confined to high-growth 'Silicon Valley'-type companies. It has worked very well in a variety of diverse contexts. For the individual, it can provide spectacular returns if the company does well; for the company, it can facilitate a strong sense of 'belonging' when there may not be much else. It can also save on cash compensation, which may well be advantageous when cash is tight.

The use of equity-based compensation works better when there is good liquidity – a publicly traded security complemented by a publicly traded option or at least the prospect of each. Indeed, the possibility of receiving shares in the company is frequently a spur towards uncommon efforts and uncommon sacrifices, to the benefit of the enterprise, its members and shareholders.

Equity compensation ought not be limited to those traditionally thought of as 'insiders' or 'employees'. Independent contractors and suppliers can, and should, be linked in where possible, indeed, in Silicon Valley, it is not uncommon for consultants, headhunters, lawyers, even landlords, to take a portion of their fees in options from newly formed pre-IPO businesses. Even customers can be included if the customer is accepting uncommon purchaser risk, as when a customer helps with early product adoption and testing or when they place a large, up front, early order to help legitimize the company and its products.

Highly flexible Silicon Valley-type firms – where there is a presumption in favour of outsourcing, but where critical knowledge assets are built and protected internally – are likely to be a favourite organizational form in some sectors of the new knowledge economy (Teece, 1996). The corollary is that the employment relationship will continue to evolve, with distinctions between 'inside' and 'outside' the firm becoming increasingly blurred.

Successful companies will always have those with whom they collaborate, be they other firms, individuals or universities. When the sources of knowledge are widely dispersed, such collaboration is likely to be extensive. Networks are thus frequently critical to the knowledge-based firm. However, while networks have been of growing importance for at least a couple of decades, one should not presume that this means that the integrated corporation is doomed. It is here to stay. As explained elsewhere (Chesbrough and Teece, 1996, for example), the corporation cannot outsource its key systems integration capability where specialized knowledge assets are required for competitive advantage; these should be developed and practised internally. However, it can outsource functions not critical to the firm's core activities. Indeed, it will frequently find providers who specialize in such 'routine' support functions. These firms can provide a level of service that the organization might not be able to provide for itself – possibly because of scale or simply because the supplier has developed other relevant knowledge. Clearly, a company is unlikely to be able to beat its competitors with respect to a function if it sources that function externally. However, if it is behind, it can certainly catch up by means of outsourcing.

Industrial Context

In this chapter, and in a series of articles written over the past decade, I have advanced the proposition that competitive advantage, or, superior profitability at the enterprise level depends on the creation and exploitation of difficult to replicate non-tradeable assets, of which knowledge assets are the most important. While, I suggest, this proposition has general applicability, its strength is likely to vary according to the industrial context. Putting to one side sectors of the economy shielded from competition by government regulation (where political access and regulatory influence are key drivers of firm performance), it would appear that other aspects of the environment also impact the strength of the proposition and affect appropriate managerial responses. In this section, the underlying cost and demand dynamics and other factors that affect knowledge management and strategic management are explored.

At one level, it is self-evident that industrial context matters. There are clearly some differences between managing a pharmaceutical company, an Internet start-up and a professional services firm. However, I propose that, in all three instances, managing knowledge assets is the key to building competitive advantage. The manner in which one can successfully manage each of the identifiable components of knowledge management – creation/ building, transfer, protection, use – will be different. In part, this is because there is variability in competitive dynamics across activities in the economy that employ knowledge assets. This is not to suggest that the knowledge economy is or will be confined to just a few activities or industries. All industries open to competition will be impacted. However, the underlying cost/success drivers are different in different contexts. Understanding the relative roles of knowledge assets and dynamic capabilities are obviously of some importance.

Perhaps we can begin by looking at extremes. Where is the new logic of organization likely to have its greatest impact; where is it likely to have the least impact? Identifying environments where there is already, or will soon be, a significant premium associated with the ownership and orchestration of knowledge assets is not difficult. Multimedia, Web services, electronic banking and brokerage are just a few obvious examples. Less obvious, but equally important, are professional services and agriculture. Technology has always been critical to agricultural productivity, but new IT coupled with satellite surveillance and active futures market participation is enabling more astute decision making with respect to crop selection and harvesting. Biotechnology is meanwhile creating a more visible revolution with respect to plant and animal selection and growth. Ironically, education is one of the least impacted sectors – in part because of its public ownership and the limited competition that exists in many locales. Traditionally low-tech activities such as retailing are undergoing a revolution, enabled by IT and, at the same time, confronted by the Internet as an alternative and competitive distribution channel.

Physical assets will, however, remain important in many industries. Consumers will still need the outputs of steel mills and petroleum refineries, though these facilities will be run in quite different ways. Take the oil business. Nowadays, crude oil and many refined products are commodities, yielding only limited opportunities (such as specialist products) for differentiation of the products themselves. Once the current wave of consolidation has levelled out gross capacity utilization differentials, the primary way in which industry participants can compete will be either in new ways of finding, transporting, refining or distributing oil or

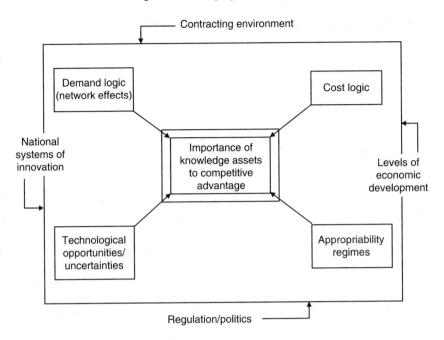

Figure 6.1 *Factors impacting knowledge management*

else political influence (that is, being better at winning in the political allocation of rights to explore for, produce and transport oil). Ownership of physical assets will not, however, provide a source of significant differentiation. Indeed, global competition and the expansion of intermediate product markets (including futures markets) means that it is possible to compete downstream as a 'virtual' refiner, outsourcing supply while protecting oneself in financial markets from the risk thereby involved.

There is no easy metric for carving out sectors of the economy that might be insulated to some degree from the fundamental dynamics described earlier. One cannot do it based on R&D in relation to sales, because so much R&D is 'outsourced' in one way or another and R&D in one industry impacts the competitive dynamics of another, as when biotechnology research impacts agriculture. Another good example is data services and telecommunications. Few service providers engage in R&D – most of the technological innovation is driven by equipment companies such as Cisco and Lucent. Nor can one do it solely on the basis of the underlying cost dynamics that characterize the industry.

There is a need to categorize environments where knowledge management skills have high utility. Figure 6.1 is an attempt to do so. The taxonomy is by no means comprehensive; but it is offered as a preliminary and tentative typology to help the uninitiated think through particular real-world situations and circumstances. Each factor that helps define relevant dimensions of industrial context is briefly described below.

Cost and demand logic

Increasing returns

In many industries today – in particular in the information industries – increasing returns are the norm. This is not just a matter of increasing returns to scale, as the phenomenon flows from both demand- and supply-side considerations. (While these are dealt with together here, they are separately identified in Figure 6.1.) The effect is that whoever gains advantage, *ceteris paribus*, gains further advantage. Whoever loses advantage will tend to lose further advantage (Apple Computers, for example, in the early 1990s). Momentum lost is difficult, though not impossible, to regain, as Apple Computers is demonstrating.

There are at least three reasons for these phenomena. The first is cost. High-tech products involve large development costs – perhaps $250+ million for the first disk of Microsoft Windows 95. The second disk could be created for almost nothing and, if distributed over the Internet could be distributed for next to nothing. While there are up-front fixed costs in many of the older industries (such as the car and steel industries), scale economies would tend to become exhausted before industry demand was substantially satisfied. The second reason is because of demand-side factors. The bigger a network gets, the more utility is associated with being on that network. This is because the product might well become a standard, actual or *de facto*. The third reason is the development of user knowledge, familiarity and skills with the product. One might become familiar with WordPerfect or Microsoft Word and so, if upgrades are available, the user will go with the product that builds on their skills.

These demand- and supply-side factors work together to produce increasing returns. They also tend to make markets unstable in that there is an absence of smooth substitution possibilities among products or platforms. The market may tip one way, then possibly another. There is a tendency for the market to 'lock in' once one firm's product gets ahead, whether due to superior acumen, small chance events, clever strategies, government regulations or judicial blundering. However, we should not think that whoever gets started first will necessarily win. Moreover, lock-ins may be quite weak and easily surmountable because switching costs are low. Like the presidential primaries in the United States, there is much that can happen between New Hampshire and California, although it typically does not hurt to win in New Hampshire. Even if one loses there, though, one can catch up by using complementary assets (such as advertising programmes), clever strategy, good luck and hard work. In product markets, one needs to focus on trying to get bandwagons going. Having a good product that is attractively priced helps immensely in increasing returns contexts.

Industry position may well become established for a while, but certainly not forever. Lotus 1-2-3 dominated spreadsheets for a while, Digital dominated minicomputers for a decade, and Microsoft may have DOS/ Windows as the standard for the PC OS for a few more years, but all eventually are overturned (unless government intervention moves in to freeze the status quo). It is not that competition stops once dominance, in the loose sense of the term, is achieved. It simply takes on a new form. Once a standard is anointed by the market, competitors push for a new standard and may have to develop a radical new technology to make it happen. Monopoly power, if attained, is transient, not permanent. Competition in the market is displaced by competition for the market.

When competition is of this kind, competitive strategies must adjust. The payoff for market insight – figuring out where the market is heading and investing heavily to get there first – is high. The strategic challenge is therefore, in part, cognitive. However, even if an organization is good at figuring out the future, to succeed one must also be good at responding quickly. Directed strategies – quickly and comprehensively implemented – are what is required. Witness Bill Gates's response at Microsoft in 1995 once he figured out the significance of the Internet. The ability to sense and then seize such opportunities is, in part, an organizational capability. It has been referred to as dynamic capability (Teece, 1998a, Teece, Pisano and Shuen, 1997, and Teece and Pisano, 1994).

In increasing returns environments, the challenge is to engineer products and services that can potentially become an industry standard. Superior technology clearly matters, but it will not succeed alone. Not only does one need complementary assets, one needs the capacity to build a bandwagon effect – suggesting the importance of disseminating information about marketplace successes, the willingness to price low to build an installed base and strong dynamic abilities to sense and then seize opportunities. Virtual structures may well be ideal early on, when the payoff to flexibility is high.

Once anointed as the flag bearer, firms must keep innovating, as staying ahead is by no means inevitable. Failure to engineer the next generation of products satisfactorily could well unseat the incumbent. The incumbent is also confronted by competition for the market. The stakes escalate as the market grows. The main reason for technology transfer is not to keep the product on the frontier of technology, but to maintain the standard by licensing others (complementors) to keep supporting and developing the established standard.

Constant returns

Large sectors of the economy are still characterized by constant returns to scale. Getting ahead is desirable, but it need not confer much advantage to profit margins, even though total profits may expand. Professional services, such as accounting, consulting, law, may well fall into this category, together with scaleable industries of the likes of food processing, book publishing, copiers, printers, paints, pharmaceuticals, adhesives and shoes. In these industries, the outcome of competitive battles depends on cost, quality and product and process innovation.

Knowledge management is important. The ability of firms to create new products that meet customers' needs requires a constant tuning of product offerings. Market share is gained in little bites, and dominance, if attained, is not protected by 'lock in' effects and/or switching costs. While brands are likely to be important, competitive advantage is built the old-fashioned way, by keeping customers happy. As competition is within the market, rather than for the market, the threat from inside the industry is relatively more important than the threat from the outside. Learning is key to staying competitive, and licensing is critical to keeping technologies and products refreshed.

Because technical expertise is of great importance in firms that compete in these contexts, the management of knowledge assets is critically important. The entrepreneurial factor is less significant. Innovation can become more of a routine. The techniques and tools of knowledge management must find their full expression here if competition advantage is to be built and maintained. Constant return environments also offer opportunities for the global expansion of the business. There are no diseconomies associated with expansion.

Management consulting appears to exhibit constant return to scale. Firms in this industry do not create new products in formal R&D activities, but create most new 'products' and services via on-the-job learning. In essence, their 'products' are usually methodologies and/or templates by which they tackle particular classes of problems. Increasingly, management consulting firms must pay attention to building, marketing and exploiting an organizational knowledge base that transcends the individuals in the firm. This knowledge base, resident as it is in the experiences of individuals in the firms, in reports, slide presentations and databases and methodologies, must be accessible to all senior personnel. However, proprietary concerns will frequently get in the way as clients will not wish studies that they have commissioned to be made available outside the consulting engagement that generated it.

Consulting firms without good knowledge management systems and protocols will frequently end up duplicating for one client what they have already done for another, even in circumstances where there are no proprietary conditions surrounding sharing. However, one should not overplay the importance of knowledge management, as the diagnosis and solution of business problems is usually highly situational.

Diminishing returns

Diminishing returns implies that the enterprise confronts rising costs as it endeavours to expand. This is because of some fixed 'factor of production', that limits profitable growth. The Napa Valley vineyard, the local sole proprietor construction contractor and the small town estate management firm are cases in point. While superior knowledge management can push back the effects of the 'fixed factor', they are unlikely to overcome it entirely.

With diminishing returns, knowledge management can be an important component of competitive strategy, as it will assist the firm in pushing the limits of its business model. Indeed, it could become the very foundation of its competitive success, as it may enable customer capital (such as customer databases) to be leveraged more effectively. In general, however, knowledge management is unlikely to enable the firm to completely unshackle itself from the disabilities of diminishing returns. The Mauna Loa Macadamia Nut Company of Hawaii may be able to improve its performance, but if there is a limited number of sites in which macadamia nuts can be cultivated, superior knowledge management is unlikely to completely remove those shackles.

Appropriability regimes

In a world of strong appropriability – that is, where patents or trade secrets and copyrights are an effective isolating mechanism – innovators can keep imitators and followers at bay, at least for a while. This gives the innovator the ability to line up complements and seek strategic partners – and do so from a position of relative bargaining strength. Lead time in the market is more confidentially assured and the chances of competitive success are higher if the firm astutely uses the intellectual property protection that it has. Dynamic abilities are therefore less critical to success, because of the protection already available via intellectual property. The converse is also true. Dynamic abilities will become more critical as the advantage from intellectual property weakens.

The advantage from intellectual property weakens if several firms have strong intellectual property rights in the same competitive space. Competitive advantage will then be eroded, although not destroyed. Cross-licensing among the owners of complementary intellectual property will lead to at least the partial dissipation of rents, but firms that have not contributed to the technology in any way will have to pay a competitive licence fee. Competitive advantage might thus be somewhat preserved, in as much as the free riders will be excluded (Grindley and Teece, 1997).

Intellectual property protection is also likely to be jurisdiction specific. The level of protection available in the US is generally higher than that in Italy, Brazil, Turkey, Japan or China. Still, an intellectual property advantage in a key market can sometimes enable the innovator to build sufficient scale and complementary assets to compete effectively where there is less intellectual property protection and possibly also in the period after the patent expires.

Compatibility standards

This is related to cost and demand logic discussed above in that one of the reasons for increasing returns to scale, at least on the demand side, is the existence of compatibility standards. When such standards exist, some degree of customer 'lock in' may exist, possibly resulting in significant switching costs for the consumer if the innovator is offering an incompatible standard.

If standards issues are not permanent, than battles over standards will not be a major strategic factor. The ability of the firm to compete by simply being better at the basics – including, of course, innovation – is likely. However, when incompatible standards are being advanced by significant contenders for a major market, the entrepreneurial and strategic abilities of top management and how well they can marshal the requisite resources, will become paramount.

In particular, the abilities of the firm to sense and possibly shape the likely course of advancement will be of particular importance. In such circumstances, there is great risk and the rules of the game are by no means transparent. With such levels of uncertainty, failure is likely to be frequent. Still, superior sensing and calibrating of the opportunities and, hence, superior decision making – will be of great importance.

Technological opportunity

Knowledge assets and dynamic abilities command a higher premium when rapid organic growth is enabled by new technology. Some environments are likely to support much greater demand growth than others. Judging from the valuation of Internet IPOs, businesses that support or use the Internet are widely regarded – at least by investors – as providing significant opportunity. Three-dimensional graphics accelerator chips are, likewise, experiencing rapid growth as performance is provided at lower prices. Demand for coffins, on the other hand, is not predicted to grow much, as the death rate appears to be quite stable in advanced countries and there is little scope for selling more than one casket for each individual deceased person. Accordingly, the mortuary and mortuary supply business is likely to be significantly more stable, and growth less robust, than Web services, multimedia, 3D graphics or computers. While there are frequently surprises with respect to traditional businesses, and an environment that has low opportunity in one epoch may have high opportunity in the next, the payoff to astute knowledge management is likely to be greater when the technological opportunity is richer.

Role of political influence

Government regulation has proven time and time again to stand in the way of innovation. That's not to say that government R&D spending doesn't sometimes provide a great assistance. However, not only does regulation tend to limit market competition, it also diverts managerial effort away from competing on merit and in favour of competing by using the regulator and the regulatory process to limit the competitive activities of one's rivals.

Accordingly, when environments are characterized by circumstances where market forces are muted by regulation, the payoff to good management – be it of knowledge assets or any other assets – is likely to be significantly compromised. However, if an environment is transitioning towards competition and away from regulation, then developing dynamic abilities is likely to be both especially difficult and especially valuable. It will be especially difficult because the basic instincts and routines of a regulated enterprise are not going to be oriented towards embracing competition. It will be especially valuable because deregulation will occasion rapid change and the opening up of commercial opportunities that have been suppressed by regulation and/or government control.

Challenges to Orthodoxy

The imperatives of the knowledge economy require new paradigms for management and a revised understanding of the role of markets and firms. Here, some of the key contentions that have been developed in this chapter are summarized.

1 Development, ownership, protection and astute utilization of knowledge assets, not physical assets, provide the underpinnings for competitive advantage in the new economy.
2 Because property rights have fuzzy boundaries and knowledge is not resident in some hypothetical book of blueprints inside the firm, figuring out how to protect and retain the firm's knowledge is a key challenge for top management. It is not just an intellectual property issue that can be delegated to the law department.
3 Today's competitive new environment favours organizations – firms – that are able to protect knowledge assets from recontracting hazards; but it also favours firms that can build, buy, combine, recombine, deploy and redeploy knowledge assets according to changing customer needs and competitive circumstances. Successful firms in the future will be 'high flex' and knowledge based.
4 It makes little sense to talk about 'labour markets', in isolation from the market for know-how. Much that is interesting about the former emerges from the study and understanding of the latter.
5 The entrepreneurial function of firms in the new economy is more critical than the administrative ones. Administrative functions can frequently be outsourced without loss of competitive advantage.

6   The globalization of financial markets and the narrowing of information asymmetries between borrowers and lenders are eroding access to capital as a major determinant of competitive advantage.
7   Compensation structures need to be more equity based. Rewards need to be geared towards individual and team outputs, not inputs.
8   Virtual structures are frequently virtuous. The presumption should be to outsource all except the development and combination of knowledge assets and knowledge routines.
9   Managing knowledge is not the same function as human resource management. Besides human resource management, knowledge management involves managing intellectual property and managing the development, transfer and further development of industrial and organizational know-how. It is far more multifaceted than simply managing people.
10 The boundaries of the firm can no longer be defined by reference to equity stakes. Networks that do not involve equity are likely to be an integral part of the firm as a functioning entity.

Conclusion

The theory put forward in this chapter is that competitive advantage flows from the creation, ownership, protection and use of difficult to imitate knowledge assets. That being so, superior performance depends on the ability of firms to be good at innovation, protecting intangible knowledge assets and using those assets. Using knowledge assets obviously conceals complicated processes surrounding:

1   the integration of intangibles with other intangibles and tangible assets;
2   the transfer of intangibles inside the firm;
3   the astute external licensing of technology where appropriate.

This set of activities requires management to refocus priorities, build organizations that are 'high flex' to accommodate such activity and display an uncommon level of entrepreneurial drive.

These challenges obviously will not simultaneously confront all firms at the same time in the same manner as context is important. However, the new norms required for success are already evident in many of the high-tech industries in the US, Europe and Japan. Those enterprises that are slow to recognize the paradigm shift and then respond appropriately can expect to experience performance declines. Many of the new start-up firms being born in Silicon Valley and elsewhere understand the logic articulated here. Many incumbents are beginning to recognize the new logic, but have as yet failed to effect transformation. Clearly, such firms are at risk.

Note

1 When its flow is impaired, it is frequently due to the poor design of incentives or pure self-interest. The latter frequently stems from the unwillingness of individuals in our organization to share information for fear of making themselves redundant.

References

Brown, J.S., and Duguid, P. (1998) 'Organizing knowledge', *California Management Review*, 40 (3): 90–111.
Chesbrough, H., and Teece, D.J. (1996) 'When is virtual virtuous? Organizing for innovation', *Harvard Business Review*, Jan.–Feb, republished in J.S. Brown (ed.) (1997) *Seeing Things Differently: Insights on Innovation*. Boston, MA: Harvard Business School Press. pp. 105–19.
Cole, R.M. (ed.) (1998) 'Special issue on knowledge and the firm', *California Management Review*, 40 (3): 15–21.
Davenport, T., Delong, D., and Beers, M. (1998) 'Successful knowledge management projects', *Sloan Management Review*, 39 (2): 43–57.
Gomory, R., and Schmitt, R. (1988) 'Science and product', *Science*, May, 11–31.
Grindley, P., and Teece, D.J. (1997) 'Managing intellectual capital: licensing and cross licensing in electronics', *California Management Review*, 39 (2): 8–41.
Leadbeatter, Charles (1998) *Living on Thin Air: The New Economy*, draft.
Mansfield, E. (1985) 'How rapidly does new industrial technology leak out?, *Journal of Industrial Economics*, 34 (2): 217–23.
Nonaka, I., and Takeuchi, H. (1995) *The Knowledge-creating Company*. New York: Oxford University Press.
Shapiro, C., and Varian, H. (1999) 'The art of standards wars', *California Management Review*, 41 (2): 8–32.
Teece, D.J. (1976) *The Multinational Corporation and the Resource Cost of International Technology Transfer*. Cambridge, MA: Ballinger.
Teece, D.J. (1980) 'Economies of scale and scope of the enterprise', *Journal of Economic Behavior and Organization*, 1 (3): 223–47.
Teece, D.J. (1981) 'The market for know-how and the efficient international transfer of technology', *The Annals of the Academy of Political and Social Science*, Nov.: 81–96.
Teece, D.J. (1982) 'Towards an economic theory of the multiproduct firm', *Journal of Economic Behavior and Organization*, 3: 153–77.
Teece, D.J. (1986) 'Profiting from technological innovation', *Research Policy*, 15 (6): 285–305.
Teece, D.J. (1996) 'Firm organization, industrial structure, and technological innovation', *Journal of Economic Behavior and Organization*, 31: 193–224.
Teece, D.J. (1998a) 'Capturing value from knowledge assets: the new economy, markets for know-how, and intangible assets', *California Management Review*, 40 (3): 55–79.
Teece, D.J. (1998b) 'Design issues for innovative firms: bureaucracy, incentives and industrial structure', in A.D. Chandler, Jr, P. Hagstrom and O. Solvell (eds), *The Dynamic Firm: The Role of Technology, Strategy, Organization, and Regions*. Oxford: Oxford University Press.

Teece, D.J. (2000a) *Managing Intellectual Capital*. New York: Oxford University Press.

Teece, D.J. (2000b) 'Strategies for managing knowledge assets: the role of firm structure and industrial context', *Long Range Planning*, 33 (1): 35–54.

Teece, D.J., and Pisano, G. (1994) 'The dynamic capabilities of firms: an introduction', *Industrial and Corporate Change*, 3: 3.

Teece, D., Pisano, G., and Shuen, A. (1997) 'Dynamic capabilities and strategic management', *Strategic Management Journal*, 18 (7): 509–33.

Williamson, O.E. (1985) *Economic Institutions of Capitalism*. New York: The Free Press.

7 Knowledge and Organization

Robert M. Grant

Introduction

Business is concerned with creating value. The challenge for business strategy is ensuring that a significant proportion of this value creation is appropriated in profit. Business creates value in two ways: commerce and production. Commerce involves arbitraging commodities in space and time. Thus, commerce includes trade, whereby a commodity is transferred from a location where it is less valued to a location where it is more valued, and speculation, which involves transferring a commodity through time from a date where it is less valued to a date when it is more valued. Production involves the physical transformation of commodities from something that is less valued, such as crude oil, to something that is more valued, such as a plastic hip replacement.

This essay concerns the problem of production. If the fundamental problem that economics addresses is that of scarcity and the need for choice, the fundamental problem that management addresses is the problem of organization: How is society to organize the production of the many thousands of the millions of goods and services required by an advanced civilization?

The analysis of organization has fallen into two major areas. The first area deals with the roles of different institutions for governing economic activity. The second area deals with the design of organizations. Historically, the former has been dominated by transaction cost economics, the latter has been dominated by sociology.

Here I argue that the recent surge of interest and flood of published work in the area of knowledge management and the 'knowledge-based view of the firm' offers considerable insight into both these areas of organizational analysis and scope for the development of new theory. Such theory is sorely needed. Within the corporate sector, we are observing rapid evolution of the organizational forms – alternatives to traditional hierarchical structures are appearing, organizational boundaries are becoming increasingly permeable, and new patterns of interfirm collaboration are emerging. Similarly rapid development is not apparent in organizational theory. The result has been a widening gap between the organizational forms that we observe and our capacity for explaining and predicting such forms. As the 'Special research forum call for papers' article in a 1999 issue of *Academy of Management Journal* notes:

In a context characterized by globalization, hypercompetition and rapid innovation, there has been a rapid evolution of organizational forms, which has generally proceeded faster than researchers' capacity either to track developments or to theorize about them. Although descriptors such as ambidextrous, hybrid, knowledge-based, transient and virtual abound, there is only a hesitant and limited understanding of the nature of new and evolving organizational forms, of the conditions under which they may merge, and of their formative processes.

Some Basic Precepts

The problem of organization is a consequence of specialization. The most fundamental principle of knowledge management is that knowledge accumulation requires human beings to specialize. This is as true in production activities as it is in intellectual activities. As Adam Smith (1937) observed about pin manufacture, if pin makers worked independently, 'they certainly could not have made the two-hundred-and-fortieth, perhaps not the four-thousand-eight-hundredth part of what they are presently capable of performing in consequence of a proper division and combination of their different operations'. A pin is an exceptionally simple product, yet huge productivity gains can be achieved by breaking up the production into a dozen different operations, with workers specializing in each stage, they develop distinctive skills. The organizational challenge is to coordinate the efforts of the different specialists whose knowledge is required to produce a product. For pin making the organizational problem is fairly straightforward: the production process can be organized as a simple sequence. For more sophisticated products – an automobile, say, or a feature-length movie – production is likely to require the combined efforts of many thousands of different specialists. Integrating such a vast range of different knowledge bases represents an immense organizational task.

These problems of organizing fall into two categories: the problems of cooperation and those of coordination. Most organizational analysis has focused on the problem of cooperation. This is true both of the analysis of alternative institutions and of organizational structure. The analysis of the relative efficiency of alternative institutions has been dominated by transaction cost economics – in particular, the costs arising from the opportunistic behaviour by the parties to a contract. The analysis of organizational structure, too, has been dominated by issues of control, goal alignment and incentives. This is true of traditional organizational theory that has been primarily concerned with issues of hierarchical control; it is also evident in organizational economics that has focused on misalignment of goals, especially between principals and agents.

The potential of a knowledge-based perspective to further our analysis of organization is primarily in relation to the problem of coordination. Even if we abstract from problems of goal conflict between individuals and groups, the problem of organizing is far from trivial. At the site of an airplane crash, all rescuers may seek the same goal, yet organizing a hastily assembled group of emergency service teams, medical personnel, local residents and passers-by in order to locate and assist survivors most effectively is a difficult task. Concentration on issues of cooperation to the neglect of coordination may stem from a tendency to interpret problems of coordination as problems of cooperation. Camerer and Knez (1996: 92) comment that 'the inefficiencies that are often attributed to cooperation problems as modeled in the PD [prisoners' dilemma] game, are in fact problems of coordination'. Within organizational theory, the analysis of authority and control within hierarchical organizations has typically failed to distinguish the role of managers in synchronizing the efforts of different specialists from the problems of ensuring cooperation with organizational goals.

Focusing on knowledge as the critical resource in the production of all goods and services helps clarify the central issues of coordination. The challenge of coordination is to devise mechanisms by means of which the knowledge resources of many different individuals can be deployed in the production of a particular product. For such deployment mechanisms to be efficient requires that they preserve the efficiencies of specialization in knowledge acquisition. Hence, any system of production that requires each individual to learn what every other individual knows is inherently inefficient. In order to make progress in either of the two main areas of organizational analysis – the analysis of different institutions of economic organization and the design of organizational structure – it is important to recognize the mechanisms that ensure coordination between individuals and groups occurs. It is here that the analysis of knowledge integration can yield key insights. Let us proceed by exploring the implications of a knowledge-based approach – first, for the analysis of alternative economic institutions and, second, for the design of organizational structures.

The Institutions of Economic Organization

Critiques of transaction costs

A central feature of the capitalist economic system is the existence of 'islands of conscious paper in this ocean of unconscious cooperation like lumps of butter coagulating in a pail of buttermilk' (Robertson, 1930). The relative roles of firms and markets and the determination of the boundaries between them has been the primary goal of 'the new institutional economics', the primary tools of which have been transaction cost economics (TCE). However, despite the success of TCE in analysing the circumstances in which markets fail, the theory offers limited insight into organizing within the firm. Although TCE offers powerful tools for analysing the transaction costs of markets, it tells us little about the factors that determine the costs of administration within firms.

The focus of TCE on the transaction as the fundamental unit of economic activity reflects the preoccupation of neoclassical economics with exchange as the predominant economic activity. By contrast, the primary focus of management is on production aspects of economic activity where the fundamental organizational challenge is achieving coordination within team-based production. Certainly, coordination within team-based production can be interpreted in terms of exchanges. Thus, Milgrom and Roberts (1992) look at the problem of synchronizing the efforts of a rowing crew in terms of exchange transactions between the individual rowers.[1] However, as this example suggests, whether a system of production is organized by market contracts between independent contractors or the creation of a firm that has employment contracts with individuals, the issue of how individuals coordinate their individual efforts remains.

The idea that the production activities of firms cannot be comprehended using the logic of the market is central to several critiques of TCE. According to Ghoshal and Moran (1996), the essence of the firm is its capacity for dynamic efficiency and innovation by means of 'purposeful adaptation'. Once we move from the static world of TCE to a dynamic world in which knowledge is continually being created, disseminated and combined into new and improved products, the limitations of TCE are even more apparent. As Williamson (1985b: 143) acknowledges. 'the study of economic organization in a regime of rapid innovation poses much more difficult issues than those addressed here . . . New hybrid forms of organization may appear in response to such a condition.'

The contribution of the knowledge-based view

Appreciating the characteristics of knowledge and the organizational challenge of integrating the knowledge assets of multiple individuals can provide considerable insight into the organizing role of firms. Certainly TCE can demonstrate clearly and unambiguously the sources of market failure in knowledge transactions (Arrow, 1962, and Choi, Raman and Ussoltseva, 1998). However, simply showing the inefficiencies of market contracts in synchronizing the efforts of an interdependent team (a rowing crew, for example) does not provide much insight into the design of an administrative system capable of maximizing team performance.

Kogut and Zander present the firm not so much as an institution that economizes on the transaction costs of markets, but as a social institution capable of coordinating human behaviour in ways that is impossible for pure market contracts. They argue that 'organizations are social communities in which individual and social expertise is transferred into economically useful products and services by the application of a set of higher-order organizing principles. Firms exist because they provide a social community of voluntaristic action structured by organizing principles that are not reducible to individuals' (1992: 384). The precise nature of these 'social communities', the 'social expertise' that they possess and the 'organizing principles' under which they operate is not made entirely clear.

Part of the problem is that Kogut and Zander, together with Nonaka and other writers on knowledge and the firm, rest much of their analysis on the concept of 'organizational knowledge'. Once we view organizations as knowing entities, it is difficult to discern the mechanisms by which individuals link their separate skills and knowledge bases to create this collective knowledge.

An alternative approach that is consistent with Simon's (1991) dictum that 'all knowledge resides in human heads' is to dispense with the notion of organizational knowledge and regard all collective knowledge as the result of aggregating and integrating individuals' knowledge.

Elsewhere, I have suggested some of the mechanisms that firms (and other organizations) might use to integrate individuals' knowledge into the production of goods and services (see Grant, 1996). The key to efficiency in knowledge integration is to create mechanisms that avoid the costs of learning. After all, if each individual has to learn what every other individual knows, then the benefits of specialization are lost. The analysis of coordination within organizations was pioneered by James Thompson (1967), who classified the types of interdependency between individuals and units. Thompson viewed the modes of interdependence between individuals as exogenously determined by the technology of production and its component processes. Using a knowledge-based perspective, we may view coordination mechanisms as choices made by the firm about how to achieve the integration of the specialist knowledge of multiple individuals. Drawing on the existing literature, I have proposed four mechanisms for knowledge integration (Grant, 1996):

1 rules and directives;
2 sequencing of tasks;
3 organizational routines;
4 joint problem solving.

The case for the existence of the firm as a unit of economic organization rests on the superiority of the firm over markets in supporting these knowledge-integration mechanisms. To achieve coordination of these different mechanisms of integration requires authority (to permit direction), centralized decision making, co-location and common knowledge (to permit communication). All these connotations are provided more readily within the firm than in any other type of organization.

The response of TCE tends to revolve around the reinterpretation of these coordination arguments using the terminology and concepts of transaction costs. Foss (1996a: 473) argues that the knowledge-based theorists 'commit the fallacy of technological determinism when they argue that the need for shared codes, languages, etc. . . . necessitates firm organization in a way that can be seen in isolation from considerations of opportunism/moral hazard.' Although the gains from 'higher-order organizing principles' may be necessary to explain the existence of the firm, they are not sufficient. According to Foss (ibid.: 473), 'Agents (human resources) could simply meet under the same factory roof, own their own capital equipment or rent it to each other, and develop value-enhancing higher-order organizing principles among themselves (as a team).' Thus, Milgrom and Roberts (1992) quote the case of the nineteenth-century English traveller in China who, shocked at the ferocity with which the overseer whipped the oarsmen of a passenger ferry, was informed that the oarsmen hired the overseer in order to prevent slacking by individual oarsmen.

Logically, transaction costs would seem essential to any theory of economic organization. The problem, however, is that too narrow a focus on transaction costs obscures the view of what firms do. Certainly, we can analyse marriage as an institution that avoids the transaction costs of spot contracts for companionship, housework and sex, but such a focus provides little insight into the nature of marriage or the reasons for some of them being more successful than others. By concentrating only on contracting costs, TCE fails to recognize the benefits associated with the richness of a bilateral relationship involving two-way exclusive sourcing of multiple services and offers no basis for the design of coordination within a marriage.

Ultimately, transaction cost analysis of the firm runs up against the problem of defining the firm. Thus, the debate between Foss (1996b), Kogut and Zander (1992) and Connor and Prahalad over knowledge-based approaches to the theory of the firm ended up with the recognition that the critical differences between the participants stemmed from different conceptions of the nature of the firm. Similarly, with marriage, one might argue that contracting individuals could establish an agreement that provided long-term exclusive sourcing of multiple physical, social and economic services without entering a legal marriage agreement. However, to all intents and purposes, such an arrangement would be marriage and, indeed, might be recognized as such by the courts (common law marriage). Because of the ambiguity of defining the firm in precise terms, Demsetz (1995) has chosen to refer to 'firm-like institutions'.

Analysing strategic alliances

If the criterion for evaluating theory is its usefulness in explaining and predicting the real world, it would seem that there is a strong case for supplementing transaction cost explanations of the efficiency of alternative institutions of economic governance with knowledge-based explanations. Such augmentation of TCE might be valuable not just in providing greater insight into the nature of the firm; it might also assist the predictive power of TCE. Casual empiricism suggests that a growing number of institutional phenomena are at odds with the predictions of TCE. Vertical partnerships of the type that characterized Japanese manufacturing industries have become increasingly prominent in the West. Whether we are looking at Chrysler's relationships with its component suppliers, the IT outsourcing arrangements between EDS and its *Fortune 500* customers or the exclusive scrap sourcing arrangements of Nucor and other steel mini-mill companies, a critical feature is growing vertical de-integration, despite increasing problems of small numbers, transaction-specific investments and information asymmetries (see Holstrom and Roberts, 1998). Similar points can be made about the rise of horizontal collaboration, such as the recent wave of airline alliances.

A key feature of these types of arrangement is that they fall somewhere between pure market contracts and internalization within a single firm. In analysing such 'intermediate' or 'hybrid' forms, knowledge-based approaches to the relative efficiencies of alternative institutional forms can be especially illuminating. Given the pervasive failure of markets for knowledge (except in the specific circumstances where knowledge has been accorded property rights and, hence, becomes an alienable commodity), the predominant choice set facing managers is not between internalization and market contracting, but between internalization and collaboration via 'relational contracts'. In general, TCE has performed poorly in analysing these 'non-market, non-bureaucratic' organizational forms. TCE can predict the circumstances in which market failure is likely to promote internalization, but is less successful in predicting the circumstances in which alliances are likely to predominate over both market contracts and internal administration. The problem is especially great for approaches that view alliances as intermediate between market contracts and full internalization. These theories point to intermediate levels of opportunism, information impact, resource specificity and the like as favouring alliances. The problem here is that quantitative information on independent variables is required in order to generate qualitative predictions (see Williamson, 1991, for example).

Most knowledge-based approaches have concentrated on alliances as vehicles for organizational learning.[2] Such characterization tends to conflict with the observation that alliance activity among companies is associated more with narrowing than broadening firms' knowledge domains. An alternative knowledge-based analysis of alliances views them as concerned more with accessing than with acquiring partners' knowledge. Such knowledge accessing permits increased utilization of knowledge resources, an advantage that is enhanced when there are uncertainties concerning technological change and early mover advantages in product markets. Even if collaborative alliances are less efficient than full internalization in supporting the knowledge integration mechanisms that form the basis of productive activity, these inefficiencies may be offset by the advantages of knowledge utilization and speed of knowledge accessing (see Grant and Baden-Fuller, 1995, for further development of this analysis).

Implications of knowledge for analysing economic institutions

To summarize the argument so far, knowledge-based approaches to the firm shift the focus of our attention from the problems of cooperation caused by opportunism and other impediments to collaboration towards the more technical problems of achieving coordination in the face of specialized human capital. By focusing on mechanisms by means of which knowledge is integrated, we establish a rationale for the firm that rests on its capacity for supporting these knowledge integration mechanisms rather than on the avoidance of opportunistic behaviour in market contracting. Ultimately, this approach leads to a focus on integration mechanisms rather than conventional economic institutions as the key issues in economic organization. While, in general, firms have certain advantages as institutions for supporting knowledge-integration mechanisms, there is no reason for inter-organizational coordination (such as that seen in Toyota's supplier system or within the small-firm networks of northern Italy) not to achieve similar efficiencies of knowledge integration as those found within the firm. Indeed, firms themselves may encounter substantial problems of replicating and integrating knowledge (Szulanski, 1996, Hart and Moore, 1990, Williamson, 1993, and Jensen, 1998).

One advantage of a knowledge-based perspective is that it shifts the focus of our analysis away from institutions and towards coordination mechanisms. A central problem of the economic theory of the firm is disagreement over the definition of the firm. Is the firm defined in terms of hierarchical authority relationships, a nexus of contracts, ownership of assets with the residual rights of control that such ownership confers or as a device for reallocating risk? If economists cannot agree on what the firm is, there is little hope of consensus among economists, sociologists and lawyers. However, if the goal of organizational analysis is to predict the most efficient structures and systems for organizing production, a knowledge-based perspective suggests that the primary consideration is not so much the institution for governing transactions (markets or firms) as the mechanisms through which knowledge integration is achieved. Thus, if the main mechanisms for integrating the knowledge required for production are rules and organizational routines, we can identify the conditions needed to support these mechanisms. We can then go on to make general hypotheses about the efficiency of particular institutions in supporting these mechanisms. For example, firms tend to outperform both markets and alliances because they permit relationships of authority between individuals and groups and provide stability of relationships conducive to the developing organizational routines. However, such analysis can also permit finer-grained analysis of why, in certain circumstances, collaborative relationships between separate firms (such as the small-firm networks of Emilia-Romagna in Italy) can achieve superior knowledge integration than that achieved in single corporations. Thus, the MIT automobile study (Womack, Jones and Roos, 1990: 127) observed:

> The make-or-buy decision that occasioned so much debate in mass production firms struck Ohno and others at Toyota as largely irrelevant as they began to consider obtaining components for cars and trucks. The real question was how the assembler and the supplier could work together smoothly to reduce costs and improve quality, whatever formal, legal relationship they might have.

Focusing on coordination mechanisms rather than economic institutions may permit a broader view for the institutions that will enable productive activity to take place. Thus, Brown and Duguid (1991) identify 'communities of practice' within which knowledge is shared and problems solved. These loose-knit informal institutions created by means of common interests and shared experiences are likely to overlap formal organizational boundaries, yet may be much more effective in integrating and transferring knowledge than the more formalized processes of the firm. One interpretation of the remarkable history of Xerox's Palo Alto Research Center (PARC) is that the communities of practice and other informal networks between the PARC researchers and the Silicon Valley microelectronics community were much more effective in transferring and integrating knowledge than Xerox's internal mechanisms.

The Design of Organizational Structures: Introductory Comments

Despite the efforts of Simon, March, Thompson, Lawrence, Lorsch and others to establish principles of organization design, a quick look at any contemporary organization theory textbook reveals the state of disarray of the theory of organizational structure. Progress has been made in specific areas and in applying individual disciplines (sociology, economics, psychology, politics, ecology, systems theory and information science), yet there has been a failure to integrate these areas and disciplines into a single body of theory. Such a theory should be comprehensive, internally consistent and capable articulating functional relationships that link the dimensions of organizational structure to a set of explanatory variables. Lex Donaldson (1995) accuses US business academics of undermining the development of a cohesive body of organization theory by 'paradigm proliferation'. In the absence of a general theory of organizations, textbook expositions of the principles of organizational structure and design have retreated into the description and comparison of specific archetypes:

'mechanistic' and 'organic' forms, and the relative merits of functional, divisional and matrix-type organizations.

Despite the absence of a dominant, well-developed theoretical paradigm, the field is one of considerable intellectual activity. Among the theoretical developments that offer considerable potential are:

1 transaction cost theory and analysis of incentives and agency issues by the 'new institutional economics';
2 applications of game theory to internal aspects of organization (Milgrom and Roberts, 1990);
3 evolutionary, co-evolutionary and capability-based approaches to organizational development (Teece, Pisano and Shuen, 1997, and Foss and Knudsen, 1996);
4 applications of systems theory, computer and information sciences, as well as generative theory to problems of coordination (Kast and Rosenweig, 1972, Masuch, 1990, Crowston, 1997, Pentland and Rueter, 1994, and Malone et al., 1999);
5 theories of complexity and self-organization (Wheatley and Kellner-Rogers, 1996, Waldrop, 1992, and Stacey, 1995);
6 organizational analysis based on principles of product design (Mahoney and Sanchez, 1996, and Gulati and Eppinger, 1996).

It is too early to point to any emerging paradigm or consensus concerning the shape of organization theory, but the pace of development lends support to Michael Jensen's (1998) view that 'a revolution will take place over the next decade or two in our knowledge about organizations'. A feature of this impending revolution in organizational theory is likely to be the central role of knowledge. Common to several of the emerging theoretical streams that are reshaping our thinking about organizational structure and design are analysis of the firm as a knowledge-processing and knowledge-integrating system.

In the following sections I review three aspects of these knowledge-based approaches to organizational structure and design:

1 the distribution of decision making;
2 the design of hierarchical structures;
3 emerging organizational forms – team-based structures in particular.

The Distribution of Decision Making Within the Firm

Some of the most valuable contributions that knowledge-based approaches to management can offer to organization theory are the ability to reinterpret existing theory from a knowledge-based perspective and, in doing so, to permit the reconciliation and integration of different strands of theory. Consider, for example, the key issue of how decision-making authority is to be distributed within the firm. To do this, let us revisit two major movements in management thinking during the twentieth century – scientific management and total quality management (TQM).

Knowledge and scientific management

Fundamental to the emergence of the modern corporation has been the development of management as a specialized body of knowledge. The earliest manifestation of this was the 'scientific management' movement during the early twentieth century. It was founded on the idea of a division of labour between workers and managers – namely, workers do the work while managers, as experts in management, specialize in decision making. However, as with all production tasks, specialization requires integration, so the managers' knowledge of organization must be brought together with the workers' skills and their familiarity with workplace conditions. As managers supposedly possess superior intelligence and specialized knowledge of the scientific principles of management, then managers must be given decision-making rights over workers. However, a critical assumption of the approach is that managers have access to all the knowledge held by the workers. Thus, Fredrick Taylor's (1987) description of the application of scientific management to shovelling coal and iron ore at Bethlehem Steel is based on the assumption that the manager has full knowledge of the skills of shovelling and of the range of situations encountered by shovellers.

This implicit assumption that managers have access to all of the knowledge of their subordinates is a striking weakness, not just of scientific management but of hierarchical models of decision making more generally. In a hierarchy, decision making concerning routine matters is delegated downwards by rules and procedures. Decision rights about complicated and strategic issues tend to be retained in the upper organizational levels. Yet, if these upper-level decision-makers do not have access to the knowledge available at lower levels of the organization, then the efficiency of the decision making is constrained not only by 'bounded rationality', but also by bounded access to relevant knowledge.

Knowledge and total quality management (TQM)

It is interesting that TQM, like scientific management, is based on the application of the principles of scientific method to decision making and the organization of work. TQM applies cause-and-effect decision trees to the diagnosis of problems and statistical analysis to the scrutinizing of defects. Yet, despite these commonalities, TQM gives rise to quite different management methods and allocations of decision rights from those of scientific management.

The critical difference between scientific management and TQM lies in their assumptions about the distribution and characteristics of knowledge. While scientific management assumed that managers are capable of accessing all the knowledge possessed by workers, TQM recognizes that knowledge is not easily transferable. Given that good decisions require the application of the knowledge relevant to those decisions, TQM favours the transfer of decision making concerning each employee's production tasks to the employees who perform the tasks. Hence, in addressing Taylor's 'shovelling problem', TQM results in a fundamentally different allocation of decision making from that recommended by Taylor. Although TQM focuses on quality as the primary performance variable, the same principles can also be applied to efficiency. If know-how about shovelling coal and iron ore accrue to those who undertake the work, and this know-how is not easily transferred to a manager or foreman, then it is the shovellers who are best able to improve productivity by improving job design and working techniques. The second assumption about knowledge implicit in TQM is that all human beings are intelligent and capable of learning. Hence, it is easier to instruct the worker in those 'principles of management' necessary for the worker to make optimal decisions concerning their work than it is to transfer the worker's knowledge to a manager. Thus, a key feature of TQM is training workers in the statistical process control and 'scientific' approaches to the analysis of problems (Wruck and Jensen, 1994).

Linking decision-making authority to knowledge characteristics

The above examples concerning scientific management and TQM point to the fact that our assumptions about the distribution of general intelligence between individuals and the characteristics of knowledge have fundamental implications for the distribution of decision making within the firm. In order to generalize our discussion, let us consider the relationship between characteristics of different types of knowledge and the optimal distribution of decision making. We begin with the premise that the quality of a decision depends on the extent to which decision making is co-located with the knowledge required for informing that decision. Co-location can be achieved in two ways: decision making can be devolved to where the knowledge resides or knowledge can be transferred to the seat of decision making authority.

The critical issue here is the mobility of knowledge, which is a function of its codifiability. Where knowledge is fully codifiable (such as information on widget inventories throughout the firm), then not only can the knowledge be transferred at low cost, but it can also be aggregated within a single location. Given economies of scale in decision making, it is desirable to decentralize such decisions. Hence, in most companies, treasury functions – including cash management and foreign-exchange hedging – are centralized in a single corporate treasury. Conversely, highly tacit knowledge is not capable of codification and is extremely difficult to transfer and aggregate. Hence, where the relevant knowledge is tacit, then decision-making power must be distributed to where the tacit knowledge is located. Thus, the productivity of lathe operators and other machinists depends critically on their tacit skills. As their sensitivity to, and awareness of, their machines cannot easily be codified, this implies that decisions about maintenance and settings should be delegated to the operatives.

Recent trends towards 'empowerment' have been justified primarily in terms of motivation and philosophies of individualism and self-determination. Our knowledge-based approach provides a purely technical basis for empowerment decisions: where knowledge is tacit or is not readily codifiable for other reasons, then decision-making quality is enhanced where authority to make decisions is delegated to those with the relevant knowledge. At the same time, it points to situations where decisions should be decentralized and situations where centralization is more efficient.

Although the dominant trend of the 1990s was towards decentralization, developments in IT and artificial intelligence promise to increase the potential for knowledge to be codified. Such a development may encourage increased centralization of decision making. Such centralization trends are apparent within fast food chains where the IT has encouraged a shift in decision making about menus, pricing and production scheduling from individual restaurant managers and franchisees to the corporate and regional headquarters.

However, as Jensen (1998) points out, a trade-off exists between benefits of co-location of decision making and knowledge and the costs of agency. As decision making devolves to those with the relevant know-how, so the costs of agency arising from the inconsistent objectives of different organizational members tend to increase. Hence, there is an optimal degree of decentralization where, at the margin, the cost reductions from distributing decision rights to individual employees is equal to the rising agency costs associated with moving decision rights further from the CEO's office.

Designing Hierarchical Structures

Hierarchy as a feature of complicated systems

I have noted that productive activity has two organizational requirements: that the activities of individuals and groups are coordinated to ensure that efforts of specialists are efficiently integrated and that individuals and groups act in concert with the goals of the organization. Hierarchy offers a way to satisfy both requirements. However, the analysis of hierarchy has been bedevilled by a failure to distinguish these two aspects of organization. Since Weber, Fayol, and the 'classical' organizational theorists, the analysis of hierarchy has focused on the organization as a hierarchy in which the conception of the organization is as a pyramid of individuals or 'offices' arranged in vertical relationships of authority. Such authority relationships have inevitably focused on cooperation rather than coordination because organizational theory has viewed organizations generically. Especially in economic organizations, the quest for efficiency of production is promoted by specialization and the division of labour, which are at the heart of the coordination problem.

Progress in the analysis of organizational structure requires separating the issues of coordination and goals alignment. While principal agent theory addresses the issues of aligning different goals, information science and general systems theory have explored the pure coordination aspects of organizing. Hierarchy is as fundamental to system-based approaches to the analysis of organizations as it is to the theory of bureaucracy. However, its rationale is quite different. Hierarchy is a feature of all complicated systems to the extent that all such systems (whether biological, mechanical or social) can be decomposed into subsystems. The primary rationale for hierarchy in these systems is that it promotes adaptation (Simon, 1962).

This approach is useful in deriving principles for grouping activities and people within complicated organizations and designing the relationships among the different groups. If hierarchy within a classical organization theory is defined in terms of delegation of authority, hierarchy within a systems perspective is defined by modularity. Activities and processes where coordination needs are most intense are organized into modules. This idea of hierarchies organized around intensity of interaction is fundamental to Simon's concept of the 'nearly decomposable' systems and Williamson's 'vertical decomposition principle' (Simon, 1982, and Williamson, 1985). The analysis of coordination and the articulation of the principles of organizing on the basis of intensity of coordination needs was developed by Thompson (1967). Thompson classifies interactions from the loosest ('pooled' interdependence) via intermediate ('sequential' interdependence) to the most intense ('reciprocal' interdependence). He argues for the design of hierarchies based, first, on identifying those tasks and activities characterized by reciprocal interdependence, then upon forming hierarchies around the successive levels of interdependence. The analysis of interdependence has been furthered by Tom Malone (1999) and his colleagues at the MIT Center for Coordination Science. Their analysis of organizational processes involves the disaggregation of processes into their individual parts and classification of dependencies on the basis of how resources are related to multiple activities.

The performance advantages of the hierarchical structure in terms of pure coordination arise from its potential for adaptability. The critical issue here is the 'loose coupling' of modules such that individual modules can innovate and adapt while not having to coordinate continually with all other modules. The concept of loose coupling between organizational units is closely associated with Weick (1976), who argued that departments that are able to vary independently promote sensitivity to environmental variation, opportunistic adaptation to local circumstances, simultaneous adaptation to conflicting demands, and the maintenance of overall organizational stability.

Modularity in product design and development

The best-developed applications of the principles of hierarchical design based on modularity and loose coupling are in relation to new product development. The problems presented by the need for fast, low-cost development of highly complicated products, such as automobiles, aircraft and computer software, has spawned a number of empirical and theoretical studies of the organization of product development. The basic idea is that product design is based on modules organized as subsystems and components, with standardized interfaces between them, and that the design process is organized in modular form to parallel the modular design of the product (Mahoney and Sanchez, 1996, and Bayliss and Clark, 1997).

Thus, in relation to computer software, Cusumano (1997) shows how Microsoft's leadership in operating system and applications software has been supported by a product development system based on modular design of the product and modular organization of the product development effort around small teams comprising a program manager, three to eight developers and a parallel feature-testing team, also with three to eight members. The entire product development team for a complicated product such as the first version of Windows NT or Windows 95 comprised some 450 people. Microsoft's Internet Explorer browser required a team of about 300, with several hundred more working on add-on features, such as Internet mail (Cusumano and Yoffie, 1998). The essential requirement for such modularization is the establishment of interfaces that permit the modules to work together. Key features of Microsoft's 'synch and stabilize' approach are imposition of rules that permit flexibility and innovation within teams but ensure coordination of the project as a whole. Critical aspects of interface management include common development languages, clearly defined goals for each module in terms of features and functions, daily and weekly 'builds' that occur at fixed times (either 2p.m. or 5p.m.) when the software is compiled and tested, and periodic stabilizations when the features of each component are fixed and then provide a common basis from which each modular team can move on to the next set of design milestones.

Such a modular approach permits flexibility in terms of innovation and adjustment that are apparent in the tortuous evolution of Netscape's

Navigator browser. Initially, the tightly coupled structure of Netscape's initial version of Navigator and the frequency of 'spaghetti code' handicapped Netscape's ability to upgrade and extend the product. The subsequent rewriting of Navigator around a modular architecture delayed the upgrading of the product and allowed Microsoft to gain leadership in the market for browsers (Cusumano, 1997).

Knowledge integration as the basis of modular design

Modular organizational designs may be viewed as efficient responses to the costs of knowledge integration. If the greater part of the knowledge used by firms is tacit, then it can be transferred only at high cost. Modularity is a means of achieving integration across a broad range of different knowledge bases while minimizing the costs of knowledge transfer. The essential efficiency benefit of modular structures is that each unit is capable of integrating knowledge among the individuals within the unit, while avoiding the need to continuously transfer it to other units. The critical issues for organizational design are then the organization of activities into modules and the definition of interfaces between the modules. The establishment of interfaces is critical as they provide the basis for knowledge integration between modules.

In the case of products, interface design relates to the physical specification of how one component fits with another. Thus, standardizing the way a lightbulb fits into a light socket permits lightbulb makers and lamp manufacturers to work independently on design and innovation. Indeed, the success of such an interface in economizing on knowledge transfer between the two is indicated by the fact that lightbulb manufacturers and lamp manufacturers are typically separate firms.

The work on modularity in organizational design has concentrated on the organization of new product development. Here the basic principle is that product development is organized around the same modular structure of the product: 'Microsoft divides projects in a way that mirrors the structure of its products. This helps teams create products with logical, efficient designs and results in project organizations with logical, efficient groupings of people' (Cusumano, 1998). The challenge for the theory of organizational structure is to extend the principles of modularity to the design of organizations in general. The principles on which modules are to be defined have been articulated fairly clearly. The essential principle is intensity of interdependence, which, from a knowledge-based perspective, means the integration of tacit knowledge in team-based tasks requiring organizational routines and/or joint problem solving.

Less progress has been made on the design of common interfaces between modular organizational units. Mahoney and Sanchez (1996) argue that 'embedding coordination in fully specified and standardized component interfaces can reduce the need for much overt exercise of managerial authority across the interfaces of organizational units developing components, thereby reducing the intensity and complexity of a firm's managerial task.' However, what are these 'standardized interfaces' between organizational units? For the most part, they are the standardized control systems by means of which overall coordination is achieved. In the case of a classical conglomerate, such as the former Anglo-American company Hanson, the main interface linking the modules was Hanson's financial management system. Because each business was deemed to be technologically and strategically independent of every other, the operation of each division as an independent entity with very little inter-divisional knowledge integration was highly feasible. Where higher levels of knowledge integration are required between modules, then interfaces need to be more complicated and less standardized. Typically, the more closely related are the businesses of a corporation then the greater the requirements for knowledge integration and the more complicated the integration mechanisms. Thus, the typical multibusiness corporation establishes formal integration via a financial control system, a strategic planning system and a human resource planning and appraisal system. In addition, a common corporate culture provides the basis for an informal system of knowledge integration. The tendency for knowledge integration requirements to be a positive function of business relatedness is evident in the fact that multibusiness corporations with closely related businesses tend to have larger corporate staffs than conglomerates.

Making Sense of New Organizational Structures

Several management scholars have commented on the inability of existing organizational theory to explain, let alone predict, the evolution of organizational forms in the business sector (see, for example, Daft and Lewin, 1993). It seems likely that the emerging knowledge-based view of the firm may permit greater understanding of emerging organizational structures, even if an integrated, comprehensive theory of organizational structure is still a distant hope. I will comment on two features of emerging organizational forms – team-based structures and non-unitary organizational structures.

Team-based structures

A growing trend in the corporate sector is for established manufacturing and service companies to emulate the team-based structure of project-based organizations, such as consulting, engineering and construction firms. Organization around teams is implied by two factors. First, the principles of modularity that were discussed above and, second, the idea that each module consists of a team of individuals with different types of specialized knowledge using multiple mechanisms to integrate their knowledge. These mechanisms cannot be managed in any detailed sense because no one outside the team has access either to the knowledge within the team or the principles that govern the team's integration mechanisms. Thus, while team-based organization reflects the need for closely inter-dependent specialists to integrate their know-how by means of routines and joint problem solving, the move towards making teams self-governing is a recognition that the knowledge necessary for designing internal coordination processes is also located within the team. The primary role of management, therefore, is not so much organizational design within teams as designing the integration across teams.[3]

A key feature of team-based organizations is a much lower dependence on authority relationships than in more traditional structures. The hier-archical structure of complicated systems, especially as applied to the firm as an institution for knowledge integration, points to desirability of a hierarchy of such integration within the firm, but does not necessarily imply the creation of an administrative hierarchy with authority relation-ships between organizational levels. In integrating knowledge, the firm may be viewed as integrating, at the first level, specific tasks. These are then integrated into closely linked processes. Processes are often grouped into broad functional areas, such as production operations, finance and marketing and sales. At the highest level of integration are cross-functional activities that integrate knowledge across multiple functions, including new product development as well as customer service and support.

The problem for the firm is that such knowledge integration cannot be achieved by an administrative hierarchy because knowledge that is integrated at one level cannot simply be transferred to a higher level to achieve broader-scale integration. For example, new product development requires the integration of knowledge concerning technology, finance, manufacturing, marketing, purchasing and several other functional areas. However, this does not imply that new product development in the firm should be undertaken by a committee comprising the vice-presidents or directors of technology, finance, marketing, manufacturing and purchas-ing. The knowledge possessed by those functional heads is the knowledge required to manage their individual functions; they are not the embodi-ment of the full range of knowledge within their particular functions. Achieving broad-scale knowledge integration requires either modular design with standardized interfaces or team-based integration where upper-level integration is still achieved by team-based groupings (Grant, 1996a).

Thus, some of the most important developments in knowledge manage-ment among US automobile companies have involved disbanding product development via committees of functional-level heads, with multifunc-tional product teams comprising lower-level personnel within each function, but, typically, led by a 'heavyweight' product manager (Clark and Fujimoto, 1991).

Non-unitary structures

The two requirements of organization referred to earlier – cooperation and coordination – can result in contradictory principles of organizational design. Effective cooperation typically requires a 'unitary chain of command'. Coordination, in contrast, is likely to require organizing around multiple groupings. Non-unitary approaches to organizing hierarchical structures have been common in business for many decades. Matrix structures were widely diffused during the 1960s and 1970s and, by the early 1980s, most large, multinational corporations were organized around three-dimensional matrices that permitted coordination within businesses, functions and geographical areas. Although matrix structures offered one solution to the need for multidimensional coordination, they failed to address some of the more fundamental needs for versatile coordination within companies. These aspects of coordination relate to the fact that different types of performance require different types of coordination, which, in turn, require different types of structure. How can these different types of structure be accommodated within a single organization?

The literature relating to non-unitary coordination structures has yielded a number of approaches and suggested several structural forms. Let me provide three examples.

1   It has long been recognized that organizations do not readily change themselves. Hence, mechanisms to promote organizational change need to exist outside the formal operating structure of organizations. From an organizational development perspective, Bushe and Shani (1991) have explored the role of parallel learning structures – structures that exist outside of the formal hierarchy and the role of which are to promote learning and innovation with a view to changing the formal structure in order to improve its effectiveness. While such parallel learning structures have traditionally been associated with promoting organizational change by means of programmes of cultural and behavioural change, some parallel structures have offered more direct assaults on formal structures. For example, General Electric's Jack Welch's (1991) 'work-out' programme created a parallel structure based around off-site, 'town hall' meetings in which the rules and conventions of the formal structure were suspended and groups of employees were empowered to make recommendations for changing processes and practices. Managers were required to accept or reject these recommendations on the spot.

2   Mike Tushman and Charles O'Reilly III (1996) address the dilemma that companies face in meeting the requirements of both evolutionary and revolutionary change. Their concept of the 'ambidextrous organization' is one in which both 'loose' and 'tight' dimensions of culture coexist. Looseness permits autonomy, creativity and pursuit of

the unknown. Tightness supports a focus on efficiency and continuous improvement. The types of structures that support organizational ambidexterity are not articulated in any detail. Tushman and O'Reilly acknowledge the need to combine top-down and bottom-up decision making and adopt structures that reconcile the responsiveness of small units with the scale and scope of the large organization. However, they say little about the kinds of structures that can achieve these goals. Drawing on the tools of chaos and complexity theory, Kauffman (1995) argues that the systems that can co-evolve to the point of chaos by combining evolutionary refinement with occasional large co-evolutionary cascades out-compete systems that adapt incrementally (see also Brown and Eisenhardt, 1998).

3   The challenge of maintaining (and perfecting) the ongoing operations of the organization while simultaneously responding to new challenges is also addressed by Nonaka and Takeuchi (1995). Their concept of a 'hypertext organization' is one that can flexibly assemble project teams that mesh the skills and know-how drawn from the 'business system' layer of the organization. Thus, the Sharp Corporation has a formal structure that is organized around business groups and specialist functions, but, for innovative priorities, has an 'urgent project system' in which employees from particular businesses and functions are assigned to project teams for a limited period of time. The electronic organizer team set up on 1 June 1985, with a goal of bringing to market the world's first electronic organizer in October 1986, was one example of this system. The team comprised five engineers from the calculator division, one from integrated circuits and one from liquid crystal displays.

These approaches to the creation of organizations that can simultaneously coordinate different types of activity reveal a common theme: James March's (1991) distinction between knowledge exploitation and knowledge exploration. Knowledge exploitation is, typically, the primary task of the formal structure. It usually requires high levels of specialization, the maintenance of standardized routines and an emphasis on efficiency and reliability. Exploration, on the other hand, not only requires less specialization, an emphasis on problem solving rather than routine and low levels of formality, but also coordination and knowledge sharing among different individuals and across different functions and departments than is required for exploitation.

Reconciling these dual processes probably means going beyond the creation of jointly 'loose–tight' organizations to the creation of distinct structures for undertaking these two categories of knowledge activities. Although the concepts of knowledge management and the terms 'ambidextrous' and 'hypertext' organizations are relatively new, their manifestations are not. A number of companies have dichotomized their operational ('exploitation') and creative ('exploration') activities. In addition to the examples of Sharp and Kao that Nonaka and Takeuchi mention, the 3M Corporation has long maintained a dual system of organization. 3M's formal structure exists to operate existing products and businesses, while an informal system of 'bootlegging' allows experimentation and the pursuit of new product ideas by individuals and teams.

Recent evidence on emerging organizational structures suggests that companies must go beyond a simple dichotomization of their structures around exploration and exploitation activities. Different dimensions of performance, even within the same productive activity, are likely to require different organizational arrangements. In the production of widgets, achieving efficiency in production is likely to require one form of knowledge integration, based heavily on specialization and sequencing, achieving quality improvement is likely to require joint problem solving across the process, and the development of new types of widget is likely to require an integrated team of specialists from different technical and functional areas.

Achieving versatility and the broadening of organizational repertoires is resulting in organizations developing parallel structures in multiple directions. In addition to their formal organization for running continuing operations, firms are increasingly relying on committees to confirm major strategic decisions, cross-functional teams for product development and taskforces for promoting organizational change. At the same time, at the informal level, a number of voluntaristic organizational groups pursue other performance goals. These include communities of practice in which individuals share experience and expertise (Brown and Duguid, 1991).

Conclusion

The emerging knowledge-based view of the firm offers a set of powerful ideas for strategy, innovation and organizational processes within the firm. The purpose of this chapter has been to show that thinking about knowledge and its application to production offers considerable scope for advancing both the role of alternative economic institutions and the design of company structures. In both cases, exploration of the characteristics of knowledge and the ways in which it is applied to the production of goods and services focuses attention on the problem of coordination in productive activity. As competition intensifies and the pace of change accelerates across most business sectors, the coordination requirements for firms becomes increasingly complicated. Firms increasingly need to simultaneously pursue multiple performance goals – cost, efficiency, quality, innovation and flexibility. Explicit consideration of the knowledge management requirements of these complicated coordination patterns can offer us insight into the choice and design of organizational structures.

Notes

1 H. Demsetz makes a similar point in *The Economics of the Business Firm: Seven Critical Commentaries* (1995), Cambridge: Cambridge University Press, pp. 1–14. Demsetz distinguishes 'transaction' and 'specialization' theories of the firm, pointing out that transaction costs are the costs of exchange while production costs are the costs of converting inputs into outputs.

2 See, for example, M.A. Lyles (1998), 'Learning among joint-venture sophisticated firms', *Management International Review* 28 (Special): pp. 85–98; C. Ciborra (1991), 'Alliances as learning experiments: cooperation, competition and change in high-tech industries', in L.K. Mytelka (ed.), *Strategic Partnerships and the World Economy*, London: Pinter, pp. 51–77; A. Mody (1993), 'Learning through alliances', *Journal of Economic Behavior and Organization*, 20: pp. 151–70; B.L. Simonin (1997), 'The importance of collaborative know-how: an empirical test of the learning organization', *Academy of Management Journal*, 40: pp. 1150–74. The outcome may be a 'competition for learning' where each alliance member seeks to learn at a faster rate than its partner in order to achieve a positive balance of trade in knowledge. See G. Hamel (1991), 'Competition for competence and inter-partner learning within international strategic alliances', *Strategic Management Journal*, 12 (Summer Special): pp. 83–103. On introducing instability to the relationship, see A.C. Inkpen and P.W. Beamish (1997), 'Knowledge, bargaining power, and the instability of international joint ventures', *Academy of Management Review*, 22: pp. 177–202.

3 Knowledge integration within teams is achieved primarily by organizational routines. The analysis of routines as ordered sequences of actions has been pioneered by Brian Pentland and Henry Rueter (1994), 'Organizational routines as grammars of action', *Administrative Science Quarterly*, 39: pp. 484–510.

References

Arrow, K. (1962) 'Economic welfare and the allocation of resources for invention', in National Bureau of Economic Research, *The Rate and Direction of Inventive Activity*. Princeton, NJ: Princeton University Press. pp. 609–25.

Bayliss, C.Y., and Clark, K.B. (1997) 'Managing in an age of modularity', *Harvard Business Review*, Sept.–Oct.: 68–77.

Brown, J.S. and Duguid, P. (1991) 'Organizational learning and communities-of-practice: toward a unified view of working, learning and innovation', *Organization Science*, 2: 40–57.

Brown, S.L. and Eisenhardt, K.M. (1998) *Competing on the Edge: Strategy as Structured Chaos*. Boston, MA: Harvard Business School Press.

Bushe, G.R. and Shani, A.B. (1991) *Parallel Learning Structures: Increasing Innovation in Bureaucracies*. Reading, MA: Addison-Wesley.

Camerer, C. and Knez, M. (1996) 'Coordination, organizational boundaries and fads in business practices', *Industrial and Corporate Change*, 5 (1): 89–112.

Choi, C.J., Raman, M., and Ussoltseva, O. (1998) 'Knowledge-based exchange: inalienability and reciprocity', discussion paper, City University Business School, London, August.

Clark, K.B. and Fujimoto, T. (1991) *Product Development Performance*. Boston, MA: Harvard Business School Press.

Crowston, K. (1997) 'A coordination theory approach to process design', *Organization Science*, 8: 157–75.

Cusumano, M.A. (1997) 'How Microsoft makes large teams work like small teams', *Sloan Management Review*, Fall: 9–20.

Cusumano, M.A. and Yoffie, D.B. (1998) *Competing on Internet Time: Lessons from Netscape and Its Battle with Microsoft*. New York: The Free Press.

Daft, R.L., and Lewin, A.Y. (1993) 'Where are the theories for the "new organizational forms"? An editorial essay', *Organization Science*, 4: i–vi.

Demsetz, H. (1995) *The Economics of the Business Firm: Seven Critical Commentaries*. Cambridge: Cambridge University Press.

Donaldson, Lex (1995) *American Anti-management Theories of Organization: A Critique of Paradigm Proliferation*. Cambridge: Cambridge University Press.

Foss, N.J. (1996a) 'Knowledge-based approaches to the theory of the firm: some critical comments', *Organization Science*, 7 (Sept.–Oct.) (5): 473.

Foss, N.J. (1996b) 'More critical comments on knowledge-based theories of the firm', *Organization Science*, 7 (Sept.–Oct.) (5): 519–23.

Foss, N.J., and Knudsen, C. (eds) (1996) *Towards a Competence Theory of the Firm*. London: Routledge.

'General Electric: Jack Welch's Second Wave (A)' (1991) HBS Case 9–391–248, Boston, MA: Harvard Business School.

Ghoshal, S. and Moran, P. (1996) 'Bad for practice: a critique of transaction cost theory', *Academy of Management Review*, 21: 13–47.

Grant, R.M. (1996a) 'Prospering in dynamically competitive environments: organizational capability as knowledge integration', *Organization Science*, 7: 375–87.

Grant, R.M. (1996b) 'Toward a knowledge-based theory of the firm', *Strategic Management Journal*, 17: 109–22; 113–17.

Grant, Robert M. and Baden-Fuller, Charles (1995) 'A knowledge-based theory of inter-firm collaboration', *Academy of Management Best Papers Proceedings 1995*, pp. 17–21.

Gulati, R.K. and Eppinger, S.D. (1996) 'The coupling of product architecture and organizational structure decisions', discussion paper 3906, Sloan School of Management, MIT.

Hart, O. and Moore, J. (1990) 'Property rights and the nature of the firm', *Journal of Political Economy*, 98: 1119–58

Holmstrom, B. and Roberts, J. (1998) 'The boundaries of the firm revisited', *Journal of Economic Perspectives*, 12 (4): 73–94.

Jensen, M.C. (1998) *Foundations of Organizational Strategy*. Cambridge, MA: Harvard University Press.

Jensen, M.C., and Meckling, W.H. (1998) 'Specific and general knowledge and organizational structure', in M.C. Jensen (ed.), *Foundations of Organizational Strategy*. Cambridge, MA: Harvard University Press. pp. 103–25.

Jensen, Michael (1998) *Foundations of Organizational Strategy*. Cambridge, MA: Harvard University Press. p. 133.

Kast, F.E., and Rosenzweig, J.E. (1972) 'General systems theory: applications for organization and management', *Academy of Management Journal*, 15: 447–65.

Kauffman, S.A. (1995) *At Home in the Universe: The Search for Laws of Self-Organization and Complexity*. New York: Oxford University Press.

Kogut, B. and Zander, U. (1992) 'Knowledge of the firm, combinative capabilities, and the replication of technology', *Organization Science*, 3: 384.

Mahoney, T. and Sanchez, R. (1996) 'Modularity, flexibility and knowledge management in product and organization design', *Strategic Management Journal*, 17 (Winter Special): 63–76.

Malone T.W., Crowston, K. and Pentland, B. et al. (1999) 'Tools for inventing organizations: toward a handbook of organizational processes', *Management Science*, 56: 621–36.

March, J.G. (1991) 'Exploration and exploitation in organizational learning', *Organization Science*, 2: 71–87.

Masuch, M. (1990) *Organization, Management and Expert Systems*. Berlin: de Gruyter.

Milgrom, P. and Roberts, J. (1990) 'Bargaining costs, influence costs, and the organization of economic activity', in J. Alt and K. Shepsle, *Perspectives on Positive Political Economy*. Cambridge: Cambridge University Press.

Milgrom, P. and Roberts, J. (1992) *Economics, Organization and Management*. Englewood Cliffs, NJ: Prentice Hall. p. 91.

Nonaka, I. and Takeuchi, H. (1995) *The Knowledge-Creating Company*. New York: Oxford University Press.

Pentland, B., and Rueter, H. (1994) 'Organizational routines as grammars of action', *Administrative Science Quarterly*, 39: 484–500.

Robertson, D.H. (1930) *Control of Industry*. London: Nisbet. p. 85.

Simon, H.A. (1962) 'The architecture of complexity', *Proceedings of the American Philosophical Society*, 106: pp. 467–82.

Simon, H.A. (1982) *Sciences of the Artificial*, 2nd edn. Cambridge, MA: MIT Press.

Simon, H.A. (1991) 'Bounded rationality and organizational learning', *Organization Science*, 2: 125–34.

Smith, Adam (1937) *An Inquiry into the Nature and Consequences of the Wealth of Nations*. New York: Modern Library Edition. chapter 1.

'Special research forum call for papers: new and evolving organizational forms' (1999) *Academy of Management Journal*, 42: 116.

Stacey, R.D. (1995) 'The science of complexity: an alternative perspective for strategic change', *Strategic Management Journal*, 16: 477–95.

Szulanski, G. (1996) 'Exploring internal stickiness: impediments to the transfer of best practices within the firm', *Strategic Management Journal*, 17 (Winter Special): 27–44.

Taylor, Frederick W. (1987) 'The principles of scientific management', *Bulletin of the Taylor Society*, December 1916, reprinted in J.M. Shafritz and J.S. Ott (1987), *Classics of Organization Theory*. Chicago: Dorsey Press. pp. 66–81.

Teece, D.J., Pisano, G., and Shuen, A. (1997) 'Dynamic capabilities and strategic management', *Strategic Management Journal*, 18: 509–33.

Thompson, J.D. (1967) *Organizations in Action*. New York: McGraw-Hill.

Tushman, M.L. and O'Reilly III, C.A. (1996) 'The ambidextrous organization: managing evolutionary and revolutionary change', *California Management Review*, 38 (4): 8–30.

Waldrop, M.M. (1992) *Complexity: The Emerging Science at the Edge of Order and Chaos*. New York: Simon & Schuster.

Weick, K.E. (1976) 'Educational organizations as loosely-coupled systems', *Administrative Science Quarterly*, 21: 1–19.

Wheatley, M.J. and Kellner-Rogers, M. (1996) 'Self-organization: the irresistible future of organizing', *Strategy and Leadership*, 24 (4): 18–24.

Williamson, O.E. (1985a) *Markets and Hierarchies*. New York: Free Press.

Williamson, O.E. (1985b) *The Economic Institutions of Capitalism*. New York: Free Press. p. 143.

Williamson, O.E. (1991) 'Comparative economic organization: the analysis of discrete structural alternatives', *Administrative Science Quarterly*, 36: 269–96.

Williamson, O.E. (1993) 'Transaction cost economics and organization theory', *Industrial and Corporate Change*, 2: 107–56.

Womack, J., Jones, D., and Roos, D. (1990) *The Machine That Changed the World*. New York: Rawson Associates.

Wruck, K.H., and Jensen, M.C. (1994) 'Science, specific knowledge, and Total Quality Management', *Journal of Accounting and Economics*, 18: 247–87.

8 How Should Knowledge be Owned?

Charles Leadbeater

Ownership issues

Each night the computers at the Sanger Research Centre near Cambridge come to life and pour long strings of letters on to the Internet. The strings of letters are unreadable to anyone but an expert, yet this code spells out the story of human heredity encoded in our DNA.

Researchers at the Sanger Centre are part of an international collaborative effort to read the human 'genome' – the, roughly, 100,000 genes that make up a human being. The book of man, as it has been called, should be complete by the year 2005, at a cost of $3 billion, mainly provided by governments and public bodies. This genetic manual could make it possible to treat a much wider range of diseases, including, perhaps, forms of cancer, heart disease and neurological disorders.

The Human Genome Project is testimony to the power of collective human intelligence to improve our well-being. Of course, the human genome may also become a cash dispenser for biotechnology and pharmaceutical companies keen to develop new medical treatments. In May 1998, a US scientist, Craig Venter, broke ranks with the project by announcing a deal with Perkin-Elmer, a US company that makes gene-sequencing machines, to compile a private account of the human genome. Perkin-Elmer's share price leapt. Other commercial exploiters of this stock of public knowledge are not far behind (Wilkie, 1998).

Who should own the human genome and the rights, if any, to exploit it for commercial purposes? If the rights were vested in governments, many people would be alarmed by the potential threats to civil liberties. A dictator or a crazed bureaucrat armed with the human genome could, in theory, wield enormous power. More prosaically, the public sector almost certainly would be less efficient than the private sector in turning this stock of know-how into widely disseminated commercial products. Yet, the idea that private companies should be given ownership over our genes is also disturbing. Human genes are like recipes – they issue instructions to cells to grow hair, digest food or fight off bacteria. These recipes were developed during millions of years of evolution – a shared human heritage of trial, error and adaptation. Unravelling what these genes do has been a vast collaborative effort. The scientist who puts the last piece of a genetic jigsaw puzzle together succeeds only thanks to the work of tens of others who have gone before. Everything suggests that ownership of human genes is fuzzy and shared. Private ownership of genes may be as morally and economically disquieting as public ownership.

The human genome is a perfect example of why issues of public policy – and ownership in particular – will be at the heart of the knowledge-driven economy, in which firms, regions and nations will compete on their ability to create, acquire, disseminate, and exploit distinctive know-how and intellectual capital. The knowledge-driven economy is not only a set of new high-tech industries, such as biotechnology and genetics, that are built on a scientific knowledge base. Nor is it just about the spread of IT and computing power, although the growth in our ability to record, store, retrieve, analyse and communicate information and explicit knowledge is certainly a force driving the new economy. The knowledge-driven economy is about a set of new sources of competitive advantage that apply to some extent, and in different ways, to all industries, whether low-tech or high-tech, from agriculture and retailing to software, depending on the nature of their market, competitive pressures and scale economies. Knowledge matters, increasingly, in all industries. However, it plays different roles in different industries – from incremental innovation in some more mature industries to radical innovation in newer, faster-moving ones. Creativity, ingenuity and talent are key to competitiveness in all parts of the service sector, but have to be organized in quite different ways depending on market conditions and where the supply of knowledge comes from. Human capital is critical in high value-added services, such as business consulting, which depend on highly trained graduates. Human capital is also critical in the so-called creative industries, such as fashion, music and entertainment, where often the most talented people are high-school dropouts armed with lots of tacit, intuitive know-how (HMSO, 1998).

Nevertheless, the key to competitiveness – whether in a vineyard, supermarket chain, engineering factory, design house or laboratory – is how know-how is marshalled and commercialized in combination with complementary skills and assets, such as the finance, manufacturing capacity and distribution needed to realize the ideas. Tangible assets, such as manufacturing plants or product features – the steel in a car, for example – will still matter in the knowledge economy. However, the value of these physical assets and products will increasingly depend on how they are combined with intangible assets and features. Take a semiconductor. The silicon from which it is made is virtually worthless. It becomes valuable only when logic is minutely inscribed on its surface. On their own, neither the abstract logic nor the dull piece of silicon is worth much to consumers. The tangible and intangible features of the product become valuable only when they are combined.

Until now, the implications of knowledge-driven competition have been mainly focused on the organization of the firm, particularly the scope for 'knowledge management' initiatives to improve a firm's capacity to innovate, learn lessons and, in general, improve 'knowledge productivity' –

which is the speed at which a firm turns information into ideas and ideas into products and services. This managerial focus is too narrow. The ability of firms to compete in the knowledge-driven economy will depend on how their internal abilities combine with a wider policy framework that conditions their activities. The implications of the knowledge-driven economy for public policy extend well beyond familiar issues to do with fiscal incentives for research and development, standards of public education or business links with universities, important though those are. The knowledge-driven economy will raise much more fundamental, far-reaching and controversial issues about how economies should be organized to increase their knowledge productivity.

A large majority of economic assumptions, institutions and regulations are designed for a primarily industrial economy. To unlock the potential of the knowledge economy, we will need to rethink many of these basic building blocks of economic policy. As an example, consider the future of taxation.

The growth of the Internet and e-commerce, combined with globalization of trade and production and shifts towards self-employment and contract work, spell the end for the twentieth century's tax system, in which large, stable organizations helped the tax authorities to collect taxes from employed people. Taxes are charged on easy-to-observe activities (King, 1997). To be effective, the tax system has to feed on the way an economy generates wealth. In the 990s, Anglo-Saxon England had an efficient tax system, designed to pay 'Danegeld' to the invading Vikings, based on a fixed rate per 'hide', as units of land where then known. Not only was land easy to observe and record, it was also the source of income and wealth. Such a land tax made sense for a largely agrarian society. In the 1890s, Britain was primarily a manufacturing economy. Many people were employed by large companies. Taxes on their pay became feasible, thanks to the emergence of the modern company and its accounts department. Capital and labour rather than land was the source of wealth. Estate duty, a tax on bequests, was introduced in 1884 to rationalize capital taxes. The tax system evolved to suit an industrialized economy.

Now look forward – not 100 years, but just 10 or 20 years into the twenty-first century. Perhaps 70 per cent of the British economy will consist of services. Most of the economy's output will be immaterial. A growing share of transactions will be conducted over the Internet and will leave no physical trail. Experiments with electronic cash will be under way. Advances in IT and communications will have created complicated international production networks, with equally complicated financial arrangements. Working out which jurisdiction should tax which activities will become more difficult. The most talented, creative and richest capital and people in the economy will be highly mobile and resistant to high marginal tax rates. A tax system, designed for a relatively ordered, industrial world, will be outmoded by the rise of the fleet-footed dematerialized economy. Industrialization shifted the tax base from land to capital and

labour. The new economy may require an equally fundamental transformation of the tax system.

Taxes are just one example of a familiar economic institution that will
be disrupted by the rise of the knowledge economy. There are many others.
Traditional accounting, for example, finds it difficult to value intangible
assets that are increasingly critical to competitiveness – people, research
and development, brands, relationships with collaborators (Leadbeater,
1998). As a result, traditional accountants find themselves competing with
a range of alternatives, from the balanced scorecard and EVA to the
Skandia navigator and other measurements of intellectual assets. Accountants and regulators may need to embark on a period of sustained innovation to make sure that investors are provided with the best possible
information. The public sector – in the United Kingdom at least – does not
yet have an accurate balance sheet of its physical assets, let alone its
intangible assets. Yet, the public sector's most valuable assets in the future
may well be intangible. Indeed, the BBC and the National Health Service,
for example, are among the strongest brands in the United Kingdom. The
public sector also owns some of the most valuable assets of the information
economy – vast databases that include information about people's income,
health and driving record. How much will these be worth to the
privatization programmes of the future?

Competition policy will need to evolve. Markets should become more
competitive. Internet-competent consumers should be armed with far more
information and many alternative sources of supply. The rapid rate of
knowledge creation in young industries – in software and genetics, for
example – should create a stream of opportunities for new entrants to
challenge incumbents, who will find their tenure as industry leaders short-
lived (Audretsch, 1995). Yet, others argue that the new economy may be
bad for competition. Software and other knowledge-like products may
enjoy increasing returns that help to lock in their position as incumbents.
Whichever line you take in this argument, it is clear that competition
policy is likely to become more contested and may require new tools and
rules (Teece, 1998).

In short, the rise of the knowledge-driven economy will have consequences for a wide range of public policies, from taxes and accounting to
regional economic policies and approaches to economic development
in emerging economies, where the focus of the World Bank's activities is
shifting from tangibles – dams, factories, roads – to the intangibles of
development – know-how, institutions and culture. This chapter focuses
on just one public policy issue, which will play a critical role in determining the kind of knowledge economies we develop: ownership.

Ownership used to provide one of the sharpest dividing lines in politics.
The traditional socialist Left favoured collective, public ownership of at
least the 'commanding heights' of the economy, in the name of the workers
who created the wealth. The Right argued that private ownership and
strong property rights combined with market competition was the key to

economic growth. In the 1980s, this argument seemed to be settled, quite decisively, in favour of the Right. Communist regimes collapsed and, around the world, State-owned enterprises were privatized, often with huge gains in efficiency. In the United Kingdom, Tony Blair's New Labour won power in 1997 after symbolically off-loading Clause Four of the Party's constitution on nationalization, which said the Party's aim was common ownership of the means of production.

Ownership will become controversial again. Conventional public and private forms of ownership may be inappropriate and inefficient in the knowledge economy. We may well need to create hybrid forms of ownership, which mix different kinds of owners and ownership structures. To understand why, take the example of the human genome a little further.

This effort to unravel our genetic inheritance is a huge collective achievement, driven by a highly competitive scientific community. Most of the research has been publicly funded. The enquiry has proceeded with scientists sharing their findings and techniques. In 1990, James Watson, one of the discoverers of the double-helix form of human DNA, extended the appealing metaphor of this shape: 'I have come to see DNA as the common thread that runs through all of us on the planet Earth'. Watson (1968) also said: 'the Human Genome Project is not about one gene or another, one disease or another. It is about the thread that binds us all.'

Yet, as we have seen, this collective uncovering of our shared genetic inheritance also creates huge opportunities for people to make money, and the case for the commercial exploitation of genetics is persuasive. It would be a huge mistake to give the job of using this knowledge base to governments, which have neither the skills nor the incentives to spread innovations efficiently. Private companies will do the job much more efficiently and creatively. The job of turning a genetic discovery into a treatment for a disease is time-consuming, risky and costly. Innovators should be given some incentive and reward for success. Since the late 1970s, the biotechnology industry has grown fastest in the United States, not just because it is home to most of the research and the richest venture capitalists, but because the United States has allowed companies to own patents on genes. This appears to have been a deliberate act of industrial policy. Intellectual property has been one of the main tools.

In 1980, the US Supreme Court overturned decades of legal precedents that said that naturally occurring phenomena, such as bacteria, could not be patented because they were discoveries rather than inventions (Sagoff, 1998). Yet, that year, the Court decided that a biologist named Chakrabarty could patent a hybridized bacterium because 'his discovery was his handiwork, not that of nature'. A majority of the judges reiterated that 'a new mineral discovered in the earth or a new plant discovered in the wild is not patentable'. Yet, they believed that Chakrabarty had concocted something new using his own ingenuity. Even Chakrabarty was surprised. He had simply cultured different strains of bacteria together in the belief that they would exchange genetic material in a laboratory soup. The then embryonic biotechnology industry used the case to argue that patents should be issued on genes, proteins and other materials of commercial value.

By the late 1980s, the US Patent Office had embarked on a far-reaching change of policy to propel the US industry forward, routinely issuing patents on products of nature, including genes, fragments of genes, sequences of genes and human proteins. In 1987, for example, Genetics Institute Inc. was awarded a patent on erythropoietin, a protein of 165 amino acids that stimulates the production of red blood cells. It did not claim to have invented the protein; it had extracted small amounts of the naturally occurring substance from thousands of gallons of urine. Erythropoietin is now a multi-billion-dollar-a-year treatment.

The industry's argument is that innovation prospers only when it is rewarded. Without rewards, innovation will not take place. The barriers to entry in biotechnology are relatively low. Biotechnology companies do not have to build costly factories or high-street retail outlets or invest in brand reputations. The basic units of production are bacteria manipulated to deliver therapeutically and commercially valuable substances. Without the protection of a patent, an innovative biotechnology company would find its discoveries quickly copied by later entrants. If ownership of the right to exploit a genetic discovery were left unclear, there would be less innovation in the economy as a whole and we would all be worse off. The biotechnology industry in the United States is larger than anywhere else, in part because innovators there have been allowed to patent their 'inventions'. In 1998, there were almost 1,500 patents claiming rights to exploit human gene sequences.

Yet, the ownership regime for industries and products spawned by genetics is far from settled. Critics of a purely private-sector approach appeal to a linked set of moral, practical and economic arguments in support of their case against private exploitation. The moral case was put most powerfully by religious leaders. In May 1995, a group of 200 religious leaders representing 80 faiths gathered in Washington DC to call for a moratorium on the patenting of genes and genetically engineered creatures. They said, 'We are disturbed by the US Patent Office's recent decision to patent body parts and genetically engineered animals. We believe that humans and animals are creations of God, not humans, and as such should not be patented as human inventions.' This point of view is not confined to the religious. A deeply ingrained assumption in Western culture is that patents establish the moral claim that someone should own an idea because he or she invented it. Yet, even the biotechnology industry does not claim to have invented its products, merely to have discovered and engineered them.

The practical argument is about what should be owned – the gene itself or the treatments. Most people would regard a drug developed from knowledge of a gene sequence as an invention that could be patented. Far more problematical is the right to own the gene itself. The cystic fibrosis gene, for example, is patented, and anyone who makes or uses a diagnostic kit that uses knowledge of the gene sequence has to pay royalties to the patent holder. Many would argue that this is too broad a patent – that it is not so much a patent as a monopoly franchise on cystic fibrosis. Because innovators will have to pay a royalty to the franchise holder, this broad patent may be excessively strong and slow down innovation. As we move into the knowledge economy, issues such as the breadth and scope of a patent, the standards or novelty, even the duration, will become more problematical. To put it another way, who should own what and for how long will become more of an issue in a knowledge-driven economy (Stiglitz, 1997).

That is because incentives to exploit knowledge need to be set against the value of sharing it. Scientific enquiry proceeds as a result of collaboration, the sharing and testing of ideas. We are lucky that James Watson and his collaborator Francis Crick did not work for Genentech or Glaxo-Wellcome because every genetic researcher would now be paying them a royalty to use their discovery. Genetics, as most sciences, is built on a bedrock of shared knowledge. The more basic the knowledge, the more inappropriate strong property rights and exclusive private ownership becomes. Privatization of knowledge may make it less likely that know-how will be shared. Perkin-Elmer will publish its research on the human genome, but only once every three months and the company will reserve at least 300 genes for its own patent programme. Publicly funded researchers share their results more openly and more frequently.

The science of biotechnology offers huge potential benefits. The political economy of ownership will be as central to its development as straightforward scientific endeavour. In biotechnology, as in many other knowledge-intensive industries, we may need to develop a new mixed economy, which could involve creating new forms of social ownership and hybrid institutions that are both public and private. A purely private-sector-led development of the industry would alarm many people on moral grounds and might not be efficient in the long run because it would undermine sharing of basic knowledge and research findings. One example of what this might involve is the venture capital fund Medical Ventures Management, which was set up with the British Medical Research Council and a set of private investors to help commercialize scientific discoveries funded by the council. The council is a profit-sharing partner in the venture, which has first call on the commercialization of any output.

The issue of ownership will be central to the interaction between publicly funded research and private exploitation, but also to knowledge creation within companies.

A New Constitution for the Company

All over the world, managers justify decisions on the grounds that they have to deliver value to the ultimate owners of the business, its shareholders. Yet, it is difficult to work out in exactly what sense share-holders own a company. The traditional idea is that a firm is founded on a set of assets – land, raw materials, buildings and machinery – that is owned by the shareholders. These are the residual assets of the business, which would be sold if it went bust. The shareholders appoint a board of directors, who appoint managers to run the business and employ labour and other factors of production to work on the capital. A firm structured in this way runs into tricky issues about how authority can be delegated from shareholders to directors and then to managers, who need to be controlled, monitored, rewarded and held to account. All power flows down from the shareholders, in theory at least.

Yet, as we know, ownership is a slippery concept. When someone owns an object – a car for example – they can use it, stop others from using it, lend it, sell it or dispose of it. Ownership confers the right to possess, use and manage an asset, earn income from it and claim an increase in its capital value. Ownership also confers responsibilities on the owners to refrain from harmful use. Owners can pass on any of these rights to other people. When a person says, 'I own that umbrella', it usually means that they can put it up, take it down, sell it, rent it or throw it away. If the umbrella were stolen, its owner could appeal to the police and the law courts for its return, yet it is far from clear that shareholders own a corporation in the way that people own umbrellas. Take the shareholders in Microsoft. Their shareholding does not give them any right to use Microsoft assets or products. They cannot turn up in Seattle and demand admittance to the offices. Microsoft's shareholders are not held accountable for its commercial behaviour, its managers are. If a Microsoft shareholder went bankrupt, Microsoft assets could not be used to pay off their debts. Shareholders in Microsoft have a largely theoretical right to appoint managers to run the business. They have some claims on the company's income and capital value, but these rights are conditioned by the claims others make.

A purely knowledge-based firm differs markedly – in theory and practice – from the traditional model of the shareholder-owned company. The core of a pure knowledge-based company – a management consultancy, advertising company, scientific research team – is the know-how of the people. Often the physical assets – the place where they work, the computers and furniture they use, the investment they have in place – is entirely secondary to their competitiveness. The critical issue is how these people combine their knowledge, expertise and customer relationships to create a viable firm. A know-how business is created when people come together, give up their individual property rights to their work and jointly invest these rights, temporarily, in the enterprise. The traditional company is based on an assertion of shareholder property rights. The know-how firm is created by knowledge capitalists agreeing to forgo their individual rights to ownership and, instead, engage in gain-sharing with one another. The larger know-how companies get, the more complicated and difficult it becomes to maintain these gain-sharing arrangements. The know-how firm is created when property rights are pooled by a social contract among peers; it is not created by the top-down delegation of power from shareholders to managers. That fundamental distinction – between social contract and hierarchy – has far-reaching implications for the way that knowledge based companies should be organized and owned.

The central issue facing a know-how firm is how to promote the cooperative pooling of knowledge – devising the knowledge-creating social contract that is at the heart of a company. In the traditional company, the central issue is nominally about how much power can be delegated from the top down and how shareholders can monitor senior managers and senior managers can monitor their juniors. In the know-how firm, the key issue is how to maintain a sense of membership and joint commitment and to prevent people from defecting or from free-riding on the efforts of others. Thus, the question of who owns the company becomes even harder to answer. A know-how company is founded on an agreement among producers to relinquish their rights to their work and work together. Property rights are inherently fuzzy and shared.

In traditional shareholder-driven companies, managers are the shareholders' agents on earth. In a know-how company, the managers have to earn respect and authority from their ability to promote cooperation and collaboration among the providers of know-how. Managers in a know-how firm have to be collaborative leaders who gain their authority by their ability to devise, revise and enforce the social contract, in order to maximize the returns to the combined knowledge of the partners in the enterprise. In a know-how company, decisions need to made by the people who have the relevant knowledge, rather than the appropriate people within a hierarchy. This implies a much more distributed and networked structure and style in know-how firms, where power should go with know-how rather than hierarchy.

These contrasts between the traditional firm and the know-how firm constitute a caricature. The real world is nowhere near so cut and dried. Most companies will be an uncomfortable mixture of these two models: they will need to deliver returns to shareholders – financial capitalists – by also engaging the commitment of the staff – the knowledge capitalists, if you will. What does this mean for the ownership of companies in the future?

As economies become more knowledge-intensive, there will be more know-how-based companies, owned by means of social contracts between knowledge workers rather than by traditional shareholders. Partnerships and ownership by employees will become more common. Companies will have to develop innovative ways to involve workers – the providers of knowledge capital – with opportunities to share in the financial wealth they create. Yet, most large companies will be rather traditional and it is difficult to convert traditional, hierarchical organizations into free-wheeling, knowledge-creating partnerships of the kind that abound in

Silicon Valley. In traditional companies, change will be evolutionary. These large organizations need structure and hierarchy to work efficiently. Global companies, operating in global product markets, will need large financial resources to compete. Knowledge capital on its own is not enough – it has to be combined with financial resources and other assets to count. If these traditional companies were designed to satisfy the interests of knowledge workers, they may well not deliver the financial performance needed to survive. If they were organized as machines to deliver shareholder value, they would not encourage the innovation they need to renew themselves. The task for companies will be to develop ownership structures and management styles that dynamically combine knowledge capital and financial capital. The most successful companies of the future will be hybrids that combine and reward financial and knowledge capital.

This tension between financial and knowledge capital underlies the 1998 debate within Goldman Sachs about turning its partnership into a public limited company. Those in Goldman Sachs who wanted the flotation argued that the partnership structure constrained the company's ability to raise financial capital, weakened its balance sheet and undermined its ability to compete with better-capitalized competitors. Those partners who did not want to become a public limited company argued that the partnership system made Goldman Sachs uniquely able to attract and motivate the brightest and the best because the partnership was designed to reward knowledge capitalists. Management was struggling to find a formula that would be the best combination of both views. Most managers in most companies are in a similar position – on uncomfortable middle ground between the old and the new, searching for structures that meet the conflicting demands of financial and knowledge capital. They will manage neither pure know-how companies nor traditional hierarchical companies, but hybrids.

Conclusion

Many societies have excelled at producing knowledge without making the most of their intellectual prowess. Ancient China produced a stream of potentially revolutionary inventions, including paper, the water-clock and gunpowder. Yet, Chinese inventiveness did not lead to a flowering of industry because there was no security for private enterprise, no legal foundation for rights outside the State, no method of investment other than in land and no social room for a class of entrepreneurs to emerge outside the State. In short, the ownership regime in ancient China was not designed to promote the commercial exploitation of a knowledge-rich society. The problem was not a lack of ideas, but a lack of incentives. Many obstacles stand in the way of inventiveness being translated into commercial success. However, one, and perhaps the most important, is whether there is the right mix of incentives to promote innovation and exploitation. Ownership and property rights play a critical role in creating those incentives. That is why innovative forms of ownership will play a critical role in the growth of the knowledge-driven economy. These innovative hybrids will combine public investment in knowledge with private exploitation, the interests of financial capitalists and knowledge capitalists and incentives to exploit and share knowledge.

These new approaches to ownership will matter not just because they provide incentives, but also because they help promote knowledge-creating cultures within companies and in society at large. A dynamic knowledge society must promote innovation and entrepreneurship alongside a respect for education and learning. Japan and Germany, for example, are outstanding knowledge economies in large part because their education systems produce well-trained workers who are orchestrated within companies to continually improve on already high levels of quality and productivity. However, Japan and Germany also have weaknesses – their companies excel at incremental innovation and they are less prolific at radical innovation. California exemplifies a radical culture of knowledge creation. California has spawned a string of innovative new companies in new industries in part because it is supportive of radical free thinking. California's laws and politics promote diversity and experimentation. The downside is that California has a dreadful basic education system, its students scoring poorly in US state rankings. California makes up for the deficiency of its basic education system by importing talent.

The ideal, perhaps, would be a hybrid economic culture that combined the best of these worlds. It would be a society that gave everyone a chance to compete in a world-class basic education system that would probably have to be largely publicly funded. Yet, it would also encourage radical innovation by virtue of an open, liberal, entrepreneurial culture in which people had the incentives to make the most of their abilities. The successful economies of the future – as much as the successful organizations – will promote hybrid, diverse and cosmopolitan cultures.

References

Audretsch, David B. (1995) *Innovation and Industry Evolution.* Cambridge, MA: MIT Press.
HMSO (1998) 'Our competitive future: building the knowledge-driven economy', Competitiveness White Paper and accompanying analytical report, December, London: HMSO.
King, Mervyn (1997) 'Tax systems in the 21st century', keynote speech at the Jubilee Symposium of the Fiftieth Congress of the International Fiscal Association, Geneva, *OECD Observer*, (208) (October/November).
Leadbeater, Charles (1998) 'Accountancy is dead', *New Statesman*, 17 April: 30–2.
Sagoff, Mark (1998) 'Patented genes: an ethical appraisal', *Issues in Science and Technology*, Spring: 37–41.

Stiglitz, Joseph (1997) 'Public policy for a knowledge economy', speech at
    Conference on the Economics of the Knowledge Driven Economy, London, Jar.
Teece, David (1998) 'Technology strategy and public policy: the meaning of monopoly
    technology industries', Third Clarendon Lecture, Oxford, 7 May.
Watson, James D. (1968) *The Double Helix: A Personal Account of the Discovery*
    Structure of DNA. New York: Atheneum.
Wilkie, Tom (1998) 'The lords of creation', *Prospect*, July: 20–4.

9 Following Distinctive Paths of Knowledge: Strategies for Organizational Knowledge Building within Science-based Firms

Fiona E. Murray

Introduction

In cases where a firm's advantage lies in the creation and application of scientific knowledge to new business opportunities, the ability to develop deep organizational knowledge of new scientific disciplines and combine this knowledge with the existing knowledge of the firm is critical. In building such capabilities, these firms face a crucial strategic question: should they commit resources to building a deep base of scientific knowledge?

In some instances, an appropriate strategy may be to do only enough research to gain access to, and understand, the science of external experts. Alternatively, it may be more effective to build deep, well-focused knowledge of one scientific discipline. A third possibility is to develop a broad knowledge base that spans a number of disciplines in such a way that insights from one discipline inform others – techniques are transferred or insights blended to develop more efficient processes or effective products. Each of these different choices represents a different knowledge path. The knowledge path is the path taken by a firm as it explores the scientific and technical knowledge that could bring new value to and expand the horizons shaped by its existing knowledge assets.

This chapter develops a taxonomy of these knowledge paths. It then develops an understanding of the processes that underlie these paths and the organizational implications for a firm intent on shaping its knowledge path more effectively. The exploration of these knowledge paths creates a richer, more dynamic understanding of how the knowledge assets of the firm are transformed, evolve, are renewed and become obsolete. The dynamic perspective presented here is at odds with much of the literature on the knowledge-based view of the firm, a view that is typically static and ignores the dynamics of knowledge change.

Firms that successfully shape their knowledge paths have developed organizational processes that allow them to shape scientific knowledge.

Creating organizational knowledge about science and technology is a complicated and multifaceted process. However, in this chapter, I argue that foundations of knowledge-building rest on two processes:

1 the search for knowledge;
2 the assembly of knowledge.

Together these two processes create different possible knowledge paths along which a firm's knowledge assets are likely to be transformed over time. Here I explore a set of dominant paths that highlight how the state of knowledge changes over time in response to these crucial organizational variables. Along each knowledge path, the knowledge assets are transformed by different combinations of knowledge-searching and assembly processes within and outside the firm.

Each knowledge path has a series of organizational implications, including the organization of research and development, the incentives provided to scientists and whether or not to focus on basic or applied research. Particular changes in organizational design will influence the production of scientific knowledge within the firm. The organizational perspective is explored in this essay by considering how to facilitate the underlying processes of search and assembly along each of the different paths.

This chapter has four parts. In the first part, I develop a framework based on control theory to distinguish between the state of knowledge and the processes that shape (control) knowledge within the firm. I then turn to the literature on the sociology of science and technological trajectories to probe the basic processes that are involved in the production of scientific knowledge. In the third section, I build a taxonomy of knowledge paths that represents different ways in which knowledge-building processes can be used together. In the fourth section, I outline the organizational implications of the different paths. This four-stage exploration of the organizational challenges associated with building knowledge assets over time should prove useful to organizations that build their competitive advantage on the creation and renewal of scientific knowledge.

Building a Model of Scientific Knowledge Paths

To understand and clarify the dynamics of knowledge paths, it is useful, first, to focus on the static state of knowledge and, second, to distinguish this static knowledge from the processes that shape knowledge. These different elements of knowledge management are too often conflated in our discussions of technological trajectories and types of innovation. Furthermore, the development of a knowledge-based theory of the firm has typically focused on the static state of this knowledge. Such a state has been characterized along dimensions of tacitness, observability, rivalry in use, degree to which knowledge is autonomous or systemic and the extent of appropriability (Nonaka, 1994, Winter, 1987, Teece, 1986, and 1998, and Chesbrough and Teece, 1996). Such detailed conceptual and empirical definitions of knowledge assets are valuable – they describe a firm's knowledge at a given point in time. None the less, these measures provide a singular and temporally bounded representation of a firm's knowledge and, therefore, poorly represent the complicated, dynamic story of knowledge change from which the asset emerged or that is the platform for future knowledge (Kim and Kogut, 1996).

A specific analytical framework from control theory clarifies the distinction between static and dynamic knowledge particularly well. According to control theory, the state of a system at any given time is distinguished from the influences that control (that is, change) the state of the system. Thus, in discussing knowledge and knowledge paths, there are two main elements that constitute the system.

1   **The state variables of a system**   The static knowledge of the firm can be thought of as the state of a knowledge system and could be described by a set of state variables, such as the number of patents.
2   **The control variables of a system**   The control variables act on the system and transform it, such that the state variables change (usually in some predictable manner). Within the firm, these variables can be thought of as knowledge change processes.

When we map the system from one state to another over time, we are mapping the path of change that the system takes. If we were to map the changing knowledge of a firm, we would be mapping the firm's knowledge path. Thus, in this essay, the definition of a knowledge path is the sequence of states of knowledge that a firm follows over time. This is similar to, but more precise than, the definitions given to a technology trajectory, although, in this context, the focus is on the trajectory of scientific knowledge within the firm. Each path arises from the influence of a particular combination of control variables – organizational processes that influence and change the state of knowledge of the firm. The general schema outlined above is illustrated in Figure 9.1.

Processes of Production: Building Scientific Knowledge

Many writers have taken a deterministic view of the dynamics of technological change. Their underlying premise is that the size, structure and performance of technology determine the nature of technological change. Further, they assume that the path of technological change is exogenous to any particular firm or individual. For example Nelson and Winter (1982)

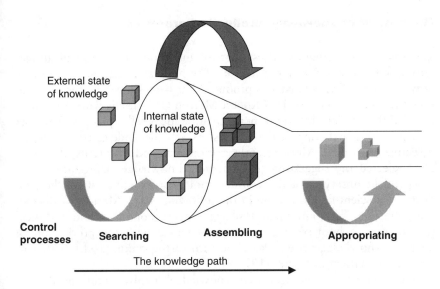

Figure 9.1   *Building knowledge by using organizational processes*

describe certain natural trajectories specific to a technological regime the frontiers of which are limited by physical, biological and other constraints. These deterministic views of the change process leave little room to explore the role of the firm in knowledge change. However, others have suggested that, although technological change may follow some external trajectory, technological opportunity (Scherer, 1965) or factors internal to the technology underdetermine this trajectory. This less deterministic view of knowledge change opens up the possibility that, within the firm, a number of different and interlocking processes simultaneously influence knowledge production and the paths of knowledge.

   A more thorough analysis of scientific and technical change suggests that complicated processes influence the trajectory of change. These processes are at once economic, sociological and psychological in their nature. They influence the interplay between technical change on the one hand and industrial and organizational change on the other. An exploration of the relevant literature in this field suggests that knowledge-production processes are strongly shaped by the context in which they are developed. The processes themselves are harder to discern from current studies. However, in this chapter, I suggest that two processes – search and assembly – underlie the production of scientific knowledge and the transformation of a firm's knowledge from one state into another. The process of searching is a quest for new knowledge or a search among existing knowledge that is not known to the firm. The process of assembling is the way in which disparate ideas, concepts and techniques are brought together or combined.

The context of knowledge-production processes

There is an increasing awareness that the institutional and organizational setting influences scientific production. The popular perception of the way in which scientific knowledge is produced has been shaped by the views of sociologists of science, such as Robert Merton (1973). His work embodied the idea that the production of new scientific ideas takes place within a set of institutions that support the scientist as an independent, truth-seeking, objective individual. More recently, sociologists and historians of science have rejected the suggestion that scientific knowledge is produced from independent observers of the world. Lenoir, for example, views the production of scientific knowledge in the following way: 'Matters of distinction, prestige, recognition, and struggle over economics and technical resources have been so inseparably intertwined with the production of scientific knowledge since at least the turn of the century, why bother to keep these matters distinct?' (1995: 4).

Lenoir points to the fact that knowledge involves both productive engagements with the world and the social and economic interests of the actors. Creating scientific knowledge is therefore a cultural practice. Thus, in order to fully understand the processes of knowledge production that shape knowledge paths, it is important to understand the cultural practice of scientists in firms.

The social community of the scientists shapes knowledge-building processes. Within and beyond the boundaries of a firm, the role of individuals or communities is crucial to an exploration of the paths and processes of knowledge change. Views on the influence of the sociological context of knowledge change – particularly as it relates to scientific knowledge – have been strongly influenced by Kuhn's *Structure of Scientific Revolutions* (1970). Most relevant is Kuhn's observation that 'normal' paths of science arise from strong social control and the socialization of each generation of young scientists. Thus, the paths or paradigms that emerge appear as the inherited knowledge of scientists (Barnes, 1985). Although some criticize his notion of a paradigm shift – either for its limited applicability within the physical sciences (Mayr, 1997) or for its universal, and therefore meaningless, applicability (Laudan, 1987) – Kuhn's view of the social and community context of knowledge change is relevant here. As Barnes has suggested:

> We need, in particular, to understand ourselves not simply as organisms but as communities. This is because knowledge is, in its very nature, a collective creation, founded not upon isolated judgements, but upon the evaluations we make together in social situations, according to custom and precedent, and in relation to our communal ends. (1985: 99)

Thus, the social context provides scientists with exemplars that, in guiding the experimental process, bring definition to the direction of knowledge

change. Within the firm, scientific and technological change will be i
enced by more complicated social dynamics than the pure form
scientific change discussed by Kuhn and Merton. A complicated se
interlocking communities is likely to influence the process of technological
change, again by means of the introduction of exemplars and expectations
(MacKenzie, 1987, and Tushman and Rosenkopf, 1992). These communities will include technical groups with a range of expertise, as well as the
wider communities that engage with the industry and the firm. For
example, the development of the science of genetics and the Human
Genome Project has been influenced by the complicated interplay of several
scientific communities, public policy makers, profit-making firms and
healthcare organizations (Cook-Deegan, 1996).

The business community plays a significant role in determining the
outcome of such change by means of its influence on industry evolution
and competition, which incorporate the market and customer communities. Abernathy and Utterback (1978) observed that the process of incremental technological change is strongly influenced by the explicit choices
of an industrial group to shape change in the direction of mass production.
This suggests that the path of technological change is influenced by the
drive towards economies of scale and mechanization (Chandler, 1977, and
Nelson and Winter, 1982). Businesses can therefore shape the processes of
technological change by means of the direction of experimentation in much
the same way that scientific exemplars can drive the process of scientific
change.

The likely determinants of business influence on the trajectory or path of
knowledge are the increasingly intertwined needs of competitors and complementors, suppliers and customers (Von Hippel, 1990, and Brandenburger and Nalebuff, 1997). For example, while multiple paths remained
viable in medical-imaging technology for a period, social and organizational processes between firms and the community of medical practitioners
were central to the path and ultimate development of technological
knowledge (Barley, 1985). Such interlocking communities play a specific
role in experimentation processes that lead to knowledge change – experimentation not only at the technical level, but also among organizations,
with market concepts and business models (Clark, 1985, and Von Hippel,
1998). Thus, industry's role in the knowledge trajectory is likely to be in
guiding the direction of experimentation by creating a context in which the
many interested parties can interact and share exemplars.

The knowledge-production processes themselves

Although the context that influences knowledge production has been
explored, the processes of knowledge production that are shaped by this
context are less clearly defined. Our understanding of organizational
learning and the routines for building organizational knowledge are the

starting point for this analysis of knowledge-production processes. The role
of the firm in building knowledge paths is based on the view of the firm as
a collection of organizational routines that are built, and amplified around,
repeated tasks (Cyert and March, 1963, and Nelson and Winter, 1982).
These 'learned' routines are invoked automatically in response to external
stimuli – the context outlined above. Thus, the path of change is arrived at
as a result of repeated, similar and local responses. These routine responses
include knowledge-production processes.

Searching for knowledge

Searching is central to knowledge change because it is the mechanism by
means of which new knowledge is identified and developed. The role of the
firm is to create, support and shape these search processes. However,
routines may arise at multiple locations within both firms and communities, and the location may shift over time (Constant, 1987). The firm,
therefore, provides a focus for routines and the search, but the firm
boundaries do not necessarily define the boundaries of the search process.

The direction and nature of the search process is crucial to knowledge
paths. As noted above, the typical view of sociologists of science suggests
that the search is shaped by exemplars. The modes and exemplars of
'normal science' – as described above – may limit and shape the search for
fundamental scientific knowledge. However, the search within the firm for
what encompasses scientific, technological and market knowledge is a
more complicated process driven by an interlocking and sometimes
contradictory set of exemplars and activities, such as intellectual traditions,
communities, social forces and failures. The ties that individuals and firms
have within a network also shape the search. Education, experience and
ties to the laboratories of others all affect to the ability of firms to pursue
science and the direction of the pursuit itself.

From an organizational perspective, exemplars (both scientific and
market) will likely shape the direction of the search process. However, a
firm's internal and external ties will also critically influence the ease of the
search process. Searching for knowledge that lies within the firm is a
different and often less costly process than searching outside the firm.
Therefore, from the perspective of the organization, the most critical
dimension in setting the direction of the search is whether the relevant
knowledge is internal or external. External knowledge may be sought
from other firms – via relationships such as alliances or joint ventures
(Chesbrough and Teece, 1996) or networks among scientists in firms and
public institutions. In some instances, firms may search as members of a
population of simultaneously searching organizations (Stuart and Podolny,
1996), but in others their search may be on the basis of unique knowledge,
which helps to build a distinctive knowledge path.

Whether it takes place within or outside the firm, the search process
identifies new knowledge. However, that knowledge is not necessarily

'digestible' by the firm until it can be integrated and combined with the firm's current knowledge base and determined to be part of an important new combination. This is the knowledge assembly process.

The process of assembling knowledge

An alternative but complementary view of the role of the firm in facilitating knowledge building comes from Schumpeter, who argued that firms involved in knowledge building combine existing knowledge and incremental learning in such a way that 'development in our sense is then defined by the carrying out of new combinations' (1934: 66). The firm's role in building combinations of knowledge has also been used to define combinative capabilities – 'the intersection of the capability of the firm to exploit its knowledge and the unexplored potential of the technology' (Kogut and Zander, 1992: 391). The process of assembling knowledge involves combining new knowledge with existing knowledge in novel ways to exploit the firm's resources (Penrose, 1959).

Exactly how assembly comes about is complicated and puzzling at both individual and organizational levels. Focusing on the organization, von Hayek asked how 'the spontaneous interaction of a number of people, each possessing bits of knowledge, brings about a state of affairs . . . which could only be brought about by the deliberate direction of somebody who possesses the combined knowledge of all of those individuals' (1948: 79).

Like the view of the search process, the firm's perspective on combining or assembling knowledge can be thought of as embedded within a social community that facilitates the process and direction of knowledge assembly. The process of assembly can take place at many levels:

1 within a well-defined scientific discipline or among disciplines;
2 as the transfer of an idea or a methodology;
3 as a new means for interpretation or applied to a new problem.

For the organization, the challenge is to link the different domains in science and the different communities of practice by the organization of skill and the management of work (Lenoir, 1995). The complexity lies in the need to create a new relationship structure each time assembly takes place. Knowledge assembly does not take place according to a 'master plan' – rather, it is spontaneous and arises within a social and professional context, particularly when the knowledge is scientific or technical (Brown and Duguid, 1998). A certain part of the assembly process is that, with few exceptions, scientific knowledge is cumulative.

However, stating that knowledge is cumulative sheds only limited light on the dynamics of the assembly process in shaping knowledge change. To give the assembly process more texture, it is helpful to think about knowledge assembly as either adding insight from within a given discipline or providing insight from outside that discipline. When assembly occurs within a given body of knowledge, problem-solvers remain within their typical 'network of possible wanderings' (Newell and Simon, 1972). Assembly is harder to achieve outside disciplinary boundaries because the exemplars, methods and equipment are less clearly defined. The challenges of assembling widely dispersed knowledge within established scientific disciplines include the rigidity of experimental methods, language that is hard to interpret and closed communities of practice. Because an established scientific discipline is frequently inaccessible to those in other areas, the ideas from that discipline are rarely applied elsewhere and the discipline is resistant to the introduction of ideas from outside its traditional boundaries (Allen, Tushman and Lee, 1979). Therefore, of the two dimensions of assembly – within and outside the discipline – the integration of knowledge from outside is more complicated and difficult.

The processes of search and assembly can be thought of as control variables that shape and transform a firm's state of knowledge. The organizational context and the broader scientific context influence the processes themselves. However, searching for, and assembling, knowledge are the fundamental processes that underlie knowledge change within the firm, and they largely determine the paths of knowledge evolution. These paths are explored in the remainder of this chapter.

Mapping the Paths of Scientific Knowledge

The notion of a knowledge path draws together often disparate research on the dynamics of change – notably the dynamics of changing scientific and technological knowledge (Kuhn, 1972), technological change and its transforming influence on industry (Rosenberg, 1986, Abernathy and Utterback, 1978, Tushman and Anderson, 1986, Tushman and Rosenkopf, 1992, and Levinthal, 1998) and technological paradigms (Dosi, 1984). However, many studies of technological change do not try to generalize about the paths of change or their organizational implications. Therefore, although rich, descriptive work on technology trajectories has yielded significant insights into the nature of technological change, the following question remains unanswered. What paths will a firm's knowledge be likely to follow? Without a description of generalizable paths of knowledge evolution, it is difficult to test basic hypotheses about the firm's knowledge evolution.

As the previous section outlined, this essay is based on the idea that search and assembly are the two organizational processes that underlie knowledge change. Over time, these processes shape a knowledge path that is both cumulative (Cohen and Levinthal, 1989) and competence building because of some familiarity and efficiency (Nelson and Winter, 1982): 'In some sense the new evolves out of the old. One explanation for this is that the output of today's searches is not merely a new technology, but also enhances knowledge and forms the basis of building blocks to be used tomorrow.'

Thus, in this chapter, I propose that a form can influence, shape and transform the search and assembly processes along different paths. This contrasts with the view that trajectories frame a certain but unknowable journey into a scientific or technological paradigm.

Distinctive knowledge paths

A knowledge path is defined by the changes that take place in the underlying knowledge states. These states are influenced, as outlined above, by dynamic organizational processes. The combination of two processes – search and assembly – together with the idea that knowledge is cumulative, creates a dynamic picture of knowledge assets and leads to the central proposition here – that there are multiple, but specific, paths along which knowledge assets typically evolve.

The driving force behind the knowledge trajectory or path is the need for the renewal of existing knowledge within the firm. This need arises as returns to investigation in the current knowledge domains of the firm decrease or perhaps because of changes in the product market or actions by competitors. The paths of knowledge are cumulative and can have a range of characteristics. The characteristics of knowledge paths are determined by whether the search for knowledge is internal or external to the firm and whether the knowledge being assembled lies within or outside the disciplinary boundaries of the firm's existing knowledge. Together, these elements provide us with an organizing framework for an analysis of knowledge paths.

The framework shown in Figure 9.2 is an organizing taxonomy for likely paths of knowledge evolution. A taxonomy is the classification or non-random organization of ideas or 'useful things or qualities' – in this instance, the things are paths of knowledge evolution (Winter, 1987). The development of a taxonomy of knowledge paths rather than one of knowledge states is closely related to the organizational issues that are central to knowledge management. Organizational concerns are often related to the transformation – renewal and accumulation – of knowledge rather than its state at any moment in time – that is, they relate to the dynamics of knowledge change rather than the statics of knowledge states.

A taxonomy of knowledge paths

The organizing framework outlined above suggests four commonly adopted paths of building knowledge assets. Each path has different characteristics of the search and assembly process and each is likely to incur different levels of effort. This section describes these paths and their attributes and illustrates each with examples.

		Searching for knowledge	
		Inside the firm	Outside the firm
Assembling knowledge	Specific to the discipline	Deep exploring	External drilling
	Outside the discipline	Internal scanning	Cherry picking

Figure 9.2   _Framework of knowledge paths_

Deep exploring path

This path is the mechanism by means of which much of our understanding of scientific knowledge has evolved. The knowledge work that has forged this path focuses on the creation of a deeper understanding of an existing knowledge base. This path is closely associated with Kuhn's notion of 'normal science', the related idea of 'normal technological progress' and the generally accepted idea of incremental innovation (Tushman and Anderson, 1986, and Dosi, 1984).

Straight and narrow path   Such a path is built from the combined processes of internal search and assembly within the knowledge discipline and, thus, is the simplest form of 'local search'. The search for new knowledge along this path is closely bounded by previous search activities, is 'problemistic' (Cyert and March, 1963) and has the lowest costs for search and assembly. The path of knowledge change may be rapid or slow, often depending on the newness of the knowledge discipline. For example, knowledge building within the domain of genetics and, in particular, the mapping of the human genome, is currently very rapid because the questions are well defined, the experimental techniques established and the language of the discipline explicit. This is often associated with traditional R&D activities in large R&D-intensive firms, as well as universities.

There is a high probability of successful (if slow) knowledge evolution when this path is chosen because the search is conducted in known areas of investigation and organizational routines can be applied (Nelson and Winter, 1982). None the less, certain rigidities in both problem solving and problem identification may develop along the straight and narrow path. Finally, decreasing returns for the knowledge path might prompt a shift, either explicitly or implicitly, to a new path (Kogut and Zander, 1992).

External drilling path

This is closely related to the deep exploring path in that the knowledge path remains with a given discipline or set of disciplines. However, the knowledge search takes place outside the boundaries of the firm. Because this search is external, the costs may be higher than those along the deep exploring path. External knowledge can be of several types:

1   public knowledge;
2   knowledge carried out externally, but funded by the firm;
3   knowledge generated in the context of external activities on the part of the firm, such as solving customers' problems.

The external drilling path is therefore common among firms that use and renew their knowledge base by undertaking projects, such as scientific consultants or the providers of scientific services. For example, Incyte uses its knowledge of genomic libraries to work with alliance partners to solve a range of biotechnology and pharmaceutical problems related to drug target identification. The continual reuse of knowledge in new (external) contexts allows the underlying knowledge assets to be updated and the knowledge path to evolve. However, in many instances, knowledge evolution does not take place automatically and knowledge management systems may be introduced to facilitate the capture and renewal of knowledge. This knowledge path is also common among firms that make extensive use of external networks, such as small biotechnology firms. The external network facilitates the renewal of their knowledge disciplines and, although it necessitates external searching, the stability and nature of network interactions reduces the search costs considerably (Liebeskind, 1996, Powell et al., 1996, and Grant, 1996). It is worth noting that, although the external drilling path is similar to the deep exploring path, the dynamic process of knowledge evolution that underlies external drilling is different.

Internal scanning

This knowledge path is one along which significant transformation of knowledge assets can take place. Firms that follow this path take knowledge from a distinctive knowledge discipline within the firm and combine it with another existing internal discipline. Thus, the existing discipline (or both) is transformed and substantially reinterpreted. The assembly costs of such a knowledge path can be high as it relies on non-routine interactions and often deliberate articulated effort. Routines cannot be easily used along the internal scanning path unless regular and repeated patterns of cross-disciplinary knowledge assembly are fostered, because routines require 'the development of a fixed response to defined stimuli' (March and Simon, 1958).

Both the response and stimuli are difficult to predict across disciplines unless interaction and assembly occur consistently (Grant, 1996). None the less, despite potentially high assembly costs, search costs can be limited because the knowledge comes from within the firm boundaries. Examples of knowledge development by an individual along the internal scanning path include that of a polymerase chain reaction (PCR) by Dr Kary Mullis at Cetus Corporation (Rabinow, 1998). At the organizational level, at Thorn-EMI, Sir Godfrey Houndshell combined the firm's expertise in image analysis with the radiography knowledge to create the CT scanner (Teece, 1986).

Returning to genetics, consider the transformation of a pharmaceutical firm's knowledge about a particular disease in the light of genetic information developed elsewhere within the firm. Patient databases compiled during clinical trials may contain valuable genetic information that can be used to build a different knowledge path for a firm's disease-based expertise. Traditionally, this information was located in two distinct knowledge disciplines, both progressing along a deep exploring path. Internal and external developments in the understanding of the genetic basis of disease gradually provided a framework for bringing these two disciplines together. As this assembly process becomes routinized, eventually the two disciplines may merge. One of the challenges of the internal scanning path is that assembly may require not only information from, for example, the knowledge of genetics, but also its experimental methods, instrumentation, language and other characteristics. The transfer and assembly of methods and language may be facilitated by the fact that it takes place within the firm. However, it is an open question as to whether or not the assembly of two distinctive bodies of knowledge is facilitated when the two relevant communities are co-located within the firm. Certainly, this is the strategy that was fostered by the traditional large-scale corporate R&D laboratories, such as Xerox PARC.

Cherry-picking path

This path is perhaps the most dramatic and, like internal scanning, it can lead to the transformation of the knowledge disciplines of the firm.

Firms pursuing the cherry-picking path search for knowledge outside the firm in different knowledge disciplines, then combine this knowledge with their existing knowledge disciplines, often in the form of complicated assembled products. The external search process can be particularly difficult when the firm has limited internal expertise in the external domain and, hence, a limited absorptive capacity (Cohen and Levinthal, 1989).

This knowledge path, like internal scanning, takes ideas from different disciplines and combines them into new knowledge and new understandings. For example, the genetic research firm Affymetrix built on its knowledge of genetics and then incorporated expertise in photolithography from outside the genetics discipline and external to the firm in order to build 'biochips'. Over time, the two knowledge disciplines were combined, at least within the firm. Such combined knowledge can be the source of unique competitive advantage because assembled knowledge paths are hard to imitate. The combinative advantage developed by Affymetrix is reinforced by the presence of scientists from the original knowledge disciplines on its scientific advisory board – Paul Berg, a Nobel Prize-winning geneticist, and R. Fabian Pease, a semiconductor expert from Bell Laboratories.

Companies such as Cisco have also developed successful cherry-picking paths that use acquisitions, alliances and joint ventures as the means of assembling outside knowledge, often in a diverse range of disciplines. Once secured, these arrangements help to overcome the problems of knowledge assembly and their contractual arrangements define the search process.

Returning to the example of an individual scientist, biographies of Albert Einstein suggest that, in the development of his general theory of relativity, he required the integration of the mathematical principles of the calculus of curved surfaces, developed some years earlier. Thus, the introduction of knowledge from other disciplines occurs widely in knowledge evolution and often from external as well as internal sources.

Organizing the Paths of Scientific Knowledge: Implications for the Firm

Each of the knowledge paths described above has been associated with different organizational challenges and competitive opportunities. Firms use specific mechanisms to overcome the organizational difficulties associated with each path, as outlined in Table 9.1. These organizational mechanisms place choices such as the use of alliances and joint ventures in a somewhat different light from that outlined by Chesbrough and Teece (1996). They have proposed a framework for the integration of innovation internal or external to the firm on the basis of the difficulties associated with capturing the value from innovation. In contrast, here I emphasize the use of intra- and extraorganizational structures on the basis of knowledge path evolution and the costs and limitations of the underlying organizational processes. In doing so, I address the challenges associated with assembling into the firm new knowledge of any type.

As Table 9.1 shows, paths focused on one central knowledge discipline pose limited assembly or coordination challenges. The external drilling path has more substantial search costs, but can be more fruitful because it is informed by customers and academics, as well as developments within and outside the firm. For example, computer chip maker Intel's R&D is, in part, driven by developments in knowledge that are undertaken by IBM and shared with equipment suppliers (see Chesbrough, Chapter 4). This path allows entrepreneurial firms to exploit the economies of scale in knowledge-building that arise in the wider community of practice. However, it requires the creation of extremely effective mechanisms of external searching.

Table 9.1   *Organizational mechanisms for building knowledge paths*

	Search mechanisms	Assembly mechanisms
Deep exploring	• Large internal R&D budgets • Dedicated basic research within established knowledge disciplines	• Common language among internal communities of practice • Knowledge-building routines
External drilling	• Networks • Funding of university research • Co-location with centres of excellence • Multiple external projects utilizing the firm's knowledge	• Common language between internal and external communities of practice • Shared exemplars of the knowledge discipline • Joint knowledge-building projects • Knowledge management systems
Internal scanning	• Internal knowledge-sharing projects • Problem-focused knowledge assembly • Key role of individuals in interdomain searching	• Multiknowledge teams • Creation of assembly routines across disciplines • Key role of individuals in interdisciplinary assembly • Development of shared language
Cherry picking	• Diverse knowledge expertise on scientific advisory boards • Alliances and joint venture activities across knowledge disciplines	• Multiknowledge teams with different knowledge sources • Key role of individuals in interdisciplinary assembly • Development of shared language across boundaries of the firm and knowledge disciplines

In contrast, internal scanning can be costly – not because of the search process, but because there are potentially high assembly costs even for those that occur within the firm. A variety of organizational mechanisms can be used to overcome these difficulties and are observed among firms that follow a knowledge evolution path akin to internal scanning. These mechanisms are closely linked to those elaborated in the product-development literature for technological integration and include multiple-knowledge teams, strong team leaders and the importance of a focus for integration (Iansiti, 1998, and Clark and Fujimoto, 1995). In the European laboratories of the consumer electronics firm Sharp, for example, teams of physicists and materials scientists from different disciplines work together on concept products and produce prototypes as a way of building common language and understanding.

Firms following the cherry-picking path must overcome both search and assembly challenges. They use organizational mechanisms that span the range from alliances and joint ventures to facilitate focused searching and to the development of a common language to improve assembly processes.

Table 9.2   *Changing knowledge paths*

	Monsanto's R&D in agrochemicals
Original knowledge path, 1950–1970s	• Deep exploring path, largely based on internal development of chemistry applied to the development of agrochemicals
Stimuli for changing knowledge path	• Decreasing returns on effort in chemicals, increasingly widespread availability of knowledge • Watson and Crick's 1953 discovery of the structure of DNA and Cohen and Boyer's work on recombinant DNA in 1973
Nature of new knowledge path	• Assembly of knowledge of chemistry, recombinant DNA methods and developments in plant cell and tissue culture
Organizational response	• 1975–1980: initially working informally via a cherry-picking path; Jaworski a biochemist at Monsanto, but working informally • 1981–87: shifting to an internal scanning path as new knowledge disciplines are created within Monsanto and then assembled • Assembly of a seed genetics knowledge discipline incorporating internal knowledge in traditional seed manipulation and external knowledge • 1995 onwards: Monsanto's acquisition of Calgene in 1997 and DeKalb Genetics in 1998; the reorganization of R&D to incorporate existing knowledge of seeds more effectively

Even when the search process takes place outside the firm, internal R&D does not stop, because the development of in-house knowledge complements rather than substitutes for external knowledge building.

Shifting knowledge paths

Firms are unlikely to maintain one knowledge path over time because the external knowledge environment is constantly shifting and subject to change. The experience of agrochemicals producer Monsanto offers some useful lessons in this regard.

Table 9.2 highlights the changing knowledge paths of Monsanto. In the 1970s, Monte Throdahl, a chemist at Monsanto, suggested that there might be a limit to the potential of chemistry. Together with Jaworski, a biochemist, they found the resources to develop knowledge in a range of emerging disciplines, including cell biology and genetics. Using different search processes generally focused on knowledge outside the firm, Monsanto developed and maintained quite separate organizational knowledge of biochemistry, seed genetics and molecular biology over a long period of time. It was only in the 1990s that this knowledge was formally assembled with the company's existing knowledge of chemistry and agrochemistry. Thus, it shifted from a deep exploring path to cherry picking, then internal scanning.

The experience of Monsanto is consistent with research suggesting that, for the majority of large firms, the diversity of technological knowledge is growing across a range of industries (Granstrand et al., 1997). These results suggest that firms are increasingly following knowledge paths that correspond to internal scanning and cherry picking. Because the searching and assembly processes are complicated and costly along these paths, a shift away from the deep exploring path is likely to occur only as a result of significant stimuli. These stimuli might include the inability of the current knowledge domain to meet customers' needs or substantially decreasing returns to knowledge building. Decreasing returns to knowledge-building can arise, as mentioned above, because of the natural limits of the scientific knowledge base or the increasing ability of firms to imitate knowledge built on the knowledge discipline renders the knowledge more commodity-like.

Conclusions

The conceptual model presented here informs our thinking about how firms build paths of knowledge to continually renew their knowledge assets. It is midway between the corporate determinism of technological change (suggested by Kodama, 1992) and the ideas of technological determinism that once informed much of the theory on management and history of technology. Its managerial implications are particularly salient for understanding the most effective organizational modes for building knowledge paths. Each mode of evolution represents a different knowledge path and each has markedly different implications for competition. Furthermore, the paths imply quite different managerial skills and organizational structures. These four paths of evolution are not mutually exclusive – they can evolve simultaneously – a fact that highlights the significant challenges of managing the full potential of knowledge assets.

The knowledge path framework, with its focus on the processes of knowledge-building, sheds light on two distinct managerial concerns to the organization. The first is the choice of appropriate organizational boundaries and processes for knowledge-building. The second is the timing and mode of transition from one path to another in response to exogenous developments in scientific knowledge.

The knowledge path analysis presented here suggests that the costs of search and assembly, their organizational requirements and the likelihood of success are crucial considerations in a firm's decisions about where to search for knowledge and how to assemble it. Specifically, a firm's choice is closely related to whether the knowledge that is sought lies within or outside the knowledge disciplines in which the firm has expertise. Viewed through the lens of knowledge paths, organizational tools such as teams, knowledge-management systems and prototyping can be considered coherent and complementary (or divergent and poorly structured) organizational choices. The suggestion that knowledge paths require a cluster of organizational processes sheds light on the second question – how might a firm might go about building a new knowledge path when there are dramatic shifts in the external knowledge context of the firm? This question is akin to asking how a firm can build new scientific capabilities.

A better understanding of these complicated paths and their underlying processes is crucial for a number of reasons. First, such an understanding is a virtual but missing element in the construction of a knowledge-based theory of the firm. Second, an understanding of the knowledge paths may improve our understanding of the economics of knowledge – in particular, the marginal costs of its use and the influence of repetitive use and imitation (Teece, 1998). Third, with a greater understanding of how knowledge evolves within firms and the economy, we will have a deeper appreciation of the managerial requirements of building, exploiting and renewing knowledge within the firm. Fourth, and perhaps most salient, knowledge evolution will be at the heart of sustainable competitive advantage for knowledge-based firms.

References

Abernathy, W., and Utterback, J. (1978) 'Patterns of industrial innovation', *Research Policy*, 8 (7): 40–7.

Allen, T.J., Tushman, M.L., and Lee, D.M.S. (1979) 'Technology transfer as a function of position in the spectrum from research through development', *Academy of Management Journal*, 22 (4): 694–708.

Barley, Stephen R. (1985) 'The alignment of technology and structure through roles and networks', *Administrative Science Quarterly*, 35 (1): 61–103.

Barnes, B. (1985) 'Thomus Khun', in W. Skinner (ed.), *The Return of Grand Theory in the Social Sciences*. New York: Cambridge University Press.

Basalla, G. (1989) *The Evolution of Technology*. Cambridge: Cambridge University Press.

Brandenburger, A., and Nalebuff, B. (1997) *Co-opetition*. New York: Doubleday.

Brown, J., and Duguid, P. (1998) 'Organizing knowledge', *California Management Review*, 40 (3): 90–111.

Chandler, A. (1977) *Strategy and Structure: Chapters in the History of the Industrial Enterprise*. Cambridge, MA: MIT Press.

Chesbrough, H., and Teece, D. (1996) 'When is virtual virtuous? Organizing for innovation', *Harvard Business Review*, January/February: 65–73.

Clark, K. (1985) 'The interaction of design hierarchies and market concepts in technological evolution', *Research Policy*, 14 (5): 235–51.

Clark, K., and Fujimoto, T. (1995) *Product Development Performance: Strategy, Organization, and Management in the World Auto Industry*. Boston, MA: Harvard Business School Press.

Cohen, Wesley M., and Levinthal, Daniel A. (1989) 'Absorptive capacity: a new perspective on learning and innovation', *Administrative Science Quarterly*, 35 (1): 128–52.

Constant, E. (1987) 'The social locus of technological practice: community, system or organization?', in W. Bijker, T. Hughes and T. Pinch (eds), *The Social Construction of Technological Systems*. Cambridge, MA: MIT Press.

Cook-Deegan, M. (1996) *Gene Wars*. New York: W.W. Norton.

Cyert, R., and March, J. (1963) *A Behavioural Theory of the Firm*. Oxford: Blackwell.

Dosi, G. (1982) 'Technological paradigms and technological trajectories: a suggested interpretation of the determinants and directions of technical change', *Research Policy*, 11 (3): 147–62.

Dosi, G. (1984) *Technical Change and Industrial Transformation*. London: Macmillan.

Granstrand, O., Patel, P., and Pavitt, K. (1997) 'Multi-technology corporations: why they have "distributed" rather than "distinctive core" competencies', *California Management Review*, 39 (4): 8–25.

Grant, R. (1996) 'Prospering in dynamically competitive environments: organizational capability as knowledge integration', *Organization Science*, 7 (4): 375–87.

von Hayek, F.A. (1948) *Individualism and Economic Order*. Chicago: University of Chicago Press.

Iansiti, M. (1998) *Technology Integration*. Boston, MA: Harvard Business School Press.

Kim, D., and Kogut, B. (1996) 'Technological platforms and diversification', *Organization Science*, 7 (3): 283–301.

Kodama, F. (1992) *Emerging Patterns of Innovation: Sources of Japan's Technological Edge*. Boston, MA: Harvard Business School Press.

Kogut, B., and Zander, U. (1992) 'Knowledge of the firm, combinative capabilities, and the replication of technology', *Organization Science*, 3: 383–97.

Kuhn, T. (1972) *The Structure of Scientific Revolutions*, 2nd edn. Chicago: University of Chicago Press.

Laudan, R. (1987) *The Nature of Technological Knowledge: Are Models of Scientific Change Relevant?* Dordrecht: Reidel.

Lenoir, T. (1995) *Instituting Science: The Cultural Production of Scientific Disciplines*. Palo Alto, CA: Stanford University Press.

Levinthal, D. (1998) 'The slow pace of rapid technological change: gradualisms and punctuation in technological change', *Industrial and Corporate Change*, 7 (2): 217.

Liebeskind, J. (1996) 'Knowledge, strategy and the theory of the firm', *Strategic Management Journal*, 17: 93–107.

MacKenzie, D. (1987) 'Missile accuracy: a case study in the social processes of technological change', in W. Bijker, T. Hughes and T. Pinch (eds), *The Social Construction of Technological Systems*. Cambridge, MA: MIT Press.

March J., and Simon, H. (1958) *Organizations*. New York: Wiley.

Mayr, E. (1997) *The Growth of Biological Thought: Diversity, Evolution, and Inheritance*. Cambridge, MA: Belknap Press.

Merton, R. (1973) *The Sociology of Science: Theoretical and Empirical Investigations*. Chicago: University of Chicago Press.

Nelson, R., and Winter, S. (1982) *An Evolutionary Theory of Economic Change*. Cambridge, MA: Harvard University Press.

Newell, A. and Simon, H. (1972) *Human Problem Solving*. Englewood Cliffs, NJ: Prentice Hall.

Nonaka, I. (1994) 'A dynamic theory of organizational knowledge creation', *Organization Science*, 5 (1): 14–37.

Penrose, E. (1952) 'Biological analogies in the theory of the firm', *American Economic Review*, 42: 804–19.

Powell, W., Koput, K., and Smith-Doerr, L. (1996) 'Interorganizational collaboration and the locus of innovation: networks of learning in biotechnology', *Administrative Science Quarterly*, 41 (1): 116–45.

Rabinow, P. (1998) *Making PCR: A Story of Biotechnology*. Chicago: University of Chicago Press.

Rosenberg, N. (1986) *Inside the Black Box*. Cambridge: Cambridge University Press.

Scherer, F.M. (1965) 'Corporate output, profits and growth', *The Journal of Political Economy*, 73 (3): 290–7.

Schumpeter, J. (1934) *The Theory of Economic Development*. Cambridge, MA: Harvard University Press.

Stuart, T., and Podolny, J. (1996) 'Local search and the evolution of technological capabilities', *Strategic Management Journal*, 17: 21–38.

Teece, D. (1986) 'Profiting from technological innovation: implications for integration, collaboration, licensing and public policy', *Research Policy*, 15 (6): 285–305.

Teece, D. (1998) 'Research directions for knowledge management', *California Management Review*, 40 (3): 289–92.

Tushman, M., and Anderson, P. (1986) 'Technological discontinuities and organizational environments', *Administrative Science Quarterly*, 31 (3): pp. 439–65.

Tushman, M., and Rosenkopf, L. (1992) 'On the organizational determinants of technological change: towards a sociology of technological evolution', in B. Staw and L. Cummings (eds), *Research in Organization Behavior*, vol. 14. Greenwich, CT: JAI Press.

Von Hippel, E. (1990) 'Task partitioning: an innovation process variable', *Research Policy*, 19 (5): 407–18.

Von Hippel, E. (1994) '"Sticky information" and the locus of problem solving: implications for innovation', *Management Science*, 40 (4): 429–39.

Von Hippel, E. (1998) 'Economics of product development by users: the impact of "sticky" local information', *Management Science*, 44 (5): 629.

Winter, S. (1987) 'Knowledge and competence as strategic assets', in D. Teece (ed.), *The Competitive Challenge: Strategies for Industrial Innovation and Renewal*. Cambridge, MA: Ballinger.

10 The Modularity Trap: Innovation, Technology Phase Shifts and the Resulting Limits of Virtual Organizations*

Henry W. Chesbrough and Ken Kusunoki

Introduction

Scholars have long noted that the technology of the firm shapes the organization of that firm (Burns and Stalker, 1961, and Woodward, 1960). More recent scholarship has shown that the organization of the firm also conditions its ability to profit from its innovation activities (Teece, 1986). A number of scholars have examined the role of the type of technology in the ability of incumbent firms to adapt to innovation opportunities (Abernathy and Utterback, 1978, Tushman and Anderson, 1986, Anderson and Tushman, 1990, Henderson and Clark, 1990, and Christensen, 1997). Some have argued that the organizational strategy of the firm must be aligned with the type of technology they choose to develop (Chesbrough and Teece, 1996, and Tushman and O'Reilly, 1997).

This interaction between technology and organization is one useful way to approach the study of knowledge management. Because technology causes the environment to change so frequently, technology-intensive settings provide researchers with abundant opportunities to observe the effects of change over a relatively short period of time. Technology provides, and indeed requires, explicitly dynamic approaches to managing knowledge, as Fiona Murray (among others) argues in Chapter 9.

This chapter builds on the prior research by developing a contingency framework firms may use to align their organizational strategy with the technology that they are pursuing. It advances the idea that the character of technology is not static. Rather, it evolves from one type, which we call 'integral' (defined below), to an opposite type, which we call 'modular' (also defined below), then cycles back. As the technology shifts from one

* We thank participants at the Second Annual Berkeley Conference on Knowledge and the Firm for useful remarks. We also wish to thank Fiona Murray and Steven Wheelwright for helpful comments on earlier drafts. Henry Chesbrough wishes to acknowledge financial support from the Division of Research at the Harvard Business School.

phase to the other, the optimal organizational configuration of the firm must also shift if it is to continue to capture value from its innovation activities.

However, the optimal alignment to a technology phase shift can be quite difficult, and often firms fall into organizational misalignment. Here we develop a conceptual framework of such organizational traps that helps explain how and why a firm fails to capture value from innovation after technology phase shifts. We apply the framework to the hard disk drive industry to illustrate the explanatory force of our framework.

Our major concern is with what we call the 'modularity trap', which is when a firm that has successfully aligned its organization with a modular phase of technology encounters difficulty capturing value from its innovation activities when the technology phase shifts from modular to integral. As discussed below, in a modular phase, firms that follow virtual organizational strategies match their internal organization to the modular technological characteristics of that phase. They coordinate much of their innovation activities via the marketplace, where independent firms come together to buy and sell technology and the components that are used to make the various items (Chesbrough and Teece, 1996). As this strategy can maximize flexibility and responsiveness in a changing marketplace, the virtual organization appears to provide a powerful and predominant model in industries that produce PCs, biotechnology, semiconductors and other technology. In these industries, many large, integrated firms have been outperformed by smaller, more focused competitors.

However, we do not think that modularity is the inevitable end state of technology. Rather, we see technology developing in cycles, where new discoveries shift the character of technology towards a more integral phase. For highly focused firms, this shift can create a serious problem, which we call the 'modularity trap'. Virtual organizations have succeeded by focusing their energies on a specific area of technology, but lack the systems expertise that can respond to new technology that rearranges the boundaries of existing technology. Their single-minded focus within a specific configuration of technology then becomes a significant liability. We will explain our reasoning about these technology shifts and the resulting organizational responses below, then illustrate their impact with examples from the Japanese hard disk drive industry.

Technology Phase Shifts and the Need for Organizational Alignment

When a new technology emerges, technological development in the industry is usually in a phase we term 'integral' (following Christensen and Chesbrough, 1999).[1] Here, the technical information about how the different elements of a system function together is not well defined and interactions between elements are poorly understood. The new technology may offer a tremendous improvement in performance or cost, but many other elements required to transform a promising idea into a commercial product have to adapt in order for this potential to be realized. This is the opposite of truly modular technology, whereby new components simply plug into the existing architectures without a hitch (Henderson and Clark, 1990).

Because the interactions between elements of this integral technology is poorly understood, developing it further is more complicated. Under these conditions, intermediate markets do not function effectively and can even be hazardous. A customer cannot fully specify their requirements to a supplier. The supplier can develop a product that meets the literal specification, only to have the customer return it because it does not work in the customer's product. Independent companies may reasonably differ about the cause of such a problem. Each may want the other to do more (and bear more of the costs) to resolve it. Customers and suppliers may also wish to avoid highly specific solutions to a particular problem for fear of being locked into doing business with each other and being exploited later on. Because the interdependencies are poorly understood, bringing in another supplier is a costly alternative that may not even solve the problem. Worse, a new supplier may introduce new technical problems, which, again, may be viewed differently by the different parties to the transaction.

To achieve close coordination and facilitate rapid mutual adjustment between pieces of interdependent technology, administrative coordination outside the market is required to develop a technology effectively. An internal or captive supplier of interdependent pieces of component technology has three general advantages over firms that coordinate via the market. One advantage is having superior access to information. The second advantage is weaker incentives to exploit temporary advantages inside the firm. The third advantage is tighter appropriability of the returns generated by the solutions to technical problems. We consider each of these in turn.

The information advantage arises from the fact that there is less 'impacted information' (Williamson, 1975) – that is, more information can be shared more quickly within the firm than can be shared between firms. Firms have access to even very detailed findings within their own walls, such as the results of specific tests and procedures, and all information created within the firm is the property of that firm. Employees have no legal right to withhold such information. Moreover, because employees usually expect to stay at a firm over time, they have an interest in cooperating today in return for receiving cooperation tomorrow on another project. Arm's-length coordination via the market has none of these advantages. One firm has no legal right to view the results of tests conducted at another firm, and firms can choose to act strategically when deciding what information to share and what information to withhold. Moreover, the very fact of dealing at arm's length means that neither party can be assured of working with the other in the future. Each firm may manoeuvre to encourage other suppliers or customers to create greater freedom of action to work with other companies in the future, in part by strategically sharing and withholding information. This reduces the 'shadow of the future' around their current dealings.

The incentive advantage is one of 'low-powered incentives' (Williamson, 1985). Individuals within different divisions that must coordinate have relatively little to gain directly from exploiting a temporary advantage over individuals in a sister division. Their division's stock is not directly traded, and the gains of one division and the losses of another are pooled together in the firm's overall stock price. Relative to firms transacting via the market, neither division has much incentive to withhold cooperation with the other or to renegotiate for better terms with the other party, as part of resolving the technical issues. The bargaining costs for coordinating technical problems become more attenuated than they would be for independent companies.

The final advantage is that of tighter appropriability (Teece, 1986). Divisions within a firm that work together to reduce complicated technical interdependencies can be fairly certain that they will benefit from the results. The likelihood that one division will hold up another is attenuated by the information and incentive advantages within firms noted above. As a result, technical problem solving can be undertaken with the confidence that the resulting solutions will not be used to undermine the position of one of the coordinating divisions in a renegotiation later on.

For these reasons, firms that follow integrated organizational strategies will match their internal organization better to the characteristics of integral technology. When innovation activities are integrated, firms can better manage the interactions between technical elements and share information freely without worrying about distortions in subsequent bargaining over the terms of exchange between business units.

However, technology may shift into a phase we call modular. In the modular phase of technology development, *de facto* and *de jure* standards develop that articulate and codify the interactions between elements of a system. These are often termed 'dominant designs' (Tushman and Anderson, 1986, and Anderson and Tushman, 1990). These standards permit even complicated components to be substituted for one another in a system. The presence of these standards and associated know-how creates enough codified information to enable markets to coordinate the integration of technology across the interfaces between stages of added value. When rival suppliers with interchangeable products discipline one another to promote strong competition within these standards, the result is more rapid technological advancement and lower prices to systems customers.

In these circumstances, virtual firms are indeed more 'virtuous' (Chesbrough and Teece, 1996) than firms that continue to manage these coordination activities inside the firm. The earlier information advantages within the firm have been rendered insignificant by the advent of technical standards. These standards codify the technological interactions, leaving relatively little technical ambiguity. The establishment of standards permits numerous firms to experiment with a variety of implementations, and the resulting diversity far exceeds what could be produced inside a single firm's walls. The very basis of competition shifts from constructing complicated systems with integral designs to more horizontal competition within individual layers of technology, bounded by these standards.

The incentive within firms remains low-powered, but this now becomes an impediment instead of a virtue. The presence of established standards permits multiple firms to compete at each level of technology. This competition disciplines each competing firm, stimulating greater risk-taking and providing an alternative source of technology should any firm attempt to hold up another. As markets can now function effectively to coordinate technical development within these standards, high-powered incentives lead to more advanced technology sooner. The presence of alternative sources similarly resolves potential appropriability problems, because suppliers have other customers and customers have other suppliers. Each can only expect to profit from the value added by its own technology.

Firms that follow virtual organizational strategies effectively match their internal organization to these modular technological characteristics. For virtual firms, focusing on a single layer of technology harnesses the strong incentives and high volumes available via the market. The ability of standards to coordinate their actions within a larger systems architecture mitigates coordination hazards and enables these firms to move fast.

These focused firms force larger firms with divisions in multiple layers of a technology to adopt more decentralized strategies themselves in order to remain competitive when the technology is in a modular phase. This decentralized organizational strategy must enable units within the firm to buy and sell components independently in the modular technology markets. In particular, decentralized organizations eschew corporate dictates to use captive sources when market conditions make this choice unwise. Similarly, they avoid corporate commands to refrain from selling technology to outside rival firms.

The overall model, therefore, is one in which phase shifts in the character of technology require an organization to reconfigure itself organizationally in order to effectively develop a technology. An important implication of the model is that the organizational strategies that integrated firms need to employ to appropriate the value of the technology they develop in their research must change in response to increasing or decreasing degrees of modularity at these interfaces. Because technological change and scientific discovery can alter the phase of a technology in an industry, firms must be prepared to adjust their organizational approach in order to profit from their technology.

To profit from innovation, therefore, firms must evaluate the condition of the technology on which their business is based and then adopt appropriate organizational policies and structures based on that evaluation. Firms that align their structures well will profit from their innovation

	Modular	Integral
Decentralized organization	Proper alignment Value realized only within technology layer No inefficient interactions	Misalignment Can't manage interactions Insufficient infrastructure
Centralized organization	Misalignment Unnecessary internal coordination Reduced scale economies	Proper alignment Value realized in the system Effective coordination of undefined interactions

Figure 10.1 *Technology–organization alignment matrix*

activities, while firms that do not will fall into the organizational traps that we describe below. These traps will frustrate their ability to capture value from their innovation investments.

The link between organizational alignment and technological phase can be depicted in a matrix, shown in Figure 10.1.

Figure 10.1 displays the interactions between organization and technology and where value can be captured or dissipated. The upper left quadrant reflects the appropriate alignment of a decentralized or virtual organizational strategy with a modular technological phase. Here, value is realized within each technology module, and the external market manages the links between the modules, avoiding inefficient internal interactions. The lower right quadrant depicts the appropriate alignment of a centralized organizational approach with an integral technological phase. Here, value is realized in the ability of internal coordination mechanisms to manage the complicated interactions of the technology. This value arises in large part because the market cannot manage these interactions itself. Here is where the information and low-powered incentive advantages within firms pay off.

The lower left and upper right quadrants indicate cases of misalignment, or organizational traps, where value can be dissipated owing to an inappropriate organizational approach to the technology. These misalignments are described and illustrated in detail below, with recent research findings from the Japanese hard disk drive industry.

The Shift to a Modular Phase and the Integrality Trap

The history of much technology reveals that the character of it is that it can cycle from very integral states to very modular states, and back, as shown

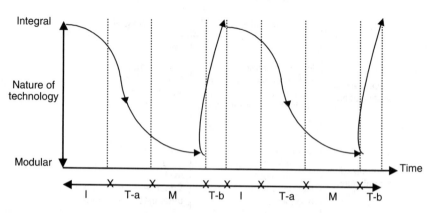

Figure 10.2   *Technology phase shifts*

in Figure 10.2 (an example of this is given below in the discussion of disk drives). In the early stage of an industry, technology underlying the product system is usually integral, implicitly encompassing substantial interdependencies between elements. At this time, how different technological elements interact with each other remains unclear. In the integral phase of technology, firms must learn and accumulate integral knowledge concerning interdependencies and interactions between technological elements at the whole product system level. However, integral knowledge is, by definition, context-specific and difficult to articulate in documents. It is tacit and usually embedded in one's experience as know-how (Nonaka and Takeuchi, 1995).

In this phase of technology, integral knowledge is a driver for an outstanding product, which sometimes results in radical or architectural innovation (Henderson and Clark, 1990). Integral innovation, based on new knowledge about how to coordinate interdependent technological elements and components within a product system, improves functionality and quality and reduces the cost of the product system. Given the tacit, context-dependent nature of integrative knowledge, however, realizing integral innovation requires a series of experiments, trial and error and continuous learning by doing, which takes a long time. By going through these experiences, firms gradually come to understand how the different technological elements and components that make up the product system interact with each other. They may develop tools, specialized equipment, testing procedures and simulations to better understand these complexities. As a result, technological interdependencies between elements lessen and interfaces between components are gradually clarified.

Hence, a technological shift to a modular phase is based on continuous, incremental accumulation of integral knowledge. The increasing understanding of technical interdependencies – and the associated creation of tools, models, simulations and equipment to manage them – all culminate in a shift of the technology towards a modular phase.

This dynamism can lead to misalignment of the organization and the technology it is developing. When technology moves from an integral state to a modular state as technological interdependencies become well known, a firm that participates in both upstream materials and downstream components (or upstream components and downstream systems) can only capture the value they add at each stage of the value chain. The shift to a modular phase effectively dissipates the earlier value obtained from coordinating these different stages of technology inside the firm.

If a firm proves unable to adapt its organizational configuration to the dictates of the phase of its technology, it will be caught in an 'organization trap'. If a firm remains integrated when a technology becomes more modular, it will be caught in an 'integrality trap' where it must rely on administrative mechanisms to accomplish technical coordination that other firms are able to accomplish in the market (see the lower left quadrant of Figure 10.1). Such misaligned firms continue to pursue internal coordination activities when these activities could be well managed via the technical interfaces and standards in the market.

Why are firms often caught in the integrality trap? The mechanism underlying this trap is closely related to the paradox that integral innovation triggers the shift to a modular phase of technology. As mentioned above, whether the innovation is based on changes within each component (modular innovation) or on new ways to coordinate and combine technological elements (integral innovation) is critical for classifying innovations. It is rather misleading to classify an innovation by looking only at its *ex post facto* configuration along the modular–integral dimension. Each innovation is, by nature, a dynamic process: a firm first perceives the source of an innovation and how it might lead to a better product and then exploits the source to realize an innovation with a particular configuration. This is shown in Figure 10.3.

Thus, an innovation can be viewed from two different angles. The horizontal dimension captures the *ex post facto* configuration of an innovation realized. As we have discussed, this dimension determines effective organizational alignments to exploit the value from innovation. The vertical dimension captures the source of the innovation, whether it consists of particular elements or by the combination of those elements. Framed in this way, an innovation can be characterized by the interaction between its source (*ex ante* expectation) and its configuration (*ex post facto* exploitation). Viewing an innovation as the interaction is important because an innovation that has its source in the progression of integral knowledge does not necessarily result in an integral innovation; nor does an innovation first realized in a specific component always result in a modular innovation. On the contrary, modular innovation often has its root in integral innovation (improved understandings of combinations of technological elements) and, conversely, integral innovation is often triggered by modular innovation (a change in a particular element or component). The important point is that such 'gaps' between a source and

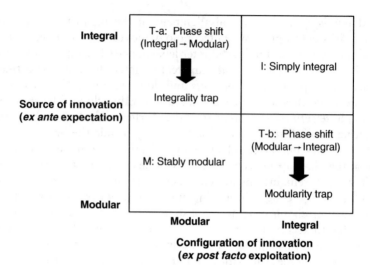

Figure 10.3 *Two views of innovation and technology phase shifts*

a configuration of innovation are typically observed when technology shifts from integral to modular or from modular to integral.

In a phase where technology is stably integral (as in Phase I in Figure 10.2), a firm will find a source of innovation as integral (a possible better way to combine elements), then it may expoit the opportunity for developing a better product via integral innovation. In this phase, therefore, an innovation is 'simply integral' and there is no gap between the *ex ante* source and the *ex post facto* configuration of the innovation (see the upper right quadrant of Figure 10.3). As firms expand their knowledge of the interdependencies of elements and components in the process of making integral innovations, technology will be in a transition phase (as in Phase T-a in Figure 10.2), gradually shifting towards the modular. In this state (the upper left quadrant in Figure 10.3), some firms may exploit the opportunity derived from preceding integral innovations so as to to realize modular innovation, but, at this time of phase transition, it is often difficult because modular innovation requires a firm to first freeze interfaces between technological elements in order to handle each element in an isolated fashion. Firms that have held leadership in the integral phase possess much integral knowledge to make the product still better. Approaching modular innovation appears perverse (at least to such firms) because this forces them to stop improving their integral knowledge, even to throw away their integral knowledge-based advantages. If they try to develop better products, it will appear much more effective and efficient for firms with rich integral knowledge to continue to pursue integral innovation. This 'rational' approach will prevent them from aligning their innovation activities with modular innovation, thus creating an organizational inertia that results in the integrality trap.

When Technology Shifts to an Integral Phase: the Modularity Trap

Organizational misalignment can work in the other direction as well. Firms that have effectively pursued virtual approaches when their technology was in a modular phase can get into trouble when the technology shifts to an integral phase if they do not also become more centralized organizationally. If a firm remains virtual as its technology shifts to a integral phase, a 'modularity trap' ensues, which is when a firm lacks the systems and experience to comprehend the new interdependencies necessary to develop the technology. The firm is no longer able to specify its needs and requirements adequately to its outside suppliers, so its familiar problem-solving routines are no longer effective. Unlike in internally organized firms, the supply chain linking the horizontal technology layers in the virtual firm is unable to achieve the coordination necessary to develop the technology.

The logic underlying this modularity trap comes from another paradox. This is that the technological shift to the integral phase can often be triggered by modular innovation. After the phase transition from integral to modular (Phase T-a in Figure 10.2), technology goes into the stably modular phase (Phase M, also in Figure 10.2). In this stage, innovation becomes simply modular. Firms try to exploit the innovation source at the component level to realize modular innovation in order to develop a better product (as shown in the lower left quadrant of Figure 4.3). However, modular innovation can sometimes reveal the need to deconstruct established ways of combining technological elements and components and, consequently, may force firms to develop new integral knowledge. Such disruptive modular innovation can result in a technology phase shift back to integral, where it again becomes unclear how different technological elements interact with each other (Phase T-b in Figure 2). At this time, the *ex post facto* configuration of innovation should be integral, while the source of innovation itself is still modular (as shown in the lower right quadrant of Figure 10.3). This distortion in the process of innovation can invite firms into the modularity trap (which is depicted in the upper right quadrant of Figure 10.1).

Firms that have enjoyed the advantages of virtual organization in the modular phase of technology will encounter great difficulties in this situation. These firms may have difficulty exploiting value from the modular innovation because it will not contribute to developing a better product without substantial coordination and interaction between technological elements.

The modularity trap is a real problem for firms with virtual organization strategies for the following two reasons. First, it would seem rational – even easy – for such firms to respond to the modular innovation opportunity by retaining their existing virtual organization. Because the innovation source lies in a specific technological element or component, the opportunity it presents seems clear. Furthermore, firms following a virtual organization approach can quickly and easily access components of a modular innovation from independent firms that began making and selling the components during the preceding modular phase. Hence, for virtual firms, the modular innovation appears to be more of an opportunity than a threat. Given the mechanism of the phase shift back to integral, virtual firms will remain virtual in order to take advantage of the abilities they have already developed. The modularity trap will become apparent only after they encounter *ex post facto* problems of interdependency and interaction between components.

Second, and very important, a technology shift back to the integral phase usually occurs over a much shorter time span than a shift to the modular phase; modularization takes a relatively long time because of the incremental nature of progress in integral knowledge. A shift back to the integral phase is triggered by a change in modular knowledge that is more explicit and context-independent. Once a firm introduces a modular innovation that requires major changes in how elements and components interact with each other, the stable interfaces between elements are broken immediately and technology moves back towards an integral phase.

This rapid shift makes it even easier for firms to fall into the modularity trap and more difficult for firms to escape from it. Firms cannot afford to gradually adapt themselves to the new phase, given its immediacy. Even if they try to develop integral knowledge by themselves to solve the coordination problems, this choice may result in a serious competitive penalty because creating integral knowledge takes a long time. Alternatively, they may rely on the problem-solving efforts of independent suppliers. However, doing so again raises the hazards of specificity and bargaining costs between the parties, making coordination still more difficult. Thus, once virtual firms fall into the modularity trap, there is no clear way out of it.

Technology Shifts and Organizational Misalignment in the Japanese Hard Disk Drive Industry: Thin Film Heads

We now examine the issues described above by looking at field research we conducted in the Japanese hard disk drive (HDD) market. The HDD industry has experienced technology phase shifts that we believe have resulted in organization traps for some firms in that market.

Hard disk drives consist of many different technological components, including read-write heads mounted at the end of an arm that flies over the surface of a rotating disk; aluminium or glass disks coated with magnetic material (often called 'media'); electric motors, including a spin motor that drives the rotation of the disks and an actuator motor that moves the head to the desired position over the disk; and a variety of electronic circuits that control the drive's operation and its interface with the computer. Although each of these component elements has evolved rapidly over the past few decades, here we focus primarily on the evolution of disk drive head technology.[2]

In the 1960s and 1970s, the HDD industry employed iron or ferrite heads that were mechanically ground to the correct tolerances for integration with iron-oxide media into a HDD. This technology was in a modular state, as the mechanical and electrical properties of ferrite heads were becoming well understood. Many companies at this time used outside suppliers and new suppliers were able to offer their heads to drive manufacturers.

There was a problem, however. The known characteristics of ferrite heads indicated that a new type of head would need to be developed if the industry were to continue to advance its technology. In anticipation of this eventual limit, IBM began developing prototype thin film heads at its Yorktown research labs in the mid-1960s and IBM announced proof of feasibility for use of this new material in magnetic recording in 1971. This announcement triggered research and development activity in other firms in that same year.

However, the new developments also caused problems. Using thin film material in a HDD required making numerous and extensive changes in other parts of the drive. The design of the head depended both on the design of other components in the system and the architecture of the system itself. Also, the designs of these other elements of the product, in turn, were predicated on the design of the head. The head–disk interface, for example, was far different from that used with the ferrite technology was used. The new head required differences in the disk media in order to reliably read and write data with the new material. Changes in the methods of error correction also had to be developed to enable the new material to record reliably.

In order to sort out the many technological interdependencies in the initial development of drives with thin film heads, product development teams had to do their work in a tightly integrated, iterative manner. The earlier, well-understood design rules that developed around ferrite head technology no longer applied as use of those rules generated error conditions that had not occurred before. The new rules that would allow thin film heads to be used in a disk drive design had to be discovered via trial and error. Depending on the problem, the solution might be implemented in the head design, the design of the head stack, the media coating or surface, the read channel electronics or the low-level software (called firmware) that controlled the disk drive functions.

The independent head companies, such as AMC, struggled mightily in the face of this technology shift. Although they were able to make a number of incremental improvements to ferrite head technology that extended its life well beyond the original anticipated limits, they were at a severe disadvantage in attempting to develop and market the new generation thin film head components to disk drive manufacturers. Customers could not fully specify the attributes they needed from AMC in their heads; nor could AMC anticipate their needs entirely. Samples of heads from AMC did not work in the new designs and determining how and where in the design and components to correct errors was an intricate process. Moreover, when AMC corrected early problems by revising its head designs, new problems cropped up in the head–disk interface, the disk surface and the associated electronics.

We view this situation as a 'modularity trap' that engulfed AMC and its drive customers. Independent head companies in this era knew how to engineer well-characterized technology such as ferrite heads and competed effectively with that technology. When that technology had matured and was starting to become obsolete, however, those same firms did not have the systems knowledge and perspective to create new technology with new materials and resolve the myriad integration issues with the other elements of the disk drive.

In contrast to AMC, IBM clearly benefited from its organizational strategy at this time in the industry. Because of its integrated organization and impressive abilities in research and development, it was able to establish a lead of many years in the deployment of thin film heads in HDDs. IBM also followed a policy of not selling its heads or its disk drives to other disk drive and systems companies respectively. This policy was also effective because the integral nature of thin film heads at the time precluded the creation of an active merchant market for them for many years to come.

The Phase Shift in Thin Film Head Technology Towards Modularity

Eventually, the mysterious attributes of thin film heads were sorted out by HDD makers and independent component manufacturers (many of whom hired key engineers from IBM, who then diffused important know-how from IBM to the independent manufacturers). As the technology became well understood, the independent firms could tool up their production lines to serve demand from any and all of their customers, giving them the potential to serve the entire market. They learned to work with suppliers of media (the disks in the disk drive) to develop new generation heads. Characterizations of the interactions were stabilized, test equipment companies developed tools to verify these characterizations and suppliers could be coordinated by their conformance to these characterizations. Joining AMC was new entrant Read-Rite, whose sales of heads mirrored the maturation of the thin film technology, rising from $28 million in 1988 to $345 million in 1992.

The development of these and other independent firms making high-quality heads in very high volume, along with the parallel development of other companies in the United States and Japan mastering the thin film technology, meant that IBM no longer enjoyed a proprietary technological edge attributable to its capabilities in the technology phase shift from modular to integral. As knowledge of that technology diffused widely throughout the industry, its character gradually changed from an integral technology to a highly modular one.

IBM's organizational strategy, however, remained inert during this phase shift in technology. It continued to restrict consumption of its heads to its own disk drive division and, similarly, limited the sale of its drives to its internal systems divisions. By eschewing outside sales of its now modular technology, IBM fell into a different organizational trap – the integrality trap. Thin film heads have high fixed development costs and require high volumes to amortize these costs. IBM's posture limited its total volume of head production to its internal needs. IBM's internal volume also suffered from other problems in its drive business at the time and resulted in rather low volumes (see Christensen 1992 and 1993). As a result, IBM became a high-cost producer of a technology it had invented.

This policy imposed a double penalty on IBM's drive business. It was not able to source heads on the merchant market and, instead, was mandated to use its own heads. Because IBM produced fewer of them, these heads were more expensive than those used by IBM's drive competitors. This cost penalty was compounded by a second effect. Because IBM could not sell its heads to other companies, it could not increase its production volumes in order to reduce its costs. As other companies' volumes and market share grew, IBM's cost disadvantage grew accordingly.

The Emergence of MR Heads: An Integral Technology Phase Shift

The continued rapid pace of technical advance in the HDD industry meant that thin film technology itself would encounter limits as well. IBM's research labs were developing a new type of head technology called 'magneto-resistive' (MR). MR heads represented another tremendous advance beyond thin film heads that promised to increase the potential recording density of disk drives tenfold, but, again, its initial character was opaque. The IBM announcement of the development of the technology quoted the lead engineering manager on the project, who said, 'We don't fully understand the physics behind the technology, but we are able to replicate it fairly consistently' (*San Francisco Chronicle*, 1992).

As with the initial thin film heads, the established design rules and models had to be thrown out. Once again, new design problems emerged.

Two common problems were electrostatic discharge (ESD) and thermal asperities (TAs), both of which illustrate the interdependencies of integral technology.

ESD was commonly encountered in the disk drive manufacturing process and every company had learned to protect the drive heads and drive electronics from it. What was new was the extraordinary sensitivity of MR heads to even minute exposures to ESD. An MR head could be processed through to completion, tested and then integrated into a HDD, but then fail to function in final test even though these processes had previously proved more than sufficient to manage ESD problems in thin film head designs. Of course, it took some time to ascertain that ESD was responsible for many of these failures, because the test procedures themselves had to be modified. Therefore 'failures' were subject to the usual Type I and Type II error problems. To resolve the problem, firms tried several changes – in the design of the head itself, the packaging for the head, the disk drive design and the manufacturing process. One firm reportedly spent over $10 million just to rip up the floor tiles of its manufacturing facility to install special flooring that inhibited even minute transmissions of ESD.

Thermal asperities are physical defects that the MR head creates in the spinning disk. This new problem results from the confluence of ever lower flying heights for the heads, higher temperatures for the writing of data by the MR head than earlier heads and texturing of the spinning disk surface. A TA is created when the flying head inadvertantly touches the disk during operation. The resulting contact generates heat, which causes the particles at that portion of the disk to swell, so distorting the signal recorded at that spot on the disk. Normal error correction codes often cannot be used to rectify these errors, because the length of the defect can exceed the length of the correction code.

Both the ESD and the TA phenomena were symptoms of a more general condition: the HDD technology had shifted back to an integral phase. Once again, independent head manufacturers and their disk drive customers had difficulty adapting to this new technology. Non-integrated US companies such as Western Digital and Maxtor, which had prospered during the modular state of thin film head technology, struggled mightily with independent head suppliers such as Read-Rite to adjust to the demands of MR head technology.

Each firm reported significant negative earning impacts from trying to adjust to the new MR technology during this period. Western Digital lost over half of its market capitalization in 1997 and analysts attributed this loss to its inability to successfully incorporate MR head technology into its next generation disk drives. Maxtor was forced to sell itself to Hyundai in order to obtain sufficient capital to remain in business. Quantum recently discontinued its captive MR head production, which it had acquired from Digital in 1994. This was the largest factor in a charge to Quantum's earnings of $190 million (*Wall Street Journal*, 1999).

Japanese firms' responses to MR technology phase shift

US firms are not the only ones to have fallen into this trap. We explored the response of the four leading Japanese HDD firms (Fujitsu, Hitachi, NEC and Toshiba) to these technology phase shifts. We learned that NEC, after more than 20 years of designing disk drives, decided in May 1997 to discontinue current generations of drive design work in MR and, instead, to partner with IBM to manufacture IBM designs in NEC's factories for NEC's systems businesses. These designs will incorporate IBM's MR components into IBM designs and allow NEC to produce competitive disk drives, albeit not of their own design. We think this decision reflects NEC's virtual approach to MR technology and its resulting inability to master MR's newly integral character.

Another Japanese drive manufacturer, Toshiba, appears to have fallen into the trap as well. Unlike NEC, Toshiba continues to develop its own disk drive designs, but relies on outside suppliers for its heads and media. Toshiba had focused its skills on rapid time to market for modular technologies for its 2.5-inch HDDs, many of which were employed in its own notebook systems. Toshiba initially treated the advent of MR heads as a minor extension of earlier head technology. When Toshiba developed its first MR drive, there were no off-the-job/on-the-job training programmes for engineers to master MR technology. In fact, the first MR drive development programme did not even have a unique project code name. Toshiba's first MR drive was just another product development following its earlier HDDs with thin film heads. Considering that the HDD technology had been in a modular phase until the MR head innovation, Toshiba's virtual organizational strategy appeared effective. One manager, mentioned the importance of component outsourcing in the HDD business:

> It was very crucial for us to have good outside suppliers of key components in order to achieve efficient product development. In-house development of key components requires heavy investments, taking effort over a long time. We have tried to have at least two suppliers for a particular key component like heads, because such an approach contributes to stable supply and cost reduction of components through competition between outside suppliers, as well as avoiding risks of investment into component development. (Kamimura, 1998)

However, Toshiba's virtual approach faced difficulties during the development of its MR drives. This same manager described the resulting problems they encountered during the development of Toshiba's first MR drive:

> We viewed HDD competition as purely a matter of speed. The advantage for first-movers is great. If you are three months late, your profit will be only 30 percent of the first-mover's. But in the case of MR heads, Toshiba could not be first. We tried to define the specs we required for our heads. But we couldn't completely specify them because we were less knowledgable about MR heads than our suppliers. When we faced technological problems unique to MR drives, we

thought that it was even wiser for us to rely on our suppliers' problem-solving efforts. For example, the process of manufacturing MR heads was so complicated that it was difficult for us to specify how to improve the performance of MR heads. It appeared more effective and efficient for us to leave the major part of head-related problem-solving in suppliers' hands simply because they were component specialists and knew more than we did. (Kamimura, 1998)

Though Toshiba's development engineers frequently communicated with suppliers by means of drawings and specifications, they did not have a working-level collaboration. When they faced problems, they relied heavily on the problem-solving efforts of each supplier. For example, when Toshiba encountered the TA problem, its engineers only attempted to control the level of particles in the drive assembly process. Indeed, they left most of the TA-related problem solving to outside suppliers of heads and media, simply setting a target of functionality and proposing that suppliers intensify their testing of component quality. This hands-off approach of Toshiba's narrowed possible paths to solutions. For example, the correction of TA only on the head side inevitably took a very long time (between three and four months) because the manufacturing process of MR heads requires many complicated steps, like a semiconductor fabrication process.

Toshiba's difficulties with MR heads in its HDDs has caused the company to change head suppliers. As of June 1998, it had tried three different head vendors. In 1998, Toshiba began using MR heads from Headway, a US supplier, because Headway's MR heads were originally designed to prevent TAs, incorporating an auto-cancelling mechanism based on technology developed by Hewlett Packard. Using Headway's heads in disk drives requires a different pre-amplifier, but it is a standard component that can be easily purchased in the marketplace.

Although Toshiba has tried to solve the MR head-related problems while retaining its virtual organizational strategy, it is still struggling to resolve technical issues related to the MR technology. Toshiba did not ship MR drives until four years after IBM, and its market share in 2.5-inch drives fell by ten percentage points from 1996 to 1998, while IBM increased its market share in 2.5-inch drives by a corresponding amount (International Data Corporation, 1998).

Not every Japanese HDD firm fell into the modularity trap. For example, Fujitsu was able to master the MR technology more effectively by investing continuously in systems knowledge, materials and component technology in its R&D labs. When the first MR drives were introduced, four different labs were engaged in MR drive development. Fujitsu Laboratory, a corporate lab, conducted long-term, MR head-related materials research. In December of 1993, 35 engineers were transferred from Fujitsu Lab to a division lab (Storage Technology Lab), including ten engineers who focused on head technology. At that time, however, only five engineers specialized in MR technology, because using MR heads had been only one option among three different technical approaches. In 1992,

Fujitsu Lab also pursued thin film heads and vertical heads as well as MR heads for possible future technology. Starting with the five engineers with MR expertise, Fujitsu gradually mastered MR technology in a learning-by-doing fashion. One engineer described Fujitsu's approach in the early stage of MR head development:

> At that time, we had neither an off-the-job nor on-the-job training programme for mastering MR technology. This was simply because most of us did not fully understand what the MR was. What we did was on-the-job learning, which included lots of trial and error. However, our in-house approach had some good things. Though we had not been so knowledgeable about MR, we could be rather careful about how to deal with the new technology when using it within the HDD product system as a whole. From the beginning, we were alert to potential interface problems between new MR heads and media. (Interview with Fujitsu engineer)

On the division side (Storage Products Group), three units conducted MR drive development from different perspectives. The Storage Technology Lab focused on future technology for key components, including heads, media, large-scale integrated circuits (LSIs) and mechanism design, as well as the HDI (head–drive interface). The Storage Component Division developed components for the next generation HDDs. Not only did it develop key components, it also built the high-end, state-of-the-art HDDs that used these components, developing systems knowledge with them. The HDD Division was responsible for developing current generation HDDs with project teams, each of which was organized for a particular model. HDDs for desktop PCs and mobile PCs were manufactured in this division.

Fujitsu's integrated organizational strategy gave it mastery over the many interdependent elements in the new MR head disk drive. Its approach to solving the noise problem is a good example. Controlling noise level was a technically subtle problem because noise was embedded in a complicated manufacturing process unique to MR heads. Fujitsu first tried to control the noise by improving the manufacturing process, but this effort did not reduce the noise level sufficiently. Hence, the company went back to materials development, which needed research-oriented technology developed at the Fujitsu Lab. In intensive collaboration with the Storage Technology Lab, the development engineers decided to speed up the use of advanced materials that had been under development at a research group in the lab for a future generation. This finally contributed to overcoming the noise problem of MR heads. Fixing errors due to TAs as well as the problem of a gap between the read and write parts of a head also required engineers to carefully understand the complicated interdependencies of heads and other parts of an HDD. Most of these technical problems were found only after assembling components into a prototype. Head engineers collaborated extensively with those on the drive side (who produced the mechanism and the LSI electronics) to coordinate the interdependencies.

Though the problem appeared on the head side, efforts on the drive side, such as error correction LSIs and controlling mechanisms, turned out to improve the quality and functionality of MR drives most effectively. One manager, described how the integral knowledge was applied to the resolution of TAs induced by the shift to MR heads:

> We saw two avenues to correct this problem, the drive side or the head itself. Seemingly, the problem was head-related. However, taking this head approach often resulted in costly and time-consuming approaches. Correction efforts on the drive system side substantially contributed to solving the problem. It was faster to think of how to recover from the asperity in the drive system than to think of how not to make the noise. This problem-solving required the coordinated efforts of many departments, such as the Fujitsu Central Lab, the Storage Technology Lab, the Storage Component Division, and the Hard Disk Drive Development Division. We were skeptical about relying on only the head suppliers to fix this problem, because they might define the problem too narrowly, which might limit their ability to find the most effective solution to the problem. (Sugihara, et al., 1998)

Fujitsu was able to leverage its capabilities in these different areas quite directly by co-locating these functions for extended periods of time until interdependencies were resolved. For this cross-functional integration, working group meetings held in the Storage Component Division located in Nagano played an important role. Engineers in the Storage Technology Lab (located in Astugi and Kawasaki) and those in the HDD Division (located at Yamagata) got together in the working group organized in the Storage Component Division. For a working group meeting, engineers from Atsugi, Kawasaki and Yamagata usually stayed in Nagano for one week in order to resolve the interdependency problems. Such working group meetings were held at least twice a month during the development of the MR drive. The Storage Component Division was a good place for the working group meetings because it had manufacturing facilities, while there was only a small-scale pilot plant in the Storage Technology Lab. It was important for the working group to verify the effectiveness of their development by actually manufacturing the HDD prototypes using the facilities in Nagano:

> Facing MR technical problems, it was critical to consider how best to recover. Should we change the head, its packaging, the mechanical assembly, or the electronics? This was difficult to answer because the MR technology was so unclear at this time. We needed to make lots of experiments and prototypes, to use trial-and-error to explore alternative solutions. Because of the strong interdependencies of the head–media interface, our head guys and media guys usually worked together in the same room to solve these problems. (Sugihara, et al., 1998)

Hitachi possessed similar capabilities in its own corporate labs, such as the Central Research Lab, the Basic Research Lab and its product development divisions' labs and advanced development groups. In 1991, the Advanced Technology Development Centre was established in the Storage Systems Division, and 100 HDD-related engineers were transferred from a variety of corporate labs to the Centre for MR drive development. They brought different strengths and perspectives to the challenges of MR.

Hitachi made extensive use of co-location and cross-functional problem solving to address problems posed by MR technology. In order to resolve the ESD, some engineers in the head design group went to Hitachi's Musashi Works of the Semiconductor Division to learn how to improve the MR head manufacturing process, which resulted in considerable improvement in yield. As for the TA problem, Hitachi pursued two ways of problem solving. First, given the experiment data from the HDI group in the Storage Systems Division, it applied the etching texture technology originally developed by its Process Technology Lab (a corporate lab) to control the surface of MR heads. Second, Hitachi tried to use its high-speed error code correction (ECC) technology, which was originally developed by Hitachi for telecommunications devices. It improved the code processing LSIs with the help of engineers from the Semiconductor Division. Engineers of head and media, as well as LSI groups of the Advanced Technology Development Centre, also conducted experimentation by collaborating with the Central Research Lab:

> We built many 'semi-prototypes' to explore MR drive technology. These usually did not work, so we often had to send the prototype from the Advanced Technology Development Center to the Product Development Group, and back again, along with much communication between the departments. While doing this, the division of labor between the two sometimes disappeared, and engineers sometimes worked in the others' areas for weeks on end in a total effort to resolve the problems. We also had formal interdepartmental meetings once a month, involving all managers. We also created a 'project team room,' where the walls were covered with data on experiments, facilitating discussion there. There were informal interdepartmental meetings almost every day in the room. (Nagai, 1998)

IBM's organizational reconfiguration

The costs to firms of being caught in the modularity trap in the HDD industry have risen since the organizational reconfiguration of IBM that began in 1993. Leveraging its technology advantage in MR heads, IBM reversed its course of many years and aggressively entered the original equipment manufacturer (OEM) disk drive market in 1993, selling its MR-based drives to numerous computer makers. It has been particularly effective in penetrating the 2.5-inch HDD market, where its market share has reached over 50 per cent (Disk/Trend, 1998).

While selling MR components gives other drive makers access to leading-edge technology, IBM likely believes that the gains from its expanded

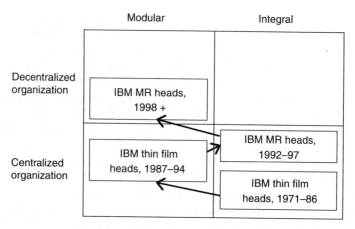

Figure 10.4   *IBM's movement along the technology–organization alignment matrix*

components sales outweigh the costs of having competing firms use its component technology. Of course, IBM's drive division benefits from this greater component volume in the form of lower costs for the heads it uses, making its drives still more competitive.

The benefits of this reconfiguration are already apparent. IBM's OEM market sales of disk drives, all of which employed IBM's MR heads, grew from zero in 1992 to almost $3 billion in 1997 (Disk/Trend, 1998). IBM's new approach means that competitors cannot rely on IBM to ignore market opportunities outside of its own systems business. Competitors that failed to keep pace with IBM in technology are now being punished by IBM's willingness to deploy its technology across the industry to serve previously unserved markets. As a result, its competitors have found it difficult to gain sufficient volume to cover their own R&D costs.

As we have discussed, IBM's organizational strategy has drifted in and out of alignment with the phase of its head technology. This movement is depicted in Figure 10.4. IBM has done well when its technology and its organization are in alignment, and it has suffered when the two have drifted apart. This suggests that there is no 'best' organizational configuration for pursuing technology through the various phase shifts. Instead, organizations must invest in systems-level knowledge and integration during integral phases, while pursuing decentralized buying and selling of technology during modular phases.

Strategies for Stimulating the Alignment of the Organization with the Phases of its Technology

We believe that firms need to develop greater organizational flexibility in order to align their organizations with the phases of their technology. We are not alone in this contention (see Tushman and O'Reilly, 1997, and Christensen, 1997). The experience of IBM, though, suggests that such flexibility is difficult to realize. IBM's organizational strategy has drifted in and out of alignment with the phase of its technology, suggesting that its organization exhibits strong inertia.

There is extensive literature on the widespread inertia of organizations (Hannan and Freeman, 1989). Thus, our model may be too ambitious in suggesting that organizations can adapt to phase-shifts in technology. Although we recognize the severity of organizational inertia, we believe that organizations none the less can develop dynamic abilities that can enable proactive responses to shifts in technology (see Teece, Pisano and Shuen, 1997). We view Fujitsu as an example of a disk drive firm that fairly nimbly aligned its organization with the phases of its technology by making important investments in its abilities.

When IBM made its MR technology announcement in 1992, Fujitsu was already planning its own research and development response. In its central research laboratory in Atsugi, Fujitsu had conducted extensive basic research into MR materials. This group had been tracking earlier IBM activities in MR and had begun to research the properties of this material. However, being integrated back into research does not automatically guarantee that a firm will avoid the modularity trap. As the technology phase shifts are cyclical, it is critical for a firm to develop dynamic abilities to utilize its integrated assets for stimulating the alignment of its organization and changing technology phases.

From this point of view, Fujitsu may provide a good example of a firm with such dynamic abilities. Besides being integrated, Fujitsu's organizational stategy was characterized by the way it managed the division of labour for developing MR drives. There were two key characteristics underlying Fujitsu's integrated organizational strategy. One was the flexible categorization of engineering activities. Though Fujitsu possessed a variety of engineering abilities, including basic research, components development, components manufacturing and HDD assembly, its definition of each engineering activity was not so rigid. To the contrary, Fujitsu's categorization of activities was flexible enough to adapt to technology phase shifts. As we have seen, Fujitsu transferred people from this central lab to its Storage Technology Laboratories in Atsugi and Kawasaki. The number of engineers in the Storage Technology Laboratories almost doubled during one year, while the number of engineers in the HDD Development Division grew by more than half. Overall, the total number of engineers grew by over 60 per cent in a single year in an alert and agile response to a phase shift in head technology. A second key feature of Fujitsu's organizational strategy was the co-location of cross-departmental working groups at the Storage Component Division, where they jointly conducted prototype-based experiments in order to identify and resolve the interdependency problems. This strategy expanded the boundaries of each engineering activity, enabling engineers with different functional tasks to focus on technical interdependencies at the drive system level.

Second, the 'system-based differentiation' was another key characteristic underlying Fujitsu's R&D organization (Kusunoki, 1997). In addition to being flexible, Fujitsu's categorization of engineering activities was based on different perspectives on the drive system over time, rather than on conventional functional differentiation. Its different R&D units, such as the Fujitsu Central Lab, Storage Technology Lab, Storage Component Division and HDD Development Division, were not simply differentiated along the functional dimension; nor were they intended to optimize engineering activities within their functional domains (research, components design, components manufacturing, drive design, assembly and so forth). In fact, each lab or division focused on its unique time perspective on the whole HDD system. For example, engineers of the Storage Technology Lab focused their activities on Fujitsu's future generation HDDs, the Storage Component Division on the next generation or high-end HDDs and the HDD Development Division targeted the current generation HDDs. Each lab or division thus possessed not only functional knowledge, but also system-level knowledge of HDD that was differentiated along a time horizon. Hence, each possessed particular knowledge for resolving technical interdependencies within itself even before it undertook coordination and communication for system-level problem solving. In this sense, Fujitsu's problem solving across departmental boundaries in the working group was more than cross-functional integration. It was cross-perspective integration in which different perspectives on the HDD systems blended with the problem solving of technical interdependencies. This system-based dimension of organizational differentiation facilitated each division's focus on the system-level interdependencies and generated an effective and efficient approach to resolving the interdependency problems. One manager of Fujitsu noted:

> Even when I was struggling with the MR technology at the Storage Technology Lab, I did not have the notion that I was doing it for MR heads alone. Rather, what I wanted to do was to develop and commercialize a totally new MR drive. My effort was not limited to the head itself. I was always thinking how we could make our HDDs better by using the MR heads under development. In this sense, there was no sharp distinction between our advanced engineering at the component level and drive development in the HDD Division. So, it was very natural for us to get together and collaborate in the working group at the Storage Component Division. However, our perspective on HDDs was more future-oriented, while the division guys concentrated on the design for a coming model. (Sugihara, et al., 1998)

The ability to access and transfer advanced technology – and the people who developed the technology – proved crucial in Fujitsu's ability to avoid the modularity trap that ensnared NEC and Toshiba. It enabled them to begin MR development sooner, get initial prototypes developed faster, creatively resolve technical issues across departmental boundaries and ship working products two years ahead of the other two firms. Fujitsu's flexible categorization and system-based differentiation of R&D activities constitute two valuable capabilities that provided it with the ability to respond to technical changes that frustrated other firms that lacked these abilities. If Fujitsu's engineering activities had been rigidly defined, functional boundaries between advanced engineering, components design and drive design could have prevented engineers from developing integral knowledge, a problem that might have caused it to fall into the modularity trap despite its integrated organizational strategy.

This, however, is only half of the organizational agility required in our model. The other imperative is to be able to adjust to technology phase shifts when the technology becomes more modular and requires greater decentralization to exploit. How can a firm with the above abilities avoid being inhibited by them when the technology phase shift obliges them to do so? How can they escape the other trap, the integrality trap?

Fujitsu again may serve as an illustration that escape is possible. As Fujitsu developed its first magneto-resistive heads internally and then created its first drives using MR heads, it deliberately shared its MR technology with a long-standing head supplier – TDK. While it continued to develop MR heads internally, it carefully nurtured TDK as a second source of MR technology. In 1992, in the early stage of MR technology development, TDK had not committed itself to MR heads because of their technological difficulty. It was Fujitsu that encouraged TDK to enter the MR head business. The Fujitsu Lab first disclosed its experimental data on its MR heads to TDK and then started intensive and extensive communication with TDK engineers. Supported by Fujitsu, TDK developed many prototype MR heads for Fujitsu. The Storage Technology Lab tested and evaluated the samples from TDK in Fujitsu's drives. Fujitsu also had a strong business commitment to TDK. Fujitsu purchased all of TDK's first volume production of MR heads. For the first model of its MR drives, Fujitsu purchased approximately half of the heads it needed from TDK, and made the other half internally. Why would Fujitsu voluntarily disclose the results of many tens of millions of dollars of research to an outside supplier, who would then sell heads based on that technology to competing disk drive manufacturers?

We see three related reasons for Fujitsu's decision, all of which helped Fujitsu avoid the integrality trap. One, Fujitsu was proactively recruiting a second source for its own internal head manufacturing division. This outside source would provide rivalry to the internal operation (Asunama, 1992) and force it to remain competitive. Two, Fujitsu acquired extensive process technology know-how from TDK as a result of sharing its MR technology. As subtle factors in the manufacturing process had substantial influence on the quality of MR heads, Fujitsu could benefit from learning TDK's know-how in order to improve its MR drives, especially when resolving the complicated interfaces between heads and other components. This increased the yields and reduced the costs of Fujitsu's internal head division. Three, the increased volumes Fujitsu's supplier would obtain from other companies would benefit Fujitsu by lowering the benchmark costs for its internal division yet again (Tatsuta and Adachi, 1998), creating an ongoing impetus for further internal cost reduction.

The division of activities between Fujitsu and external suppliers was also flexible. TDK was not simply an outside head supplier for Fujitsu, nor was the division of activities rigidly fixed. The role of TDK gradually changed in the process of MR drive development, which was based on mutual commitment and trust created by long-term collaboration. As for the sourcing of heads, Fujitsu's strategy may appear to have been 'outsourcing', but its dynamic division of activities with TDK enabled it to escape from the integrality trap in which integrated firms without dynamic abilities were often caught.

Fujitsu also empowered its HDD division to aggressively pursue outside sales of disk drives to other systems companies. Doing so meant that – at both the drive level and the systems level – Fujitsu was simultaneously buying technology from outside companies and selling its own to outside companies. This decentralized approach forced each division within Fujitsu to stand on its own value added feet and unshackled Fujitsu's components and disk drives from restraints at the corporate level.

Fujitsu's strategies build on long-standing investments in research, flexible categorization of boundaries of inside and outside engineering activities, system-based differentiation of R&D organization and proactive decentralization policies. These appear to have given the company some agility. Because firms pursuing virtual strategies, such as NEC, Toshiba, Western Digital and Maxtor, had no such dynamic flexibility, their ability to incorporate MR technology in its integral phase state was severely curtailed.

Conclusion

We think that technology evolves in cycles, emerging initially in an integral form in which the various technological interdependencies are opaque. Gradually, after extensive processes of experimentation, trial and error, these interactions become well understood. This understanding causes the character of the technology to become modular in nature. However, further research and discovery can generate new breakthroughs that start the cycle over again and such breakthroughs are often triggered by specific modular innovations.

To profit from innovation in these different phases of technology, we offered a model of how firms need to align their organizations with the character of the technology they are pursuing. Modular technology phases require decentralized or virtual organizational approaches that coordinate technical adjustments in the market to capture value from innovation. Integral phases require much more centralized or integrated organizational structures that leverage managerial processes to coordinate poorly understood interdependencies inside the firm.

Firms that do not so align themselves are at risk of falling into one of two organizational traps. One is an integrality trap, in which a centralized firm continues to rely on managerial coordination in a modular phase of technology to manage its technology development. The other trap is a modularity trap, in which firms that achieved success by means of decentralized coordination via the market continue to rely on those methods for resolving integral technology issues.

Given the recent enthusiasm for virtual firms, we think it worth emphasizing this latter trap. Firms such as Toshiba and NEC relied on outside suppliers' capabilities to incorporate MR technology, effectively ignoring the importance of the technology phase shift of MR towards greater integrality. The lack of strong systems integration knowledge, combined with deep component knowledge, caused them to underestimate the challenge of the MR technology shift and forced them to rely on outside suppliers to respond to the challenge. These outside firms similarly lacked the required systems knowledge. The resulting problems in coordination resulted in late shipments of the technology, leading to the loss of market share for Toshiba and the decision of NEC to stop designing disk drives. Firms such as IBM and Fujitsu, which possessed the technical ability at the systems and component levels and employed a centralized organizational strategy to manage the technology transition of disk drive heads to an integral phase, have been able to profit handsomely from their competitors' weaknesses. As MR technology becomes well established, both firms are also adopting flexible organizational strategies that will allow them to continue to profit from this technology.

Virtual organizations are widely believed to be speedy and agile This is certainly true in some industries where technology is in a modular phase. If technology is integral, as it is in the automobile industry, integrated organizational strategies work better to produce profit from innovation opportunities. Similarly, industries in which the technology is stably modular may benefit more from delayed, horizontally organized, more virtual approaches.

While this contingent perspective is common among academic scholars and practitioners, our point of view emphasizes that such a static contingency framework may overlook the dynamic aspects of technology. Even if technology is currently in a modular phase, it can move back to integral and vice versa. The technology phase shifts can bring about considerable impacts on firms' competitiveness. Our concept of the modularity trap may therefore carry an important insight for the virtuousness of virtual firms.

Notes

1 We adopt the term 'integral' to highlight the organizational implications of this type of technology and dispel any potential confusion between 'systemic' technology and 'systems' technology that might arise for readers with engineering and scientific backgrounds. In an earlier paper, one of us termed this type of technology 'systemic' (Chesbrough and Teece 1996), which might generate such confusion.
2 Our account of the introduction of thin film heads in this section draws heavily from Christensen's extensive research programme in hard disk drives. See Christensen, 1992, 1993 and 1997 and Christensen and Chesbrough, 1999.

References

Abernathy, William, and Utterback, James (1978) 'Patterns of industrial innovation', *Technology Review*, June/July: 40–7.

Anderson, Philip, and Tushman, Michael (1990) 'Technological discontinuities and dominant designs: a cyclical model of technological change', *Administrative Science Quarterly*, 35: 604–33.

Asunama, B. (1992) 'Japanese manufacturer–supplier relationships in international perspective', in P. Sheard (ed.), *International Adjustment and the Japanese Economy*. St Leonards, Australia: Allen & Unwin.

Burns, Tom, and Stalker, George (1961) *The Management of Innovation*. London: Tavistock.

Chesbrough, Henry W. (1999a) 'Arrested development: the experience of European hard disk drive firms in comparison with US and Japanese firms', *Journal of Evolutionary Economics*, 9: 287–329.

Chesbrough, Henry W. (1999b) 'The differing organizational impact of technological change: a comparative theory of national institutional factors', *Industrial and Corporate Change*, 8 (3): 447–86.

Chesbrough, Henry, and Teece, David (1996) 'When is virtual virtuous? Organizing for innovation', *Harvard Business Review*, Jan.–Feb.: 65–74.

Christensen, Clayton (1992) 'The innovator's challenge: understanding the influence of market environment on processes of technology development in the rigid disk drive industry', PhD dissertation, Harvard Business School.

Christensen, Clayton (1993) 'The rigid disk drive industry: a history of commercial and technological turbulence', *Business History Review*, 67 (Winter): 531–88.

Christensen, Clayton (1994) 'Industry maturity and the vanishing rationale for industrial research and development', working paper 94–059, Graduate School of Business, Harvard University.

Christensen, Clayton (1997) *The Innovator's Dilemma*. Cambridge, MA: Harvard Business School Press.

Christensen, Clayton, and Chesbrough, Henry (1999) 'Technology, organization, and the returns to research' (mimeo), Harvard Business School.

Disk/Trend Report–Rigid Disk Drives, Disk/Trend, Mountain View, CA. Annual reports 1977–1997.

Grchowski, Edward (1998) 'History of disk technology at IBM', IBM Almaden Labs web site: www.storage.ibm.com.technolo/grochows/

Hannan, Michael, T. (1977) 'The population ecology of organizations', *American Sociology*, 82: 929–64.

Hannan, Michael T., and Freeman, John (1989) *Organizational Ecology*. Cambridge Harvard University Press.

Henderson, Rebecca, and Clark, Kim (1990) 'Architectural innovation: the reconfigurati existing product technologies and the failure of established firms', *Administrative Sci Quarterly*, 35: 9–30.

International Data Corporation (1998) 'Storage systems: 1998 Winchester market forecast and review', Framingham, MA: IDC.

Isozaki, Ichiro, and Mukuta, Takayuki (1998) Personal interview at NEC Corporate offices, Fuchu City, Japan, 16 March.

Kamimura, Hiromi (1998) Personal interview at Toshiba Corporate offices, Tokyo, Japan, 17 March.

Kusunoki, Ken (1997) 'The phase variety of product system and system-based differentiation: an alternative view on organizational capabilities of the Japanese firm for product innovation', working paper 97–10, Hitotsubashi University Institute of Innovation Research.

Kusunoki, Ken, and Numagami, Tsuyoshi (1998) 'Interfunctional transfers of engineers in Japan: empirical findings and implications for cross-functional integration', *IEEE Transactions*, Washington, DC.

Leonard-Barton, D.A. (1992) 'Core capabilities and core rigidities: a paradox in managing new product development', *Strategic Management Journal*, 13: 111–25.

Nagai, Hideo (1998) Personal interview at Hitachi offices in Odawara, Japan, 18 March.

Nonaka, Ijuhiro, and Takeuchi, Hirotaka (1995) *The Knowledge-creating Company*. New York: Oxford University Press.

Odagiri, Hiroyuki (1992) *Growth Through Competition, Competition Through Growth*. Oxford: Clarendon Press.

Odagiri, Hiroyuki, and Goto, Akira (1993) 'The Japanese system of innovation: past, present and future', in Richard Nelson (ed.), *National Innovation Systems: A Comparative Analysis*, Oxford: Oxford University Press. pp. 76–114.

San Francisco Chronicle, August 15, 1992, D1.

Sheard, Paul (1991) 'Delegated monitoring among delegated monitors: principal agent aspects of the Japanese main banking system', working paper 274, Center for Economic Policy Research, Stanford University.

Sugihara, J., Adachi, S., and Hashizume, H. (1998) Interview with senior Fujitsu Storage Products Group management, Fujitsu offices, Kawasaki, Japan, 20 March.

Tatsuta, T., and Adachi, S. (1998) Personal interview at FDK Corporate Offices, Tokyo, Japan, 19 March (FDK is a subsidiary of Fujitsu).

Teece, David J. (1986) 'Profiting from technological innovation: implications for integration, collaboration, licensing and public policy', *Research Policy*, 15 (Dec.): 285–305.

Teece, David J., Pisano, Gary P., and Shuen, Amy (1997) 'Dynamic capabilities and strategic management', *Strategic Management Journal*, 18 (7): 509–33.

Tushman, Michael, and O'Reilly, Charles (1997) *Winning Through Innovation*. Cambridge, MA: Harvard Business School Press.

Tushman, Michael, and Anderson, P. (1986) 'Technological discontinuities and organizational environments', *Administrative Science Quarterly*, 31: 439–65.

Wall Street Journal, February 23, 1999, C1.

Williamson, Oliver E. (1985) *The Economic Institutions of Capitalism*. New York: The Free Press.

Williamson, Oliver E. (1975) *Markets and Hierarchies: Analysis and Antitrust Implications.* New York: The Free Press.

Woodward, Joanne (1960) *Management and Technology.* London: Her Majesty's Stationery Office.

PART III
MANAGING KNOWLEDGE AND TRANSFORMATION

---

11 Can Knowledge Management Deliver Bottom-line Results?

Charles E. Lucier and Janet D. Torsilieri

Introduction

In late 1996, NatWest Markets – the investment banking arm of Britain's NatWest Group – appointed the well-regarded banker Victoria Ward as its first Chief Knowledge Officer (CKO). Her goal? To improve the productivity of 7,000 employees around the world by giving them access to each other's knowledge – ideas, lessons learned, specific client understandings, the locations of experts and so on. Recognizing that the driven and accomplished investment bankers would resist being told by a CKO what knowledge mattered most, Ward enlisted champions from various business unit line organizations who shared her conviction that by enabling sharing among investment bankers, productivity would improve. Ward and her small team of seven worked with these champions to rapidly launch a series of sharing and collaboration pilots. However, the investment bank, unconvinced of the value of these pilots, ended its foray into knowledge management less than a year after appointing Ward as CKO. Frustrated, but convinced of the power of knowledge management, Ward left and started her own knowledge management consulting business.

According to John Browne, CEO of British Petroleum, 'to generate extraordinary value for shareholders, a company has to learn better than its competitors and apply that knowledge through its businesses faster and more widely than they do' (Prokesch, 1997). BP has outperformed competitors in recent years – in part by continually launching initiatives to leverage the knowledge of customers, contractors, vendors and employees.

Examples include a programme reducing average drilling days (a major driver of deepwater drilling costs) from 100 days per well to only 42 days by systematically sharing lessons learned across wells; the joint development of a new logging tool with Schlumberger that enabled BP to more productively drill horizontal wells long before the competition; and a virtual network that generated $30 million in value in its first year by linking experts to critical decisions – this was subsequently embraced and funded by business unit managers across the company.

The Promise of Knowledge Management

Knowledge management offers a compelling promise.[1] As strategists agree that knowledge is increasingly the source of companies' competitive advantage, it is logical to expect that more effective management of the creation and use of knowledge would accelerate a company's natural rate of learning, allow it to outpace competitors and create value for both customers and shareholders (Lucier and Torsilieri, 1997). And equally compelling is the human element: boring repetitive tasks and layers of management control – hallmarks of Taylorism and scientific management – would be replaced with learning, creativity, collaborative communities of practice and opportunities to take ownership of results – both individually and in teams. It could be the dawn of a new management paradigm.

Confirmation that knowledge management is indeed a harbinger of a new era is easy to find. The business press widely publicized early successes at consulting firms such as Booz Allen and applications engineering companies like Buckman Labs. More than 100 conferences held in the United States and Europe in 1998 focused on knowledge management or intellectual capital, 25 new books on the subject were published between 1996 and 1998 and 4 periodicals dedicated to knowledge management have been established in recent years. Since 1990, many of the world's leading companies – two-thirds of Booz Allen's clients among them – have launched learning or knowledge initiatives. Also, CEOs, including GE's Jack Welch, Allied Signal's Larry Bossidy, Monsanto's Bob Shapiro, BP's John Browne and Lend Lease's Stuart Hornery, extol the virtues of learning and knowledge in their annual letters to shareholders. Finally, the Gartner Group estimates that the knowledge management software and consulting market reached $1.5 billion in 1998 and forecasts a $5 billion market by 2002.

At the same time, some observers have declared that knowledge management is a fad that does not produce results (*The Economist*, 1997). A survey conducted in 1998 (Bain & Co.) concluded that, of all contemporary management techniques, knowledge management demonstrates the biggest gap between promise and results realized. Knowledge management practitioners know that for every widely publicized story about a

CEO who is successfully leveraging knowledge to transform a company (such as GE's Jack Welch and BP's John Browne), there seems to be an unpublicized, but equally significant, failure (such as at NatWest Markets).

Is knowledge management delivering on its promise? The answer hinges on what we mean by results. If we only mean an adequate return on investment, where knowledge management contributes enough to a team's ability to achieve its objectives that the small investment in software and time is justified, then the size and growth of the knowledge management market suggests that, indeed, we are realizing the promise. For many – not only software vendors and consultants selling knowledge management services, but also individuals excited by the promise of knowledge management – this very broad interpretation of results is appropriate.

However, we believe that the promise of knowledge management demands a much higher standard than merely an adequate return on investment. The promises of competitive advantage, accelerated learning and value creation clearly imply significant bottom-line improvements. In today's demanding environment, a company cannot sustain a new organizational model (the human side of the promise) that does not yield bottom-line results.

Is knowledge management achieving significant bottom-line results? Recognizing that sometimes it does, the real question is whether or not knowledge management is likely to create a big enough impact that top management should pursue it. If knowledge management is not yet reliably – and consistently – delivering significant results, how should we change our approach to ensure that the promise is realized?

Knowledge Management Fails to Deliver Significant Results

Across the 108 companies we studied, we found no correlation between systematic management of knowledge and improved bottom-line performance. That is, we found that companies with extensive knowledge management programmes were not more likely to achieve improved bottom-line performance than companies without extensive knowledge management initiatives. In other words, when top management pulls the knowledge management lever and funds a major initiative, on average there is no increase in the company's performance.

As we expected to find a reasonably strong relationship – certainly the major programme we led at Booz Allen delivered significant impact – we explored a variety of different measures and statistical techniques. We finally decided that our negative result was accurate. In fact, we now wonder how we ever could have expected anything else. We were persuaded less by the statistical evidence than by an understanding of the experiences of individual companies (see Figure 11.1).

Large	*North-west quadrant* • Ford • Global Building Products Co. • Monsanto	*North-east quadrant* • GE • BP • Buckman Labs
Small	*South-west quadrant* • Dow Chemical • NatWest Markets • Digital	*South-east quadrant* • Automotive Supplier • Global Oil Company • Global Facilities Manager
	Small	Large

Scope of knowledge initiative

Figure 11.1   *Performance map for sample of cases*

North-east quadrant: large initiative, large bottom-line results

At General Electric, Jack Welch's stated strategy is to improve performance faster than competitors – by learning. Explaining his rationale for learning in a 1996 address, Welch told shareholders, 'When the rate of change outside exceeds the rate of change inside, the end is in sight.' Welch drives performance by adapting knowledge from outside the company in the form of powerful new paradigms – such as demand flow manufacturing, quick service/quick response and, more recently, Six Sigma quality – to GE's disparate businesses. Although the initial search for these methodologies is relatively unsystematic (Jack just picks them), the adaptation and application of the new paradigms leverages GE's disciplined performance management systems. Leaders of each business unit – from GE Capital to GE Plastics – are expected to use the new approach, and their performance targets are adjusted accordingly. Learning occurs in executive meetings as results and lessons are shared and then transmitted down the line. GE's corporate university at Crotonvile provides the resources to teach methodologies to people across the organization. GE's outstanding results reinforce employees' willingness to adopt (and adapt) the new paradigms, as evidenced by GE's early successes with Six Sigma. Management is quick to acknowledge that GE's ongoing performance improvement is explicitly learning-based.

Buckman Labs, the small specialist chemical company based in Memphis, Tennessee, has become famous among knowledge management practitioners for its successful implementation of a broad knowledge transfer capability. Buckman's 1,200 associates deliver tailored solutions to customers in over 90 countries. CEO Bob Buckman launched the knowledge capability in the late 1980s with two goals: accelerate problem resolution and increase the percentage of sales from new products by enabling associates to spend more time with customers. To motivate change, Buckman began measuring associates on the percentage of time spent directly with customers. Associates now have access to cases, lessons learned, expert directories and on-line discussions, which they leverage in tackling problems on their customers' behalf. For example, the resolution of a problem with a fungus growing on equipment in a tomato canning plant can provide important lessons for associates tackling similar fungi in different manufacturing environments. The improved solutions (and reduced time taken to resolve problems) create immediate value for customers, which contributes to Buckman's growth. Via its knowledge network, Buckman Labs has reduced its response time from weeks to hours and increased the percentages of sales of new products from 14 per cent in 1987 to 34.6 per cent in 1996.

South-west quadrant: small initiative, small bottom-line results

We expected, and found, many programmes in this quadrant. The programmes fell into three categories. The first category comprised small, 'sharing-enabled' efforts such as the one at NatWest Markets. They either failed even to deliver a return adequate to justify costs or were curtailed for lack of promise.

The second group entailed small, 'results-driven' initiatives that generated demonstrable impact within their target area, but were too narrow in scope to affect the company concerned as a whole. For example, Dow Chemical Company's intellectual asset management initiative targeted reduced costs and improved patent utilization by cataloguing, maintaining and disseminating knowledge about more than 29,000 existing patents. Dow has saved an estimated $50 million over 10 years by eliminating maintenance costs on obsolete patents and better managing viable ones. In addition, higher usage enhanced the value of the patent portfolio an estimated 400 per cent. These results, while real and important, are simply too small to have a significant impact on a $20 billion company like Dow. Attempts to extend the knowledge management approach across the company have failed.

The final group in the south-west quadrant includes small, sharing-enabled efforts that successfully fostered a new, more collaborative culture and generated adequate returns, but that, unlike Buckman Labs, did not generate significant bottom-line impact Most of the companies in this category set out to enable the sharing of ideas, lessons learned and prior work by means of some combination of an experts directory, knowledge base and collaboration tool. In general, the tools created are viewed by staff as valuable and have changed how people work and continue to evolve. However, there is no evidence of impact (either small results like Dow's or the significant impact of those in the north-east quadrant). For example, in 1996, Digital's Network and Systems Integration Services business unit set out to create 'higher margin repeatable solutions' by enabling the staff to share work. The team quickly created a database of examples and then began identifying best practices. The effort is valued by staff and, though they cannot quantify results, they continue to invest the small amounts required to enable the programme's evolution.

North-west quadrant: small initiative, large financial results

One group of companies in the north-west quadrant demonstrated huge bottom-line impact from relatively small knowledge initiatives – a full order of magnitude more than the level of results generated by successful programmes like Dow's in the south-west quadrant. For example, one leading building products manufacturer has consistently outperformed competitors since implementing a knowledge-based pricing initiative. To replace a time-consuming process that relied on expert judgement and multiple hand-offs, the company developed an analytically based pricing structure that could be used for about 80 per cent of the bids. To encourage use of the new pricing understandings, the salesforce was trained, equipped with laptop computers and given new profit-based incentives to replace the old volume-based ones. Price realization increased by more than one percentage point in the first year and even more in the second and third years.

A second group of initiatives, exemplified by Ford, generated real bottom-line results that, while important, represent only a fraction of the performance initiatives underway. By using the sharing-enabled knowledge management programme in Ford's manufacturing division, workers collaborate in communities of practice, identifying and implementing best practices. The programme is achieving results – a claimed $450 million in savings over 3 years. However, these improvements are a small part of Ford's overall productivity improvement. In one year, 1997, Ford achieved $3 billion in cost savings – the majority of which came from sourcing and other productivity improvement initiatives, including an innovative metric-driven programme to drive best practices in engineering.

Of course, managers have a host of approaches for achieving improvements in productivity, from 'Chainsaw' Dunlop's wholesale elimination of positions to popular initiatives, such as strategic sourcing and business process re-engineering, to recent megamergers, such as the joint venture between Shell and Texaco, designed to enable further cost reduction. Companies that successfully use these other approaches, but also have a small knowledge effort in progress, typically fall in the north-west quadrant.

Calling these efforts 'knowledge management', however, stretches the definition of the term so far as to be meaningless.

The rest of the companies in the north-west quadrant are successfully driving bottom-line improvements and using knowledge as the basis of competitive advantage. However, these strategic successes are unrelated to small efforts also underway to systematically manage knowledge, despite the claims of some in the knowledge management community. For example, before its merger with Pharmacia & Upjohn Inc. Monsanto was a knowledge-age company clearly on the path to becoming a learning organization. Knowledge management efforts in different parts of the company had met with varying degrees of success, but, in general, were in areas unrelated to the significant value creation then underway at Monsanto.

South-east quadrant: large initiative, small financial results

The south-east quadrant includes two kinds of companies with extensive knowledge management efforts. These two are those that successfully change people's behaviour but do not find an effective way to capture the value of the effort and those that fail to create or capture any value at all.

An automotive component supplier is an example of those companies that failed to capture the value created. This company successfully identified and adopted best practices on a large scale – processes were changed, set-up times reduced, work flows optimized and workers cross-trained. However, neither customers nor shareholders benefited from these measurable improvements in operations. To capture the value from greater flexibility and shorter lead-times in reduced inventory, both master schedules and inventory targets would have had to be revised. They were not. Similarly, labour productivity did not increase because demand remained constant and management did not take advantage of the operational improvements to reduce the headcount. In some plants, worker participation was motivated by the promise that the headcount would remain unchanged – laudable, but in an industry with no growth in volume, this promise virtually ensured that no value would be captured.[2]

Even if companies successfully achieve productivity improvement, in slow-growth, asset-intensive industries, profitability may decline. In these industries, the typical focus of knowledge management is better asset utilization, usually by increasing the output of the asset. If the industry is growing no faster than the GNP (such as is the case for retailing, chemicals, refining and building products in most developed countries), then effective knowledge management enables increases in output greater than the increases in demand – that is, it triggers industry overcapacity, puts downward pressure on prices and forces consolidation. Of course, this scenario is a Prisoner's Dilemma. In short, a firm is better off systematically managing knowledge, whether or not its competitors do so, but the industry as a whole would be better off if no one managed knowledge effectively!

In addition to successful, yet ill-fated initiatives, the south-east quadrant also includes large, sharing-enabled efforts to foster learning organizations or collaborative cultures. Sadly, these create little value and capture none. They are the sharing-enabled programmes of the south-west quadrant writ large. For example, one leading oil company hoping to achieve performance levels that would put it squarely in the north-east (with competitor BP), implemented a set of corporate wide learning and knowledge initiatives to stimulate collaboration. While many middle and senior managers have benefited personally from opportunities to develop listening, communication and leadership skills, top management has no evidence of results and has turned its attention to other issues. Other initiatives deep in the business units have generated real results, but champions disassociate their programme from the failed corporate initiatives.

A global facilities management company launched a large-scale collaborative best-practice programme including dedicated staff, internal conferences and a technology infrastructure. Excited about the potential of this programme, senior salespeople told a key customer about it in a sales pitch. The customer's response was, 'You guys aren't very good, so don't waste any of my money on doing something like that.' The programme was curtailed because of a lack of results – not only for the company, but also for the customers.

Achieving Results, Delivering the Promise

Despite the lack of relationship between systematic knowledge management efforts and bottom-line results, we believe that the critics are wrong: knowledge management is more than a fad. The successes at GE, Buckman Labs and BP, as well as and our own efforts at Booz Allen demonstrate that the promise can be redeemed. Effective management of the creation and use of knowledge can stimulate both individual and organizational learning, accelerate the company's rate of performance improvement and provide a basis for competitive advantage.

Results have been limited because we in the knowledge management community misread the promise. Excited by the insight that knowledge and learning represented potential sources of competitive advantage, it was only a small step for those of us educated in the era of management science to set out to manage knowledge. However, that was the wrong approach. The real promise of knowledge management – achieving significant results with significant effort, as the companies in the north-east quadrant have done – calls for knowledge to be integrated into management – not the other way around. Three lessons from results-driven programmes illustrate the integration of knowledge with management.

First, while the knowledge management community has developed far better practices for the systematic creation and use of knowledge than traditional management practice, many traditional practices remain valid. These include driving only one or two priorities at a time, selecting priorities that have strategic impact and measuring results. To achieve significant results, we must synthesize the new knowledge management disciplines with many traditional management practices. Except for consulting firms and engineering companies, all of the companies in the northeast quadrant achieved this kind of integration by having a team of visionary senior line managers who drove focus and results (often in very traditional ways) and applied the new practices to systematically manage the creation and use of knowledge (either directly or in partnership with a knowledge management professional).

Second, we must be more explicit about the link between the improved creation and use of knowledge and the benefit to customers and shareholders. Does improved throughput create value or just add to industry overcapacity? Will headcount be adjusted to yield increased productivity? Can prices be increased to capture part of the improved value to customers? How will the sharing of ideas create/benefits for customers?

For example, GE's awesome management system to drive improved productivity ensured that at least part of the value of the improved use of knowledge would reach the bottom line. By focusing on price structure and price realization, the building products manufacturer drove results to the bottom line with only a small initiative. Even the successful initiatives with adequate returns in the south-west quadrant, such as Dow, explicitly targeted areas for improvement and managed to capture some value. Buckman Labs captured value by identifying and measuring relationships between investments enabling collaboration and sharing, time spent with customers, rapid problem resolution, sales from new products and overall growth (both in size and profitability).

Sometimes companies get lucky, the benefits are realized and they end up in the north-east quadrant. For example, the consulting industry environment has enabled many consulting firms to realize benefits from knowledge management, even though few of us were explicit about expected benefits up front:

- With industry growth in excess of 15 per cent and business models that ensure high utilization of people, no special effort was required to adjust hiring targets to capture the benefits of improved productivity.
- Brand image with both prospective clients and prospective recruits is enhanced by accelerated publication of leading ideas without additional effort.

Finally, integrating knowledge into management means that we have to embrace a new view of change. With knowledge management, change can't drive results, results drive change. In the traditional approach to management, executives first design what they want employees to do and

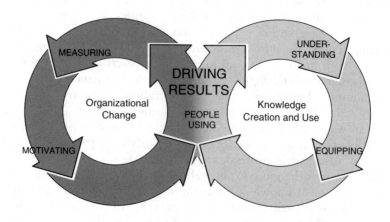

Figure 11.2   *The learning dynamic*

then craft a change management programme to induce them to do it. Many executives tasked with establishing a knowledge programme try that same sequential approach. They create knowledge first, then try to figure out how to get people to use it. However, the sequential approach does not work with knowledge in today's organizations. We are harnessing a dynamic, not managing a static set of activities. Together, knowledge creation and use drive change; change drives knowledge creation and use. Results drive the dynamic (see Figure 11.2 for an illustration of the 'learning dynamic' and Lucier and Torsilieri, 1997).

With today's pressure on performance, people use what helps them achieve results; they do not have time to contribute to initiatives that do not help them succeed in their jobs. However, people will be motivated to use and share understandings (such as GE's new paradigms and the lessons learned in applying them), if they are equipped to do so (that is, trained and given the tools or the time) and if the measurements demonstrate value in accordance with company goals.

Our findings suggest a prediction about the future of knowledge management. Two fundamentally different schools of thought will evolve: sharing-enabled knowledge management and results-driven knowledge management. Those who adhere to the sharing-enabled school will reject our conclusion that a buttoned-down, results-driven approach is the only path to achieving significant input from knowledge for the vast majority of companies. Building on the successes of consulting companies and applications engineering firms such as Buckman Labs, they will continue to argue that broad sharing initiatives can stimulate creativity across a corporation, drive performance improvement and create competitive advantage. We expect the differences in these schools of thought to increase, creating two increasingly distinct communities of practice. This bifurcation will add to the already high levels of confusion among people trying to manage in the knowledge age.

The sharing-enabled community of practice has come to define popularized knowledge management. It is easy to celebrate the successes of knowledge programmes that have generated sufficient improvements in morale and team effectiveness to justify relatively small investments in IT and top management consultants' time. This community of practitioners will continue to increase, stimulated by their experience of the power of collaboration and by vendors (both IT and consultants) who serve them. Despite their successes, these practitioners will be increasingly frustrated – both by their inability to achieve the promise of the learning organization and the chorus of critics who unfairly question the degree of success.

The results-driven practitioners will increasingly disassociate themselves from the term 'knowledge management'. This group will focus on achieving significantly improved results by integrating knowledge into management. In most cases, line managers will use knowledge to achieve their critical strategic priorities. In a few cases – generally in applications engineering oriented businesses such as consulting and specialty chemicals – broad initiatives to enhance sharing and collaboration will be helpful. In the learning organizations they build, the highly successful practitioners will find themselves focusing less on new software and techniques and more on a set of fundamentally new questions. Instead of the traditional scientific management question – 'What is the best way for my employees to get the job done?' – the north-east quadrant practitioner asks, 'What do my employees (or customers or vendors) need to know to make the best decision?' Instead of the traditional strategy question – 'How can I build barriers against my competitors?' – the north-east quadrant practitioner asks, 'How can we leverage knowledge to create more value for customers faster than our competitors?'

These two schools of thought represent two distinct choices. They are not the ends of a continuum, nor the first and second steps of a process. Except in the specialized cases of consulting firms and applications engineering companies, there is not a path to the north-east quadrant via sharing-enabled programmes. Even for those kinds of companies, sharing-enabled initiatives are almost always grounded in results-driven principles (that is, knowledge is integrated into management). Unfortunately, the early successes that shaped our understanding of the promise of knowledge management grew out of these exceptions. While the confusion is understandable, the reality is that, for virtually all other types of businesses, the only path to the north-east quadrant is a results-driven approach. Small-scale sharing-enabled programmes remain a viable management practice, generating, as we have seen, adequate returns. However, despite the hopes of the popular knowledge management culture, scaling up a sharing-enabled programme leads invariably, to small bottom-line results.

Companies, not understanding that there is a choice, are increasingly launching programmes with north-east quadrant goals but a sharing-enabled approach. This leads to no results, disappointment, mass confusion and disillusionment with the promise of knowledge management. A long-tenured CEO of an $8 billion service company, having driven double-digit growth for many years, embraced the promise and assigned a top manager to launch a knowledge management programme. This results-minded senior manager assembled a team to set the direction for the new programme. The team leader, after attending several conferences and reading material in the popular knowledge press, inevitably came away equipped to implement the sharing-enabled approach. It only took one conversation in which we shared these perspectives for the senior manager, with his 20 years of experience in some of the world's most performance-oriented companies, to recognize the danger and redirect the thinking. Most companies are not so lucky.

CEOs and managers have to decide how to respond to the promise of knowledge management. For CEOs and other top mangers, the choice is clear. They may support sharing-enabled initiatives within various parts of the organization, leaving implementation to others, but to achieve strategic impact, the only choice is the results-driven approach – and responsibility cannot be delegated. For knowledge practitioners and other managers in the knowledge age, the choice is less clear. Many may choose to be rewarded by the changes in culture and morale wrought by small, sharing-enabled programmes. For those who aspire to the north-east quadrant, the answer lies in finding – or becoming – a senior line manager to champion the cause.

Notes

1 Popularized in 1990 by Peter Senge with his best-selling book *The Fifth Discipline: The Age and Practice of Learning Organization*, London: Century Business, the concept of a learning organization has captured the imagination of many CEOs. By 1995, with the publication of Ikujiro Nonaka and Horitaka Takeuchi's acclaimed *The Knowledge-creating Company*, New York: Oxford University Press, the promise of knowledge and learning as competitive weapons was well accepted.
2 In theory, even if value had not been captured in increased productivity, the company might have benefited from increased price or volume. No attempt was made to increase prices. Volume not only did not increase, but market share actually declined because a competitor that increased its productivity passed part of the benefit to customers in the form of lower prices.

References

Bain & Co. (1998) '1998 management tool utilization and satisfaction survey', summarized by *Consultant's News*, November: 8.

'Face Value: Mr Knowledge' (1997) *The Economist*, 31 May: 63.

Lucier, Charles E., and Torsilieri, Janet D. (1997) 'Why knowledge programs fail: a CEO's guide to managing learning', *Strategy and Business*, Fourth Quarter: 14.

Prokesch, Stephen E. (1997) 'Unleashing the power of learning: an interview with British Petroleum's John Browne', *Harvard Business Review*, Sept.–Oct.: 147.

12 How Tacit Knowledge Explains Organizational Renewal and Growth: the Case of Nokia

Seija Kulkki and Mikko Kosonen

Introduction

This chapter discusses knowledge as a major source of renewal and growth of the firm.[1] We argue that the contextually embedded and future-oriented nature of knowledge may explain growth in terms of organizational dynamism and renewal, even on an international and global scale. The dynamic nature of knowledge as a growth engine is derived from its tacitness. The Nokia Corporation is of interest because of the exceptional growth and renewal capability it demonstrated during the 1990s while profitably transforming itself from a diversified European conglomerate into a focused global telecommunications company.[2]

Multinational organizations are of special interest because they can create and exploit knowledge in a variety of culturally, socially and economically different environments. They have the worldwide opportunity to recombine and recompose knowledge-based assets in an international or global network and can deploy strategies that reflect variations in global knowledge intensity and extensity (Hedlund, 1996).[3] This suggests that multinational corporations deploy managerial and organizational ways and means to bring about an international or global scale of knowledge creation and exploitation (Doz, et al., 1996, and Kulkki, 1996, 1998). Dunning (1997) discusses new organizational modalities and a shift away from hierarchical forms towards new relational, collective or stakeholder-based alliance forms within the knowledge-based global economy. Dunning discusses entering an era of the knowledge-based global capitalism after the machine- and finance-based capitalism of the nineteenth and twentieth centuries.

We argue here that knowledge can, in fact, be an engine of renewal and growth, provided that it is consciously and holistically managed. There may, however, be limits to what management can do. At best, it can fuel and facilitate the intertwined coexistence of knowledge creation and exploitation.[4] This again opens new insights into how to manage emergent structures and processes of creation[5] simultaneously, as well as mechanistic structures and processes of implementation.[6]

This chapter addresses three questions.

1 What are the managerial and organizational mechanisms that facilitate the emergence of new individual and organizational tacit knowledge on a global scale?
2 What are the managerial and organizational ways and means that facilitate the conversion of tacit knowledge to explicit knowledge?
3 What are the managerial and organizational ways and means that facilitate the efficient exploitation of knowledge simultaneously with emergent and convergent structures and processes?

This chapter extends the discussion of knowledge conversion (Nonaka and Takeuchi, 1995, and Nonaka and Konno, 1998) and innovations (Leonard and Sensiper, 1998) to address the contextual nature of knowledge and its consequent managerial and organizational implications. In their discussion of communities of practice, Brown and Duguid (1998) say that knowledge management concerns not only the processes of knowledge creation and exploitation, but also the underlying organizational, institutional and structural properties that enable them to emerge and flourish – or else prevent them from doing so.

In our view of knowledge as meanings and mental models, we emphasize the role of individual minds in knowledge creation, conversion and exploitation (Nonaka and Takeuchi, 1995). Knowledge as meaning also raises the issue of context – that is, how individuals create reality within an organizational context (Kulkki, 1996).[7] This is a reason to address the question of how a company operating globally provides opportunities for individuals to create and exploit knowledge.

This chapter is organized as follows. We first discuss the future-oriented and contextual nature of tacit knowledge in order to identify the dynamic organizational characteristics that enable its emergence and conversion to explicit knowledge. We next address the managerial and organizational mechanisms for the creation and exploitation of knowledge using the example of the Nokia Corporation. That example leads us to propose that a knowledge-based view of the renewal and growth of the firm may lead managers to reconsider the nature and roles of individuals, underlying values, strategies, structures, processes and actions, as well as external and internal boundaries within the firm. All of these things affect the relationship of the individual to the organization as well as the relationship of the organization to its environment. The challenges raised by this new view of the firm are particularly great for companies that operate globally.

Future-oriented Tacit Knowledge

Tacit knowledge is commonly discussed as personal, non-articulated, silent, hidden, experience-based and skill-type bodily knowledge (Polanyi, 1958).[8] From an organizational point of view, individual tacit knowledge is a source of knowledge creation (Nonaka and Takeuchi, 1995). Thus, tacit knowledge is a latent, not yet activated reservoir for explicit knowledge, based on experiences and practice. While tacit knowledge is derived from personal experience, it contains subjective qualities that make it difficult to articulate (Nonaka and Takeuchi, 1995). Thus, tacit knowledge reflects an idiosyncratic history of a person and, consequently, of an organization. This view emphasizes the stock of knowledge derived from experience over time.

There has been less discussion about the future-oriented nature of tacit knowledge, although Polanyi also gives a reason for that interpretation.[9] He discusses learning, based on tacit latent knowledge, as a heuristic act of insight where the mind is in contact with a still-hidden reality (Polyani and Prosch, 1975). In that condition, the mind may be anticipating an indeterminate range of the yet unknown and inconceivable. Contextual learning theories discuss the nature of individual tacit meanings and argue that tacit meaning perspectives contain, among others, orientation models for the future, horizons of expectations and orientation models for ambiguity, risk and uncertainty.[10] Tacit meaning perspectives may have a strong orientation towards the future, depending on the context (Kulkki, 1996).[11] Hence, they may be prescientific and preconceptual by nature (Polanyi, 1958).

Kulkki (1996 and 1998) discusses the multidimensional nature of tacit knowledge and the capacity of the individual mind to create the future. She argues that tacit meaning perspectives contain open-ended orientation and problem-solving models for the future, risks and uncertainties and horizons of expectations intertwined with the self-concept and ideographic social and cultural history of an individual. The tacit meaning perspectives contain not only cognitive elements, but also integrative and intertwined conative and affective dimensions (see Figure 12.1). Thus, tacit meaning perspectives are integrated or imprinted by values, affections, feelings, and emotions (Nonaka and Takeuchi, 1995). This is why tacit knowledge combines experience-based, skill-type knowledge with individual capacity to give intuitive forms to new things – that is, to anticipate and preconceptualize the future. This also may explain why tacit knowledge combines bodily knowledge and knowledge of the mind.

At one end of the knowledge continuum is tacit knowledge, which may be deeply contextually embedded, existential and ontological, then, at the other end, explicit knowledge of concepts, things, models, manuals and definitions. At that end, knowledge enters the epistemological and linguistic arena of articulation and justification. However, explicit knowledge may also contain meanings with tacit elements (Polanyi, 1958). Explicit knowledge may change into information, which Nonaka and Takeuchi (1995) define as a flow of messages. They distinguish knowledge from information by stating that knowledge may be created from the flow of information, but that it is anchored in the beliefs and commitments of its holder.

The domain of tacit meaning perspectives involves the ability of the individual to differentiate space, time, direction, dimensions, sequences,

Explicit knowledge

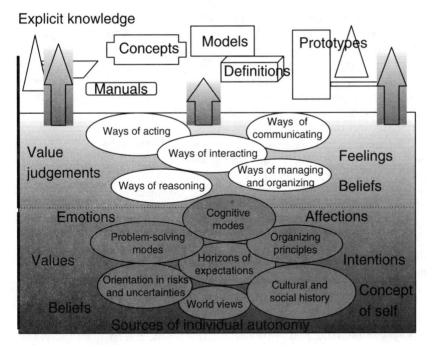

Tacit knowledge

Figure 12.1   *The multidimensional nature of knowledge (Kulkki, 1998, p. 26)*

entities, focus, states, moods and feelings. It is here where the individual can identify the beginnings and ends of events. Thus, the strategic capacity of the individual to understand complicated phenomena and create future lines of actions based on them, lies within the domain of tacit meaning perspectives. Mezirow (1994) states that knowledge creation means changes in meaning perspectives.

Consequently, tacit knowledge is both of the past and for the future. It is historical and experience-based, but it may also be stretched over the discontinuity between the past and the future if it is open-ended and used in open-ended problem solving for future actions. With tacit knowledge, one can fill in the blanks of explicit knowledge. Tacit knowledge offers an open window to the future.[12]

The Contextuality of Tacit Knowledge

We believe, based on the nature of the tacit meanings, that individual knowledge is inextricably linked to context.[13] It mirrors or reflects a context. Hedlund (1993 and 1994) discusses the mirroring of knowledge, people and actions, as well as the reflective relationship of the struc-ture and knowledge construction of the firm. Kulkki (1996) discusses the contextuality of knowledge based on contextual learning theories. According to that viewpoint, individuals or groups create knowledge based on experiences derived from actions and interactions. Experiences are seen as events that have meaning as a whole. They are also described as a totality of events, with qualities of continuous activity and change. The quality of experiences as events is a product, an outcome, of the interaction between individual(s) and their context. Thus, experiences are strongly affected by subjective and organizational elements.

Consequently, context-specific tacit knowledge may be both subjective and 'objective', personal and social, individual and organizational or collective (Spender, 1996, and Tsoukas, 1996). Tsoukas argues that knowledge is inherently indeterminate and continually emerging; it is not self-contained. This gives knowledge an unstable and fluid nature. The fluidity of the knowledge base may reflect the context of the firm (Kulkki, 1996) and explain the context-dependent emergence of meanings. It may also explain how tacit knowledge is a by-product of actions, as well as an intertwined outcome of intellectual processes of perception (see, for example, Hurley, 1998).

Giddens (1984) discusses social renewal and his view is that reality is neither the experience of the individual nor a determination by context. Giddens emphasizes that reality is created by the interplay of individuals and context, in a series of times and spaces where the reflection and knowledge of human beings is deeply involved in practices and reality. Giddens emphasizes the ontology of time and space and reflection in action. He claims that a co-presence exists, that individuals have the capacity to act and tacitly reflect at the same time[14] – that is, he says human beings can continuously 'monitor' the flow of their activities, as well as the social, psychological and physical aspects of the contexts in which they move. People routinely maintain a continuing 'theoretical understanding' of the grounds for their actions. This relates to Nonaka and Konno's (1998) discussion of the mental, virtual and/or physical phenomenological 'places' in time and space where something new may emerge and happen.

With experiences being deeply subjective and perceived holistically as a total flow of events, the organization–environment relationship may largely depend on the interactive and creative capacity of the individuals who deal with customers, partners, competitors and others. Individuals are 'the eyes and ears' of the firm – that is, the individual (I) is in an intermediate, creative and constitutive position between the organization (O) and the environment (E) (see Figure 12.2). The environment 'flows into' the organization via individual minds.

Hurley (1998) argues that the mind perceives reality while acting, and acts while perceiving. Lakoff and Johnson (1999) put forward the view that even reasoning is intertwined with perception and action. From the organizational viewpoint, this means that individuals may act as a creative strategic capacity of the firm when perceiving and acting.[15] This means that individuals are not only the eyes and ears, but also the brains, mouths

Figure 12.2 *A knowledge-based view of the relationship of organization (O) and environment (E), based on individuals (I)*

and hands of the firm. This view differs from the rational and linear information-processing viewpoint, which sees the firm as a collector of information from the environment via market analysis that then perceives and reasons, only later acting. According to this view, the brains are separate from the hands. Consequently, the firm may lack enough speed to live on the market pulse.

Dispersed Knowledge

Following the thoughts of von Hayek,[16] Tsoukas (1996) discusses the fact that knowledge is dispersed primarily because it is an individual possession. Although the stock of knowledge of the firm is a reflection of individuals' stock of knowledge, it is destined to stay dispersed and local because there are few means to control processes when knowledge is emerging all over the firm. Tsoukas (1996) declares that 'rational economic calculation' cannot take into account the factual knowledge of the particular circumstances of time and space.[17]

Hagström and Hedlund (1998) discuss the lateral dispersion of knowledge within multinational corporations as a consequence of the horizontal linking of positions, knowledge and actions that form the main structural dimensions from the knowledge-creation viewpoint. They view knowledge as an archipelago where the islands are distinct from each other, rather than a mountain, where from the top you can see all the rest.

Knowledge within a globally operating firm is, hence, strongly dispersed among cultures and locations. This fact has traditionally caused multinational corporations to emphasize control and ways to diminish the variety of knowledge rather than benefit from it. They have claimed to be good at exploiting existing knowledge-based assets, but not at all as good at creating novelty (Hagström and Hedlund, 1998).

Characteristics of a Knowledge-based Global Firm

Hedlund (1996) addresses the question of how a company can benefit from the increasing intensity and extensity of global knowledge. He reasons that high knowledge intensity is the outcome of increasing content demand and complexity of knowledge, which can also be interpreted as an increasing diversity, tacitness and contextual embeddedness of knowledge.[18] Wide extensity of knowledge reflects the ability of a company to create, transfer and exploit knowledge globally among many activities, processes and knowledge areas. Hedlund says that Silicon Valley companies have deep (tacit) involvement in a few local environments in their development of high technology. Global 'hamburgers' are companies with low knowledge intensity, but wide knowledge extensity – that is, these companies are effective in the transfer and exploitation of knowledge; they transfer explicit standardized and globalized concepts as meaning schemes (brands, franchising concepts, quality standards and operational procedures).[19] Global innovators, in turn, can organize and manage deep (tacit) involvement in knowledge creation in many locations as well as transfer and exploit that knowledge over borders. The latter is what Doz, et al. (1996 and 1997) discuss as a 'metanational strategy' in which the company acts globally as the orchestrator of its knowledge and capabilities.

Nonaka (1997) discusses individual-based knowledge creation in interaction with the local environment.[20] Interaction may concern:

1   explicit knowledge of products and services;
2   it may also concern tacit knowledge of hidden needs or concepts for new or revised products and services;
3   even more deeply cooperative and co-creative ways if acting where new tacit meaning perspectives are sensed and anticipated.

By means of this interaction, the company can perceive future R&D trends, as well as future trends in technology and businesses. Also, new visions and worldviews, as well as new values, ideas and ideals, may be sensed, perceived or creatively anticipated and preconceptualized. Nonaka (1997) states that this type of interorganizational and interpersonal interaction is a basis for real-time knowledge creation within the firm. He discusses real-time knowledge creation as an organic process to develop markets, not as mechanistically split segments, but by understanding the underlying deep patterns that constitute markets. This view emphasizes the need for tacit understanding of the constitutive powers behind the future.

Consequently, globally innovative companies seem to know how to organize and manage for deep involvement in many international locations for the creation and exploitation of new knowledge, as well as how to activate individual abilities for knowledge-based interpersonal and interorganizational interaction.

The Recent History of the Nokia Corporation

Nokia is one of the leading companies in telecommunications and mobile phones. The issue at hand is how a company can manage individual and corporate-wide knowledge to stimulate organizational renewal and global growth. The Nokia case comprises aspects of the intertwined development of its two main businesses, Nokia Mobile Phones (NMP) and Nokia Telecommunications (NTC).

Telecommunications network equipment and mobile phones are both high-tech businesses characterized by rapid growth and turbulence. This is based on highly competitive and also 'co-opetitive' behaviour among companies, the aim of which is to create new communication businesses.[21] Such creative global 'market maker' behaviour has led to very short product lifecycles, particularly in mobile phones, and strong standardization- and technology-based competition in both businesses. All of these tendencies emphasize the importance of the right timing as well as speed in bringing new innovations into the global marketplace. In the case of mobile communications, these market conditions have led to the creation of an entirely new industry in less than ten years.

Today's Nokia has emerged from four major business phases.

1   The development of competence in radio technology products and systems, together with very advanced Scandinavian telecommunications operators as its main customers during the 1970s and 1980s.
2   The decision to create an international cellular system and mobile phone business based on GSM technology (the pan-European digital global standard for mobile telecommunications) in the late 1980s.
3   The decision to focus on telecommunications-oriented global businesses in 1992. This, in turn, enabled the fast and determined creation of a leading global position in mobile phones and GSM-network business by the mid-1990s.
4   From the mid-1990s onwards, the creation and further leveraging of a leading global position in mobile communications by means of the conscious exploitation of new knowledge-based ways to operate and grow.

Phase 1: learning to create new technology at the customer interface

Nokia's history in telecommunications dates back to the early 1960s, when it began experimenting with electronics in the back office of its then core cable business. This experimentation soon evolved into active development of telecommunications, especially mobile communications technology, in close cooperation with the leading Scandinavian operators during the 1970s and 1980s.

New managerial and organizational ways of acting emerged during this phase. First, Nokia learned to appreciate a close and open customer interface when developing new products and systems in cooperation with demanding customers. Second, Nokia learned to create new technology quickly and efficiently by utilizing commercially available components and open standards. For instance, the DX technology that is incorporated in GSM technology was based on Intel components at the beginning of the 1980s. Nokia did not have major ASIC production and technology in house at the time.

The opportunity to innovate with the market has always been highly appreciated in the company. At Nokia, individual tasks are largely perceived as open-ended and continuously changing, requiring an innovative approach to problem solving. From the knowledge viewpoint, this means that the basic structural 'component' of the firm – action based on individual knowledge – is creative and innovative by nature and subject to being continuously challenged by its customers.

Phase 2: building a common mindset for going global

At the end of the 1980s, Nokia began developing GSM technology, including an international GSM system and mobile phone business. A new business unit was established within Nokia Telecommunications (NTC) around GSM network technology and all the related in-house technologies and resources were transferred to this new unit. Nokia saw that, for a small company, mobile communications provided an interesting new international growth opportunity in an industry that was just starting to deregulate. Nokia had a strong technology base and was used to creating new business concepts in cooperation with its customers. Nokia also expected that its small but advanced home market would provide an excellent stepping stone to international markets. At the same time, Nokia's larger competitors perceived this emerging business area as a small niche market in comparison to their 'mainstream' fixed telecommunications businesses.

Parallel to NTC's development and based on largely the same strengths, Nokia began developing an international mobile phone business (NMP) that would require high volume and low costs. This would not have been possible without wide geographic and standards scope as well as unified brand identity. Thus, NMP decided to focus on all optional cellular standards and create a truly international presence quickly. This decision can later be characterized as a brave move for a Finnish technology company that had very little experience in consumer marketing and volume business.

Nokia based its growing mobile communications on two different business approaches. NTC built an international presence by cooperating with customers around the world to create new system solutions. NMP, in turn, built an efficient volume business with strong regional R&D, manufacturing and logistical capabilities.

These different approaches to internationalization were a natural result of the nature of the two businesses. NTC had to stretch its R&D

'mentally', because the volumes did not allow R&D to be placed in every market. This 'mental' globalization of the core R&D took place by having various R&D people – including top managers – participate in customer projects. The key requirements of different customers were then brought back to the R&D home base and embedded in the core product. Thus, the product was made modular and flexible for various needs, which, in turn, created additional speed and cost advantages. NMP, for its part, internationalized by building up regional R&D centres in all its main markets in order to support local end-user preferences and different cellular standards. This approach also provided sufficient speed and cost efficiency at a time when no one else was operating truly globally. As markets have gradually globalized, NMP's regional R&D centres have been given a more global and specialized role in order to have enough critical mass for the creation of new global knowledge.

Nokia as a corporation started to accumulate knowledge about how to combine local responsiveness with global efficiency by creating global product platforms that could be quickly localized. This was an important move from both strategic and operational points of view at a time when markets were deregulating and just about to open up. Nokia's management learned that it could actually 'jump over' several internationalization phases and build a globally configured organization right from the beginning, while Nokia's competitors were still operating in a multidomestic way.[22]

This development phase strengthened Nokia's sense of direction and global operation. It also provided the common experiences that created the basis for a corporate culture based on focused vision and strategy as well as strongly shared values and ideals.

Phase 3: focus on telecommunications and fast globalization

At the beginning of 1992, Nokia decided as a corporation to focus on global telecommunications-oriented businesses. This decision was made by the new CEO and his new management team, which had been appointed from within the telecommunications part of the company. It was based primarily on the strong related core competence and the attractive market opportunities offered by a growing wireless industry. Behind the decision was also an intuitive belief that 'voice will go wireless' and that the mobile phone could one day become everybody's phone. This decision soon led to an accelerated globalization of NTC's and NMP's businesses. Focusing on mass markets also meant that Nokia needed to invest heavily in creating a uniform global brand.

Nokia's rapid transformation and globalization was accomplished primarily by ambitious and technically competent, but relatively young and inexperienced, people. During a short period of time, Nokia sent hundreds of employees abroad to temporary assignments in order to address the market challenges and growth as close to their source as possible. Out of necessity, the company had to take big risks and place its trust in its people, especially its front-line people.[23] Those people learned to take responsibility for the whole business, not only the task at hand, because there were simply no senior people around to lean on. They also learned to solve problems and make decisions on the spot without bureaucracy or much guidance.

The shared assignment and target of Nokia's employees was to create new markets by opening up long-term customer relationships and, ultimately, selling new telecommunications solutions and products. This shared assignment also forced Nokia to create new ways of operating. In the system business, these included multiskilled teams that operated in close cooperation with customers and global R&D teams. In other words, Nokia created organizational mechanisms to meet customers' needs by means of combined knowledge and resource 'packages' to reflect and anticipate the current and future problems of their customers' businesses.

Nokia's solutions were created as a result of close cooperation of individuals from the front line, customers and senior management. Senior management travelled from one place to another to solve problems with the customer-facing employees. Again, there were no other organizational ways and means to support and facilitate global operations and share and accumulate knowledge.

During this phase, Nokia learned lessons that today are still strongly affecting its knowledge-based renewal and growth capacity:

1 management learned to trust the problem-solving abilities and foresight of their front-line people;
2 management learned to trust intuition and rapid decision making;
3 the whole organization learned to act and prioritize on the basis of intuitive anticipation of the future;
4 the whole organization learned to trust and like the opportunity to learn new things and stretch its competence;
5 NTC learned to build new global markets and, consequently, the managerial and organizational ways and means to operate globally in close cooperation with its customers; NMP learned to build globally brand-based market positions that benefited from interlinked R&D centres and a cost-efficient network of high-quality manufacturing and logistics.

These lessons did not come easily. People made many small mistakes, but usually learned before making bigger mistakes. The corporate culture became one that accepted failure and saw it as a learning opportunity. Nokia employees also learned over time to see problems as part of the business and problems that could be solved more quickly than competitors could solve them created new business opportunities.

The hands-on management style also strengthened the competence-based, egalitarian organizational culture and rapid decision making that had already existed in the company when it was smaller. The common experiences of management and individuals on the front lines anchored a common mindset and values. The resulting Nokia way of acting is based on respect for individuals and customers and an emphasis on customer and employee satisfaction, continuous learning and high levels of aspiration and achievement.

Such ambitious target setting and activity established a corporate culture of co-creation between the people on the front line and the senior management. From the knowledge viewpoint, this co-creation led to shared organizational tacit knowledge. The outcome was widely shared worldviews, cultural, social and intellectual modes of perceiving and acting, as well as new problem-solving modes, organizing principles, cognitive modes, attitudes and feelings. By means of mutual intensive problem-solving processes, individuals on the front line and senior management started to develop tacitly the same rhythms and feelings about the future, which they derived from the market pulse. One can argue that once managers started to use their 'hands', the organization could begin using its 'brain'. This may be the foundation for organization-wide conscious action – that is, the organization acts and perceives, perceives and acts, at the same time.

Phase 4: leveraging a global leadership position

Nokia is today the largest mobile phone manufacturer and one of the two biggest GSM-based cellular systems providers in the world. This position provides Nokia with a good opportunity for fulfilling its next-generation vision of creating a 'mobile information society' by further leveraging its position in the converging digital communications industry. A prerequisite for future success is, however, that the company is continuously able to renew itself.

Many of Nokia's past experiences provide a good basis for strong renewal and, hence, ability to grow. Nokia has learned to create, convert and exploit new technology and systems solutions in close cooperation with customers worldwide. The company has also learned to live with very short product lifecycles and volatile markets, as well as severe price competition (Ala-Pietilä, 1998). It has also learned to build globally linked R&D activities as well as a global logistical configuration for the most efficient low-cost and high-quality manufacturing and delivery. The company has also been able to create a strong brand recognition in the minds of consumers.

The two internally different business models of NTC and NMP have presented Nokia with new options for the internal fusion of abilities. As the industry as a whole continues to converge and become more open, NTC needs to learn from NMP and vice versa. Thus, in 1998, the CEO of Nokia changed the jobs of the most of the firm's Executive Board members in order to transfer knowledge and experiences from one business to another and move people away from their 'comfort zones'.[24]

In order to keep its current businesses out of those comfort zones, Nokia has established a new venture organization and Board to challenge current thinking and accelerate the development of new growth businesses.[25] It has also established its own venture fund to place minority ownership in interesting emerging small- and medium-sized companies that create new technology and business concepts in line with Nokia's future vision.

Nokia has faced additional new challenges as a large global company. It has had to figure out how to maintain and further improve its innovative, individual-based and egalitarian corporate culture, as well as the hands-on management style that has strongly contributed to its ability to renew itself thus far. Consequently, there is pressure to institutionalize some of the organizational and managerial mechanisms that had been previously taken care of purely by individuals. High-quality global operations require standardized processes in addition to shared values and management principles. The greatest challenge is to combine these in such a way that the vitality and creativity of the organization can be sustained.

As a result, Nokia is continuously considering new ways and means to interlink people, actions and knowledge globally.

Shared visioning and the strategy-creation process

Nokia interlinks and upgrades individual and organizational tacit knowledge and converts it into explicit knowledge by means of a continuous companywide shared visioning and strategy-creation process. This process involves hundreds of people within the company, as well as some visionary thought leaders from outside the company, in order to tap the widest possible knowledge base and commit people to the actual strategy implementation. The outcome of the process – an aligned and shared strategy – provides people with a common direction and an in-depth understanding of the assumptions behind the strategy. The latter, in turn, is needed to give people a 'map' with which to read the markets themselves.[26] The visioning and strategy process, as well as management education within Nokia, are organized to be widely interactive forums to create common foresight, 'digest' new knowledge and information and agree on future actions.[27] The highly egalitarian and 'straightforward' management culture also offers a good opportunity for anyone to challenge the future directions, at any time throughout the year. Thus, Nokia deploys managerial and organizational mechanisms that keep strategy continuously intertwined with implementation.

Interlinked R&D

The corporate R&D at Nokia concentrates on long-term research and advanced development, together with business units and universities.[28] It focuses on corporatewide core competence, as well as on mutually identified disruptive technologies. The corporate R&D is closely interlinked with Nokia's businesses. Indeed, it has many ongoing research projects that are primarily financed and carried out in cooperation with the business units. This cooperation is strengthened by transferring people – dozens of people from corporate R&D move to business units, together with their projects, every year. These tactics have accelerated the taking of new technology into use. Consequently, corporate R&D is not a separate research institute, but, rather, an integral part of corporatewide R&D activity.

The same highly cooperative and integrative way of acting is also applied in the global R&D of the business units. People from the geographically dispersed R&D centres participate actively in customer projects all over the world in order to remain in touch with real-life problems and help solve them quickly. This is also very important from the global product-creation viewpoint: one can only create truly global products by combining lessons from many markets. The basic structure of Nokia's R&D consists of a chain of specialized competence centres that are located in leading countries from the business and/or technology development viewpoint. For instance, the third-generation cellular technology development is based in Japan, because Japan will probably be the first country to take this new technology into use. Thus, Nokia aims at creating modular global technologies and products that can be customized to local needs with a minimum amount of change. This, in turn, enables global economies of scale to be combined efficiently with local responsiveness.

Transparency by means of common modular processes and IT solutions

Nokia's business process development and IT have traditionally served the standardization and re-engineering of information and activity flows in each of the Nokia businesses. Today, Nokia's process and information management architecture is being designed to gain additional speed, flexibility and cost-efficiency using modular business processes and related information systems. This 'plug and play' organizational architecture should enable Nokia to configure new types of global business systems in an efficient way. Nokia also strives for maximum information transparency, which means universal real-time access to all critical codified business information within the company. The purpose of this transparency is to simultaneously increase global learning, integration and local responsiveness.

The information management architecture of Nokia has been constructed with different value-adding layers. The 'bottom' layer includes a transparent information management platform for the transaction processing of codified data and information. The second layer is for planning and decision making based on the transparent information. The third layer is for informal communication and sharing of knowledge related to Nokia's internal and external worlds.

Nokia also actively combines IT with its own communications products and activities in order to create new communication products and solutions. Furthermore, Nokia invests in exploiting new e-business technologies to expand interaction with customers and partners. Nokia believes that mobile communication technologies can add great value to more 'traditional' e-commerce solutions.

Virtual societies coexist with 'real' societies in the form of 'social webs' that are encouraged by the company. Indeed, Nokia facilitates the self-organization of social webs where Nokia people can discuss and create new ideas and opportunities with people from other cultures. Interaction with competitors and scientists from universities and research institutions has also been widely used.

Organization in time and space

We have discussed knowledge-based renewal and growth of innovative global companies that can anticipate and create new knowledge and future markets by ensuring openness at all levels of the organization. This is a contextual quality according to which individual actions, the activities of teams and the action lines of the whole organization are open-ended and in 'breathing' interaction with the environment. This quality also provides an organization with the greatest possible speed and flexibility because all of its activities are naturally time-paced.

A capacity for time-paced action means that a globally innovative company has structures, processes and actions that make it possible to deal with current tasks as well as foresee future needs. Thus, one may argue that a globally innovative company can leverage speed and flexibility by using managerial and organizational mechanisms that interlink its creative *ba* on a global scale (Nonaka and Konno, 1998). However, in the Nokia case, the creative *ba* are not only different places or contexts of its global operations, but also discontinuities in time and space caused by the very nature of their individual and collective actions and interactions.

Nokia has made this possible by giving individuals creative, innovative and open-ended space to develop or revise ways of acting for the future. Thus, individual actions may be reflective and create new tacit and explicit knowledge even though they are disciplined for effective implementation. In the same way, different problem-solving teams and groups can be innovative and apply effective ways to create and innovate, even though they are performing according to specified goals in specified time frames.[29]

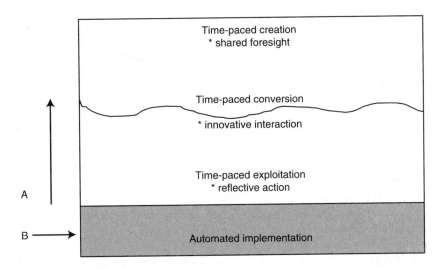

Figure 12.3   *Time-paced organization*

Figure 12.3 illustrates a company that has intertwined the creation, conversion, and exploitation processes of knowledge, based on multi-layered, time-paced interaction with the environment. The knowledge-based renewal ability of the company (A) is supported by intertwined structures, processes and activities that are standardized and automated for implementation (B).

Based on this principle individuals can, through their actions and problem solving, change their focus between 'tacitly present' future market and customer needs and the 'explicitly present' requirement to implement current tasks. The figure also illustrates how common future foresight can be achieved companywide, such as during the strategy process or in a management-development forum. During these shared activities, people's insights about the future are converted into a common vision, strategic directions and actionable milestones and measures (Nonaka and Takeuchi, 1995).

Concerning the concept of time-paced organization, the principle of intertwined action, perception and reasoning is applied to all ontological levels of context: individuals, groups and teams, the whole organization and the interorganizational level. In principle, each ontological level may consist of emergent structures and processes of creation, as well as communicative and interactive structures and processes of conversion and implementation.[30]

Unified action, perception and reasoning, in time, can be translated into an ability to deploy creative and interactive strategies, structures, processes and actions that draw their substance simultaneously from different markets and environments. This is the organization living as time-paced in time and space. We believe that such an organization can best exploit market discontinuities globally and, consequently, renew itself and grow. This is the contextual quality of a globally operating company that helps to capture the essence of dispersed knowledge in the global marketplace.

The role of individuals is crucial in time-paced organizations because they interact with their environment through individuals. The multilayered openness with the environment comprises many ways and means to sense and create future markets based on individuals and teams. At Nokia, for instance, the company relies much more on its people and networks for business intelligence than on traditional market research and analysis, which is based on an information-processing approach focused on the external environment.[31]

The 'interface' or difference between innovative strategy and its rapid implementation is transparent, almost non-existent, in a time-paced organization. The company has the ability to 'flow' or live proactively in time all the time. This means that the future is present as an aspect, in tacit or explicit form, in every reflective action. Time is the unifying pace-making factor within the organization. Ideally, the whole global company can 'breathe' and act in the same time-paced rhythm.

Modular processes and information systems are also crucial in a time-paced organization because they allow the rapid global implementation of agreed explicit actions – that is, automated implementation.

Conclusions

The Nokia case illustrates the exceptionally rapid knowledge-based growth of a globally innovative company. This differs essentially from contingent, organic, evolutionary, social or institutional views on growth (see, for example, Lawrence and Lorsch, 1967, Scott 1995, and Nelson and Winter, 1982). First, one may argue that, until the knowledge-based view of the organization emerged, individuals were 'faceless' – they were veiled behind managerial and organizational mechanisms, task structures or the distribution of labour within the firm. Second, earlier views emphasized only the role of management and strategy or structure as a means to adapt to the environment. Third, earlier scholarship tended to view growth as a result of adaptation to, and not as a mutually constitutive and creative interaction with, the environment.

Nonaka and Takeuchi (1995) discuss knowledge creation as a means of explaining organizational change, innovation and renewal. They consider organizational dynamism and abilities for renewal from the following viewpoints:

1 the capacity of individual minds to create new tacit knowledge;
2 the organizational capacity to convert that explicit knowledge by means of self-organizing teams and processes of socialization, communication and dialogue.

They also emphasize the role of middle management as a mediator of the visions and ideals of top management to people on the front line. Thus, Nonaka and Takeuchi view individuals as being very important. They are the 'working knowledge archive' of the firm and added value for the organization.

At Nokia, growth has been an outcome of market-maker behaviour – that is, a mutually constitutive creation of markets with customers has been driven by the common intentional actions of management and individuals on the front line. This view of knowledge-based growth emphasizes a conscious and holistic, time-paced interaction between management and individuals.[32] They may be considered to be autonomous knowledge workers interacting with the environment.[33]

A challenge for a globally operating company is how to interlink, worldwide, the foresight of both individuals and management for time-paced strategies, as well as for time-paced innovative interaction and reflective actions. At Nokia, this challenge is quite significant because the company emphasizes, from the renewal viewpoint, the role of individual reflective actions more than that of structures or even processes. However, the Nokia case also shows that business processes may at least partly replace organizational structure, in its traditional meaning. Processes can provide both flexibility and discipline if they are based on modular knowledge and activity cores that are supported by information technology.

Giddens (1984) argues that, from the viewpoint of dynamic change, structures should be viewed as allowing 'bindings' of time and space in social systems. He views structures as 'virtual or mental orders' of relations. This means that there is no need for structures in a traditional sense, but, rather, for 'structural properties'. Structures may only be present as 'virtual entities', either as memory traces or by virtue of their time–space presence. At Nokia, the 'binding' for common reasoning, perception, and global action was first achieved via hands-on management that was later supported by global forums for dialogue and discussions, as well as by global information and communications systems.

Penrose (1959/1980) emphasizes actions as activators of knowledge, but she mainly considers the existing latent 'surplus' knowledge within the firm.[34] She argues that managers build the firm to reflect their own perceptions of the world and reality. Here, however, we discuss growth and renewal based on future-oriented tacit knowledge that reflects the shared vision and strategy of both management and individuals on the front line. Thus renewal and growth are intentional, even intuitive actions that are based on shared tacit understanding.

The Nokia case shows that the emergence of individual and, consequently, organizational tacit knowledge may be accelerated if the company offers opportunities for individuals to learn and experience demanding new things, stretching themselves. Thus, the firm becomes a growth platform for individuals. This may relate to what Nonaka and Takeuchi (1995) discuss as an opportunity for a knowledge-creating company to offer individual transcendental renewal. Individual growth results in organizational growth and vice versa. However, the Nokia case is about accelerated growth and renewal based on high levels of aspiration which has involved the whole company, not only temporary teams for innovative tasks. The Nokia case shows that this type of challenging individual and organizational renewal and growth may strengthen both individual and organizational self-identity and autonomy. This encourages widely autonomous behaviour and abilities for independent problem solving and responsibility taking. The Nokia case also demonstrates ways of acting that cause individuals to be interested in and concerned about the future. Such individuals are alert and 'in a sensing mode', as well as in a proactive mode to anticipate and create future markets.

The Nokia case supports the importance of common values and ideals that Nonaka and Takeuchi (1995) also discuss. One may argue that, in particular, trust has been the most important factor to offer stability over the discontinuities of accelerated growth.

The knowledge-based view of a firm challenges previous theoretical discussion and management practice, based, for instance, on transaction-cost and game theories. These older theories draw on assumptions that:

1 resources are scarce and markets are limited, circumstances that lead to competition for existing resources and markets and not to the creation of new ones;
2 knowledge is mostly 'out there' or developed only in company laboratories;
3 the main objective of the firm is the efficient exploitation of knowledge that is explicit, manageable, tradeable and subject to 'packaging' and transferring.

These views objectify and simplify the issue of knowledge and neglect its tacit and embedded human and organizational nature. They assign only an instrumental value to people and knowledge – and even to the whole organization. The underlying assumption is that people are not necessarily worth trusting and are, in fact, a potential source of problems. This has led to emphasizing control, a detailed distribution of labour, traditional information processing and hierarchical structures.

The knowledge-based view of a firm is about to change these underlying assumptions.

Notes

1   Edith T. Penrose (1959) in *The Theory of the Growth of the Firm*, London: Basil Blackwell, views knowledge as a resource of the firm that is latent, waiting for a wake-up call, but offering productive services when activated by

use (pp. 67–87). According to her view, 'productive services' are contributions that knowledge (and other resources) can make to the productive operations of the firm. As long as any resource is not fully utilized in current operations, there is an incentive for a firm to find a way to use it more fully. Penrose argues that the dynamic and generative nature of knowledge (and other resources) is a productive service (p. 68) and that the firm will never reach an 'equilibrium position' in which there is no further incentive to expand. A 'state of rest' is precluded by three significant obstacles: the indivisibility of resources, the opportunity to use them differently under different circumstances and the opportunity to use them in a 'specialized' manner.

2   Some basic facts about the Nokia Corporation. In 1999, the firm had net sales of EUR 19.8 billion. At year end 1999, Nokia had 52 R&D centres in 14 countries and 17134 R&D employees, approximately 31 per cent of Nokia's total personnel. Nokia's global production comprises 12 manufacturing factories in five countries and ten mobile phone manufacturing facilities in eight countries.

3   Gunnar Hedlund (1996) in 'The knowledge intensity and extensity and the MNCs as nearly recomposable systems (NRS)', a paper presented at the annual meeting of the Academy of International Business, Banff, Canada, Sept. 26–29, discusses two tendencies in the world economy: increasing 'knowledge intensity' – that is, the increasingly demanding content of knowledge, including increasing complexity and increasing 'knowledge extensity' – that is, a rapid extension (or distribution or delivery) of knowledge globally via information and communication networks. Hedlund discusses how this may affect the ways and means of multinational companies to organize and manage international and global operations. He proposes an organizational form that is nearly capable of 'composing' knowledge and new competences by flexibly combining and recombining its resources over the global network of units.

4   James G. March (1991) in 'Exploration and exploitation in organizational learning', *Organization Science*, 2 (1): pp. 71–87, discusses the exploration for knowledge as including search, variation, risk taking, experimentation, play, flexibility, discovery and innovation. The exploitation of knowledge includes such things as refinement, choice, production, efficiency, selection, implementation and execution.

5   Gunnar Hedlund (1994) in 'A model of knowledge management and the N-Form corporation', *Strategic Management Journal*, 15: pp. 73–90, discusses knowledge as being structured formally, according to work processes and actions. He also discusses ordering principles for the experimentation of knowledge and the organization as a mirroring and reflective structure of knowledge, action and social phenomena (1993, 'Assumptions on hierarchy and heterarchy, with application to the management of the multinational corporation', in S. Ghoshal and D. Eleanor Westney (eds), *Organization Theory and Multinational Corporations*, New York: St Martin's, p. 226). He views organizational structures as an intertwined outcome of the dynamic interaction of knowledge, actions and people. Ikujiro Nonaka and Hirotaka Takeuchi (1995) in *The Knowledge-creating Firm: How Japanese Companies Create Dynamics of Innovation*, New York: Oxford University Press, discuss the hypertext structures of business as usual (the business layer) the creative processes of knowledge creation (the project team layer), and knowledge construction (the knowledge base layer of the firm).

6   David Bohm (1998) in Lee Nichol (ed.), *On Creativity*, London: Routledge, distinguishes between creative processes and mechanical processes and reflects on the nature of the creativity and on what distinguishes creative processes from those that are merely mechanical (pp. vii–viii). He argues that the human being is in a unique position of being able to perceive the dynamism and movement of the world around him, while at the same time realizing that the perceptive mind is of an equivalent order of creativity, participating intimately with the world it observes. To the extent that one's perceptions of the world affect 'reality' – and the evidence for this is considerable – people have a corresponding responsibility to attempt to bring thought processes and the world they emerge from and interpret into a coherent relationship. In enquiring into the nature of creativity, Bohm does not shy away from questions of beauty, truth or what is 'good'. Rather, he supports the idea of a creative apprehension of 'a certain oneness and totality, or wholeness, constituting a kind of harmony that is felt to be beautiful'. The creative enquiry is richly aesthetic.

7   Michael Polanyi and Harry Prosch (1975) in *Meaning*, Chicago: University of Chicago Press, p. 3, enter the discussion on meanings by stating that an achievement of meaning cannot properly be divorced from intellectual freedom. Thus, the creation of meanings may depend on the quality of the context of creation.

8   Polanyi and Prosch (1975, pp. 37–45) discuss the nature of personal knowledge from the point of view of tacit bodily knowledge or skill. Two kinds of skilful knowing are interwoven: a skilful handling of things must rely on our understanding them, while intellectual comprehension can be achieved only via the skilful scrutiny of a situation. The kinship between the process of tool-using and that of perceiving a whole has been so well established already by gestalt psychology that it may be taken for granted. Thus, the structure of tacit knowing includes a joint pair of constituents – that is, a functional structure of from–to knowing includes jointly 'from' knowing and a focal 'to' or 'at' knowing. Where one focuses is determined by the act of a person, who integrates one with the other.

9   Michael Polanyi (1958) in *Personal Knowledge: Towards a Post-critical Philosophy*, London: Routledge, pp. 69–77) discusses, among other things, trick learning, sign learning and latent learning. He discusses latent learning as an act of interpretation that may contain heuristic insights and innovations.

10 Jack Mezirow (1994) in *Transformative Dimensions of Adult Learning*, San Francisco: Jossey-Bass, discusses the creation of new meanings and transformative future ways of acting. Contextual learning theories discuss meaning schemes and meaning perspectives. The discussion is partly based on the findings of the schema theories.

11 Polanyi (1958, preface) discusses gestalt psychology and the nature of personal knowledge. Such knowledge is derived from the personal participation of the knower in all understanding. However, he argues, this does not make one's understanding subjective. Comprehension is neither an arbitrary act, nor a passive experience, but a responsible act claiming universal validity. Such knowing is indeed objective in the sense of establishing contact with a hidden reality – a contact that is defined as the condition for anticipating an indeterminate range of yet unknown (and perhaps yet inconceivable) true implications. Polanyi calls this fusion of the personal and the objective 'personal

knowledge'. This knowledge contains intellectual commitment. He argues that into every action of knowing there enters a passionate contribution of the person knowing what is being known. Thus, Polanyi describes comprehension and knowing as a passionate intellectual commitment to the yet unknown and inconceivable.

12   Tacit knowledge consists of tacit meaning perspectives and partly tacit and partly explicit meaning schemes. Tacit meaning perspectives become converted meaning schemes (Mezirow, 1994, p. 44) in socialization, interaction and dialogue. Meaning schemes consist of particular knowledge, concepts, ideas, beliefs, value judgements and feelings that may become articulated in interpretations. Meaning schemes are concrete manifestations of meaning perspectives. Thus, they can be partly tacit in nature. When translated into specific norms and ways of acting, they directly guide actions. The nature of meanings causes tacit and explicit knowledge to be intertwined and never 'at rest' – knowledge is fluid, in dynamic movement, while it is challenged by actions and experiences derived from actions within a context.

13   Jean Grondin (1995) in *Sources of Hermeneutics*, Albany, NY: State University of New York Press, discusses the prime questions of hermeneutics and theory of interpretation. He places the relationship of context and knowledge – that is, contextuality and the problem of objective truth, the context and value of truth claims – at the very centre of hermeneutics: 'It is only if one enquires into the underlying motivation of what is being said that one can hope to grasp the truth. Contextuality and knowledge (truth) belong together in a way that does not entail any kind of relativism, because the knowledge (truth) that emerges out of a given situation and urgency remains one that can be shared by others, provided they are attentive to the unsaid side of the discourse' (p. ix).

14   We use the term 'tacit reflection' (or 'perception'), based on Giddens (1984) in *The Constitute of Society*, London: Polity Press, pp. 1–16. Giddens discusses 'practical consciousness' (tacit reflection) in connection with the nature of action. He says that action cannot be discussed separately from the body, its mediations with the surrounding world and the coherence of an acting self. He says that the acting self involves treating the reflexive monitoring, rationalization and motivation of action as embedded sets of processes. The vast bulk of 'stocks of knowledge', or mutual knowledge incorporated in encounters, is not directly accessible to the consciousness of the actors. Unconscious motivational components of action have an internal hierarchy of their own, a hierarchy that expresses the 'depth' of the life history of the individual actor. Giddens discusses a 'discursive consciousness' of actions – that is, human beings can report their intentions in, or reasons for, acting as they do (articulation, explicit reflection) – and he discusses practical consciousness, which concerns unconscious motivation and other subtle treatments (non-articulation, tacit reflection) that affect actions and human conduct (pp. 6–7).

15   George Lakoff and Mark Johnson (1999) in *Philosophy in the Flesh: The Embodied Mind and its Challenge to Western Thought*, New York: Basic Books, pp. 9–44, discuss cognitive consciousness and the embodied mind. They discuss the nature of reason as inextricably entwined with body and bodily experiences, both of which precondition the conceptual systems of the mind – that is, the structures and processes of the mind that perceive and create reality. Lakoff and Johnson base their discussion on new discoveries of

cognitive science. They discuss especially the nature of cognitive unconsciousness, arguing that cognitive unconsciousness is vast and intricately structured.
Unconscious thought may be more than 95 per cent of all thoughts. Cognitive
unconsciousness includes not only all automatic cognitive operations, but also
implicit knowledge. Lakoff and Johnson argue that knowledge and beliefs are
framed in terms of a conceptual system that resides mostly in the cognitive
unconsciousness. They argue that the unconscious conceptual system functions
like a 'hidden hand' that shapes how we conceptualize all aspects of our
experience.

16 F.A. von Hayek (1945) in 'The use of knowledge in society', *American Economic Review*, 35 (4), pp. 519–30, discusses the dispersed nature of knowledge
in society. He argues that a rational economic order is determined precisely by
the fact that no one person possesses all of the knowledge necessary to act.
Instead, separate individuals possess dispersed bits of incomplete and
frequently contradictory knowledge. This raises the problem of the utilization
of knowledge that is not given to anyone in its totality. See C. Nichijama and
K. Leube (eds) (1984) in *The Essence of Hayek*, Stanford, CA: Hoover
Institute Press, p. 212.

17 Haridimos Tsoukas (1996) in 'The firm as a distributed knowledge system: a
constructionist approach', *Strategic Management Journal*, 17 (Winter Special),
p. 12, discusses critically the neoclassical view of firms and a behaviourist
concept of human agents. He leans on the views of von Hayek (see Nichijama
and Leube, 1984, pp. 266–77) and argues that assumptions of rational economic order are synonymous with attempting to find the best way of allocating
given resources, which leads to seeing the economic problem as a simple one of
logic and economic calculus.

18 Hedlund (1996) discusses the fact that increasing knowledge intensity is the
result of accelerated growth of new knowledge as well as increasing levels of
education worldwide.

19 J.C. Spender and Robert M. Grant (1996) in 'Knowledge and the firm:
overview', *Strategic Management Journal*, 17 (Winter special), p. 8, discuss
knowledge transfer between and within firms. They reason that the success of
companies such as Wal-Mart and McDonald's is dependent on their ability to
transfer the knowledge embodied in organizational routines from one establishment to another.

20 Ikujiro Nonaka (1997) in 'Knowledge creation and sustainable competitive-
ness of the firm', a paper presented at a seminar organized by LIFIM (the
Finnish Institute of Management) on Organizational Knowledge Creation, 23
March, reported by Veijo Sahiluoma, *Kauppalehti*, 1 April 1997, 61, p. 32,
discusses 'real-time' knowledge creation with the examples of Microsoft and
Toshiba in the computer and multimedia industries.

21 Adam M. Brandenburger and Barry J. Nalebuff (1996) in *Co-opetition*, New
York: Doubleday, describe co-opetition as a revolutionary mindset that combines competition and cooperation – a game theory strategy that is changing
the game of business.

22 This conclusion is supported by two doctoral theses on global growth and
internationalization by Nokia managers (see Matti Alahuta (1990) 'Global
growth strategies for high technology challenges', PhD dissertation, Helsinki
University of Technology, and Mikko Kosenen (1991) 'Internationalization
process of industrial systems suppliers with special emphasis on strategy and

organization', PhD dissertation, Helsinki School of Economics and Business Administration).

23   Interview with Sari Baldauf, president of Nokia Telecommunications (NTC) (at that time President of Cellular Systems), in Seija Kulkki (1996) 'Knowledge creation of multinational corporations: knowledge creation through action', PhD dissertation, Helsinki School of Economics and Business Administration.

24   CEO Jorma Ollila shuffled the jobs of Nokia's top managers in order to promote renewal and growth within the corporation. The former President of NTC became President of NMP, the President of NMP became President of New Venture Businesses, and the former Senior Vice-president responsible for Asian markets became President of NTC.

25   The New Venture Board's role is to keep new ventures linked with current businesses and, thus, renew the whole organization, not just the ventures in the new venture organization.

26   Nokia's vision and strategy process consists of, first, visioning the outside world, second, creating a strategic intent and strategy and, third, defining the strategic action lines and key measures for each business. The corporatewide visioning process comprises a few hundred people, whereas the strategy-creation process comprises thousands of people from all over the organization. The role of Nokia's annual five-year visioning and three-year strategy-creation process is to update, align, document and share, once a year, the companywide knowledge in business and technology. The visioning work focuses on three to five corporatewide interest areas and is carried out by focused multifunctional and multicultural teams headed by senior management. This approach combines both commitment and expertise in an efficient way. The visions are then challenged in various vision workshops before being communicated to all businesses as the basis of their strategy work. The 'final' visions and strategies act as reference points against which the whole organization evaluates its experiences and new knowledge throughout the year.

27   Nokia organizes many management education programmes and forums for its cross-functional and cross-cultural teams. For newcomers, however, Nokia only gives a short introduction to the company. It lets people learn their jobs and build their personal network by means of action. The company also does not distribute many written instructions to its employees. It emphasizes international orientation and open minds, as well as a high quality of (academic) education and maturity as personal characteristics, but, otherwise, the company lets people 'tacitly learn through action'. Nokia has found it advantageous to have a substantial annual flow of new people with new ideas coming in, without too much preconditioning of their thinking.

28   Corporate R&D comprises close to 10 per cent of all R&D personnel of the company.

29   In its management development, Nokia emphasizes methods of creative and innovative working, problem solving, concept creation and logical argumentation. Compare Nonaka and Takeuchi (1995) on the spiral (SECI) process of knowledge creation, where they discuss the means to convert tacit knowledge to explicit knowledge as well as combine and recombine explicit knowledge.

30   This reflects Nonaka and Takeuchi's (1995) idea of the spiral process of knowledge creation from tacit to explicit and back to tacit again on the ontological levels of individuals and groups, as well as intra- and inter-organizationally. Nonaka and Takeuchi describe a process in which individual

tacit knowledge is converted to organizational explicit knowledge, which is assimilated throughout the organization and, by means of cooperation, even to the interorganizational domain. However, Nonaka and Takeuchi also discuss an organizational context in which the business structure (of business as usual) is hierarchically ordered, which may mean that the basic structure of the firm is not very time-sensitive or reflective.

31 Nokia uses traditional market and competition analysis, as well as analysis of technology trends, mainly to verify and check its direction.

32 Dan Schendel (1996) in 'Knowledge and the firm', *Strategic Management Journal*, 17 (Winter Special): pp. 1–4, views knowledge as a key source of competence and the creation and utilization of knowledge in organizations as the key resource managers need to appreciate and understand in order to achieve sustainable competence. Spender and Grant (1996) argue that the key to understanding organizational renewal lies in understanding the relationship between abstract knowledge and individual and organizational practices.

33 Peter Drucker (1998) in 'On knowledge workers', keynote speech at the Knowledge Forum, Haas School of Business, University of California, Berkeley, 25 Sept., described the nature and role of knowledge workers as quite autonomous and independent when offering their knowledge-based services to the firm.

34 Penrose says that growth is based on knowledge, but as a latent opportunity for generative growth.

References

Ala-Pietilä, Pekka (1998) 'Strategy when uncertainty goes beyond probability', keynote speech at the Strategic Management Society Conference in Orlando, Florida, 3 March.

Baker, Stephen, Crockett, Roger O., and Gross, Neil (1998) 'An interview with CEO Jorma Ollila of Nokia Corporation', *Business Week*, 10 Aug. (European ed.): 38–44.

Brown, John Seely, and Duguid, Paul (1998) 'Organizing knowledge', *California Management Review*, 40 (3): 90–111.

Doz, Yves, Asakawa, Kaz, Santos, José F.P., and Williamsson, Peter (1996, rev. 1997) 'The metanational corporation', INSEAD working paper.

Dunning, John (1997) 'The changing nature of the firm in a knowledge-based globalizing industry', paper presented at the Conference on Knowledge in International Corporations, Rome, Italy, November.

Giddens, Anthony (1984) *The Constitute of Society*. London: Polity Press.

Hagström, Peter, and Hedlund, Gunnar (1998) 'The dynamic firm: a three-dimensional model of internal structure', in A.D. Chandler, P. Hagström and Ö. Söllvell (eds), *The Dynamic Firm*. New York: Oxford University Press.

Hedlund, Gunnar (1993) 'Assumptions on hierarchy and heterarchy, with application the management of the multinational corporation', in S. Ghoshal and D. Eleanor Westney (eds), *Organization Theory and Multinational Corporations*. New York: St Martin's.

Hedlund, Gunnar (1994) 'A model of knowledge management and the N-form corporations', *Strategic Management Journal*, 15: 73–90.

Hurley, S.L. (1998) *Consciousness in Action*. Cambridge, MA: Harvard University Press.

Kulkki, Seija (1996) 'Knowledge creation of multinational corporations: knowledge creation

through action', PhD dissertation, Helsinki School of Economics a.
Administration.

Kulkki, Seija (1998) 'Knowledge creation and dynamism of governance struc
multinational corporations: a research design', INSEAD working paper 24.2.

Lakoff, G. and Johnson, M. (1999) *Philosophy in the Flesh: The Embodied Mind a*
Challenge to Western Thought. New York: Basic Books.

Lawrence, Paul R., and Lorsch, Jay W. (1986 [1967]) *Organization and Environment.* Boston,
MA: Harvard Business School.

Leonard, Dorothy, and Sensiper, Sylvia (1998) 'The role of tacit knowledge in group
innovation', *California Management Review*, 40 (3): 112–32.

Mezirow, Jack (1984) *Transformative Dimensions of Adult Learning.* San Francisco: Jossey
Bass.

Nelson, Richard A., and Winter, Sidney (1982) *An Evolutionary Theory of Economic Change.*
Cambridge, MA: Harvard University Press.

Nonaka, Ikujiro, and Konno, Noboru (1998) 'The concept of "*ba*": building foundation for
knowledge creation', *California Management Review*, 40 (3): 40–54.

Nonaka, Ikujiro, and Takeuchi, Hirotaka (1995) *The Knowledge-Creating Firm: How
Japanese Companies Create Dynamics of Innovation.* New York: Oxford University Press.

Penrose, Edith T. (1959/1980) *The Theory of the Growth of the Firm.* Oxford: Basil
Blackwells.

Polyani, Michael (1958) *Personal Knowledge: Towards a Post-critical Philosophy.* London:
Routledge.

Scott, W. Richard (1995) *Institutions and Organizations.* Thousand Oaks, CA: Sage.

Spender, J.-C. (1996) 'Making knowledge the basis of a dynamic theory of the firm', *Strategic
Management Journal*, 17 (Winter Special): 45–62.

Tsoukas, Haridimos (1996) 'The firm as a distributed knowledge system: a constructionist
approach', *Strategic Management Journal*, 17 (winter special): 12.

13 Knowledge is Commitment

Haruo Naito

Introduction

'The more money the company makes, the better employees will be rewarded.' One day in the mid-1980s, I asked my employees whether that message inspired them. I found out that this message no longer motivates most employees today. This is one of the reasons for my becoming so enthusiastic about the knowledge creation theory.

The conventional, classical and financial-oriented message does not make sense any more. In addition, the personal objectives and goals of employees are no longer the same as those of the company – the era in which the purpose of the company was the same as that of its employees is over. I realize that we need to construct a system that synchronizes or harmonizes the purposes and goals of both employers and employees. Because at Eisai we have dramatically expanded operations worldwide in recent years (2,000 employees out of the total of 7,300 are now non-Japanese), the company's perspective must transcend nationality, culture, language and habit and unify worldwide employees. Without such a common perspective, good communication within the company will not be possible.

Knowledge-creation activities provide the framework in which an employee as an individual and a company as an organization can collaborate and unify the business processes. In other words, the purpose of each employee and that of the company could be synchronized and harmonized by means of knowledge-creation activities. I think that knowledge creation is an approach to solving new or historically unresolved issues. I believe that socialization is the most important knowledge-creation activity. Socialization is particularly important for Eisai, as a pharmaceutical company. The answers to our unsolved problems lie with the market.

In 1988, I took over the office of company President from my father, Yuji Naito. Eisai had sales of 15.9 billion yen when my grandfather passed the torch to my father and by the time I succeeded my father, the company had grown to 3,692 employees with sales of 167.0 billion yen. Before I became the President, I was the Head of the Research and Development Division at the Tsukuba Research Institute.

The Tsukuba Research Institute

In 1983, I was appointed Head of the Tsukuba Research Institute. Coming as I did from a liberal arts background, I was not completely comfortable with the details of science. In fact, when I went to the institute, I felt the withering gaze of the veteran researchers, who seemed to be wondering, 'Well, what can you do?' At the same time, among them were those who felt a vague dissatisfaction that they did not have the understanding of the top executives or an appreciation of the company's management.

I first tried explaining what the whole company expects of the Institute and that the fate of the company depends on having new products. I wanted everyone to realize that the Institute is the most important part of the company. Although I am not a trained scientist, I thoroughly discussed with key researchers the ideas and projects that scientists were working on. During the approximately 4 years I worked at the Institute, I spent many 24-hour days there and did my best to communicate via MBWA (management by wandering around) on a one-on-one basis.

While there, I came up with the concept of 'the mechanism of the interesting', which is based on the idea that people do their best work when they find it interesting. I thus became fascinated with how to foster interest. This includes, for example, building a sharp relationship between effect and effort invested, encouraging in-house competition, setting milestones for the fine-grained evaluation of research results and establishing a system of rewards for milestones achieved.

During this period, the Institute was aflame with activities, producing in four years more successes (and failures) than the company had had over the previous decade. We developed drugs that will be global products for the next generation, including Aricept® (for the treatment of Alzheimer's disease) and Aciphex/Pariet® (for the treatment of gastrointestinal disorders/ diseases).

The research and product development process that led to Aricept® was especially important in the globalization of the company. This compound was discovered and developed by Dr Hachiro Sugimoto, who was determined to find and develop a drug to treat dementia. The research and development process of a new drug is very time-consuming and difficult. Dr Sugimoto's dedicated efforts were supported by the firm and his commitment to the project was also a personal one – he was caring for his mother, who suffered from dementia. His 15-year effort finally bore fruit with the development of donepezil hydrochloride (Aricept®) – one of the first prescription drugs for the treatment of Alzheimer's-type dementia. Dr Sugimoto is working on the next step – a drug to cure dementia.

The EI (Eisai Innovation) Declaration

When I became Vice-president in 1987, I was required to think about the future of Eisai. We were nearing the 50th anniversary of the company in

1991 and looking ahead to another half-century.

In the late 1980s, the entire healthcare environment began to undergo a major transformation in Japan. The business environment in which drug companies found themselves was in the midst of tumultuous changes, including the diversification of patients' needs, attempts to hold down total medical expenses, decreases in officially established drug prices, inroads by foreign-owned companies, entry into the pharmaceuticals field by companies from different industries, the development of ICH (the International Conference on Harmonization of Technical Requirements for Registration of Pharmaceuticals for Human Use) and higher research and development costs. Greater attention was being devoted to the quality of life of patients and their families, the quality of medical services, the medical system and the safety and cost of pharmaceuticals. What was demanded of a company like Eisai changed as well – this was the era of a transformation from simply pursuing sales and profits to pursuing a corporate ideal that included contributing to society by satisfying the diverse needs of patients and their families, consumers, the general public and employees, while devoting ample attention to environmental concerns.

Amidst these great changes, while always considering what kind of company Eisai should become, I settled on two themes:

1 formulating a medium-term managerial plan;
2 creating a concept for the new Eisai – that is, a long-term management plan for the twenty-first century and beyond.

My first task as Vice-president was to formulate a new medium-term managerial plan. Since 1957, Eisai had practised planned management based on three-year medium-term plans. That Eisai succeeded in becoming one of the top ten drug companies in Japan in such a short period of time is a tribute to this planned management. I formulated 'new strategic 5-year plans' instead of 3-year plans to build our position as a world-renowned drug company by 2001, the end of a 15-year period divided into phase I, phase II and phase III. This 'new strategic five-year plan' was not a top-down plan from the management level, but a bottom-up one, in which individual employees developed five-year plans for their own work, reflecting their dreams for the future of Eisai. This five-year planning naturally encouraged employees' sense of inclusion and made the whole company more active than before.

Phase I was 'the period of strengthening our domestic business', phase II was 'the period of globalization' and phase III was 'the period of soaring progress'. Phase I was the time for building up the domestic business system and laying the groundwork for development abroad. Within Japan, the system of branches was increased from 10 to 21, a sales system was created to facilitate area marketing with close ties to local regions and the new products Myonal®, Selbex® and Azeptin® were built into major products. At an early stage, we gave each medical representative (MR) a laptop computer to use in developing a system that would allow each MR to provide high-quality information about pharmaceutical products to medical professionals. At the same time, parallel with the opening of laboratories in the US and UK, clinical development companies were established in both countries, forming an international research and development system for conducting clinical research and obtaining approval for new candidate drugs in Japan, America and Europe simultaneously.

Phase I of the five-year strategic plan began in 1987 and, even after succeeding my father as President in 1988, I continued to mull the remaining management theme of 'creating new concepts'. This means new concepts that, along with the founding spirit that motivates Eisai, will build the present and lead to the still-unknown future. In 1990, I distributed the following personal message to the entire company as the Eisai Innovation Concept.

Eisai Innovation Concept

'The world is changing. Let us change along with it.'

Eisai regards the patient, his family and, moreover, people in general as the most important 'participants' in the healthcare process. We take great pride in improving the healthcare of society. Eisai's goal of playing a unique role in society can only be accomplished by pursuing the 'Eisai Way', that is, fostering entrepreneurship among its employees. To become a company which can contribute significantly to society under any medical care system, we must continually repeat the process of strategy formulation, implementation and review at all levels of our organization. It is also vital for us to recognize the feelings of these important healthcare 'participants' and to empathize with them. Our corporate principle challenges us to be the leader in responding to their needs. Thus, we must seize every business opportunity to fulfil this objective. We merely cannot be preoccupied with the creation and distribution of pharmaceuticals, but need to tackle new business opportunities in healthcare. In order to be among the 20 leading pharmaceutical companies in the world by the year 2001, I feel we must able to offer something new and beneficial to people in need of healthcare, in addition to pharmaceutical products in the broad sense of the term.

Striving to establish the ideal corporate culture, Eisai encourages all of its members to develop and exhibit their abilities to the fullest extent. Each member should continually evaluate whether he or she is making maximum contribution to the well-being of the healthcare 'participants'. It is our aim that everyone at Eisai finds a clear-cut sense of purpose in their work. In a spirit of close contact and cooperation, all are encouraged to work together as a team, while, at the same time, devoting themselves to becoming knowledgeable and experienced in the company's business practice.

In recognition of the fact that people are Eisai's most valuable resource, all employees should treat each other with respect and maintain open lines of communication. Each person must take the responsibility to support his or her colleagues by contributing ideas and constantly encouraging one another. Everyone at all levels should clearly recognize his or her own goals and what is needed to attain them. Eisai provides unlimited opportunities for everyone to experience a sense of achievement as they strive to meet these goals. Under our concept of 'Integrated Group Operations', or IGO, which links the entire Eisai organization, I want to create a corporate environment in which all members of Eisai share a common mission and set of values, while having the freedom and responsibility to set their own goals and decide how best to accomplish them.

Society expects us to be an innovator. One of our strengths is that we are a young, dynamic organization with future potential, something that does not exist in many older companies. Every one of us at Eisai must meet society's expectations. We must demonstrate our obligation to society by identifying with the healthcare 'participants', developing a response to their needs, verifying the social benefits of this response and, finally, making this response available to the world before anyone else. To meet this challenge, every element of our organization, including our employees, our corporate atmosphere and emphasis and our style of doing business, must continually renew itself. It is in this manner that we will succeed in achieving our highest goals in the 1990s and on into the next century. This is 'Eisai Innovation'.

Haruo Naito
President and Chief Executive Officer

The Japanese pharmaceutical industry was approaching a period fraught with the many problems cited above. As extolled in the founding principles, Eisai needed a new concept to enable it to turn its attention on the world, not limit itself to Japan. In this period of transition, I believed that the direction Eisai should take in the future was to serve not just physicians, pharmacists or other medical providers as we did previously, but also the ultimate consumers of pharmaceuticals – namely patients and their families.

The content of Eisai innovation, summarized in a single phrase, is to be a human healthcare company. I believe that the activities involved in this include sharing in the joys and sorrows of patients and their families and focusing on the question 'What do they want?' As a drug company, Eisai is part of society. After disseminating the EI (Eisai innovation) declaration throughout the whole company, I formulated the 'Corporate Concept' and the 'Corporate Image' we are aiming for as follows.

The Corporate Concept

'We give first thoughts to patients and their families and contribute to increasing their benefits.'

This corporate concept is rooted in the founding principles and restates the values desired by Eisai towards the twenty-first century. The aim is to clearly focus on patients and consumers as the main object of the corporate activities of Eisai and raise the significance of Eisai as a company by realizing improved benefits to patients and consumers. All of Eisai's corporate activities are planned and conducted on the basis of whether or not they contribute to this goal.

The Corporate Image

The corporate image we aim for is to be a human healthcare company that earns recognition from society in any healthcare system.

Eisai, which has worldwide goals, does not operate solely under the current system within Japan. No matter how the healthcare environment changes, by providing continually improved patient benefits worldwide, Eisai aims to become a company the unique significance of which is recognized, irrespective of time and location.

Towards the realization of 'knowledge'

The entire company began a search towards a new quickening in my own 'EI' declaration. I had some trepidation about the new concept of human healthcare. Conditions of creative chaos had been stirred up in the whole company by the request for each individual to pursue their own human healthcare goals. However, the concept is nothing more than a metaphor, a symbol. I decided to adopt the knowledge-creation theory, substituting human healthcare for knowledge. If Eisai is to adopt the image of a human healthcare company, knowledge creation is the process for doing so. In other words, 'knowledge' is the innovation Eisai needs and knowledge creation is a method of creating revolutionary innovations.

The first thing I did after making the EI declaration was to train core managers who would create new 'knowledge' and be the key to promoting EI. Those people might be called the first generation of knowledge workers in the company. I set 1990–91 as the two-year period for training these core managers. In a training session known as the 'EI conference', young core manager candidates from all the divisions of the company, including R&D, production, sales and administration, were trained as the nucleus for promoting EI.

The EI conference included 5 groups of about 20 people each (totalling 103 people) in 4 parts:

1 the Gotemba conference;
2 practical training in hospital wards;
3 individual practical training on the front lines of healthcare;
4 the Koishikawa conference (at the head office).

I myself participated in the first Gotemba conference, which involved a week-long stay at a training camp in Gotemba. By means of lectures and case studies, the trainees came to understand that 'a company must constantly innovate' and gained a thorough grounding in 'how to put a new viewpoint to use in one's own work'.

Following the Gotemba conference, two-night, three-day practical hospital training was conducted at Ome Keiyu Hospital (in Ome, Tokyo), which is a leader in medical care for the elderly. At the Hospital, the trainees experienced new levels of concern for others by participating in practical care of the elderly, including helping them bathe, assisting with meals and changing diapers. This practical hospital work, which familiarized trainees with the needs of patients and got them to see things from the patients' perspective, was an invaluable part of making human healthcare a reality. Thereafter, many other employees were recruited for this practical hospital experience and, by December 1998, more than 600 people had participated.

The third part – individual practical training – involved three nights and four days of off-site training on the front lines of medical treatment. Participants each experienced, separately from other trainees, giving medical treatment at patient-oriented medical institutions, emergency medical treatment sites and clinics on isolated islands and in remote mountain areas.

Finally, at the Koishikawa conference, each member presented, before me and other company officers, a proposal for 'how the company must change', expressed their views on 'how I will change myself' and concluded their training as an EI manager – that is, as a knowledge manager.

Individual employees and human healthcare

Once the core managers have been trained, they form the nucleus for a whirl of human healthcare activities companywide, leading to the creation of new knowledge.

Since 1992, these trained managers have assumed leadership roles and we have begun a total of 74 human healthcare projects in divisions throughout the company. Employees in each division search for new ways to improve the benefits associated with their principal responsibilities in the conduct of their daily duties. The main projects have included:

1 in the medical pharmaceuticals division, preparation of notebooks and medical staff support for improving the quality of life of rheumatism patients;
2 in the consumer healthcare division, preparation of easy-to-understand explanations of general drugs and the provision of health information by holding consumer meetings;
3 in the drug research division, the development of elderly-friendly dosage forms and packaging;
4 in the medical information division, enquiry and consultation services for customers via Freefone telephone numbers.

The activities begun by about 200 core managers towards the realization of hunan healthcare concept were shared and created a great stir in all divisions of the company. A new movement had begun, in which each employee keeps asking themselves, 'What is my principal role, and how can I improve the results and benefits – to society, customers and the company – that are a product of my daily activities?'

In parallel with the promotion of these projects, new programmes have been developed for general employees, including practical employee training in hospitals, human healthcare conferences with university researchers and other companies and cross-training between divisions to exchange information. This has all been about allowing the human healthcare concept to permeate the day-to-day work of each employee.

Results of human healthcare activities

Eight years of activities in sales, R&D, production and administration have produced many results. The sales division has prepared medication guidance videos for patients, easy-to-understand, illustrated, over-the-counter package inserts and English-language product information for foreigners. In addition, a 'customer hotline' has been set up to answer questions from customers 365 days a year via a Freefone line and collect information on market needs.

In the production division, the main focus was proclaimed to be downstream processes, and efforts were made to ensure quality and make sure that the production environment conforms to the ISO 9000 series certification requirements.

In the administration division, which is quite remote from patients and consumers, the accounting department considers the convenience of the salesforce in the payment and/or reimbursement of expenses to be its main focus. It has also attempted to make accounting procedures easier to understand. The personnel department considers its main focus to be 'all the employees and their families' and has developed a new personnel system ('For You') to serve employees' needs, focusing on making it easy and convenient for them to do their work.

Practical hospital training led to the development of tablets for elderly patients that dissolve quickly in the mouth with just a small amount of saliva. The experiences at hospitals also led to the establishment in April 1996 of the new company Elmed Eisai, which specializes in pharmaceuticals for the elderly. Elmed Eisai has attracted much attention as a new drug company that anticipates changes in the market and manufactures and sells value-type generics that have added value in terms of dosage form, information and price.

Promotion of human healthcare activities uses the latest information technology. Product information centres that handle customer enquiries and consultation have built information databases and a companywide intranet allows employees to exchange information. Information gathered from the customer hotline office has led to the development of over-the-counter tablets for children and syrups for infants that were formerly available only in adult dosages.

Promotion of globalization

In 1995, Eisai walked on to the global stage with a view to selling worldwide – particularly in Europe and America – the promising new drug Aricept® for the treatment of Alzheimer's-type dementia. As I mentioned earlier, Aricept® typifies human healthcare at Eisai, for it was developed by a researcher who himself was caring for a relative who suffered from dementia. Strange to say, Aricept® was the first step in the realization of global human healthcare. At the time, Eisai had research centres in Boston and London and a clinical development company in the United States. In anticipation of the sales of Aricept®, Eisai set up sales companies in the United States, Britain, Germany and France. Eisai has also built a drug manufacturing plant in Research Triangle Park in North Carolina, which will also have research functions for promising drugs. Eisai is one of the first Japanese drug companies to have a full-function operation in America, including production and sales as well as research and development.

The globalization of the business has been accompanied by a sharing of the human healthcare concept in the worldwide Eisai network. Since 1996, this concept has been promoted worldwide at conferences in Europe, the United States and Asia, via local companies and projects designed to make it a part of everyday activities. In Europe and the United States, human healthcare activities bore fruit all at once with the marketing of Aricept®. Active exchanges are under way in various countries with support groups of Alzheimer patients and nurses, in which the sharing of tacit knowledge with patients and their families is encouraged. This has led to the creation of care programmes for Alzheimer's-type dementia, for which Eisai has gained international recognition. In autumn 1998, Eisai participated in the Alzheimer's Association's 'Memory Walk', held in cities all across the United States to bring patients' families and concerned caregivers together in the fight against Alzheimer's disease.

Establishment of the Knowledge Creation Department

In 1997, the Knowledge Creation Department was established under the direct control of the company President as the nucleus for promoting innovation in the worldwide Eisai network. Knowledge Creation Department managers are assigned to all the divisions in the company to support human healthcare activities and promote planning for knowledge creation in each division, serve as a liaison for global personnel exchanges and projects that span different organizations and plan and promote the training of those who will carry out human healthcare.

The theory of practical knowledge creation for making human healthcare a reality is put into detailed practice by the Knowledge Creation Department, which holds a human healthcare conference and meetings for the exchange of activities and ideas and introduces programmes by means of various training activities.

In November 1997, the Knowledge Creation Department conducted a survey to ascertain the state of the everyday processes of knowledge creation at Eisai and identify the strengths and weaknesses in each division and organization, with an objective of turning the company into a 'global human healthcare enterprise'.

The knowledge creation survey consisted of approximately 200 questions focused on the 4 modes of knowledge conversion – socialization, externalization, combination and internalization (Nonaka and Takeuchi, 1995). It was administered to Eisai and its network companies in Japan in 1997 and, in 1998, to local Eisai companies in Asia, Europe and the United States; approximately 5,000 employees participated in the survey. Our intention is to conduct knowledge creation surveys at regular intervals to ensure the further permeation and stimulation of knowledge creation activities that will support global human healthcare.

The survey results in Japan may be characterized in a phrase as 'dynamic bureaucracy'. In the four modes of knowledge creation, the score for internalization was very high, regardless of age group or job rank, while the scores for socialization, externalization and combination were average. These results are inferred to be typical of the drug manufacturing industry, in which there is rapid progress in medicine and pharmacology and it takes a great deal of time to acquire this knowledge. It is also inferred that, although individual employees actively acquire knowledge and are highly motivated, the same is not true for the organization as a whole. It was observed in Japan that we are still too much influenced by empiricism, which is justified by previous successes.

Future activities will need to include more deliberate socialization and externalization, along with the creation of new knowledge that is not dependent on past experience. We need to put more effort into identifying needs and problems from the customer's standpoint while maintaining a highly motivated human healthcare vision and will, and into having an interactive forum for obtaining customer and market knowledge. We also need to develop and verify our own hypotheses and build on successful experiences.

Future directions

Based on the results of the knowledge creation survey, Eisai will continue to create innovations for the realization of a global human healthcare enterprise. Because the environment surrounding the pharmaceutical industry is changing and because we have the products to contribute to the people in the world now, such as Aricept® and Aciphex/Pariet®, it is time to depart from past experience, think from a zero base and create new knowledge to realize our corporate philosophy.

The primary objective of our knowledge creation activities is to activate the modes of socialization and externalization. In response to the results of the survey, I have instituted two changes. One is organizational, the other is a new internal training system that focuses on new core leaders.

In 1999, Eisai changed the organizational structure of the domestic salesforce to adjust to the prescription drug market. We closed the regional offices and branch offices to eliminate the regional marketing system and renewed the salesforce to match the market segments more closely. We created four sales groups, one for each market segment:

1 university hospitals, which practise highly sophisticated medication;
2 large regional hospitals, which are the medical centres of their areas;
3 general practitioners, who prescribe daily medication;
4 pharmacies, which dispense drugs.

This organizational change is intended to bring us closer to the front lines of medication in order to better understand patients' needs. Opportunities to socialize with customers will, we hope, help us acquire tacit knowledge of the market. This is our attempt to change a bureaucratic organization into an autonomous organization for knowledge creation. This type of organization will, we believe, provide a better environment for the development of socialization and externalization. Further, as Eisai's sales activities more successfully transcend time and space as a result of highly sophisticated IT communication, the roles of MRs as 'knowledge workers' to socialize tacit knowledge of the market, and middle managers, who moderate and activate knowledge creation, will become even more important. We intend to strengthen the support for middle managers, who are the key to success in this organizational structure.

Second, we modernized our internal training system to bring up new core managers, or 'super captains'. We changed the focus of the training system from nurturing many employees who have identical business skills to creating many kinds of 'knowledge workers'. First, we revised training programmes to introduce human healthcare concept and allow each employee to participate freely based on individual motivation and enthusiasm. Second, to support this objective, many types of *ba* (place, space, opportunity) are provided for employee development. We established the Knowledge Creation Conference to develop new core managers. Among the important skills needed by future managers, we focused on externalization – the skill to become a 'knowledge leader'. The programme has three training sessions and one correspondence session. At the final stage, the managers present their proposals for innovation to top management.

By means of this training programme, we intend to nurture new 'super captains' for the promotion of global human healthcare.

Professor Ikujiro Nonaka has noted that 'personal thought and enthusiasm bear knowledge.' I would like to pursue and create systems in which individual employees contribute to the knowledge and innovations that further the realization of Eisai's corporate philosophy – global human healthcare.

Eisai now faces several challenges in knowledge creation. The first is how to promote exchanges with patients and consumers on the level of tacit knowledge. One method, of course, is practical training in hospital wards, but surely there are other ways to make direct contact with patients and consumers. In order to make our concept a reality, we must increase the feedback from patients and improve direct contact with them. In America, we have expanded our contacts with patients and families suffering from Alzheimer's-type dementia, but, in the future, we must search for a wider variety of methods.

Another challenge is to make use of the technology of the Internet in carrying out knowledge creation activities. IT is obviously of great benefit in the mode of combination, but perhaps the same technology can be harnessed for the mode of socialization as well. For example, sometimes a letter is a better way to express heartfelt gratitude than direct conversation. In communicating with children and family members, writing is sometimes more effective than speaking. Perhaps the young people of the world who use the Internet can use it for the efficient socialization of tacit knowledge. This is one challenge that we must solve in order to reap further benefits from knowledge creation.

Conclusion

As a conclusion, let me say a few personal words about the practice of knowledge management. My long involvement in knowledge creation activities has been a very enjoyable and worthwhile experience. I look forward to going to work every morning and the results I have discussed thus far have benefited me personally as well as the company. Knowledge creation activities are frequently a trial-and-error process and I do not know whether knowledge creation activities will bring immediate profits. However, I am sure that, in the long term, knowledge creation activities will be essential for managing the company and running its organizations. This is because profits, which are the fruit of corporate activities, result only from improving the benefits for our customers and incorporating their knowledge as an integral component of our activities. Moreover, knowledge creation activities teach us the importance of maintaining an interactive relationship with our customers.

It is clear to me that middle managers hold the key to knowledge creation. Good middle managers bring organizational knowledge creation to life – not just by facilitating socialization, but especially by externalization and combination. A CEO's message may be misunderstood. The CEO may be thinking of a stallion, but by the time this word reaches the employees, the original thought may have been translated to elephant, rooster, fox, seahorse or bull. By means of interactive communication and participation by as many employees in the organization as possible, we can define, achieve and implement the company's mission. This is what we mean by knowledge creation. The larger the company, the more important are interactions among middle management, top executives and subordinates. Middle managers at Eisai are no longer just intermediate administrators. The middle managers who have acquired the skills of knowledge creation by participating in EI conferences and new knowledge creation conferences are innovation leaders who will build a new future for the company.

Corporate activities are a matter of goals and results. We refer to the goals of corporate activities as our 'mission' or 'ideal'. If we are able to accomplish our mission, the company will profit. The goal and mission of Eisai is human healthcare. Of course, goals and results are equally important, but we must be aware that they are clearly different.

As Eisai continues to expand globally, I think that goals and mission will become even more important in the coming age of diversity of values. Human healthcare is intended to be the common mission or goal of Eisai employees worldwide, regardless of national borders, what language we speak or whether we are male or female. I do not think we will find such commonality in monetary and financial results or theories. If we, as human beings, can share thoughts that transcend borders, languages and cultures, I think those thoughts can be a kind of aesthetic, like truth, virtue or beauty. Such thoughts induce commitment. These common thoughts will be found in our mission and goals and in the knowledge creation that unfolds in our daily work towards their realization.

Reference

Nonaka, I., and Takeuchi, H. (1995) *The Knowledge-creating Company*. New York: Oxford University Press.

14 The Knowledge Perspective in the Xerox Group

Kazue Kikawada and Dan Holtshouse

A Xerox Group Perspective – Independent but Parallel Paths Lead to the Same Place: the Human Face of Work

When Fuji Xerox and the Xerox Corporation first began applying the concepts of knowledge management to their businesses in the mid-1990s, they did so on independent but somewhat parallel tracks. Each company was driven in its own way by the same challenge: to learn how to compete more effectively in a global information economy that runs more and more on knowledge-based intangibles and less on land, labour and capital.

Xerox and Fuji Xerox have worked together as business partners for more than 35 years, collaborating on research, product design and development, sharing manufacturing responsibilities and selling each other's printers, copiers, software and other office equipment in their respective Eastern and Western markets.

Together, the companies shared an early adoption of the quality movement, using it to revitalize their businesses in the 1980s. At the beginning of the 1990s, they co-created a unified, worldwide group identity and market position as The Document Company. They discovered, several years ago, that they also shared a common interest – indeed, common strategic ground and early activity – in a new business concept built on knowledge and knowledge management.

With knowledge management, the companies are on their third major journey of the past 20 years. We believe the ideas and practices behind knowledge can raise the businesses to a new level of growth, helping to create thriving work environments in which people's knowledge, talent, energy and creativity can be focused on building new value for customers.

The two companies have a rich history and a reputation for technological innovation, community, social commitment and leadership in global markets. Sometimes they exchange knowledge and collaborate with each other; other times, they go it alone. They are applying a similar practice to knowledge initiatives, working together to grow cumulative knowledge about the movement and the market, and co-developing academic expertise and thought leadership on the subject. At the same time, the companies are working independently to put knowledge ideas into practice within their business units. Even here, however, they keep a strong peripheral awareness of each other's activities and this is facilitated by a regular series of in-person forums and exchanges.

As a result of these mutual and independent efforts – which have attended to the philosophical and the theoretical as well as the practical – the companies have garnered a significant amount of valuable knowledge about knowledge in the workplace. Of particular interest, we believe, is an understanding of what is happening and how early adopters have put knowledge to work in their businesses, for what purpose and with what results. From this understanding has come a suggestion – a model, maybe – of what the knowledge-driven company of the future might look like. It is helping Fuji Xerox and the Xerox Corporation to be credible and tangible in a movement that some see as vague, soft or prone to hype. It is also giving the companies something to aspire to as they develop abilities in knowledge, both as a discipline to improve internal effectiveness and as the foundation for a growing number of services and products for customers.

We think our perspective is unique – in part, because of the effort we have made to study the knowledge movement, but, more importantly, because of the history and values our two companies have shared for more than three decades. Our perspective on knowledge blends technology with a strong focus on the human – the social and cultural sides of work – and it embraces the visions of East and West.

What follows, then, is an examination of the areas – we call them 'domains' – in which we have discovered knowledge to be at work within business, along with a look at the paths that brought Xerox and Fuji Xerox to a common view on knowledge.

Ten Domains – the Pulse of the Knowledge Movement

As we explore in greater detail later in this chapter, Xerox and Fuji Xerox have made a considerable effort to understand the practices of knowledge management as they have been applied in the workplace by early adopters worldwide.

Together and separately, the companies have backed third-party research, held international forums and even formed a panel of 100 knowledge managers – people whose responsibilities are primarily to facilitate the sharing of knowledge in their businesses or organizations. We have researched more than 40 case studies and learned such things as how much money companies are spending on knowledge, how many people are working on knowledge within companies, how knowledge pioneers define their jobs, how they measure success and where they see the movement going.

Our research into the thoughts and behaviour of these early adopters has found many cases of organizations that are achieving or expecting significant benefits from knowledge-management initiatives. These include improving the performance of client services, increasing customer value, generating new licensing revenue, expanding markets and shortening cycle times. This discovery was important to us because it validated the knowledge movement and its potential. Companies were not simply making toe-in-the-water efforts to see if knowledge could prove itself on the periphery before being shown the main stage; they were applying knowledge management to core elements of their businesses and expecting big things from it.

A crucial piece of work was to map dozens of seemingly diverse efforts to see if there was any commonality to them or their application. Maybe companies had learned, for example, that knowledge works well in one aspect of a business or in a particular process, but not in others. We found that these initiatives, as well as our own, fell roughly into ten domains, namely:

1   sharing knowledge and best practices;
2   instilling responsibility for knowledge sharing;
3   capturing and reusing past experiences;
4   embedding knowledge in products, services and processes;
5   producing knowledge as a product;
6   driving knowledge generation for innovation;
7   mapping networks of experts;
8   building and mining customer knowledge bases;
9   understanding and measuring the value of knowledge;
10 leveraging intellectual assets.

After studying and working with these domains for some time, we started to believe that we had identified a framework for the knowledge-driven organization of the future. It is our hunch now that the successful company of the twenty-first century will have to be a master of all ten domains (see Figure 14.1). Because of their importance, let us look at them one by one.

Knowledge sharing

The first two domains – both of which concern the sharing of knowledge – emerged as the most dynamic of the ten. We think this is because many companies are looking for better ways to use, share and reuse the knowledge that they know already exists in their organizations.

We think that, of all the possible applications, knowledge sharing is likely to make the biggest initial contribution to knowledge-worker

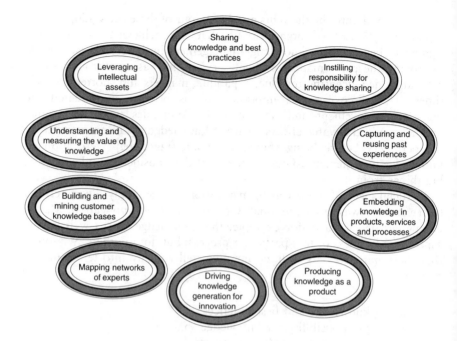

Figure 14.1 *The ten domains of knowledge management*

productivity, competitiveness and growth. In fact, we believe that creating systematic ways to share existing organizational knowledge will become a business imperative in the early part of the twenty-first century. Why? Because much of companies' explicit knowledge is ripe for sharing and a growing portion of the technological infrastructure for people to share it is in place, if they have the proper environment and incentives to do so.

A study by the Delphi Consulting Group indicated that only about 12 per cent of the organizational knowledge in any company is in some sort of structured knowledge base where it can be readily accessed by others who need it. The largest amount – 46 per cent – lies scattered about organizations in the form of paper and electronic documents. This should be available for sharing but isn't because of problems such as paper-to-digital exchange and incompatible computer systems. Documents are the most common vehicle used by people to share knowledge, but the barriers between paper and digital documents are among the greatest inhibitors to achieving this.

The connection between knowledge and documents, by the way, appears to be growing increasingly tighter. One market research group found that 70 per cent of senior executives believe that more than half of their companies' knowledge is contained in documents. Our conviction is deepening that document management is an essential, if not core, element of knowledge management.

Instilling responsibility for knowledge sharing

Our research turned up another, perhaps more significant, barrier to knowledge sharing: a human resistance to sharing in most business environments. When people see their knowledge as a source of job security or power, they are often reluctant to share it. Consequently, we believe knowledge sharing must have a cultural component to it. Companies need to create an environment that is conducive to sharing and then support it with strong technology and improved work processes.

The most effective efforts at Xerox have been the ones that have drawn not just on technological innovativeness, but also on anthropological experience gained from decades of workplace studies as well. We shall look at several examples drawn from Fuji Xerox and Xerox later in the chapter. All of them use technology, but all also depend on cultural underpinnings for their success.

Capturing and reusing past experiences

Most companies are seeking ways to make knowledge gained from past experience available in the present, either to those who were part of the initial experience or to an entirely new set of people.

Our studies identified a car manufacturer that, in 1997, was trying to capture peripheral knowledge – trade-offs made, assumptions and analyses and disagreements – that it created but usually discarded in its final product design specifications. The company believes it can shorten its design cycle, lower costs and bring products to market faster by capturing and retaining this knowledge for reuse in subsequent projects.

Embedding knowledge in products, services and processes

Some companies are attempting to discover where their most valuable knowledge lies in their products, services and processes. Understanding this can help them make better strategic decisions, such as where to focus their business to take advantage of unique strengths.

Companies are making conscious, strategic choices about how to embed knowledge in products and services to generate the highest revenues and profits. For example, an agricultural company found that its greatest knowledge value is in the recipe for the DNA at the heart of each crop seed. As a result, the company recognizes that its strategic options include the ability to outsource everything in its value chain except the formulation and ownership of the DNA recipe.

Producing knowledge as a product

Many companies that once saw their market as one for tangible products or services are learning that their real value may lie in the knowledge that went into developing the product in the first place or, perhaps, in how to use the product.

For example, several of the biggest firms offering professional services sell their knowledge via the Internet. Doing so both enhances their ability to serve existing clients and helps them reach new customers. Pharmaceutical companies are discovering that knowledge about how to administer drugs, avoid complications and manage side-effects is as desirable to customers as the drugs themselves. A global bank has found value in selling customers' knowledge about how to most effectively use the money it lends them.

Driving knowledge generation for innovation

We know that innovative companies can emerge from an environment that strongly supports individuals' creativity. However, we have found few real-world examples of attempts to understand or systematically manage the conversion of personal creativity into organizational innovation. Nevertheless, some companies – including Fuji Xerox – are pursuing this as an area that may pay big dividends in the coming years.

There are many different viewpoints on this matter. For example, should firms concentrate only on explicit knowledge that can be technologically assembled and distributed or else embrace the entire social, cultural and environmental atmosphere in which one person exchanges tacit knowledge with another? In fact, can the creative aspects of knowledge or the knowledge aspects of creativity ever be explicit at all?

We expect this domain to be the focus of more academic and business research and believe that insight here will some day help companies radically improve the productivity of knowledge work. To this end, Fuji Xerox and Xerox are trying to learn more about the flow of knowledge and its relationship to creativity by means of a variety of efforts. These include the New Work Way in Japan and the endowment of a professorship in knowledge at the University of California, Berkeley, in the United States.

Mapping networks of experts

Knowledge is essentially invisible and that's a problem. If you cannot see what knowledge is available to you, how can you possibly put it to use? One way of overcoming this is to create maps so people can locate and access the knowledge or expertise held by certain people in an organization.

We have seen three types of maps in use. One gives help desk staffers a path through their organization so they can find answers to customers' questions. Another shows relationships in the company's decision-making process – bringing to life the interdependencies among contributors to, say, software development and the flow of knowledge among them. Yet another is a map that makes visible the specialized communities that are tied together not by organizational bonds, but by the work they do or the interests they share. These communities usually grow up on their own with little corporate or organizational sanction or support, yet are valuable sources of knowledge that can be put to use both inside and outside the community.

The more time we spend studying and practising knowledge management, the more convinced we become of the essential role that communities play in the success of business. We may once have thought of them as loose-knit networks tangential to the core work of most companies, but communities may, in fact, turn out to be organizations' most important engines of innovation. For it is within communities – outside the boundaries of organizational hierarchy and politics – that people share vision, passion, language, traditions and a sense of context and common purpose. They appear to eagerly share what they know in a spirit of safety and collegiality towards some mutual good, readily displaying their expertise and knowledge, building social capital among their peers in the process.

Building and mining customer knowledge bases

As IT becomes more sophisticated, exploiting knowledge about customers – their needs and desires, buying habits, interests – becomes an important asset in the creation and delivery of products and services.

We found good examples of customer-focused knowledge management in a benchmark study conducted by the American Productivity and Quality Center. A software company, for example, has developed a system in which non-technical employees can support customers over the telephone and customers themselves can solve their own problems by using the Internet. Likewise, a firm organizing temporary staff offers its client companies a service where they can use the Internet to track every project the firm runs for them around the world, including project summaries, costs, locations and success stories.

Understanding and measuring the value of knowledge

Can knowledge actually be measured? If so, how? Such questions are at the centre of a debate that we think will take some time to resolve. In the meantime, most organizations are focusing their measurement efforts on tangible assets, such as patents and trademarks, using traditional yardsticks, such as changes in cost, usage rates, customer satisfaction, accuracy in problem solving and customer response time. For example, a chemical company has assigned specific, ten-year dollar values to its patent portfolio. This firm figures it can earn $125 million in licensing fees and save $40 million by reducing the number of patents it manages.

However, the greatest potential, we feel, lies in the tacit knowledge that remains difficult, if not impossible, to measure. That is why we urge organizations to make a priority of making knowledge visible – identifying where in the company the tacit knowledge resides, then developing a way to make it explicit. By knowing what the knowledge is, who has it, where it is and how it contributes to the business, companies will be in a better position to come up with new ways to measure its value.

Leveraging intellectual assets

Patents, copyrights, invention proposals and licensing agreements are all documents that visibly embody a company's knowledge, which it can then buy, sell or trade at will. Managing these assets is getting attention in an environment in which businesses are pressured to focus on core strengths, bring products to market quickly and reap the best possible return on their intellectual property.

Xerox and Fuji Xerox are among the companies reinventing their intellectual-property management processes in recognition of this view. They are re-evaluating their entire combined patent portfolios against their business strategy to identify areas of strength as well as weakness. This work is being done by a new business unit, the role of which is to manage and market the company's intellectual property. The goals for this unit are to improve the rate of innovation, increase patent licensing revenue and take a tougher stance on those who infringe on the company's patents. It has already helped the firm identify and take action against several infringing companies.

Using the knowledge domains

Our work with the domains has brought us a number of important benefits. For one, it has helped us define knowledge management. Admittedly, knowledge can be a soft concept. By understanding what companies and knowledge managers are doing and what they are getting for their efforts, we have been able to craft definitions of knowledge and knowledge management that make business sense to us and our customers. We therefore have something with which we can look at the myriad of things being promoted as knowledge management solutions today and make intelligent judgements about what is and is not a true knowledge tool or solution. These are our definitions.

Knowledge is the accumulated experience and actionable information that exists within an organization. It is information in action or the capacity to take action

For example, it is what people know – about their work, how to get things done, their products and services, customers, competitors and abilities. It is in people's heads, documents and, often, hidden in the processes that connect people.

Managing for knowledge (we prefer this phrase to 'knowledge management') means creating a thriving working and learning environment that fosters the continuous creation, aggregation, use and reuse of both personal and organizational knowledge in the pursuit of new business value

It involves helping people find and share that actionable experience and information and put it to use. First and foremost, this involves people, their work processes and the culture in which people work – also, ultimately, technology to support people, the culture and the work.

Conclusion

The domains have also given us a template for thinking about what a truly knowledge-driven company needs to become and for evaluating our own internal efforts. If one assumes (and we do) that the knowledge-driven company will have to master all ten domains, it is relatively easy to use the template to see where one's strongest practices are and where additional emphasis is needed. Building from what the domains have shown us, we have roughed out an architecture for the structure of a knowledge-focused company. It has four building blocks: communities, knowledge repositories, knowledge navigation and access, and knowledge flow.

As an IT vendor with a focus on documents and knowledge, the domains have helped us make decisions about what products and services might be needed to support customers' activities and desires. For example, after recognizing the importance of knowledge mapping, we brought forward tools from the company's research community that could detect and manage knowledge flow. On a larger corporate scale, the interest and activity in the knowledge-sharing domains told us that we would be well served by placing short-term strategic emphasis on knowledge-sharing tools, products and services.

The domains are a foundation of Xerox's thinking on the application of knowledge concepts in the business world. One might wonder what brought us here. As we said at the beginning of this chapter, the paths of Fuji Xerox and Xerox to date have been more independent than parallel, but are growing ever closer together. Before we look at these paths, it might be helpful to understand a little more about their shared history.

Xerox Group History: Co-destiny, Quality and the Document

The roots of knowledge: a struggle to compete in the 1970s

In speaking of our companies, we frequently use the name the 'Xerox Group'. This refers to two separate but related entities that often conduct business as one. The Xerox Corporation, based in the United States, does business in North America, South America, Europe, Africa and much of Asia. Fuji Xerox, a Tokyo-based joint venture between Xerox and the Fuji Photo Film Company, is the hub of operations in Japan and throughout the Pacific Rim. Fuji Xerox was formed in 1962.

Although the sales territories of the two are clearly delineated, they share many research, design, product development and manufacturing efforts. For example, Fuji Xerox supplies colour copiers and printers as well as low-end black-and-white printers for Xerox worldwide. Xerox's production-class publishing and printing systems, laser printers and multifunction office systems are sold by Fuji Xerox. Yet, even these are often the result of an iterative product design effort involving engineers from both companies.

It would be false to claim that the Xerox Group's knowledge initiatives are anything but a few years old, but the foundation for its approach in knowledge was laid in the mid-1970s as the core business came under pressure from new rivals. It was further established in the 1980s and 1990s as the company crafted a shared vision of the future, embraced quality, set a core strategic focus on the document and re-engineered its businesses.

Co-destiny: global partnership around a shared future

Recognizing the strengths and efficiencies we could realize by working towards a shared future, the companies undertook a project called Co-destiny in 1982. The aim of the project, which was put forward by Fuji Xerox, was to set a single direction for the Xerox Group – strategically uniting the competences of the entire group in light of accelerating globalization.

The two companies created a multicore global strategy targeting the worldwide market. This attempt was very different from the unipolar strategy typically employed by most large organizations in the United States and Japan at the time. This is because it sought to build a cooperative relationship in which each company existed on equal footing with the other – their skills complementing each other, their product and market strengths displayed where they would be most effective.

The relationship was built on trust. The companies avoided focusing on potential conflicts. They carried on dialogue at virtually every level, including at a semi-annual corporate summit meeting where the top executives of Xerox and Fuji Xerox exchanged information and ideas and developed shared goals and strategies. The two companies learned from each other in a process that continues to this day.

Quality: management knowledge moves East to West in the 1970s and 1980s

It was well before 'co-destiny', however, that the companies recognized their mutual dependence and the benefits of exchanging knowledge, ideas, information and strategies. At no time was this more evident than during the mid-1970s, when Xerox's patent on the basic xerographic technology – its most important asset – expired. Japanese companies wasted no time entering the plain paper copier market; the Xerox Group's market share plummeted in the face of competition from new, fleet-footed and low-cost rivals.

Yotaro Kobayashi, then Deputy President of Fuji Xerox, saw from his vantage point within Japan that his company would need fundamental reform if it was to match its new competitors. Under the leadership of Kobayashi, who later became the company's president and is now its Chairman and CEO, Fuji Xerox embraced Total Quality Management (TQM) in 1976 and redefined itself in a companywide initiative known as the New Xerox Movement. Quality thus became the basic business principle for Fuji Xerox and, by 1980, had improved itself enough to win Japan's coveted Deming Prize.

In the United States, however, Xerox faced a more serious predicament. Under a vigorous offensive from the Japanese companies, market share losses were greater than those in Japan, yet it took the company until the early 1980s to recognize the problem's severity. Encouraged by Fuji Xerox's successful counterattack in Japan, Xerox turned to its Japanese partner for help.

Xerox put the ideas of quality into practice under a programme known as Leadership Through Quality. It was built in large measure on the basic philosophy and methods – especially benchmarking and best practices – of Fuji Xerox's New Xerox Movement, but adapted to the culture of a Western company. The adoption of quality, combined with the lessons learned from Fuji Xerox about Japanese design practices, manufacturing processes and cost structures, helped reverse the market share losses by employing Japanese rivals' own tactics against them. Dubbed an 'American Samurai', Xerox won the United States' Malcolm Baldrige National Quality Award in 1989.

These practices were introduced in Europe, and Xerox's then partner, Rank Xerox limited, became the first winner of the European Quality Award in 1992. By then, quality had become a central management tenet shared by the entire Xerox Group worldwide. Quality was a unifying idea, a global sharing and conversion of organizational knowledge that began in

Japan and spread to the rest of the Xerox world. Xerox Group companies have since won a national quality award in every country in which such awards are given.

Discovery of the document: the knowledge flow reverses in the 1990s

Around 1990, as personal computers and networks started to form a new communication infrastructure in the office, Xerox began to rethink the role of its products in the way people work.

The company was about to launch a new line of all-digital machines that had the ability to electronically scan, manipulate and combine images, print them at high speeds and digitally assemble entire booklets on the fly. By hooking these machines up to networks, Xerox could revolutionize the way people share, store and retrieve information by making paper and digital documents available anywhere in the world.

The strategic planning process called Xerox 2000 identified the document as the key vehicle for people to exchange ideas and knowledge at work. The company reviewed its history of helping people share information using paper documents, anticipated a digital future, redefined its place in people's work lives and labelled itself The Document Company. Its portfolio of offerings now include a range of hardware, software and services that allow people to capture, copy, print, view, manipulate, store, retrieve and distribute documents, as well as distil or extract the knowledge that lies within them.

Mundane as the machine sometimes seems, the copier has played an important role in the culture of society by democratizing information and launching a communication revolution. Peter Drucker, in the 1994 Top Forum organized by Fuji Xerox, said, 'The communication revolution really began with the copier of Xerox. Not because it was the first modern office machine, basically, but because it opened up the vision and made us aware of the fact of the central importance of communication.'

With networks now spanning the globe, near-instant communication is at the heart of most work processes. As a large percentage of what is communicated – corporate and organizational information – is in documents, we think that applying digital document technology in line with the concepts of knowledge management has a similar potential to bring about a revolution in the way people work.

'The Document Company' evolved into the first market positioning to be shared by the entire Xerox Group. The knowledge and ideas behind it spread to Europe and Asia, where Fuji Xerox set up its own document business strategy, along with a far-reaching study of the corporation and management in the upcoming knowledge society.

At Fuji Xerox a cross-functional group known as the Document Design Forum examined new concepts and customer values built around the document. This group agreed that 'Knowledge is the essential value of information, and corporate activities can be understood as organizational knowledge creation in which new customer values are added and enriched.' The group, in fact, defined a document as 'knowledge in visible form with which people think, express themselves, understand, make decisions and act'.

Thus, documents have grown in stature, being seen now throughout the Xerox Group as essential media by means of which knowledge workers have conversations, with which they connect with each other to share knowledge and ideas, ultimately improving their effectiveness and productivity. As we have refined our strategies at Xerox and Fuji Xerox, we have grown to see knowledge as the core concept that allows us to differentiate our products and services from those of our competitors and helps us improve our internal business activities.

By focusing on the document as the vehicle for knowledge-generating and knowledge-sharing conversations among communities of people at work, the goal of the Xerox Group is to create a new communication culture – indeed, a new work environment – for customers and the company itself.

Fuji Xerox: A New Work Way Leads to Knowledge

The new work way: connecting knowledge with creativity

Although quality was an essential component in the successful transformation of the company's business, Fuji Xerox has been convinced for some time that conventional TQM must be developed into a new, knowledge-based management concept that we call Creative Quality Management.

The philosophy of Creative Quality Management is that companies' creativity emerges from people's innovation, which, in turn, depends on the effective use and exchange of personal and organizational knowledge. The roots of this idea can be found in the New Work Way – a way of working that Fuji Xerox first proposed in 1988. The New Work Way can reasonably be seen as the firm's initial step on the path to knowledge, although it may not have been recognized at the time.

The New Work Way, Fuji Xerox's third major long-range corporate policy, was developed in response to significant changes in the business environment. Younger Japanese workers had a different relationship to work and different working styles than their seniors. The workplace was increasingly being built on highly intelligent new office environments. Meanwhile, employees were becoming complacent about proposing new ideas and taking initiative under TQM.

The New Work Way was an attempt to build a responsive and proactive company, one the innovations of which could help it cope with rapid change in a fast-paced world. Fuji Xerox sought to complement the scientific, logical and control-oriented methods of TQM with a way of working that would fit the styles and attitudes of a new generation. What was noteworthy about the New Work Way was that, within a society that traditionally emphasized collective effort, it placed importance on the motivation and contribution of individuals, encouraging them to display originality and creativity in their work.

Fuji Xerox created policies, processes, systems and environments to facilitate this new way of working. Our overriding intent was to establish *ba* – the Japanese word for places or opportunities that nourish people's optimal creativity, knowledge creation and knowledge sharing. This effort involved three elements.

First, believing that workers' knowledge is grown and their creativity inspired by interacting with people different from themselves, the company offered employees at all levels paid social service sabbaticals and other chances to spend time beyond the company's walls.

Second, the company provided the first network and information systems-equipped satellite offices in Japan to remove from workers' lives the stress of long commutes, give employees more time to spend with their families and encourage self-innovating work styles.

Finally, the company increased the amount of direct interaction between workers and executives. In 1988, Yotaro Kobayashi, then President, hosted the first 'Talknade' sessions in which groups of about 250 employees met directly with Fuji Xerox senior executives. The employees frankly expressed complaints, asked questions and suggested creative changes to strategies, processes and policies. Many improvements in such areas as communication and employee evaluation have emerged from these sessions. At the time of writing, in late 1999, 'Talknade' sessions have been held 24 times throughout Japan.

From its origins in the New Work Way movement, Fuji Xerox's approach to knowledge has been largely a strategic one, focused on creating environments in which individual imagination and creativity gives birth to new knowledge that can then be shared among groups of workers, thus leading to group innovation. In fact, its new mission statement explicitly points to the role of knowledge in contributing positively to a diverse global community.

A new mission statement speaks of knowledge

Almost a decade before the New Work Way was adopted, in 1979, Fuji Xerox had adopted the Corporate Philosophy and Action Guidelines – these clarified the company's reason for existence and specified its aims and goals. This statement was intended to help employees understand Fuji Xerox in relationship to the communities in which they lived and worked.

The philosophy and guidelines played a significant role in the growth of Fuji Xerox and in its various achievements, including the Deming Prize, the New Work Way, territorial expansion and overseas business development, as well as the transition to digitization ahead of its competitors. However, almost 20 years later, the philosophy and guidelines felt dated. For one thing, they failed to embrace the firm's new reach into the Asia-Pacific region and the United States. In addition, many were concerned that the many English-speaking people with whom they were now working might not fully appreciate or understand translated versions of the Japanese-language documents.

In an effort to update the firm's philosophical underpinnings, Fuji Xerox spent a year reviewing the philosophy and guidelines. The result? The new Mission Statement and Shared Values, which was introduced to employees in January 1998.

These were the culmination of a process that started with a group of highly motivated young volunteers (the 'Excellent 21'), closely involved Fuji Xerox senior executives and drew heavily from 4 months of dialogue among Japanese and non-Japanese employees in Japan, the Asia-Pacific region and the United States. We see the process as a global knowledge conversion in which a diversity of personal beliefs, images and values were converted by means of dialogue into collective knowledge, which was then codified as corporate knowledge (in the mission statement).

The new mission statement reads, 'We, the Fuji Xerox Group, will strive to build an environment for the creation and effective utilization of knowledge.' It commits the company to contributing to a global community 'by continuously fostering mutual trust and enriching diverse cultures'. Thus, it positions Fuji Xerox as playing an important role in an emerging, global knowledge society.

Equally important, the new mission statement encourages employees to pursue their own self-fulfillment and growth and demands that the results of these pursuits be shared to improve the living standards of everyone. Young people involved in the initial mission statement discussions repeatedly stressed that this was one of its most important components. So as not to let the mission statement stand as an isolated philosophical document, the company backed it up with a list of ten humanity-based shared values that each employee is expected to respect. They are customer satisfaction, environmental consciousness, high ethical standards, scientific thinking, professionalism, team spirit, cultural diversity, trust and consideration, joy and fulfilment and an adventurous, pioneer spirit.

The Knowledge Design Initiative and the Global Leaders Forum

As knowledge has become an increasingly attractive value for Fuji Xerox, the role of the Document Design Forum – the group that had led the firm's strategic effort concerning documents – has changed. In 1997, in fact, the group changed its name to the Knowledge Design Initiative in recognition of a new mission – to help Fuji Xerox achieve strong leadership in the future knowledge business, becoming a force for the kind of transformation that will be required to accomplish this leadership.

Throughout much of the 1990s, knowledge was part of the strategic dialogue at Fuji Xerox, if not a highly visible practice or position. For example, in 1993 the company held the first of a series of annual executive forums under the theme 'Documents and Knowledge Creation'. This was intended to offer a *ba* in which employee participants and customers' companies' senior executives could think collectively about business aspects of knowledge.

The first forum featured a dialogue between Hitotsubashi University Professor and author Ikujiro Nonaka and John Seely Brown, the head of Xerox's Palo Alto Research Center in California. In the second year, the forum presented a dialogue between Chairman Kobayashi and management guru Peter F. Drucker. In subsequent years, each of these events, held under the name Global Leaders Forum, has attracted more than 400 people and involved such knowledge notables as Ikujiro Nonaka, Karl Erik Sveiby, Hirotaka Takeuchi, Stephen Denning, Carla O'Dell and the chairs of major Japanese companies and the Aspen Institute.

These forums – especially with their exchange of Eastern and Western ideas on knowledge – have inspired the Xerox Group to pursue a new kind of knowledge-driven productivity as a core customer value.

Knowledge Dynamics™ and Knowledge Work Space™

European and American companies appear to have been quicker than most of their Japanese counterparts to embrace knowledge management as an essential element of business. About 8 per cent of American and European companies listed among the 1999 *Fortune* 500 had a senior executive with the title of chief knowledge officer, whereas none of the major Japanese companies had an equivalent post.

Of course, the mere appointment of someone with the word 'knowledge' in their title may have little effect on a company's competitive position. Yet, Fuji Xerox does believe that if Japanese companies are to improve their global competitiveness, its senior executives will have to develop an intense interest in the subject and must support their employees in creating and sharing knowledge.

We have observed that although Western companies are quick to adopt knowledge management, they have focused predominantly on explicit knowledge – that which is already out in the open and available for shared use or consumption. Their efforts often lack insight on tacit knowledge – the kind that is in people's heads or invisibly embedded in processes and relationships. We believe that aspects of both explicit and tacit knowledge must be understood and that knowledge offers its most attractive advantage when explicit and tacit versions of it interact with each other.

With Professor Ikujiro Nonaka's spiralling knowledge-creation process in mind, the Knowledge Design Initiative has been studying the interplay between explicit and tacit knowledge under the title 'knowledge dynamics'. Our findings are tending to reject conventional ideas of 'management' when it comes to creating and using knowledge. Rather, we are drawn towards softer, more human-friendly words, such as 'facilitate' or 'support'. We are finding that perhaps the most meaningful way to systematically or holistically approach knowledge in all its forms will be to effectively 'direct' the contexts or the environments in which knowledge dynamics take place – that is, in which knowledge is created, used and shared. We refer to these environments as 'knowledge work space'.

Our strategic representation of knowledge dynamics is a conceptual model that depicts the process of creating and using knowledge and the relationships among individuals, groups and organizations. Built on Nonaka's ideas, it has four quadrants, with each quadrant representing one of four basic human actions involved in the flow of knowledge – creating, expressing, sharing and utilizing. It also has two movement axes – the 'movement axis of organizational evolution of knowledge', representing the creation and memorization of knowledge; and the 'movement axis of organizational ecology of knowledge', representing the dissemination and enrichment of knowledge. The model shows that new values are produced when these two axes work in tandem.

The study and use of this model has helped reveal specific functions that can be emphasized and methods that can be used for the creation and use of knowledge under certain circumstances. We are researching the constituent elements of the knowledge work space and it is our intention to offer products and services that help the firm's customers create and take advantage of such environments.

Internal knowledge work space practices at Fuji Xerox

Fuji Xerox is pouring ideas about knowledge work space into a number of solutions that support field service engineers, customer telephone-support staff and salespeople.

Using the Technical Information Search System (TISS), Fuji Xerox technicians can electronically share tips for fixing office machines. The system, modelled after a similar Xerox solution (called Eureka) developed in France, consists of a searchable on-line database of repair solutions that are not contained in the company's printed manuals. All of the tips are written by the technicians themselves and validated by their peers.

As of mid-1999, the system had about 2,500 users and a database of 3,000 tips. The technicians were contributing about 100 tips per month and were accessing the database to look for solutions about 2,000 times a month. The TISS has helped reduce by 10 to 20 per cent the number of service calls that have to be escalated to a higher level for resolution.

A different type of knowledge solution is in use by the seven staff members of the Nandemo Sodan Centre (NSC), who support 15,000 Fuji Xerox employees in providing answers to customers' enquiries. All of the queries and the responses to them are converted to a searchable database accessible to the NSC staffers and to Fuji Xerox salespeople. The database helps sales people give customers accurate answers to even those questions that go beyond the salesperson's knowledge and expertise.

Salespeople are also aided by a knowledge repository named *Musashi*. This digital storehouse of knowledge about customers is designed to support an environment in which Fuji Xerox acts as a partner with its customers, gaining and maintaining in-depth knowledge of them and collaborating to solve even their tacit needs in an atmosphere of mutual trust.

ZEIS: an holistic engineering information system

One of the toughest challenges for manufacturing companies in today's business environment is the never-ending pressure to improve product quality while lowering costs and shortening development cycle times. We project, for example, that, by 2000, Fuji Xerox will have achieved a minimum of 50 per cent improvement in product reliability, a 40 per cent cut in unit manufacturing cost and a 40 per cent cut in cycle time over its performance in 1994.

As the pressure continues, however, companies will be able to gain only a finite amount using conventional or even updated TQM and product development models. Breakthroughs are possible, though, with the creative implementation of knowledge solutions – particularly those that foster the conversion of tacit knowledge to explicit knowledge.

Fuji Xerox has been evolving a model of just such a system since 1995. Under the name Zen'in-Sekkei Engineering Information System (ZEIS), the company has created a technologically supported process and environment for sharing knowledge among the entire engineering community working on any product.

ZEIS brings together engineers working on industrial design, manufacturing, customer support, asset recycling, product safety and other issues. It offers them opportunities and spaces to interact with each other and a common information resource. It is a classic example of a *ba* that supports the continuous creation of new knowledge along with the efficient distribution and effective use of that knowledge.

ZEIS contains two crucial elements: a combined physical and virtual space and a central information repository. Engineers from all disciplines can gather remotely via their PCs to exchange information and knowledge, but they can also meet in special rooms created to capture tacit knowledge in motion. These rooms are equipped with two 70-inch screens that display such information as quality checklists and three-dimensional computer design drawings.

The computers that drive the displays – and the engineers' own work-stations – are connected to a huge central information resource. Comprising a document and image repository along with a database, it gives all engineers access to a vast amount of explicit knowledge: technology and development programme information, design data, patents and standards, recycling guides, parts catalogues, marketing and planning information, preparation and production notes, programme management details and schedules, cost parameters and inspection, evaluation and quality results. About 5,000 Fuji Xerox engineers have access to this system.

The system benefits the company by:

1 giving designers more time for product development by shortening and improving the up-front information-gathering and knowledge-sharing processes;
2 increasing the amount of innovation by using job-oriented information in the development process;
3 providing a *ba* for the creation of new knowledge;
4 preventing the recurrence of trouble by registering and using designers' know-how.

ZEIS has become popular among the company's engineers, most of whom have voluntarily registered as users and 40 per cent of them regularly access the system. It has become a crucial component of the time-to-market process and is facilitating unprecedented collaboration among engineers from a variety of disciplines, bringing more tacit knowledge to bear to address present and future development challenges.

Building Momentum for Knowledge at Xerox

Corporate and grass roots efforts begin a movement at Xerox

In adopting its identity and business strategy as The Document Company, Xerox had become well versed in the role that documents play in the capture and transfer of workplace knowledge as early as the late 1980s. Our hunch, looking at the nascent knowledge management movement, was that it would be a natural extension of document management – a logical next step, if you will, for organizations that had embraced quality, re-engineered business processes and downsized, so were now ready for a new phase of growth.

The knowledge movement within Xerox began to take form in the 1995–96 timeframe by at least two paths. A corporate-wide initiative was launched to explore the strategic implications for the company's current and future marketplace. At about the same time, grass roots initiatives were springing up internally within organizations and other functional areas to meet emerging challenges for creating better knowledge-based work environments.

The Xerox knowledge initiative

The Corporate Knowledge Initiative was established in February 1996. It was begun by Xerox Chairman and CEO Paul Allaire and, from the start, it was positioned as a strategic initiative affecting both internal and external activities. It was made a part of Xerox 2005 (X2005) – the company's strategic long-term planning process – and it has reported directly to the Chief Strategy Officer since its inception.

The Knowledge Work Initiative (we called it such to emphasize the importance of the knowledge worker) had several purposes:

1 to develop a deep understanding of the knowledge phenomenon;
2 to determine implications for Xerox for both enriching and expanding the positioning of our current businesses as well as preparing for new market spaces likely to emerge as a result of a new focus on knowledge;
3 to create a Xerox framework for conceptualizing new market opportunities for knowledge-based technologies, products and services.

At the end of 1996, the knowledge team recommended to Allaire and the senior executives on the X2005 strategy team that Xerox establish itself as a leader in the emerging knowledge movement. Since then, the emphasis has been on building awareness, buy-in and organizational momentum for knowledge within Xerox. Its work has included coordinating and championing new research programmes for the development of knowledge-based technology in research centres around the world. It has also included working with customer business units to help them prepare for the professional services and consulting offerings that will be needed to address emerging customers' knowledge-management problems. Finally, it has involved cross-leveraging Xerox's internal knowledge practices with its experiences from customer engagements in order to make the best use of resources inside the company.

Shortly after being given its high-level sanction, the Knowledge Work Initiative sponsored an extensive market research programme in order to better understand the underlying complexities of the knowledge movement. This research, which continues today, helps build knowledge about emerging customer needs and helps the firm judge the quality of its internal knowledge initiatives. As part of the research, the initiative has achieved the following.

1   Conducted in-depth interviews with 60 non-Xerox knowledge workers from across the United States. The interviews brought home the need to continually link specific information with specific knowledge so that, as new information comes into any system or community, a signal indicates that old knowledge should be updated and replaced.

2   Established a panel of 100 knowledge managers from the United States, Europe and eight other countries, most of whom work for *Fortune 500* companies. Their job responsibilities include managing knowledge of one sort or another. The panelists have agreed to be surveyed once a year to help Xerox identify trends and map success factors for knowledge initiatives and investments.

3   Co-sponsored basic market research and best practices benchmarking in the industry by means of Ernst & Young's Managing Knowledge for the Organization – a multiclient consortium focused on advancing research on knowledge – and six, separate American Productivity & Quality Center studies of best knowledge practices in the United States and Europe.

4   Facilitated the building of a worldwide Xerox community of more than 40 working knowledge champions from such areas as research, engineering, advertising, sales, marketing, planning, management information and professional services. This group meets at least once a year in a two-day forum to share ideas and advance the overall knowledge movement within the Xerox Group.

5   Conducted an active thought leadership programme to advance basic understanding and awareness of knowledge issues. This includes co-sponsorship with Fuji Xerox of the United States' first ever professorship in knowledge; co-sponsorship of annual knowledge conferences with Ernst & Young; and publication of a series of case studies about Xerox's knowledge practices and solutions. The thought leadership programme also includes an effort to place articles about the company's insights and experiences in selected trade publications.

6   Established a Web-based virtual meeting place for knowledge leaders to stay connected with each other and find information about what Xerox knows, what it is saying and doing in the knowledge arena. The website, called *The Knowledge Horizon*, is a work space for self-organizing communities. It contains a searchable datebase of research reports, case studies, presentations and daily news articles about knowledge. The site débuted in late 1997 by providing semi-live coverage of the Ernst & Young Knowledge Advantage conference. Between 1,500 and 2,000 employees tuned in from remote locations during the two-day event.

7   Created an internal newsletter – *Knowledge Newsline* – about knowledge at Xerox, which reports what the company knows about

knowledge management, what it is doing internally and what it is offering customers. The newsletter has been important in helping to build awareness, provide learning and create a shared vision for knowledge.

Knowledge managers panel: tracking the knowledge movement

This first of its kind panel of knowledge managers drawn from nine countries began with the need to find the leaders who were working to develop knowledge management abilities in their organizations. The goal was to gain insight into emerging market needs involving knowledge. It was important to find out who the early adapters of the knowledge movement were. By keeping track of their activities, we hoped to keep our finger on the pulse of this business trend. In return for their participation, we shared our findings with the panelists and invited them to submit questions for future surveys.

The research is being conducted by an internal Xerox business research group. The group conducted the first survey in the autumn of 1997 and quickly encountered a major obstacle: finding bona fide knowledge managers. Researchers first tried using the Internet for recruiting, but many respondents turned out to be unqualified impostors (one was a teenager whose mother said he was taking a nap). We ultimately used telephone screening, but this was not without its problems. Because this is an emerging field, many knowledge managers are not visible in normal organizational structures. In the end, we tracked down about 100 knowledge managers – people who said their primary responsibility was to facilitate the sharing of knowledge in support of some business value – and enlisted them for the project.

Here is how the survey is conducted: Each panelist participates in a semistructured, one-on-one telephone interview, providing narrative-rich answers to open-ended questions. The answers are recorded and transcribed, then analysed with a proprietary computer-based process that displays the connections between words. This extensive linguistic analysis is based on the proximity and frequency of words, as well as their nature – whether visual, auditory or kinesthetic. The program analyses the content of the verbatim responses, then generates a diagram or 'mind map'. Because respondents' specific words are captured electronically, researchers are able to do keyword searches and track how the views and experiences of knowledge managers change over time.

One of the first questions explored was 'What is knowledge?' Among the more interesting things we learned was that knowledge is considered information until it becomes internalized as a result of action. You can receive information, but, until you use it, you do not have knowledge. One panelist said he could give someone a recipe, which he considered information, but not until that person actually prepares a meal does the recipe become knowledge. Likewise, a person with a map has information, but, until they use it to get somewhere, they don't actually have the knowledge of how to get there.

The survey also found that there are several strata to knowledge management. The first involves incorporating knowledge into products. In the second, people share information, generating knowledge within an organization. The third level involves helping customers' customers become more knowledgeable.

The panel also identified major obstacles to the knowledge movement. The top obstacle often seems to be the lack of support from the top. A close second is resistance to sharing among the ranks. This implies that there is a need for a culture change.

The findings so far highlight the importance of creating environments that encourage people to share information. Knowledge is seen as power, and people are unlikely to share it without some kind of incentive, fearing someone else will get the credit for what they know.

Our panel confirmed our belief that overcoming this anti-sharing mentality requires knowledge managers to act as catalysts for change. In fact, a high percentage of knowledge managers who saw their role as that of a change agent also reported a greater sense of satisfaction with their progress.

Tracking the evolution of knowledge management over time is a major goal of the project and provides a quantitative aspect to the study. The research group plans to poll panelists at least once a year for the foreseeable future. The growth and development of the knowledge movement depends, in large part, on the success of these kinds of panelists – the pioneers of their profession. Xerox hopes to stay in touch with what they are thinking and doing.

Smart service: leveraging knowledge from the field

Xerox technicians worldwide make more than a million visits to customers' sites every month to service machines. Enabling these service engineers to capture and share the knowledge they amass from their experiences is the aim of Eureka – a project that began in a collaboration between Xerox France and researchers at the Xerox Palo Alto Research Center (PARC).

Based on an understanding of how a community of practice works, Eureka leverages social systems to build knowledge, providing processes and technologies that enhance lateral communication among technicians. The project was inspired in part by a seminal PARC ethnographic study that revealed how technicians use 'war stories' to teach each other to diagnose and fix machines. In contrast to conventional training systems that emphasize top-down delivery of information, Eureka supports engineers in sharing those stories electronically in the form of tips.

The impetus behind Eureka was the realization that service manuals, which were updated infrequently, were out of date almost as soon as they were printed. When an engineer sees a new problem and comes up with a solution, he needs to be able to share it quickly and usefully with others – this helps the community reuse its knowledge better.

Researchers worked closely with the service technicians to design Eureka, which is about 90 per cent social process and 10 per cent infrastructure. Indeed, the social aspects of Eureka are what make it unique. The system has been shaped by a decade of research at PARC on participatory design, which involves knowing how to engage the practitioners themselves in co-developing work practices, processes and technology. Participating in such a community-based design process gave the technicians ownership of the system and a stake in sustaining its overall success.

Instead of financial incentives, Eureka relies on personal recognition to motivate workers to share their knowledge, contribute ideas and take responsibility for building and maintaining the community knowledge base. By notifying tip authors when a designated peer receives a tip or validates it and by placing the names of both author and validator on the tips and passing along feedback, Eureka helps foster people's natural desire to contribute, building social capital and intellectual capital simultaneously.

The system, which initially focused on high-end copiers, was field tested in 1995 by about 1,500 service technicians. The result was a 5 per cent saving in both parts usage and labour in France. Technicians now access more than 5,000 tips per month. More than 15 per cent of the technicians have contributed validated tips. New tips are generated at the rate of about one per 1,000 service calls, with 70 per cent of the tips validated in fewer than five days. Using laptop computers linked to the Internet, Eureka is being rolled out worldwide to 24,000 Xerox service technicians. Also, the company has begun to share it selectively with customers.

The system is based on a recognition that service technicians are not just the eyes and hands of the corporation; they are also its brains. They are the people who come up with new ideas and solutions. Eureka provides the tools and techniques to capitalize on that local knowledge more effectively, less expensively and more quickly than previous methods of sharing knowledge (see Figure 14.2). Eureka is entirely self-sustaining – users take it on themselves to build and maintain the knowledge base with no pushing or help from outside managers, reporters, or editors. Eureka is being extended into new communities such as product design, call centre support and sales.

DocuShare: sharing community-based knowledge

Many tools aimed at supporting electronic collaboration fall short because they do not provide an environment that truly helps people work together.

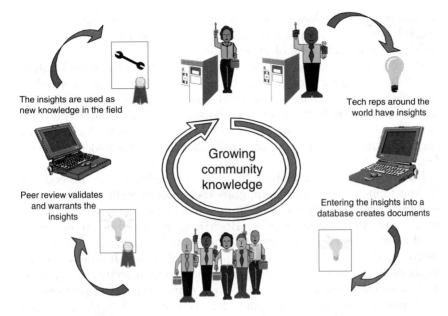

The insights are used as new knowledge in the field

Tech reps around the world have insights

Growing community knowledge

Peer review validates and warrants the insights

Entering the insights into a database creates documents

Figure 14.2 *The Eureka knowledge sharing process*

Source: Xerox Corporation

DocuShare – a technology that has been in wide use within Xerox since 1997 and has since been introduced as a product – lets people create a virtual work space in which they can easily share information, collaborate on documents and stay connected with co-workers.

This collaborative environment, initially called AmberWeb, was especially designed to support communities of workers and was originally conceived as a new tool to help scientific researchers share files electronically. However, it has become much more. Tapping a latent corporatewide need for an easy-to-use intranet-based knowledge-sharing system, the technology spread to more than 60,000 Xerox employees since inception.

There are several keys to the success of DocuShare, which was developed by researchers at Xerox's Joseph C. Wilson Center for Research and Technology in up-state New York. First, the system, which enables people to access repositories of shared documents, calendars, bulletin boards and databases, is community owned and community maintained. There is no central administration or authority to go through – anyone within a community can easily create an account and users can manage their own work spaces. It also offers a very fast learning curve – the result of its designers' close work with the initial community of users to understand their desired look, feel and functionality.

Also crucial to the success of DocuShare is that it was designed for the Web. It is a layer of software that sits on a server enabling any standard Web browser to provide desired services. At the back end, it stores documents and provides security and access rights. Users have complete control over security parameters and can easily designate 'write' or 'read only' access at every level of information.

DocuShare was designed to give the 500 scientists and professionals at the Wilson Center a greater sense of awareness of each other's activities and, thus, more of a feeling of community. The system's 'what's new' feature makes people aware of activities throughout the centre and keeps them up to date on their colleagues' work. Users can learn who has joined the community and take note of any file changes or new folders that have been added.

DocuShare's quick adoption by Xerox's employees far beyond the Wilson Center was a bottom-up, grass roots process with no formal promotion – spurred only by word-of-mouth reports about work improvements that the system enables. DocuShare makes the intranet more productive. It manages security and can be used by anyone, regardless of where they are or what computing platform they use. It works with all kinds of documents – word processing, presentation software, hypertext and multimedia. Also, DocuShare does not require extensive customization or support, nor does it demand that people go through a systems administrator or change the way they work. Users can put the tool to work quickly and begin leveraging their knowledge assets almost immediately.

FIRST: providing knowledge resources to the field

When Xerox's sales representatives and analysts in the United States encounter a question they can't answer, they pull out their laptop computers to access the Xerox Field Information Research Systems Team (FIRST) website. FIRST's users are teams of sales reps and analysts who sell systems solutions. These often involve configuring complicated software and hardware to work with customers' networks and equipment – work that can present thorny new and unexpected problems.

The teams rely on each other's experiences to solve these problems and share those experiences with each other in the form of 'tech notes' that are made accessible to all via FIRST's website. The system now includes more than 7,000 tech notes spanning years of experience working with Xerox systems.

Keeping knowledge up to date is a primary concern in the fast-moving systems world. FIRST's editorial process involves automatic flagging of documents every six months. At that point, a human has to review flagged documents and either regenerate them, give them a new update date or delete them.

Another automatic process is a survey form presented to FIRST users after their tenth query. The most important question asked is, 'How much time did you save?' The most frequent answer? An average of more than two days per enquiry.

The FIRST experience tells us that people who can quickly retrieve information and turn it into knowledge – relevant, useful and actionable – are ahead of the game. Some of the lessons learned from FIRST are the following.

1 *Analyse needs first* Carefully analyse why you are capturing the information and what you hope to accomplish with it.
2 *Determine customer retrieval requirements* Find out what information is really valuable for the users and, more important, what they (or you) will want to do with the information later.
3 *Select the proper tools* Ask what tools will best allow you to get out what you put in. You may be able to purchase off-the-shelf tools or you may have to write your own software.
4 *Set up a monitoring procedure* In today's fast-paced world, old information is bad information. It leads to old knowledge and ill-informed decisions. Keeping information fresh requires a continuous monitoring and review process. This includes monitoring user feedback so the system continually improves.

Intellectual property management: a strategic approach

A company's intellectual assets exist on many levels. Xerox established a dedicated Corporate Office for Management of Intellectual Properties (COMIP) to protect and leverage the most tangible of those knowledge resources – patents, invention proposals, copyrights and licensing arrangements.

COMIP's responsibilities encompass a range of intellectual capital, including patents, trade secrets, know-how, software and copyrights. Patents – one of the most important and visible of Xerox's intellectual assets – have been the initial focus. Xerox generates about 800 patents a year and frequently ranks among the top ten US patent holders. The intellectual capital strategy will help ensure that Xerox's technology directly supports its present and future business goals – and generates a valuable return.

To shape the strategy, Xerox formed a cross-company working group, drawing representatives from all business divisions, as well as the corporate, legal and strategy groups. The team began by defining a new set of technology categories – ways of classifying patents into areas that fit into the firm's future businesses as identified by the Xerox 2005 strategic planning process.

The group came up with 42 categories, which were then whittled down to 5. The company has set patent-filing targets for each category, consistent with the business strategy: 80 per cent have been distributed among the 5 categories, while 20 per cent were assigned to a 'miscellaneous' category to provide flexibility for handling the unexpected.

The new process, put into action in 1998, involves reclassifying a portfolio of nearly 7,000 patents and developing information on the expected use and relative value of each patent within its new category. An annual renewal and update process lets the company reset targets if it seems necessary.

In addition to managing the patent portfolio, COMIP manages the worldwide licensing of all Xerox's intellectual property. A corporate infringement laboratory is also a part of this activity. Its role is to maximize the value of the patent portfolio by improving the company's ability to discover and demonstrate infringement. It also collects royalties or gains access to cross-licensing agreements by knowing about infringements.

Xerox places a high value on its intellectual property and recognizes that, if it is properly managed as an asset, it will become an increasingly important contributor to the company's success.

Taking knowledge to market: positioning plus new products and solutions

A steadily growing emphasis on knowledge over a period of about three years put Xerox in a position where, by late 1998, it was ready to become more publicly visible regarding knowledge. Although the company chose not to refer to itself as The Knowledge Company, it did begin to build a market position around the idea, defining its mission as helping customers share knowledge via documents. The tag line of a new advertising campaign was 'Keep the Conversation Going. Share the Knowledge' – a testimony to Xerox's focus on the human, community-oriented aspects of knowledge work.

In the autumn of 1998, the company introduced and detailed its new concepts of knowledge, laying out a rationale for its positioning, launching new products designed to enhance knowledge sharing in the office and announcing a knowledge-sharing technology and marketing partnerships with IBM's Lotus Development unit and Microsoft. These partnerships combine the paper and electronic document-handling abilities of the multifunctional Document Centre machines with the distribution, filing and retrieval features of Lotus Domino, Lotus Notes and Microsoft Exchange.

In early 1999, 'Share the Knowledge' became part of Xerox's annual corporatewide direction to employees and the firm launched several internal knowledge-sharing initiatives – one of them intended to foster long-term cultural change in the way that quality initiatives had done two decades earlier. At the time of writing, this effort is still in the early stages of development and so detailed results are not available.

Externally, however, Xerox has continued to build a presence and reputation as a knowledge-driven company. It has announced partnerships with Microsoft and IBM Lotus Notes to pair Document Centre devices with Microsoft's Exchange and Lotus Notes software and the launch of the first knowledge-sharing offerings with the theme 'Competing Through Knowledge'. In fact, the company has announced a significant long-term reorientation as a solutions provider that will ultimately earn much of its revenue from software and services that help people share knowledge.

The new offerings include a suite of software-driven applications, technology, practices, services and solutions – all designed to facilitate the sharing of knowledge in solving customers' problems, improving their work processes and helping them create new markets and gain competitive advantages. The solutions include some we have addressed in this chapter – Eureka and DocuShare, for example. They have been drawn from a diversity of Xerox sources – from grass roots efforts to improve work productivity and effectiveness in customer service and environment, health and safety, from Xerox research labs in the United States and Europe, from the company's network services subsidiary (Xerox Connect) and outsourcing unit (Xerox Business Services) and from the entrepreneurial spin-off firms that Xerox calls New Enterprise Companies.

The knowledge momentum at Xerox has thus grown in less than four years from a handful of grass roots projects and a small 'official' corporatewide initiative into a full-blown internal business-improvement project and market positioning, supported by a range of products, services, technology and solutions. The effort has been strengthened by permission from the top of the company to experiment and learn. The knowledge idea was adopted and sponsored early on by Chairman and CEO Paul Allaire. Managing for knowledge has become a core business focus for Xerox.

Collaborative Initiatives

While Xerox and Fuji Xerox have blazed a considerable portion of their knowledge trails independently, they have stayed aware of each other's actions and collaborated on several projects – both to increase their knowledge about the knowledge movement and further the market's understanding of the subject.

The Berkeley professorship

To increase understanding of knowledge and its impact on business, Fuji Xerox and Xerox jointly sponsored the United States' first academic professorship dedicated to the study of the subject. The Xerox Distinguished Professorship in Knowledge in the Haas School of Business at the University of California, Berkeley, was endowed by a $1 million grant from the two companies.

It was initiated by Fuji Xerox and supported by Xerox as a way to study knowledge as it is an increasingly important theme in the twenty-first century. Work done under the professorship is intended to go beyond management theories developed in the twentieth century, bridge the gap between Western and Eastern knowledge and contribute new management theories and language.

Professor Ikujiro Nonaka – a long-time collaborator and adviser to Fuji Xerox in the areas of business management and organizational design – was appointed as the first Xerox Knowledge Professor. Nonaka, one of Japan's foremost authorities on knowledge management, received both his MBA and PhD from Berkeley.

The professorship was a catalyst for establishing of the annual UC Berkeley Forum on Knowledge and the Firm. Begun in 1997, this small but powerful conference brings the world's leading knowledge theorists and practitioners together for two days of immersion in thoughts about the state of knowledge in business. The first day has the atmosphere of an intimate think-tank in which the leaders share ideas among themselves; the second features presentations and exchanges that are open to the public.

The first Berkeley Forum looked at the goals of knowledge work, identified a common knowledge vocabulary, highlighted gaps between the theory and practice of knowledge, and addressed the question of how organizations might measure the value of their knowledge. The second Forum helped attendees gain a new understanding of the importance of knowledge to competitiveness and of the connection between knowledge and creativity.

The Berkeley Forum has served as a sort of incubator for new ideas on knowledge, advancing the movement's learning edges while fostering more widespread understanding about its concepts and practices.

Continual knowledge exchange

In addition to collaborating on external and public projects, such as the Berkeley professorship, Xerox and Fuji Xerox take part in an ongoing exchange of knowledge in a series of internal forums and workshops.

Since 1994, Xerox's Corporate Strategy Group and Fuji Xerox's Corporate Marketing and Business Planning Department have held joint concept marketing workshops. In recent years, these have been dedicated to exploring the relationship between information and knowledge.

Xerox also has sponsored an annual learning exchange called the Xerox Knowledge Forum, in which knowledge leaders, knowledge practitioners and other executives from throughout the Xerox Group participate. Held since 1997, the Knowledge Forum brings together an increasingly important internal community – people who are helping move the knowledge idea forward within the company and with customers. The two-day Forum features nearly two dozen talks and discussions highlighting knowledge-based initiatives throughout the company. In 1999, for example, the presentations covered efforts underway in customer locations and, inside Xerox, in areas such as customer service, information management, intellectual capital management, corporate strategy and corporate culture. Presentations also showcased the latest knowledge-themed Xerox advertising and communication programmes for general and specialized external audiences.

The forums introduce Xerox and Fuji Xerox attendees to information, experiences and knowledge from the outside. The 1999 Forum, for example, featured presentations by IBM's leading knowledge authority, Larry Prusak, and an executive from the Gartner Group, which had recently completed a major market study of knowledge management. Professor Nonaka has also attended and addressed the Forum.

Summary

A shared long-term interest in knowledge

As Xerox and Fuji Xerox pursue and build knowledge strategies and initiatives, they collaborate where practical, just as they have done since becoming partners in 1962. We recognize that – especially as knowledge contains such an important cultural dimension – it is important that knowledge-sharing efforts be focused on, and carefully tailored to, the communities they are designed to help. At the same time, we see the benefits in shared learning and the pooling of growing worldwide knowledge and expertise on the subject of knowledge. We are already seeing the competitive need to systematically manage for knowledge on a global basis. Our efforts at Xerox and Fuji Xerox will undoubtedly move ever closer together. As Kobayashi has said, 'Knowledge is a value shared by the entire Xerox Group conducting business in the global market. Knowledge unites the members of the Group into one and strengthens the ties among them.'

Without the different lenses that our Eastern and Western viewpoints provide, we would not have the unique perspective that we do. Because of our blend of theory, philosophy, sociology, work practice study, nuts-and-bolts business pragmatism and a global viewpoint, Xerox and Fuji Xerox have crafted a business framework for knowledge that we can rally around as a company. We have also backed it with strategies for adopting it internally and externally.

With an understanding of what is happening in the knowledge market, what benefits people are getting from it and how companies of the future might structure for optimal knowledge use, the Xerox Group is learning how to go forward, how to be real and credible and what products and services to offer the market to best meet customers' needs – even those that have not yet been identified.

Thus, it is a firmly held view at Xerox and Fuji Xerox that the ability to leverage knowledge resources will be critical to every company's success in the new millennium. The companies' expertise and experience in managing documents and the knowledge they contain is an ideal springboard from which to play a leadership role in this increasingly vital field.

We have high aspirations for the role that knowledge will play in defining what Xerox and Fuji Xerox know and stand for, what they do, the way they work and what products and services they provide their customers.

15 Towards a Universal Management Concept of Knowledge

Hirotaka Takeuchi

Introduction

Knowledge has been a central subject of debate in philosophy and epistemology since the days of Plato and Socrates. An old concept, dating back to 400 BC is being heralded today as one of the newest ideas in management.

What is new is the idea of capturing knowledge gained by individuals and spreading it to others in the organization. Although a consensus has emerged around the world on what to call this idea – knowledge management – different countries have run off with it in divergent directions during the early stages of its development. European companies have been primarily concerned with *measuring* knowledge, while American companies have been much more focused on *managing* knowledge effectively by using IT and Japanese companies on creating new knowledge organizationally.

There was a danger a few years ago that knowledge management, which hit the West like lightning, would end up being just a buzzword, as have many management ideas in the past. Recall what happened to re-engineering, which started out as a perfectly sensible management idea when first written about in 1990. The hype that subsequently developed in the West (re-engineering never actually took off in Japan) meant that the human factor was too quickly ignored, and re-engineering degenerated into little more than a fad.

Knowledge management is now moving into a new era. European companies are beginning to move beyond measuring knowledge and looking for ways of better applying knowledge to work. American companies are beginning to realize the limitations of the IT-driven approach and incorporating the human factor into knowledge management. Japanese companies, on the other hand, are beginning to move beyond the tacit dimension of knowledge and exploring how databases can improve productivity.

What began as three divergent approaches to knowledge management are coming together in this new era of synthesis to form a universal foundation. Metaphorically speaking, it is as though three different roots are becoming intertwined to form a solid trunk of a tree.

This chapter will start with a brief review of the early approaches adopted by European and American companies, followed by a more detailed description of the Japanese approach. It will then show how the three approaches are becoming synthesized to form a universal management concept of knowledge.

Measuring Knowledge

European companies have taken the lead in developing measurement systems for their intangible assets and reporting the results publicly. They include Skandia AFS, a subsidiary of the Skandia insurance and financial services company, WM-data, a computer software and consulting company, Celemi, a company that develops and sells creative training tools, and PLS-Consult, a management consulting firm. All of these companies are Scandinavian – the first three being Swedish and the fourth Danish. They have all been influenced by the pioneering work of Karl Erik Sveiby (1997) of Sweden, who developed a method of accounting for intangible assets in companies in the late 1980s.

Collectively, these companies developed hundreds of indices and ratios in an effort to provide a comprehensive view of intellectual assets at hand. For example, they measure such things as 'business development expenses as a percentage of total expenses', 'percentage of production from new launches', 'information technology investments as a percentage of total expense', 'information technology employees as a percentage of total employees', 'percentage of employees working directly with customers' and other data as indicators of intellectual capital.

In addition, these companies actually include this data in their annual reports to show how effectively intellectual assets are leveraged. Skandia AFS' annual report, for example, highlights the process of transforming 'human capital', which is an asset the company cannot own, into 'structural capital', which can be owned by the company (Edvinsson and Malone, 1997). Human capital is defined as the combined knowledge, skill, innovativeness and ability of the company's individual employees to meet the task at hand. It also includes the company's values, culture and philosophy. Structural capital is defined as the hardware, software, databases, organizational structure, patents, trademarks and everything else of organizational capability that supports those employees' productivity – that is everything left at the office when the employees go home. Structural capital also includes customer capital and the relationships developed with key customers.

Managing Knowledge

American companies have taken the lead in managing knowledge effectively using IT. The best practices in service industries – where knowledge is effectively the product – come mostly from American management consulting firms. The roles that 'knowledge integrators' at Andersen Consulting play in managing knowledge are well documented (Stewart, 1997). These knowledge managers are responsible for keeping the knowledge database orderly (such as, Knowledge Xchange in the case of Andersen Consulting), categorizing and formatting documents and deleting the obsolete. They are also charged with cajoling consultants into using the system and identifying topics that ought to become research projects.

At Ernst & Young's Centre for Business Knowledge, 250 people manage the electronic repository and help consultants find and use information (Hansen, Nohria and Tierney, 1999). In addition, Ernst & Young has a staff member in each of its 40-plus practice areas who helps codify and store documents. The resulting databases created at all the practice areas are linked in a network. Hansen, Nohria and Tierney call this a codification strategy. Knowledge is carefully codified and stored in databases, where it can be accessed and used easily by anyone in the company. Codification takes place using a 'people to documents' approach, in which knowledge is given by the person who developed it, made independent of that person and reused for various purposes.

Of manufacturing industries, I have had first-hand experience of working with GE and Hewlett-Packard, both of which have received favourable press coverage in the knowledge management field. At GE, I served as one of the facilitators of its Work-Out programme, which began in 1989. Work-Out exemplifies an attempt on the part of large companies to create the opportunity for hidden knowledge to be made public (Tichy and Sherman, 1993).

Hewlett-Packard has embarked on a number of knowledge management initiatives in recent years to create a purposeful process for capturing, storing, sharing and leveraging what employees know. One of the outcomes of this work is the formation of KnowledgeLinks, in which an internal consultancy group located at headquarters collects knowledge from one Hewlett-Packard business and translates it so that the other businesses can apply it. An on-line version of KnowledgeLinks is now available, enabling managers to receive a screenful of documents, war stories and best practice on how others have dealt with key management issues in the past such as decreasing time-to-market, outsourcing manufacturing, managing retail channels and others. The KnowledgeLinks websites not only provide access to what others have done, but who to contact as well (Stewart, 1997).

Creating Knowledge

As is evident from the above, the focus in the West is not on knowledge per se, but on measuring and managing knowledge. Where does Japan stand with respect to knowledge management? (Remember, knowledge management is about capturing knowledge gained by individuals and spreading it to others in the organization.)

Japanese companies did not jump on the bandwagon in the early stages of the knowledge management boom. This is not because they do not fully recognize the importance of knowledge as the resource and key source of innovation. They do, as Nonaka and Takeuchi (1995) have pointed out. What they are not convinced about is the value of simply measuring and managing existing knowledge in a mechanical and systematic manner. They doubt if that alone will enhance innovation.

Japanese companies' reluctance to accept the data-based and mechanical approach to knowledge management reflects Ikujiro Nonaka's influence. Nonaka's thoughts about knowledge are different from the popular Western view in two respects, according to *The Economist* (1997: 31, p. 71)

> The first is his relative lack of interest in information technology. Many American companies equate 'knowledge creation' with setting up computer databases. Mr Nonaka argues that much of a company's knowledge bank has nothing to do with data, but is based on informal 'on-the-job' knowledge – everything from the name of a customer's secretary to the best way to deal with a truculent supplier. Many of these titbits are stored in the brains of middle managers – exactly the people whom re-engineering replaced with computers. The second thing that makes Mr Nonaka stand out is his insistence that companies need plenty of slack to remain creative.

Nonaka seems to be posing two fundamental questions about knowledge management here. Can you measure the titbits of knowledge stored in the brains of managers? Can you really create new knowledge by trying to micro-manage this knowledge?

Nonaka draws a clear distinction between knowledge management and knowledge creation, as illustrated by the following episode. In naming the first chaired professorship dedicated to the study of knowledge and its impact on business, the Haas School of Business at the University of California, Berkeley, initially recommended the title 'Xerox Distinguished Professorship of Knowledge Management'. Nonaka enquired if the title could be changed to 'Xerox Distinguished Professorship of Knowledge Creation'. As a compromise, they agreed to call it 'Xerox Distinguished Professorship in Knowledge'.

The Japanese approach to knowledge differs from the Western in a number of ways. We will highlight three fundamental differences here:

1   how knowledge is viewed: knowledge is not viewed simply as data or information that can be stored in the computer; it also involves emotions, values, hunches;
2   what companies do with knowledge: companies should be creating new knowledge, not just managing it;

3 who the key players are: everyone in the organization is involved in creating organizational knowledge, with middle managers serving as key knowledge engineers.

Two kinds of knowledge

There are two kinds of knowledge.[1] One is explicit knowledge, which can be expressed in words and numbers and shared in the form of data, scientific formulae, product specifications, manuals, universal principles and so forth. This kind of knowledge can be readily transmitted to individuals formally and systematically. This has been the dominant form of knowledge in the West. The Japanese, however, see this form as just the tip of the iceberg. They view knowledge as being primarily tacit, something not easily visible and expressible.

Tacit knowledge is highly personal and hard to formalize, making it difficult to communicate or share with others. Subjective insights, intuitions and hunches fall into this category of knowledge. Furthermore, tacit knowledge is deeply rooted in an individual's actions and experience, as well as in the ideals, values or emotions they embrace.

To be precise, there are two dimensions to tacit knowledge. The first is the 'technical' dimension, which encompasses the kind of informal and hard-to-pin-down skills or crafts often captured in the term 'know-how'. Master craftsmen or three-star chefs, for example, develop a wealth of expertise at their fingertips, after years of experience, but they often have difficulty articulating the technical or scientific principles behind what they know. Highly subjective and personal insights, intuitions, hunches and inspirations derived from bodily experience all fit into this dimension.

Tacit knowledge also contains an important 'cognitive' dimension. It consists of beliefs, perceptions, ideals, values, emotions and mental models so ingrained in us that we take them for granted. Though they cannot be articulated very easily, this dimension of tacit knowledge shapes the way we perceive the world around us.

The difference in the philosophical traditions of the West and Japan shed light on why Western managers tend to emphasize the importance of explicit knowledge whereas Japanese managers put more emphasis on tacit knowledge. Western philosophy has a tradition of separating 'the subject who knows' from 'the object that is known', epitomized in the work of the French rationalist Descartes. He proposed a concept that is called after him – Cartesian dualism – which is the separation between the knower and the known, mind and body, subject and object.

Descartes argued that the ultimate truth can be deduced only from the real existence of a 'thinking self', which was made famous by his phrase 'I think therefore I am'. He assumed that the 'thinking self' is independent of body or matter, because while a body or matter does have an extension we can see and touch but doesn't think, a mind has no extension but thinks.

Thus, according to the Cartesian dualism, true knowledge can be obtained only by the mind, not the body.

In contrast, the Japanese intellectual tradition placed a strong emphasis on the importance of the 'whole personality', which provided a basis for valuing personal and physical experience over indirect, intellectual abstraction. This tradition of emphasizing bodily experience has contributed to the development of a methodology in Zen Buddhism dubbed 'the oneness of body and mind' by Eisai, one of the founders of Zen Buddhism in medieval Japan.

Zen profoundly affected samurai education, which sought to develop wisdom in the process of physical training. In traditional samurai education, knowledge was acquired when it was integrated into one's 'personal character'. The education placed a great emphasis on building up character and attached little importance to prudence, intelligence and metaphysics. Being a 'man of action' was considered more important than mastering philosophy and literature, although these subjects also constituted a major part of samurai education.

The Japanese have long emphasized the importance of bodily experience. A child learns to eat, walk and talk as a result of trial and error. They learn with the body, not only with the mind. Similarly, a student of traditional Japanese art – for example, calligraphy, the tea ceremony, flower arrangement or Japanese dancing – learns by imitating the moves of the master. A master becomes a master when the body and mind become one while stroking the brush (calligraphy) or pouring water into the kettle (the tea ceremony). A sumo wrestler becomes a grand champion when he achieves *shingi-ittai* – when the mind (*shin*) and technique (*gi*) become one (*ittai*).

There is a long philosophical tradition in the West of valuing precise, conceptual knowledge and systematic sciences, which can be traced back to Descartes. In contrast, the Japanese intellectual tradition values the embodiment of direct, personal experience. It is these distinct traditions that account for the difference in the importance attached to explicit and tacit knowledge.

Knowledge creation, not knowledge management

The distinction between explicit knowledge and tacit knowledge is the key to understanding the differences between the Western approach to knowledge (knowledge management) and the Japanese approach to knowledge (knowledge creation). As we have seen, the West has placed a strong emphasis on explicit knowledge and Japan on tacit knowledge.

Explicit knowledge can easily be 'processed' by a computer, transmitted electronically or stored in databases. The subjective and intuitive nature of tacit knowledge makes it difficult to process or transmit the acquired knowledge in any systematic or logical manner. For tacit knowledge to be communicated and shared within an organization, it has to be converted into words or numbers that anyone can understand. It is precisely during the time this kind of a conversion takes place – that is, from tacit to explicit – that organizational knowledge is created.

The reason Western managers tend not to address the issue of organizational knowledge creation can be traced to the view of knowledge as necessarily explicit. They take for granted a view of the organization as a playing field for 'scientific management' and a machine for 'information processing'. This view is deeply ingrained in the traditions of Western management, from Frederick Taylor to Herbert Simon.

Frederick Taylor prescribed 'scientific' methods for the workplace, the most important being time and motion studies. Such studies encourage 'a preoccupation with allocating resources, . . . monitoring and measuring performance, and manipulating organizational structures to set lines of authority' (Kim and Manborgne, 1997: 71). Taylor developed 'an arsenal of tools to promote efficiency and consistency by controlling individuals' behaviour and compelling employees to comply with management dictates.' Scientific management had little to do with encouraging the active cooperation of workers. As Kim and Mauborgne point out, 'Creating and sharing knowledge are intangible activities that can neither be supervised nor forced out of people. They happen only when people cooperate voluntarily.'

Nonaka also contends that the creation of knowledge cannot be managed. The notion of creating something new runs counter to the 'control' mentality of traditional management science. 'Given a certain context, knowledge emerges naturally. You have to give your employees a lot of latitude, not try to control them', says Nonaka (Takeuchi, 1997). He sees the experiences and judgements of employees, their commitment, ideals and way of life as an important source of new knowledge. This tacit dimension is ignored by Taylor's scientific management.

Herbert Simon developed a view of organization as an 'information-processing machine'. He built a scientific theory of problem solving and decision making based on the assumption that human cognitive capacity is inherently limited. He argued that effective information processing is possible only when complicated problems are simplified and organizational structures are specialized. This Cartesian-like rationalist view led him to neglect the human potential for creating knowledge. He did not see human beings as those who actively discover problems and create knowledge to solve them.

The Japanese emphasis on the cognitive dimension of knowledge gives rise to a wholly different view of the organization. It is seen not as a machine for processing information, but as a 'living organism'. Within this context, sharing an understanding of what the company stands for, where it is going, what kind of a world it wants to live in and how to make that world a reality become much more crucial than processing objective information. Highly subjective, personal and emotional dimensions of knowledge have virtually no chance for survival within a machine, but have ample opportunity to grow within a living organism.

Once the importance of tacit knowledge is realized, then one begins to think about innovation in a wholly new way. It is not just about putting together diverse bits of data and information. The personal commitment of the employees and their identifying with the company and its mission become crucial. Unlike information, knowledge is about commitment and beliefs ('justified, true belief', in fact – a concept first introduced by Plato); it is a function of a particular stance, perspective or intention. In this respect, the creation of new knowledge is as much about ideals as it is about ideas and that fact fuels innovation. Similarly, unlike information, knowledge is about action – it is always knowledge 'to some end'. The unique information an individual possesses must be acted on for new knowledge to be created. This voluntary action also fuels innovation.

Although we have made a clear distinction between explicit and tacit knowledge, they are not totally independent of each other. Rather, they are mutually complementary. They interact with each other in the creative activities of human beings. Our theory of knowledge creation is anchored to a critical assumption that human knowledge is created and expanded via social interaction between tacit knowledge and explicit knowledge. This interaction gives rise to four modes of knowledge conversion:

1   from tacit to tacit, which is called socialization;
2   from tacit to explicit – externalization;
3   from explicit to explicit – combination;
4   from explicit to tacit – internalization.

Knowledge conversion is a 'social' process between individuals as well as between individuals and an organization, but, in a strict sense, knowledge is created only by individuals. An organization cannot create knowledge by itself. What the organization can do is support creative individuals or provide the contexts for them to create knowledge.

Organizational knowledge creation, therefore, should be understood as a process that 'organizationally' amplifies the knowledge created by individuals and crystallizes it as part of the knowledge network of the organization

The infatuation in the West with knowledge management reflects the bias towards explicit knowledge, which is the easier of the two kinds of knowledge to measure, control and process. Explicit knowledge can be much more easily entered into a computer, stored in a database and transmitted on-line than the highly subjective, personal and cognitive tacit knowledge. Knowledge management deals primarily with existing knowledge. However, in order to create new knowledge, we need the two kinds of knowledge to interact with each other in the actions of individuals within the organization.

Middle managers as key players

In Japan, creating new knowledge is not the responsibility of the selected few, but of everyone in the organization. No one department or group of experts has the exclusive responsibility for creating new knowledge. Front-line employees, middle managers and top management all play a part. However, this is not to say that there is no differentiation in the roles that these three play. In fact, the creation of new knowledge is the product of dynamic interactions among the three kinds of players.

Front-line employees are immersed in the day-to-day details of particular technology, products or markets. While they have an abundance of highly practical information, they often find it difficult to turn that information into useful knowledge. For one thing, signals from the marketplace can be vague and ambiguous. For another, these front-line employees can become so caught up in their own narrow perspective that they lose sight of the broader context. Moreover, even when they do develop meaningful ideas and insights, it can still be difficult to communicate the importance of that information to others. People don't just receive new knowledge passively, they interpret it actively to fit their own situation and perspectives. Thus, what makes sense in one context can change or even lose its meaning when communicated to people in a different context.

Top management provides a sense of direction for where the company should be headed. It does so, first of all, by articulating a 'grand theory' for what the company 'ought to be'. In highly universal and abstract terms, the grand theory set forth by top management helps to link seemingly disparate activities or businesses into a coherent whole. Second, top management provides direction by establishing a knowledge vision in the form of a corporate vision or policy statement. Its aspirations and ideals determine the quality of knowledge the company creates. Third, top management provides direction by setting the standards for justifying the value of the knowledge that is being created. It needs to decide strategically which efforts to support and develop.

Middle managers serve as a bridge between the visionary 'ideals' of the top and the often chaotic 'reality' of those on the front line of business. Middle managers mediate between the 'what ought to be' mindset of the top and the 'what is' mindset of the front-line employees by creating middle-level business and product concepts. In other words, if top management's role is to create a grand theory, middle managers create more concrete concepts that front-line employees can understand. The mid-range theory created by middle managers can then be tested empirically within the company with the help of front-line employees.

Middle managers, who often serve as team leaders of the product development team in Japan, are in a key position to remake reality according to the company's vision. In remaking reality, they take the lead in converting knowledge. Although they facilitate all four modes of knowledge conversion, middle managers make their most significant mark in converting tacit images and perspectives into explicit concepts. They synthesize the tacit knowledge of both front-line employees and top management, make it explicit and incorporate it into new technologies, products or systems. In this sense, middle managers are the true knowledge engineers of what we call 'the knowledge-creating company'. Middle managers are the key to continuous innovation in Japan. They are at the very centre of a continuous iterative process involving both the top- and the front-line- (that is, bottom-) level employees called middle-up-down. In the West, however, the very term 'middle manager' has become one of contempt, synonymous with 'backwardness', 'stagnation' or 'resistance to change'. Some have argued that middle managers are 'a dying breed' or 'an unnecessary evil'.

Another impression we have is that the responsibility for knowledge management initiatives in the West rests with the selected few, not with everyone in the organization. Knowledge is managed by a few key players in staff positions, including information processing, internal consultancy or human resources management. In contrast, knowledge is created by the interactions of front-line employees, middle managers and top management, with middle managers in line positions playing the key synthesizing role in Japan.

With a few exceptions, notably GE and Hewlett-Packard, front-line employees are not an integral part of knowledge management. This situation is similar to the days of Frederick Taylor, which did not tap the experiences and judgements of front-line workers as a source of knowledge. Consequently, the creation of new work methods for scientific management became the responsibility of the selected few in managerial positions. These élites were charged with the chore of classifying, tabulating and reducing the knowledge into rules and formulae and applying them to daily work. The danger of knowledge management is in having the responsibility for capturing the knowledge gained by individuals and spreading it to others in the organization resting in the hands of a selected few.

Moves Towards a Synthesis

Rudyard Kipling once wrote, 'Oh, East is East, and West is West, and never the twain shall meet' ('The Ballad of East and West', 1892). This, however, may not necessarily apply to the field of knowledge management today, where East and West are beginning to become more synthesized. In particular, a sea change is taking place among companies in the West, which are beginning to realize the limitations of their singular focus on the IT-based approach to knowledge management.

Signs of this realization are becoming quite visible in the West. In an article in *California Management Review*, Richard McDermott (1999), a consultant who specializes in designing and implementing knowledge management strategies, points out in no uncertain terms that leveraging knowledge is very hard to achieve by means of IT tools and concepts alone. He makes a clear distinction between knowledge and information and identifies the following unique characteristics of knowledge in a vernacular reminiscent of Nonaka and myself:

1   knowledge always involves a person who knows;
2   knowledge comes from experience that we have reflected on, made sense of and tested against others' experiences;
3   knowledge is invisible and often comes to mind only when we need it to answer a question or solve a problem;
4   knowledge flows through communities, from one generation to the next;
5   knowledge circulates via stories, chance hallway meetings and other informal, undocumented practices and artifacts;
6   new knowledge is created at the boundaries of old knowledge.

Similarly, for academics in the UK – Swann, Newell, Scarbrough and Hislop (1999) – have written an article that illustrates three fundamental problems with IT-driven approaches to knowledge management. First, they tend to ignore tacit knowledge and focus only on explicit or codified knowledge. Second, they end up tapping existing knowledge at the expense of trying to create new knowledge. Third, they concentrate on capturing, codifying and transmitting knowledge without really thinking about how it will be used or applied by others.

The spotlight today is on companies in the US and Europe that are employing a more human and personal approach to knowledge management. For example, strategy consulting firms, such as Bain, Boston Consulting Group and McKinsey, are featured in an article in the *Harvard Business Review* by Hansen, Nohria and Tierney (1999). The firms are adhering to what the authors call a personalization strategy. They contend that knowledge is closely tied to the person who developed it and is shared mainly by means of person-to-person contacts within these firms. The firms attach more importance to transferring knowledge that has not been codified or couldn't be codified and resort to brainstorming sessions or one-on-one conversations as a medium of exchange. IT is utilized primarily to help consultants communicate knowledge, not to store it.

Outside of the consulting industry, Hewlett-Packard best exemplifies the 'East meets West' phenomenon. As mentioned earlier, it was one of the first companies to establish an IT-based on-line knowledge sharing system called KnowledgeLinks. At the same time, it has been proactively seeking ways to foster person-to-person exchanges of knowledge, as described below.

1   Hewlett-Packard has an expert directory system at its central research lab that enables individuals to register themselves and describe their

areas of expertise and special competency. Anyone in the company can then search through the profiles, find people who may be able to help and make a direct contact with them (Sieloff, 1999).

2 One division developed a successful electronic oscilloscope with a Windows operating system and interface. To make sure that other divisions understood and applied the interface, the division decided to take the person-to-person approach and sent its development team members to face-to-face meetings at divisions around the world (Hansen, Nohria and Tierney, 1999).

3 Product delivery consultants within North America hold monthly teleconferences to discuss problems that are directly related to High Availability – a software product that minimizes computer downtime for customers. Participants, who join in on a voluntary basis, talk openly about their own experiences installing the product, share their ideas on how to work more effectively with clients or discuss ways to deal with a persistent bug in the software. The monthly call ends up being an active give-and-take session as well as a story-telling session (Wenger and Snyder, 2000).

4 Every employee at Hewlett-Packard has access to corporate airplanes, which travel daily to different offices. Engineers often use these planes to visit other divisions and share ideas about new products or new technology (Hansen, Nohria and Tierney, 1999).

5 The physical office environment is considered an important contributor to making knowledge sharing spontaneous and effortless. Hewlett-Packard shuns the trend towards 'ice cube tray' floor layouts of small, individual cubicles with high partitions and little or no shared space. Instead, it favours a much more open office environment with low or no internal partitions, ample team space with provisions for continuous information displays and special enclosed areas for occasional privacy and concentration (Sieloff, 1999).

Hewlett-Packard's efforts clearly demonstrate why the company is at the leading edge of the East meets West phenomenon. It understands the value of tacit knowledge (direct, personal experience), views the organization not solely as a machine for processing information, but as a living organism, provides the proper contexts to facilitate a 'social' process between individuals and between individuals and the organization and values the involvement of everyone in the organization. Again, these traits closely resemble the approach to knowledge espoused by Nonaka and myself.

In Europe, Shell has gained a reputation for its ability to tap tacit knowledge in creative ways (McDermott, 1999, and Wenger and Snyder, 2000). In its Deepwater Division, engineers hold collaborative problem-solving meetings facilitated by a community coordinator. These engineers, engaged in deepwater drilling, form a 'community of practice' or a group of people informally bound together by shared expertise and passion. By solving problems in the public forum, they develop a common understanding of the tools, approaches and solutions for deepwater drilling. The community coordinator's role is to gather anecdotal evidence systematically. At Shell, the community coordinator conducts interviews to collect stories and publishes them in newsletters and reports. Stories are easy to remember and are 'live', contain huge amounts of tacit knowledge.

In contrast to the West – where companies are leaning more towards the human and personal approach – many Japanese companies are aggressively pursuing the IT-based approach to knowledge management. Asahi Beer ('Nikkei Computer', 1999) and Shiseido ('Nikkei Jouhou Strategy', 2000) are representative of such companies. Last year, Asahi Beer distributed laptop personal computers to 900 salespeople who are sending in about 200 bits of market information a day into the company's newly constructed intranet system. Knowledge captured by the salespeople is codified and stored in databases, where it can be accessed and used easily by anyone in the company. The intranet system at Asahi Beer features 'must see' and 'recommended' marks on information deemed important by the sales headquarters as well as interviews with top salespeople. Shiseido's on-line customer database features a voice-net system that allows everyone in the organization to listen to customers' complaints and enquiries live.

Conclusion

In retrospect, the fact that different countries have run off with knowledge management in divergent directions in the 1990s has been a blessing in disguise. The saplings that took root in Europe, the US and Japan have become intertwined to form a strong trunk that is serving as a solid foundation for future development.

Measuring knowledge has become increasingly important as the company's market value is being determined more and more by its intangible assets rather than its tangible assets. Microsoft's market capitalization, for example, does not depend on the value of the premises it owns, nor its machinery/equipment and goods in stock. It depends on the value attached to its intangible assets, such as patents, business networks, human capital and brands (McKinsey & Co., 2000). Thus, we need to capitalize on our European strength and continue refining how we should measure the value of these intangible assets.

Databases are becoming increasingly sophisticated as we move from simply capturing, storing and leveraging what employees know into building databases involving customers, competitors, suppliers and other stakeholders. Sophistication will also have to be enhanced as sound and images will become an integral part of data, together with numbers and words. In addition, sophistication will have to increase as infrastructures for the Internet, intranets and extranets keep being updated. Thus, we need to build on the American strength to match advancements in IT.

The tacit dimension of knowledge, which was largely ignored in the West, holds the key to whether or not knowledge management will end up being just a fad, as many new management ideas have proved to be in the past. As this chapter has pointed out, the signs are very encouraging. Companies now realize that explicit knowledge simply represents the tip of the iceberg. They are trying to come to grips with tacit knowledge that is still largely untapped. People are beginning to realize that knowledge is far more complicated than it appears. No wonder it has been the central subject of philosophy and epistemology since 400 BC.

A study conducted by McKinsey & Company and Darmstadt University of Technology (2000) reveals the complicated and dynamic nature of knowledge. After more than 400 personal interviews with people at 39 companies around the world (18 in Europe, 11 in North America and 10 in Japan), they discovered that knowledge is an asset:

1   that means different things to different people;
2   that can become outdated instantaneously;
3   that initially is often tacit, not codified;
4   the value of which increases when it is shared among people;
5   the generation of which cannot be planned scientifically;
6   that can be recycled independently of ownership of physical assets.

Thus, we need to fully utilize our Japanese strength to make this rather intriguing concept operational within management.

Having formed a solid trunk from three intertwined saplings, knowledge management is now positioned to branch out and bear its fruits in the field of management. It may blossom to become the most universal management concept in history.

Notes

An earlier version of this chapter appeared in 1998 as 'Beyond knowledge management: lessons from Japan', in *Monash Mt Eliza Business Journal*, 1 (1).

1   As we will see later, conversions from explicit to tacit, explicit to explicit and tacit to tacit are also possible. However, the biggest 'bang' in organizational knowledge creation comes from converting tacit to explicit.

References

'Nikkei Computer', 16 August, 1999: 132.
'Nikkei Jouhou Strategy', January 2000: 74.
Economist, 31 May 1997: 71.
Edvinsson, Leif and Malone, Michael S. (1997) *Intellectual Capital: Realizing Your*

Company's True Value by Finding Its Hidden Brainpower. New York: Harp
pp. 10–15.

Hansen, Morten T., Nohria, Nitin, and Tierney, Thomas (1999) 'What's your st
managing knowledge?', *Harvard Business Review*, March–April: 108–9, 112.

Kim, W. Chan, and Mauborgne, Renée (1997) 'Fair process: managing in the k
economy', *Harvard Business Review*, July–Aug.: 71.

McDermott, Richard (1999) 'Why information technology inspired but cannot deliver
knowledge management', *California Management Review*, Summer: 103–17.

McKinsey & Co. (2000), unpublished report Darmstadt University of Technology, 24
February.

Nonaka, Ikujiro, and Takeuchi, Hirotaka (1995) *The Knowledge-creating Company: How
Japanese Companies Create the Dynamics of Innovation.* New York: Oxford University
Press.

Sieloff, Charles G. (1999) '"If only HP knew what HP knows": the roots of knowledge
management at Hewlett-Packard', *Journal of Knowledge Management*, 3 (1): 53.

Stewart, Thomas A. (1997) *Intellectual Capital: The New Wealth of Organizations.* New
York: Doubleday. pp. 124–7.

Sveiby, Karl Erik (1997) *The New Organizational Wealth: Managing and Measuring
Knowledge-based Assets.* San Francisco: Berrett-Koehler Publishers.

Swan, Jacky, Newell, Sue, Scarbrough, Harry, and Hislop, Donald (1999) 'Knowledge
management and innovation: networks and networking', *Journal of Knowledge Management*, 3 (4): pp. 262–75.

Takeuchi, Hirotaka (1997) personal interview with Ikujiro Nonaka, in Tokyo, 24 June.

Tichy, Noel, and Sherman, Stratford (1993) *Control Your Destiny or Someone Else Will.* New
York: Currency Doubleday.

Wenger, Etienne C., and Snyder, William M. (2000) 'Communities of practice: the organizational frontier', *Harvard Business Review*, Jan.–Feb.: 143.

16 Research Directions for Knowledge Management

Ikujiro Nonaka and David J. Teece

The Need for Transdisciplinary Enquiry

The emerging interest in knowledge management requires, and will probably receive, considerable attention and be a focus of scholarly enquiry. As research advances, it ought to be especially sensitive to preserving and building on the already significant literature concerning the management of technology, entrepreneurship, innovation and business strategy. Indeed, there is a real danger that knowledge management will become discredited if it proceeds in ignorance of this large body of existing literature, as it would thereby create unnecessary intellectual clutter and confusion. Properly understood, the knowledge management umbrella can be a convenient rubric for integrating important work in accounting, economics, entrepreneurship, organizational behaviour, philosophy, marketing, sociology and strategy. Each of these fields provides important insights into one aspect or another of knowledge management, whereas standing alone none provides an integrating framework. What is required is transdisciplinary research that goes beyond mere interdisciplinary activity.

Some Research Issues

While there are many potentially valid research issues that be could identified, there are several topics that are particularly salient and warrant special attention. These are the following.

The assembling of evidence to test the proposition that firm-level competitive advantage in open economies flows from difficult-to-replicate knowledge assets

This proposition, advanced by the editors, is one that may not be uniformly accepted. The empirical evidence needs to be further developed.

There clearly is some seemingly contradictory evidence, but perhaps this tends to prove the rule. For example, regulations (such as state and federal telecom regulations in the US) create rent-seeking opportunities that arise from the ability to out-lawyer or out-influence one's rivals in the courts and political arenas. Witness the success of MCI in entering the long-distance phone markets in the United States in the 1970s or the political alliance against Microsoft that has leaned on the US Department of Justice to cripple Microsoft. Such instances illustrate that government regulations, which frequently serve to limit competition, create incentives for firms to expend resources to influence regulation in ways that favour particular competitors over others.

As another example, trade barriers are still ubiquitous in many countries, and there are domestic policies that shield competitors (such as government restrictions) on entry into particular markets. Accordingly, there are more than a few nooks and crannies where rents still flow from old-fashioned restrictions on trade (the protected French automobile industry and US dairy industry, for example). Domestic competitors may compete away some of these rents unless there are further restrictions on entry or if there are scale effects that favour incumbents.

However, surveys of industries exposed to global competition (and not shielded by governmentally imposed controls) will demonstrate that superior profits stem from intangible assets, such as know-how, customer relationships, brands and superior business processes. One indicator of the new regime is how the sources of wealth creation have changed over time. John D. Rockefeller, Andrew Carnegie, Henry Ford and other capitalists in the late nineteenth and early twentieth centuries, gained wealth in ways rather different from Bill Gates (Microsoft), Richard Branson (Virgin), Lawrence Ellison (Oracle), Michael Dell (Dell Computers) and Gordon Moore (Intel). An analysis of industrial and business wealth creation today might be rather suggestive of the role of intangible assets and dynamic capabilities.

The task is quite challenging methodologically. To analyse these issues quantitatively, one would need to establish measures for intangible assets as well as dynamic capabilities (the entrepreneurial way in which such assets are deployed). However, as an interim step, qualitative historical comparisons can be made. More quantitative approaches are also possible, such as using histories of matched pairs of leading firms analysed with non-parametric statistics, where the 'treatment' is investment in intangibles or some other such proxies for intangible assets (see Teece, 1981). Other approaches that are initial steps in this direction include Hirschey and Weygandt (1985), who demonstrated that Tobins Q ratios are cross-sectionally correlated with R&D intensity.

Making greater efforts to quantify the value of intangible assets

Balance sheets prepared under Generally Accepted Accounting Practices endeavour to represent the firm's tangible assets, but completely omit intangibles – with the exception of goodwill. As a consequence, balance sheets are, at best, a poor guide to the value of an enterprise: at worst, they can be almost useless and quite misleading.

There have been various efforts to create adjusted balance sheets by capitalizing the value of income streams earned by certain intangibles, most notably technological know-how, brands and customer relationships (see Lev and Songiannis, 1995). This is a very useful beginning and is suggestive of further work that can be done.

The value of some types of intellectual property can be observed when certain rights of use are sold (licensed) or exchanged (cross-licensed) in arm's-length transactions. Patent, trade secret and copyright licences are not infrequently granted. Royalty rates are sometimes reported publicly, and vary considerably by sector and the strength of the intellectual property rights involved. The orders of magnitude – into double digits as a percentage of sales for very valuable patents and patent portfolios – suggest that intellectual property can have great value. Brands, likewise, can have great value.

Understand generic inputs, idiosyncratic inputs and profitability

The information/knowledge/competences dimensions of inputs (especially intangibles) used to create products remains almost completely unexplored in economics and strategy. There is some recognition that information economics does not conform too much to standard economic theory (see Arrow, 1962). Indeed, the economics of knowledge and competence (which is distinct from the economics of information) is even more primitive.

As with information, the development of knowledge and competence involves certain important costs, but it is different in that the marginal cost of subsequent use is by no means zero. As with ordinary (generic) inputs, knowledge assets and other intangibles are required in production on a repetitive/continuous basis. Another difference is that the costs of transfer are generally high and, as noted, such assets are difficult to trade.

Also, because these 'inputs' cannot be purchased on the market, the growth of the firm is limited in the short run by the 'stock' of such intangibles and competences possessed by the firm. In the longer run, investment in training can soften these restraints.

Further research is clearly needed on imitation and replication. Relevant research now exists in the form of the study of the replication of quality processes and best practices (see Szukanski, 1993, and Cole, 1995). Because of the tacit elements of knowledge, replication can only be accomplished internally; imitation from the outside is difficult. Thus, value flows from a profitable business model undergirded by intangible assets and supported by business processes with a high tacit component.

It is obviously desirable to test such a theory. However, if it is possible to identify circumstances where these factors are at play, then investment opportunities abound. Put differently, any researcher who can work this out can also make money on Wall Street, assuming such characteristics are not already fully understood by investors. Accordingly, the internal credibility of any published statistical analysis is questionable. Nevertheless, empirical work along these lines would be of great interest and ought to be strongly encouraged. An important starting point will be coming up with acceptable operational indices of superior financial performance. Market-based approaches (such as Tobins Q) are likely to be preferable.

Explore the importance of entrepreneurial versus administrative capabilities

In today's world of converging technology and markets, rapid innovation can transform markets overnight. Administrative systems that effect organizational control, while necessary, no longer provide the under-pinnings of value creation. Control of internal cash flow is, likewise, of marginal value. If not astutely crafted, administrative systems can stifle initiative and weaken performance-based incentives. Moreover, they no longer suffice for value creation because the relevant organizational skills are so ubiquitous.

Accordingly, performance differentials should open up between firms that excel at the entrepreneurial, while nevertheless possessing administrative skills. Firms that are more entrepreneurial are likely to rely on more high-powered incentives, are likely to be more decentralized and have open and transparent governance. Such firms are likely to favour investment in innovative activities, but not necessarily by establishing centralized R&D facilities. A changing kaleidoscope of alliances and joint ventures is also likely to characterize firms that elevate the entrepreneurial over the administrative. Characteristics of such 'high flex' Silicon Valley-type organizations are identified elsewhere (Teece, 1996), suggesting obvious possibilities for empirical research.

Reflections on the Berkeley Initiative

Throughout this book and in the Berkeley Forum, it has been clearly demonstrated that researchers and practitioners from diversified fields have been involved in developing knowledge-based theories and practices. In the era of the knowledge society, nothing much can be explained without the concept of knowledge. While management researchers initiated the present wave of research, scholars and practitioners from other fields – such as psychology, linguistics, cognitive science, philosophy, anthropology, city and regional planning, sociology and economics – are now joining the fray.

As these fields branched out from philosophy, the interrelationships among them have been vague and messy. The knowledge paradigm can encourage researchers to escape from out of this jungle.

Looking back over the past three years of the Berkeley Forum, we note that the first year's Forum was mainly populated by strategy and management researchers. In the second year, quite a few renowned economists and psychologists joined. In the third year, additional researchers from anthropology, city and regional planning, as well as sociology joined. While research in management may have stimulated initial breakthroughs, insights and methodologies from other well-established fields are now driving much of the enquiry. The challenge now is whether or not we can unify them into a new paradigm of social science that would help us understand a wide variety of human activities in the emerging knowledge economy.

There are quite a few hurdles standing in the way of a new paradigm. In these closing remarks, we will briefly discuss three important requirements for future success.

First, as noted earlier, we need to conduct transdisciplinary research – that is, integrate different disciplinary approaches. Insightful enquiry into the nature of knowledge often requires flexible combinations of different disciplines. Transdisciplinary research is, however, not just interdisciplinary (merely combining two or more different approaches) – it goes further, integrating existing approaches and creating a new view of human behaviour. These approaches include cognition, group activities, and corporate management. For example, knowledge-based theories of the firm and organization may be constructed by integrating the theories concerning firm boundaries, cognition and action, language, knowledge creation and leadership.

Second, we need to further expand the unit of analysis for knowledge-based theories and practices. In particular, it should range from individual to group, firm to industry and region to nation. Currently, while some areas are well researched, others are not. An even harder challenge is to coherently connect research with different units of analysis. Although each unit is expected to provide important insights, all must be integrated in order to provide the entire picture of the new paradigm.

Third, we need to deepen our understanding of different types of 'group' epistemology, which is a shared discipline of knowledge creation within a group. While, traditionally, philosophers have been working on individual epistemology, knowledge-based theorists from management fields have introduced the concept of corporate epistemology. The concept has helped us understand the diversification of different management styles among successful firms. This 'group' can be an organization, community, region, city or nation, as well as a corporation. As traditional social science fields such as psychology, sociology, anthropology and economics have been working on these units, insights from such fields would be helpful in enhancing our understanding of different levels of 'group' epistemology.

They should be fully integrated if our understanding of the knowledge-creation processes is to be comprehensive.

We hope that interested researchers and practitioners are all heading towards the establishment of a new paradigm. We are especially optimistic that more philosophers will find this initiative interesting and regard it as an opportunity. We believe that building a philosophical foundation is the key to the development of a unified theory.

The journey may be long, but the torch has been well and truly lit. We believe that a new paradigm will be a major driving force, enabling a better understanding of the business firm in our Internet-enabled knowledge-based economy.

References

Arrow, K. (1962) 'Economic welfare and the allocation of resources for invention', in R. Nelson (ed.), *The Rate and Direction of Inventive Activity*. Princeton, NJ: Princeton University Press.

Cole, R. (1995) *The Death and Life of the American Quality Movement*. New York: Oxford University Press.

Hirschey, M., and Weygandt, J. (1985) 'Amortization policy for advertising and research and development expenditures', *Journal of Accounting Research*, 23: 326–35.

Lev, B., and Sougiannis, T. (1995) 'The capitalization, amortization, value relevance of R&D', unpublished working paper.

Szulanski, G. (1993) 'Intrafirm transfer of best practice, appropriate capabilities, organizational barriers to appropriation', working paper, INSEAD.

Teece, D. (1981) 'Internal organization and economic performance: an empirical analysis of the profitability of principal firms', *Journal of Industrial Economics*, 30 (2): 173–99.

Teece, D. (1996) 'Firm organization, industrial structure, and technological innovation', *Journal of Economic Behavior and Organization*, 31: 193–224.

Index